Clojure for Data Science

Statistics, big data, and machine learning for
Clojure programmers

Henry Garner

BIRMINGHAM - MUMBAI

Clojure for Data Science

First published: September 2015

Production reference: 1280815

Published by Packt Publishing Ltd.
Livery Place
35 Livery Street
Birmingham B3 2PB, UK.

ISBN 978-1-78439-718-0

www.packtpub.com

Credits

Author
Henry Garner

Reviewer
Dan Hammer

Commissioning Editor
Ashwin Nair

Acquisition Editor
Meeta Rajani

Content Development Editor
Shubhangi Dhamgaye

Technical Editor
Shivani Kiran Mistry

Copy Editor
Akshata Lobo

Project Coordinator
Harshal Ved

Proofreader
Safis Editing

Indexer
Monica Ajmera Mehta

Graphics
Nicholas Garner

Disha Haria

Production Coordinator
Arvindkumar Gupta

Cover Work
Arvindkumar Gupta

About the Author

Henry Garner is a graduate from the University of Oxford and an experienced developer, CTO, and coach.

He started his technical career at Britain's largest telecoms provider, BT, working with a traditional data warehouse infrastructure. As a part of a small team for 3 years, he built sophisticated data models to derive insight from raw data and use web applications to present the results. These applications were used internally by senior executives and operatives to track both business and systems performance.

He then went on to co-found Likely, a social media analytics start-up. As the CTO, he set the technical direction, leading to the introduction of an event-based append-only data pipeline modeled after the Lambda architecture. He adopted Clojure in 2011 and led a hybrid team of programmers and data scientists, building content recommendation engines based on collaborative filtering and clustering techniques. He developed a syllabus and copresented a series of evening classes from Likely's offices for professional developers who wanted to learn Clojure.

Henry now works with growing businesses, consulting in both a development and technical leadership capacity. He presents regularly at seminars and Clojure meetups in and around London.

Acknowledgments

Thank you Shubhangi Dhamgaye, Meeta Rajani, Shivani Mistry, and the entire team at Packt for their help in bringing this project to fruition. Without you, this book would never have come to pass.

I'm grateful to Dan Hammer, my Packt reviewer, for his valuable perspective as a practicing data scientist, and to those other brave souls who patiently read through the very rough early (and not-so-early) drafts. Foremost among these are Éléonore Mayola, Paul Butcher, and Jeremy Hoyland. Your feedback was not always easy to hear, but it made the book so much better than it would otherwise have been.

Thank you to the wonderful team at MastodonC who tackled a pre-release version of this book in their company book club, especially Éléonore Mayola, Jase Bell, and Elise Huard. I'm grateful to Francine Bennett for her advice early on—which helped to shape the structure of the book—and also to Bruce Durling, Neale Swinnerton, and Chris Adams for their company during the otherwise lonely weekends spent writing in the office.

Thank you to my friends from the machine learning study group: Sam Joseph, Geoff Hogg, and Ben Taylor for reading the early drafts and providing feedback suitable for Clojure newcomers; and also to Luke Snape and Tom Coupland of the Bristol Clojurians for providing the opportunity to test the material out on its intended audience.

A heartfelt thanks to my dad, Nicholas, for interpreting my vague scribbles into the fantastic figures you see in this book, and to my mum, Jacqueline, and sister, Mary, for being such patient listeners in the times I felt like thinking aloud. Last, but by no means least, thank you to the Nuggets of Wynford Road, Russell and Wendy, for the tea and sympathy whenever it occasionally became a bit too much. I look forward to seeing much more of you both from now on.

About the Reviewer

Dan Hammer is a presidential innovation fellow working on Data Innovation initiatives at the NASA headquarters in the CTO's office. Dan is an economist and data scientist. He was the chief data scientist at the World Resources Institute, where he launched Global Forest Watch in partnership with Google, USAID, and many others. Dan is on leave from a PhD program at UC Berkeley, as advised by Max Auffhammer and George Judge. He teaches mathematics at the San Quentin State Prison as a lead instructor with the Prison University Project. Dan graduated with high honors in economics and mathematics from Swarthmore College, where he was a language scholar. He spent a full year building and racing Polynesian outrigger canoes in the South Pacific as a Watson Fellow. He has also reviewed *Learning R for Geospatial Analysis* by Packt Publishing.

> Thanks to my wonderful wife Emily for suffering through my terrible jokes.

www.PacktPub.com

Support files, eBooks, discount offers, and more

For support files and downloads related to your book, please visit www.PacktPub.com.

Did you know that Packt offers eBook versions of every book published, with PDF and ePub files available? You can upgrade to the eBook version at www.PacktPub.com and as a print book customer, you are entitled to a discount on the eBook copy. Get in touch with us at service@packtpub.com for more details.

At www.PacktPub.com, you can also read a collection of free technical articles, sign up for a range of free newsletters and receive exclusive discounts and offers on Packt books and eBooks.

https://www2.packtpub.com/books/subscription/packtlib

Do you need instant solutions to your IT questions? PacktLib is Packt's online digital book library. Here, you can search, access, and read Packt's entire library of books.

Why subscribe?

- Fully searchable across every book published by Packt
- Copy and paste, print, and bookmark content
- On demand and accessible via a web browser

Free access for Packt account holders

If you have an account with Packt at www.PacktPub.com, you can use this to access PacktLib today and view 9 entirely free books. Simply use your login credentials for immediate access.

For Helen.

*You provided support, encouragement, and welcome
distraction in roughly equal measure.*

Table of Contents

Preface

"Statistical thinking will one day be as necessary for efficient citizenship as the ability to read and write."

- H. G. Wells

"I have a great subject [statistics] to write upon, but feel keenly my literary incapacity to make it easily intelligible without sacrificing accuracy and thoroughness."

- Sir Francis Galton

A web search for "data science Venn diagram" returns numerous interpretations of the skills required to be an effective data scientist (it appears that data science commentators love Venn diagrams). Author and data scientist Drew Conway produced the prototypical diagram back in 2010, putting data science at the intersection of hacking skills, substantive expertise (that is, subject domain understanding), and mathematics and statistics knowledge. Between hacking skills and substantive expertise—those practicing without strong mathematics and statistics knowledge—lies the "danger zone."

Five years on, as a growing number of developers seek to plug the data science skills' shortage, there's more need than ever for statistical and mathematical education to help developers out of this danger zone. So, when Packt Publishing invited me to write a book on data science suitable for Clojure programmers, I gladly agreed. In addition to appreciating the need for such a book, I saw it as an opportunity to consolidate much of what I had learned as CTO of my own Clojure-based data analytics company. The result is the book I wish I had been able to read before starting out.

Clojure for Data Science aims to be much more than just a book of statistics for Clojure programmers. A large reason for the spread of data science into so many diverse areas is the enormous power of machine learning. Throughout the book, I'll show how to use pure Clojure functions and third-party libraries to construct machine learning models for the primary tasks of regression, classification, clustering, and recommendation.

Approaches that scale to very large datasets, so-called "big data," are of particular interest to data scientists, because they can reveal subtleties that are lost in smaller samples. This book shows how Clojure can be used to concisely express jobs to run on the Hadoop and Spark distributed computation frameworks, and how to incorporate machine learning through the use of both dedicated external libraries and general optimization techniques.

Above all, this book aims to foster an understanding not just on how to perform particular types of analysis, but why such techniques work. In addition to providing practical knowledge (almost every concept in this book is expressed as a runnable example), I aim to explain the theory that will allow you to take a principle and apply it to related problems. I hope that this approach will enable you to effectively apply statistical thinking in diverse situations well into the future, whether or not you decide to pursue a career in data science.

What this book covers

Chapter 1, Statistics, introduces Incanter, Clojure's primary statistical computing library used throughout the book. With reference to the data from the elections in the United Kingdom and Russia, we demonstrate the use of summary statistics and the value of statistical distributions while showing a variety of comparative visualizations.

Chapter 2, Inference, covers the difference between samples and populations, and statistics and parameters. We introduce hypothesis testing as a formal means of determining whether the differences are significant in the context of A / B testing website designs. We also cover sample bias, effect size, and solutions to the problem of multiple testing.

Chapter 3, Correlation, shows how we can discover linear relationships between variables and use the relationship to make predictions about some variables given others. We implement linear regression—a machine learning algorithm—to predict the weights of Olympic swimmers given their heights, using only core Clojure functions. We then make our model more sophisticated using matrices and more data to improve its accuracy.

Chapter 4, Classification, describes how to implement several different types of machine learning algorithm (logistic regression, naive Bayes, C4.5, and random forests) to make predictions about the survival rates of passengers on the Titanic. We learn about another test for statistical significance that works for categories instead of continuous values, explain various issues you're likely to encounter while training machine learning models such as bias and overfitting, and demonstrate how to use the clj-ml machine learning library.

Chapter 5, Big Data, shows how Clojure can leverage the parallel capabilities in computers of all sizes using the reducers library, and how to scale up these techniques to clusters of machines on Hadoop with Tesser and Parkour. Using ZIP code level tax data from the IRS, we demonstrate how to perform statistical analysis and machine learning in a scalable way.

Chapter 6, Clustering, shows how to identify text documents that share similar subject matter using Hadoop and the Java machine learning library, Mahout. We describe a variety of techniques particular to text processing as well as more general concepts related to clustering. We also introduce some more advanced features of Parkour that can help get the best performance from your Hadoop jobs.

Chapter 7, Recommender Systems, covers a variety of different approaches to the challenge of recommendation. In addition to implementing a recommender with core Clojure functions, we tackle the ancillary challenge of dimensionality reduction by using principle component analysis and singular value decomposition, as well as probabilistic set compression using Bloom filters and the MinHash algorithm. Finally, we introduce the Sparkling and MLlib libraries for machine learning on the Spark distributed computation framework and use them to produce movie recommendations with alternating least squares.

Chapter 8, Network Analysis, shows a variety of ways of analyzing graph-structured data. We demonstrate the methods of traversal using the Loom library and then show how to use the Glittering and GraphX libraries with Spark to discover communities and influencers in social networks.

Chapter 9, Time Series, demonstrates how to fit curves to simple time series data. Using data on the monthly airline passenger counts, we show how to forecast future values for more complex series by training an autoregressive moving-average model. We do this by implementing a method of parameter optimization called maximum likelihood estimation with help from the Apache Commons Math library.

Chapter 10, Visualization, shows how the Clojure library Quil can be used to create custom visualizations for charts not provided by Incanter, and attractive graphics that can communicate findings clearly to your audience, whatever their background.

What you need for this book

The code for each chapter has been made available as a project on GitHub at `https://github.com/clojuredatascience`. The example code can be downloaded as a zip file from there, or cloned with the Git command-line tool. All of the book's examples can be compiled and run with the Leiningen build tool as described in *Chapter 1, Statistics*.

This book assumes that you're already able to compile and run Clojure code using Leiningen (`http://leiningen.org/`). Refer to Leiningen's website if you're not yet set up to do this.

In addition, the code for many of the sample chapters makes use of external datasets. Where possible, these have been included together with the sample code. Where this has not been possible, instructions for downloading the data have been provided in the sample code's README file. Bash scripts have also been provided with the relevant sample code to automate this process. These can be run directly by Linux and OS X users, as described in the relevant chapter, provided the curl, wget, tar, gzip, and unzip utilities are installed. Windows users may have to install a Linux emulator such as Cygwin (`https://www.cygwin.com/`) to run the scripts.

Who this book is for

This book is intended for intermediate and advanced Clojure programmers who want to build their statistical knowledge, apply machine learning algorithms, or process large amounts of data with Hadoop and Spark. Many aspiring data scientists will benefit from learning all of these skills, and *Clojure for Data Science* is intended to be read in order from the beginning to the end. Readers who approach the book in this way will find that each chapter builds on concepts introduced in the prior chapters.

If you're not already comfortable reading Clojure code, you're likely to find this book particularly challenging. Fortunately, there are now many excellent resources for learning Clojure and I do not attempt to replicate their work here. At the time of writing, *Clojure for the Brave and True* (`http://www.braveclojure.com/`) is a fantastic free resource for learning the language. Consult `http://clojure.org/getting_started` for links to many other books and online tutorials suitable for newcomers.

Conventions

In this book, you will find a number of text styles that distinguish between different kinds of information. Here are some examples of these styles and an explanation of their meaning.

Code words in text, database table names, folder names, filenames, file extensions, pathnames, dummy URLs, user input, and Twitter handles are shown as follows: "Each example is a function in the `cljds.ch1.examples` namespace that can be run."

A block of code is set as follows:

```
(defmulti load-data identity)

(defmethod load-data :uk [_]
  (-> (io/resource "UK2010.xls")
      (str)
      (xls/read-xls)))
```

When we wish to draw your attention to a particular part of a code block, the relevant lines or items are set in bold:

```
(q/fill (fill-fn x y))
(q/rect x-pos y-pos x-scale y-scale))
(q/save "heatmap.png"))]
(q/sketch :setup setup :size size))
```

Any command-line input or output is written as follows:

```
lein run -e 1.1
```

New terms and **important words** are shown in bold. Words that you see on the screen, for example, in menus or dialog boxes, appear in the text like this: "Each time the **New Sample** button is pressed, a pair of new samples from an exponential distribution with population means taken from the sliders are generated."

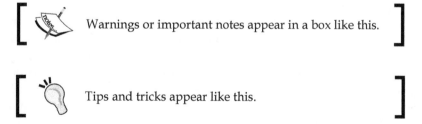

[Warnings or important notes appear in a box like this.]

[Tips and tricks appear like this.]

Reader feedback

Feedback from our readers is always welcome. Let us know what you think about this book—what you liked or disliked. Reader feedback is important for us as it helps us develop titles that you will really get the most out of.

To send us general feedback, simply e-mail feedback@packtpub.com, and mention the book's title in the subject of your message.

If there is a topic that you have expertise in and you are interested in either writing or contributing to a book, see our author guide at www.packtpub.com/authors.

Customer support

Now that you are the proud owner of a Packt book, we have a number of things to help you to get the most from your purchase.

Downloading the example code

You can download the example code files from your account at http://www.packtpub.com for all the Packt Publishing books you have purchased. If you purchased this book elsewhere, you can visit http://www.packtpub.com/support and register to have the files e-mailed directly to you.

Downloading the color images of this book

We also provide you with a PDF file that has color images of the screenshots/diagrams used in this book. The color images will help you better understand the changes in the output. You can download this file from https://www.packtpub.com/sites/default/files/downloads/Clojure_for_Data_Science_ColorImages.pdf.

Errata

Although we have taken every care to ensure the accuracy of our content, mistakes do happen. If you find a mistake in one of our books—maybe a mistake in the text or the code—we would be grateful if you could report this to us. By doing so, you can save other readers from frustration and help us improve subsequent versions of this book. If you find any errata, please report them by visiting http://www.packtpub.com/submit-errata, selecting your book, clicking on the **Errata Submission Form** link, and entering the details of your errata. Once your errata are verified, your submission will be accepted and the errata will be uploaded to our website or added to any list of existing errata under the Errata section of that title.

To view the previously submitted errata, go to https://www.packtpub.com/books/content/support and enter the name of the book in the search field. The required information will appear under the **Errata** section.

Piracy

Piracy of copyrighted material on the Internet is an ongoing problem across all media. At Packt, we take the protection of our copyright and licenses very seriously. If you come across any illegal copies of our works in any form on the Internet, please provide us with the location address or website name immediately so that we can pursue a remedy.

Please contact us at copyright@packtpub.com with a link to the suspected pirated material.

We appreciate your help in protecting our authors and our ability to bring you valuable content.

Questions

If you have a problem with any aspect of this book, you can contact us at questions@packtpub.com, and we will do our best to address the problem.

1
Statistics

"The people who cast the votes decide nothing. The people who count the votes decide everything."

– Joseph Stalin

Over the course of the following ten chapters of *Clojure for Data Science*, we'll attempt to discover a broadly linear path through the field of data science. In fact, we'll find as we go that the path is not quite so linear, and the attentive reader ought to notice many recurring themes along the way.

Descriptive statistics concern themselves with summarizing sequences of numbers and they'll appear, to some extent, in every chapter in this book. In this chapter, we'll build foundations for what's to come by implementing functions to calculate the mean, median, variance, and standard deviation of numerical sequences in Clojure. While doing so, we'll attempt to take the fear out of interpreting mathematical formulae.

As soon as we have more than one number to analyze it becomes meaningful to ask how those numbers are distributed. You've probably already heard expressions such as "long tail" and the "80/20 rule". They concern the spread of numbers throughout a range. We demonstrate the value of distributions in this chapter and introduce the most useful of them all: the normal distribution.

The study of distributions is aided immensely by visualization, and for this we'll use the Clojure library Incanter. We'll show how Incanter can be used to load, transform, and visualize real data. We'll compare the results of two national elections—the 2010 United Kingdom general election and the 2011 Russian presidential election—and see how even basic analysis can provide evidence of potentially fraudulent activity.

Downloading the sample code

All of the book's sample code is available on Packt Publishing's website at http://www.packtpub.com/support or from GitHub at http://github.com/ clojuredatascience. Each chapter's sample code is available in its own repository.

 The sample code for *Chapter 1, Statistics* can be downloaded from https://github.com/clojuredatascience/ch1-statistics.

Executable examples are provided regularly throughout all chapters, either to demonstrate the effect of code that has been just been explained, or to demonstrate statistical principles that have been introduced. All example function names begin with ex- and are numbered sequentially throughout each chapter. So, the first runnable example of *Chapter 1, Statistics* is named ex-1-1, the second is named ex-1-2, and so on.

Running the examples

Each example is a function in the cljds.ch1.examples namespace that can be run in two ways—either from the **REPL** or on the command line with **Leiningen**. If you'd like to run the examples in the REPL, you can execute:

lein repl

on the command line. By default, the REPL will open in the examples namespace. Alternatively, to run a specific numbered example, you can execute:

lein run --example 1.1

or pass the single-letter equivalent:

lein run -e 1.1

We only assume basic command-line familiarity throughout this book. The ability to run Leiningen and shell scripts is all that's required.

 If you become stuck at any point, refer to the book's wiki at http://wiki.clojuredatascience.com. The wiki will provide troubleshooting tips for known issues, including advice for running examples on a variety of platforms.

In fact, shell scripts are only used for fetching data from remote locations automatically. The book's wiki will also provide alternative instructions for those not wishing or unable to execute the shell scripts.

Downloading the data

The dataset for this chapter has been made available by the Complex Systems Research Group at the Medical University of Vienna. The analysis we'll be performing closely mirrors their research to determine the signals of systematic election fraud in the national elections of countries around the world.

 For more information about the research, and for links to download other datasets, visit the book's wiki or the research group's website at `http://www.complex-systems.meduniwien.ac.at/elections/election.html`.

Throughout this book we'll be making use of numerous datasets. Where possible, we've included the data with the example code. Where this hasn't been possible — either because of the size of the data or due to licensing constraints — we've included a script to download the data instead.

Chapter 1, Statistics is just such a chapter. If you've cloned the chapter's code and intend to follow the examples, download the data now by executing the following on the command line from within the project's directory:

```
script/download-data.sh
```

The script will download and decompress the sample data into the project's data directory.

 If you have any difficulty running the download script or would like to follow manual instructions instead, visit the book's wiki at `http://wiki.clojuredatascience.com` for assistance.

We'll begin investigating the data in the next section.

Inspecting the data

Throughout this chapter, and for many other chapters in this book, we'll be using the Incanter library (`http://incanter.org/`) to load, manipulate, and display data.

Incanter is a modular suite of Clojure libraries that provides statistical computing and visualization capabilities. Modeled after the extremely popular R environment for data analysis, it brings together the power of Clojure, an interactive REPL, and a set of powerful abstractions for working with data.

Each module of Incanter focuses on a specific area of functionality. For example `incanter-stats` contains a suite of related functions for analyzing data and producing summary statistics, while `incanter-charts` provides a large number of visualization capabilities. `incanter-core` provides the most fundamental and generally useful functions for transforming data.

Each module can be included separately in your own code. For access to stats, charts, and Excel features, you could include the following in your `project.clj`:

```
:dependencies [[incanter/incanter-core "1.5.5"]
               [incanter/incanter-stats "1.5.5"]
               [incanter/incanter-charts "1.5.5"]
               [incanter/incanter-excel "1.5.5"]
               ...]
```

If you don't mind including more libraries than you need, you can simply include the full Incanter distribution instead:

```
:dependencies [[incanter/incanter "1.5.5"]
               ...]
```

At Incanter's core is the concept of a dataset—a structure of rows and columns. If you have experience with relational databases, you can think of a dataset as a table. Each column in a dataset is named, and each row in the dataset has the same number of columns as every other. There are a several ways to load data into an Incanter dataset, and which we use will depend how our data is stored:

- If our data is a text file (a CSV or tab-delimited file), we can use the `read-dataset` function from `incanter-io`

- If our data is an Excel file (for example, an `.xls` or `.xlsx` file), we can use the `read-xls` function from `incanter-excel`

- For any other data source (an external database, website, and so on), as long as we can get our data into a Clojure data structure we can create a dataset with the `dataset` function in `incanter-core`

This chapter makes use of Excel data sources, so we'll be using `read-xls`. The function takes one required argument—the file to load—and an optional keyword argument specifying the sheet number or name. All of our examples have only one sheet, so we'll just provide the file argument as string:

```
(ns cljds.ch1.data
  (:require [clojure.java.io :as io]
            [incanter.core :as i]
            [incanter.excel :as xls]))
```

In general, we will not reproduce the namespace declarations from the example code. This is both for brevity and because the required namespaces can usually be inferred by the symbol used to reference them. For example, throughout this book we will always refer to `clojure.java.io` as io, `incanter.core` as I, and `incanter.excel` as xls wherever they are used.

We'll be loading several data sources throughout this chapter, so we've created a multimethod called `load-data` in the `cljds.ch1.data` namespace:

```
(defmulti load-data identity)

(defmethod load-data :uk [_]
  (-> (io/resource "UK2010.xls")
      (str)
      (xls/read-xls)))
```

In the preceding code, we define the `load-data` multimethod that dispatches on the `identity` of the first argument. We also define the implementation that will be called if the first argument is :uk. Thus, a call to `(load-data :uk)` will return an Incanter dataset containing the UK data. Later in the chapter, we'll define additional `load-data` implementations for other datasets.

The first row of the `UK2010.xls` spreadsheet contains column names. Incanter's `read-xls` function will preserve these as the column names of the returned dataset. Let's begin our exploration of the data by inspecting them now — the `col-names` function in `incanter.core` returns the column names as a vector. In the following code (and throughout the book, where we use functions from the `incanter.core` namespace) we require it as i:

```
(defn ex-1-1 []
  (i/col-names (load-data :uk)))
```

As described in running the examples earlier, functions beginning with ex- can be run on the command line with Leiningen like this:

```
lein run -e 1.1
```

The output of the preceding command should be the following Clojure vector:

```
["Press Association Reference" "Constituency Name" "Region" "Election
Year" "Electorate" "Votes" "AC" "AD" "AGS" "APNI" "APP" "AWL" "AWP"
"BB" "BCP" "Bean" "Best" "BGPV" "BIB" "BIC" "Blue" "BNP" "BP Elvis"
"C28" "Cam Soc" "CG" "Ch M" "Ch P" "CIP" "CITY" "CNPG" "Comm" "Comm
L" "Con" "Cor D" "CPA" "CSP" "CTDP" "CURE" "D Lab" "D Nat" "DDP"
"DUP" "ED" "EIP" "EPA" "FAWG" "FDP" "FFR" "Grn" "GSOT" "Hum" "ICHC"
"IEAC" "IFED" "ILEU" "Impact" "Ind1" "Ind2" "Ind3" "Ind4" "Ind5" "IPT"
"ISGB" "ISQM" "IUK" "IVH" "IZB" "JAC" "Joy" "JP" "Lab" "Land" "LD"
"Lib" "Libert" "LIND" "LLPB" "LTT" "MACI" "MCP" "MEDI" "MEP" "MIF"
"MK" "MPEA" "MRLP" "MRP" "Nat Lib" "NCDV" "ND" "New" "NF" "NFP" "NICF"
"Nobody" "NSPS" "PBP" "PC" "Pirate" "PNDP" "Poet" "PPBF" "PPE" "PPNV"
"Reform" "Respect" "Rest" "RRG" "RTBP" "SACL" "Sci" "SDLP" "SEP" "SF"
"SIG" "SJP" "SKGP" "SMA" "SMRA" "SNP" "Soc" "Soc Alt" "Soc Dem" "Soc
Lab" "South" "Speaker" "SSP" "TF" "TOC" "Trust" "TUSC" "TUV" "UCUNF"
"UKIP" "UPS" "UV" "VCCA" "Vote" "Wessex Reg" "WRP" "You" "Youth"
"YRDPL"]
```

This is a very wide dataset. The first six columns in the data file are described as follows; subsequent columns break the number of votes down by party:

- **Press Association Reference**: This is a number identifying the constituency (voting district, represented by one MP)

- **Constituency Name**: This is the common name given to the voting district

- **Region**: This is the geographic region of the UK where the constituency is based

- **Election Year**: This is the year in which the election was held

- **Electorate**: This is the total number of people eligible to vote in the constituency

- **Votes**: This is the total number of votes cast

Whenever we're confronted with new data, it's important to take time to understand it. In the absence of detailed data definitions, one way we could do this is to begin by validating our assumptions about the data. For example, we expect that this dataset contains information about the 2010 election so let's review the contents of the Election Year column.

Incanter provides the i/$ function (i, as before, signifying the `incanter.core` namespace) for selecting columns from a dataset. We'll encounter the function regularly throughout this chapter—it's Incanter's primary way of selecting columns from a variety of data representations and it provides several different arities. For now, we'll be providing just the name of the column we'd like to extract and the dataset from which to extract it:

```
(defn ex-1-2 []
  (i/$ "Election Year" (load-data :uk)))

;; (2010.0 2010.0 2010.0 2010.0 2010.0 ... 2010.0 2010.0 nil)
```

The years are returned as a single sequence of values. The output may be hard to interpret since the dataset contains so many rows. As we'd like to know which unique values the column contains, we can use the Clojure core function `distinct`. One of the advantages of using Incanter is that its useful data manipulation functions augment those that Clojure already provides as shown in the following example:

```
(defn ex-1-3 []
  (->> (load-data :uk)
       (i/$ "Election Year")
       (distinct)))

;; (2010 nil)
```

The 2010 year goes a long way to confirming our expectations that this data is from 2010. The nil value is unexpected, though, and may indicate a problem with our data.

We don't yet know how many nils exist in the dataset and determining this could help us decide what to do next. A simple way of counting values such as this it to use the core library function `frequencies`, which returns a map of values to counts:

```
(defn ex-1-4 [ ]
  (->> (load-data :uk)
       (i/$ "Election Year")
       (frequencies)))

;; {2010.0 650 nil 1}
```

In the preceding examples, we used Clojure's thread-last macro `->>` to chain a several functions together for legibility.

Along with Clojure's large core library of data manipulation functions, macros such as the one discussed earlier—including the thread-last macro - >> — are other great reasons for using Clojure to analyze data. Throughout this book, we'll see how Clojure can make even sophisticated analysis concise and comprehensible.

It wouldn't take us long to confirm that in 2010 the UK had 650 electoral districts, known as constituencies. Domain knowledge such as this is invaluable when sanity-checking new data. Thus, it's highly probable that the `nil` value is extraneous and can be removed. We'll see how to do this in the next section.

Data scrubbing

It is a commonly repeated statistic that at least 80 percent of a data scientist's work is data scrubbing. This is the process of detecting potentially corrupt or incorrect data and either correcting or filtering it out.

 Data scrubbing is one of the most important (and time-consuming) aspects of working with data. It's a key step to ensuring that subsequent analysis is performed on data that is valid, accurate, and consistent.

The `nil` value at the end of the election year column may indicate dirty data that ought to be removed. We've already seen that filtering *columns* of data can be accomplished with Incanter's `i/$` function. For filtering *rows* of data we can use Incanter's `i/query-dataset` function.

We let Incanter know which rows we'd like it to filter by passing a Clojure map of column names and predicates. Only rows for which all predicates return true will be retained. For example, to select only the `nil` values from our dataset:

```
(-> (load-data :uk)
    (i/query-dataset {"Election Year" {:$eq nil}}))
```

If you know SQL, you'll notice this is very similar to a WHERE clause. In fact, Incanter also provides the `i/$where` function, an alias to `i/query-dataset` that reverses the order of the arguments.

The query is a map of column names to predicates and each predicate is itself a map of operator to operand. Complex queries can be constructed by specifying multiple columns and multiple operators together. Query operators include:

- `:$gt` greater than
- `:$lt` less than
- `:$gte` greater than or equal to
- `:$lte` less than or equal to
- `:$eq` equal to
- `:$ne` not equal to
- `:$in` to test for membership of a collection
- `:$nin` to test for non-membership of a collection
- `:$fn` a predicate function that should return a true response for rows to keep

If none of the built-in operators suffice, the last operator provides the ability to pass a custom function instead.

We'll continue to use Clojure's thread-last macro to make the code intention a little clearer, and return the row as a map of keys and values using the `i/to-map` function:

```
(defn ex-1-5 []
  (->> (load-data :uk)
       (i/$where {"Election Year" {:$eq nil}})
       (i/to-map)))

;; {:ILEU nil, :TUSC nil, :Vote nil ... :IVH nil, :FFR nil}
```

Looking at the results carefully, it's apparent that all (but one) of the columns in this row are `nil`. In fact, a bit of further exploration confirms that the non-nil row is a summary total and ought to be removed from the data. We can remove the problematic row by updating the predicate map to use the `:$ne` operator, returning only rows where the election year is not equal to `nil`:

```
(->> (load-data :uk)
     (i/$where {"Election Year" {:$ne nil}}))
```

The preceding function is one we'll almost always want to make sure we call in advance of using the data. One way of doing this is to add another implementation of our `load-data` multimethod, which also includes this filtering step:

```
(defmethod load-data :uk-scrubbed [_]
  (->> (load-data :uk)
       (i/$where {"Election Year" {:$ne nil}})))
```

Now with any code we write, can choose whether to refer to the :uk or :uk-scrubbed datasets.

By always loading the source file and performing our scrubbing on top, we're preserving an audit trail of the transformations we've applied. This makes it clear to us — and future readers of our code — what adjustments have been made to the source. It also means that, should we need to re-run our analysis with new source data, we may be able to just load the new file in place of the existing file.

Descriptive statistics

Descriptive statistics are numbers that are used to summarize and describe data. In the next chapter, we'll turn our attention to a more sophisticated analysis, the so-called **inferential statistics**, but for now we'll limit ourselves to simply describing what we can observe about the data contained in the file.

To demonstrate what we mean, let's look at the Electorate column of the data. This column lists the total number of registered voters in each constituency:

```
(defn ex-1-6 []
  (->> (load-data :uk-scrubbed)
       (i/$ "Electorate")
       (count)))
```

```
;; 650
```

We've filtered the nil field from the dataset; the preceding code should return a list of 650 numbers corresponding to the electorate in each of the UK constituencies.

Descriptive statistics, also called **summary statistics**, are ways of measuring attributes of sequences of numbers. They help characterize the sequence and can act as a guide for further analysis. Let's start by calculating the two most basic statistics that we can from a sequence of numbers — its mean and its variance.

The mean

The most common way of measuring the average of a data set is with the mean. It's actually one of several ways of measuring the **central tendency** of the data. The mean, or more precisely, the arithmetic mean, is a straightforward calculation— simply add up the values and divide by the count—but in spite of this it has a somewhat intimidating mathematical notation:

$$\bar{x} = \frac{1}{n} \sum_{i=1}^{n} x_i$$

where $\bar{x}$ is pronounced *x-bar*, the mathematical symbol often used to denote the mean.

To programmers coming to data science from fields outside mathematics or the sciences, this notation can be quite confusing and alienating. Others may be entirely comfortable with this notation, and they can safely skip the next section.

Interpreting mathematical notation

Although mathematical notation may appear obscure and upsetting, there are really only a handful of symbols that will occur frequently in the formulae in this book.

Σ is pronounced *sigma* and means *sum*. When you see it in mathematical notation it means that a sequence is being added up. The symbols above and below the *sigma* indicate the range over which we'll be summing. They're rather like a C-style `for` loop and in the earlier formula indicate we'll be summing from *i=1* up to *i=n*. By convention *n* is the length of the sequence, and sequences in mathematical notation are one-indexed, not zero-indexed, so summing from *1* to *n* means that we're summing over the entire length of the sequence.

The expression immediately following the sigma is the sequence to be summed. In our preceding formula for the mean, x_i immediately follows the sigma. Since *i* will represent each index from *1* up to *n*, x_i represents each element in the sequence of *xs*.

Finally, $\frac{1}{n}$ appears just before the sigma, indicating that the entire expression should be multiplied by *1* divided by *n* (also called the **reciprocal of n**). This can be simplified to just dividing by *n*.

Name	Mathematical symbol	Clojure equivalent
	n	(count xs)
Sigma notation	$$\sum_{i=1}^{n} x_i$$	(reduce + xs)
Pi notation	$$\prod_{i=1}^{n} x_i$$	(reduce * xs)

Putting this all together, we get "add up the elements in the sequence from the first to the last and divide by the count". In Clojure, this can be written as:

```
(defn mean [xs]
  (/ (reduce + xs)
     (count xs)))
```

Where xs stands for "the sequence of *xs*". We can use our new mean function to calculate the mean of the UK electorate:

```
(defn ex-1-7 []
  (->> (load-data :uk-scrubbed)
       (i/$ "Electorate")
       (mean)))

;; 70149.94
```

In fact, Incanter already includes a function, mean, to calculate the mean of a sequence very efficiently in the incanter.stats namespace. In this chapter (and throughout the book), the incanter.stats namespace will be required as s wherever it's used.

The median

The median is another common descriptive statistic for measuring the central tendency of a sequence. If you ordered all the data from lowest to highest, the median is the middle value. If there is an even number of data points in the sequence, the median is usually defined as the mean of the middle two values.

The median is often represented in formulae by $\tilde{x}$, pronounced *x-tilde*. It's one of the deficiencies of mathematical notation that there's no particularly standard way of expressing the formula for the median value, but nonetheless it's fairly straightforward in Clojure:

```
(defn median [xs]
  (let [n     (count xs)
        mid (int (/ n 2))]
    (if (odd? n)
      (nth (sort xs) mid)
      (->> (sort xs)
           (drop (dec mid))
           (take 2)
           (mean)))))
```

The median of the UK electorate is:

```
(defn ex-1-8 []
  (->> (load-data :uk-scrubbed)
       (i/$ "Electorate")
       (median)))

;; 70813.5
```

Incanter also has a function for calculating the median value as s/median.

Variance

The mean and the median are two alternative ways of describing the middle value of a sequence, but on their own they tell you very little about the values contained within it. For example, if we know the mean of a sequence of ninety-nine values is 50, we can still say very little about what values the sequence contains.

It may contain all the integers from one to ninety-nine, or forty-nine zeros and fifty ninety-nines. Maybe it contains negative one ninety-eight times and a single five-thousand and forty-eight. Or perhaps all the values are exactly fifty.

The variance of a sequence is its "spread" about the mean, and each of the preceding examples would have a different variance. In mathematical notation, the variance is expressed as:

$$s^2 = \frac{1}{n}\sum_{i=1}^{n}\left(x_i - \overline{x}\right)^2$$

where s^2 is the mathematical symbol often used to denote the variance.

This equation bears a number of similarities to the equation for the mean calculated previously. Instead of summing a single value, x_i, we are summing a function of $\left(x_i - \overline{x}\right)^2$. Recall that the symbol $\overline{x}$ represents the mean value, so the function calculates the squared deviation of xi from the mean of all the xs.

We can turn the expression $\left(x_i - \overline{x}\right)^2$ into a function, square-deviation, that we map over the sequence of xs. We can also make use of the mean function we've already created to sum the values in the sequence and divide by the count.

```
(defn variance [xs]
  (let [x-bar (mean xs)
        n     (count xs)
        square-deviation (fn [x]
                           (i/sq (- x x-bar)))]
    (mean (map square-deviation xs))))
```

We're using Incanter's i/sq function to calculate the square of our expression.

Since we've squared the deviation before taking the mean, the units of variance are also squared, so the units of the variance of the UK electorate are "people squared". This is somewhat unnatural to reason about. We can make the units more natural by taking the square root of the variance so the units are "people" again, and the result is called the **standard deviation**:

```
(defn standard-deviation [xs]
  (i/sqrt (variance xs)))

(defn ex-1-9 []
  (->> (load-data :uk-scrubbed)
       (i/$ "Electorate")
       (standard-deviation)))

;; 7672.77
```

Incanter's implements functions to calculate the variance and standard deviation as
s/variance and s/sd respectively.

Quantiles

The median is one way to calculate the *middle* value from a list, and the variance
provides a way to measure the spread of the data about this midpoint. If the entire
spread of data were represented on a scale of zero to one, the median would be the
value at 0.5.

For example, consider the following sequence of numbers:

```
[10 11 15 21 22.5 28 30]
```

There are seven numbers in the sequence, so the median is the fourth, or 21. This
is also referred to as the 0.5 quantile. We can get a richer picture of a sequence of
numbers by looking at the 0, 0.25, 0.5, 0.7, and 1.0 quantiles. Taken together, these
numbers will not only show the median, but will also summarize the range of the
data and how the numbers are distributed within it. They're sometimes referred
to as the *five-number summary*.

One way to calculate the five-number summary for the UK electorate data is shown
as follows:

```clojure
(defn quantile [q xs]
  (let [n (dec (count xs))
        i (-> (* n q)
              (+ 1/2)
              (int))]
    (nth (sort xs) i)))


(defn ex-1-10 []
  (let [xs (->> (load-data :uk-scrubbed)
                (i/$ "Electorate"))
        f (fn [q]
            (quantile q xs))]
    (map f [0 1/4 1/2 3/4 1])))

;; (21780.0 66219.0 70991.0 75115.0 109922.0)
```

Quantiles can also be calculated in Incanter directly with the s/quantile function.
A sequence of desired quantiles is passed as the keyword argument :probs.

Incanter's `quantile` function uses a variant of the algorithm shown earlier called the **phi-quantile**, which performs linear interpolation between consecutive numbers in certain cases. There are many alternative ways of calculating quantiles—consult `https://en.wikipedia.org/wiki/Quantile` for a discussion of the differences.

Where quantiles split the range into four equal ranges as earlier, they are called **quartiles**. The difference between the lower and upper quartile is referred to as the **interquartile range**, also often abbreviated to just **IQR**. Like the variance about the mean, the IQR gives a measure of the spread of the data about the median.

Binning data

To develop an intuition for what these various calculations of variance are measuring, we can employ a technique called **binning**. Where data is continuous, using `frequencies` (as we did with the election data to count the nils) is not practical since no two values may be the same. However, it's possible to get a broad sense of the structure of the data by grouping the data into discrete intervals.

The process of binning is to divide the range of values into a number of consecutive, equally-sized, smaller bins. Each value in the original series falls into exactly one bin. By counting the number of points falling into each bin, we can get a sense of the spread of the data:

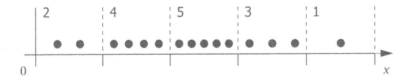

The preceding illustration shows fifteen values of x split into five equally-sized bins. By counting the number of points falling into each bin we can clearly see that most points fall in the middle bin, with fewer points falling into the bins towards the edges. We can achieve the same in Clojure with the following `bin` function:

```
(defn bin [n-bins xs]
  (let [min-x    (apply min xs)
        max-x    (apply max xs)
        range-x  (- max-x min-x)
        bin-fn   (fn [x]
                   (-> x
                       (- min-x)
```

```
                        (/ range-x)
                        (* n-bins)
                        (int)
                        (min (dec n-bins))))]
        (map bin-fn xs)))
```

For example, we can bin range 0-14 into 5 bins like so:

```
(bin 5 (range 15))


;; (0 0 0 1 1 1 2 2 2 3 3 3 4 4 4)
```

Once we've binned the values we can then use the `frequencies` function once again to count the number of points in each bin. In the following code, we use the function to split the UK electorate data into five bins:

```
(defn ex-1-11 []
  (->> (load-data :uk-scrubbed)
       (i/$ "Electorate")
       (bin 10)
       (frequencies)))


;; {1 26, 2 450, 3 171, 4 1, 0 2}
```

The count of points in the extremal bins (0 and 4) is much lower than the bins in the middle—the counts seem to rise up towards the median and then down again. In the next section, we'll visualize the shape of these counts.

Histograms

A histogram is one way to visualize the distribution of a single sequence of values. Histograms simply take a continuous distribution, bin it, and plot the frequencies of points falling into each bin as a bar. The height of each bar in the histogram represents how many points in the data are contained in that bin.

We've already seen how to bin data ourselves, but `incanter.charts` contains a `histogram` function that will bin the data and visualize it as a histogram in two steps. We require `incanter.charts` as c in this chapter (and throughout the book).

```
(defn ex-1-12 []
  (-> (load-data :uk-scrubbed)
      (i/$ "Electorate")
      (c/histogram)
      (i/view)))
```

The preceding code generates the following chart:

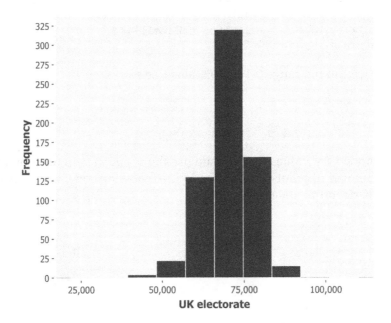

We can configure the number of bins data is segmented into by passing the keyword argument :nbins as the second parameter to the histogram function:

```
(defn ex-1-13 []
  (-> (uk-electorate)
      (c/histogram :nbins 200)
      (i/view)))
```

The preceding graph shows a single, high peak but expresses the shape of the data quite crudely. The following graph shows fine detail, but the volume of the bars obscures the shape of the distribution, particularly in the tails:

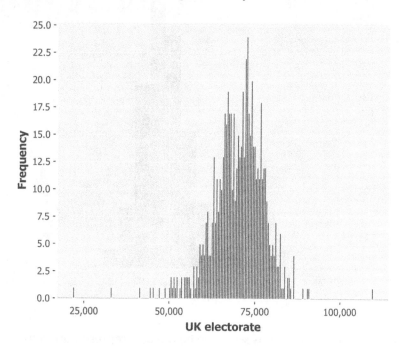

Choosing the number of bins to represent your data is a fine balance — too few bins and the shape of the data will only be crudely represented, too many and noisy features may obscure the underlying structure.

```
(defn ex-1-14 []
  (-> (i/$ "Electorate" (load-data :uk-scrubbed))
      (c/histogram :x-label "UK electorate"
                   :nbins 20)
      (i/view)))
```

The following shows a histogram of 20 bars instead:

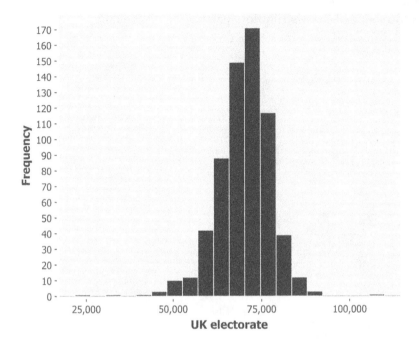

This final chart containing 20 bins seems to be the best representation for this data so far.

Along with the mean and the median, the *mode* is another way of measuring the average value of a sequence—it's defined as the most frequently occurring value in the sequence. The mode is strictly only defined for sequences with at least one duplicated value; for many distributions, this is not the case and the mode is undefined. Nonetheless, the peak of the histogram is often referred to as the mode, since it corresponds to the most popular bin.

We can clearly see that the distribution is quite symmetrical about the mode, with values falling sharply either side along shallow tails. This is data following an approximately normal distribution.

The normal distribution

A histogram will tell you approximately how data is distributed throughout its range, and provide a visual means of classifying your data into one of a handful of common distributions. Many distributions occur frequently in data analysis, but none so much as the normal distribution, also called the **Gaussian distribution**.

 The distribution is named the normal distribution because of how often it occurs in nature. Galileo noticed that the errors in his astronomical measurements followed a distribution where small deviations from the mean occurred more frequently than large deviations. It was the great mathematician Gauss' contribution to describing the mathematical shape of these errors that led to the distribution also being called the Gaussian distribution in his honor.

A distribution is like a compression algorithm: it allows a potentially large amount of data to be summarized very efficiently. The normal distribution requires just two parameters from which the rest of the data can be approximated – the mean and the standard deviation.

The central limit theorem

The reason for the normal distribution's ubiquity is partly explained by the central limit theorem. Values generated from diverse distributions will tend to converge to the normal distribution under certain circumstances, as we will show next.

A common distribution in programming is the *uniform* distribution. This is the distribution of numbers generated by Clojure's rand function: for a fair random number generator, all numbers have an equal chance of being generated. We can visualize this on a histogram by generating a random number between zero and one many times over and plotting the results.

```
(defn ex-1-15 []
  (let [xs (->> (repeatedly rand)
                (take 10000))]
    (-> (c/histogram xs
                     :x-label "Uniform distribution"
                     :nbins 20)
        (i/view))))
```

The preceding code will generate the following histogram:

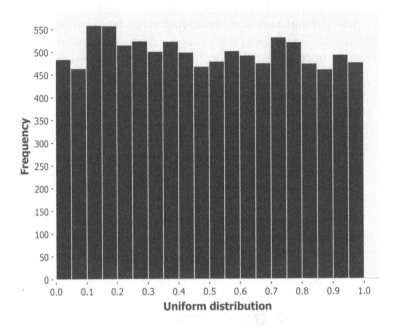

Each bar of the histogram is approximately the same height, corresponding to the equal probability of generating a number that falls into each bin. The bars aren't exactly the same height since the uniform distribution describes the theoretical output that our random sampling can't mirror precisely. Over the next several chapters, we'll learn ways to precisely quantify the difference between theory and practice to determine whether the differences are large enough to be concerned with. In this case, they are not.

If instead we generate a histogram of the means of sequences of numbers, we'll end up with a distribution that looks rather different.

```
(defn ex-1-16 []
  (let [xs (->> (repeatedly rand)
                (partition 10)
                (map mean)
                (take 10000))]
    (-> (c/histogram xs
                     :x-label "Distribution of means"
                     :nbins 20)
        (i/view)))))
```

The preceding code will provide an output similar to the following histogram:

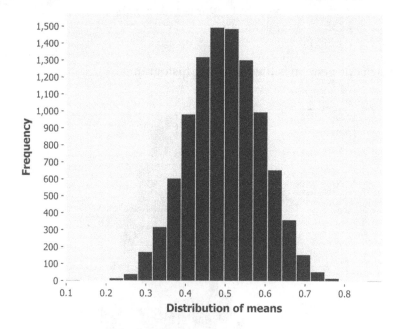

Although it's not impossible for the mean to be close to zero or one, it's exceedingly improbable and grows less probable as both the number of averaged numbers and the number of sampled averages grow. In fact, the output is exceedingly close to the normal distribution.

This outcome — where the average effect of many small random fluctuations leads to the normal distribution — is called the **central limit theorem**, sometimes abbreviated to **CLT**, and goes a long way towards explaining why the normal distribution occurs so frequently in natural phenomena.

The central limit theorem wasn't named until the 20th century, although the effect had been documented as early as 1733 by the French mathematician Abraham de Moivre, who used the normal distribution to approximate the number of heads resulting from tosses of a fair coin. The outcome of coin tosses is best modeled with the binomial distribution, which we will introduce in *Chapter 4, Classification*. While the central limit theorem provides a way to generate samples from an approximate normal distribution, Incanter's `distributions` namespace provides functions for generating samples efficiently from a variety of distributions, including the normal:

```
(defn ex-1-17 []
  (let [distribution (d/normal-distribution)
        xs (->> (repeatedly #(d/draw distribution))
```

```
                         (take 10000))]
        (-> (c/histogram xs
                         :x-label "Normal distribution"
                         :nbins 20)
            (i/view))))
```

The preceding code generates the following histogram:

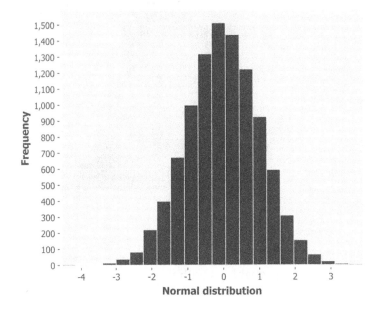

The d/draw function will return one sample from the supplied distribution. The default mean and standard deviation from d/normal-distribution are zero and one respectively.

Poincaré's baker

There's a story that, while almost certainly apocryphal, allows us to look in more detail at the way in which the central limit theorem allows us to reason about how distributions are formed. It concerns the celebrated nineteenth century French polymath Henri Poincaré who, so the story goes, weighed his bread every day for a year.

Baking was a regulated profession, and Poincaré discovered that, while the weights of the bread followed a normal distribution, the peak was at 950g rather than the advertised 1kg. He reported his baker to the authorities and so the baker was fined.

The next year, Poincaré continued to weigh his bread from the same baker. He found the mean value was now 1kg, but that the distribution was no longer symmetrical around the mean. The distribution was skewed to the right, consistent with the baker giving Poincaré only the heaviest of his loaves. Poincaré reported his baker to the authorities once more and his baker was fined a second time.

Whether the story is true or not needn't concern us here; it's provided simply to illustrate a key point—the distribution of a sequence of numbers can tell us something important about the process that generated it.

Generating distributions

To develop our intuition about the normal distribution and variance, let's model an honest and dishonest baker using Incanter's distribution functions. We can model the honest baker as a normal distribution with a mean of 1,000, corresponding to a fair loaf of 1kg. We'll assume a variance in the baking process that results in a standard deviation of 30g.

```
(defn honest-baker [mean sd]
  (let [distribution (d/normal-distribution mean sd)]
    (repeatedly #(d/draw distribution))))

(defn ex-1-18 []
  (-> (take 10000 (honest-baker 1000 30))
      (c/histogram :x-label "Honest baker"
                   :nbins 25)
      (i/view)))
```

The preceding code will provide an output similar to the following histogram:

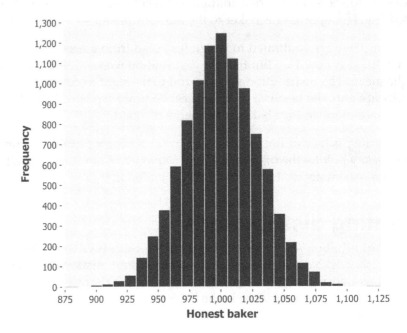

Now, let's model a baker who sells only the heaviest of his loaves. We partition the sequence into groups of thirteen (a "baker's dozen") and pick the maximum value:

```
(defn dishonest-baker [mean sd]
  (let [distribution (d/normal-distribution mean sd)]
    (->> (repeatedly #(d/draw distribution))
         (partition 13)
         (map (partial apply max)))))

(defn ex-1-19 []
  (-> (take 10000 (dishonest-baker 950 30))
      (c/histogram :x-label "Dishonest baker"
                   :nbins 25)
      (i/view)))
```

The preceding code will produce a histogram similar to the following:

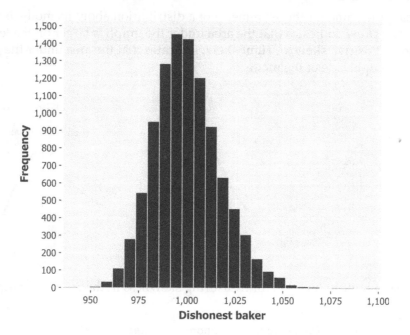

It should be apparent that this histogram does not look quite like the others we have seen. The mean value is still 1kg, but the spread of values around the mean is no longer symmetrical. We say that this histogram indicates a **skewed normal distribution**.

Skewness

Skewness is the name for the asymmetry of a distribution about its mode. **Negative skew**, or **left skew**, indicates that the area under the graph is larger on the left side of the mode. **Positive skew**, or **right skew**, indicates that the area under the graph is larger on the right side of the mode.

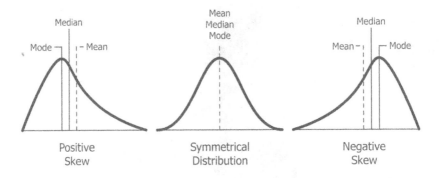

Incanter has a built-in function for measuring skewness in the `stats` namespace:

```
(defn ex-1-20 []
  (let [weights (take 10000 (dishonest-baker 950 30))]
    {:mean (mean weights)
     :median (median weights)
     :skewness (s/skewness weights)}))
```

The preceding example shows that the skewness of the dishonest baker's output is about 0.4, quantifying the skew evident in the histogram.

Quantile-quantile plots

We encountered quantiles as a means of describing the distribution of data earlier in the chapter. Recall that the `quantile` function accepts a number between zero and one and returns the value of the sequence at that point. 0.5 corresponds to the median value.

Plotting the quantiles of your data against the quantiles of the normal distribution allows us to see how our measured data compares against the theoretical distribution. Plots such as this are called **Q-Q plots** and they provide a quick and intuitive way of determining normality. For data corresponding closely to the normal distribution, the Q-Q Plot is a straight line. Deviations from a straight line indicate the manner in which the data deviates from the idealized normal distribution.

Let's plot Q-Q plots for both our honest and dishonest bakers side-by-side. Incanter's `c/qq-plot` function accepts the list of data points and generates a scatter chart of the sample quantiles plotted against the quantiles from the theoretical normal distribution:

```
(defn ex-1-21 []
  (->> (honest-baker 1000 30)
       (take 10000)
       (c/qq-plot)
       (i/view))
  (->> (dishonest-baker 950 30)
       (take 10000)
       (c/qq-plot)
       (i/view)))
```

The preceding code will produce the following plots:

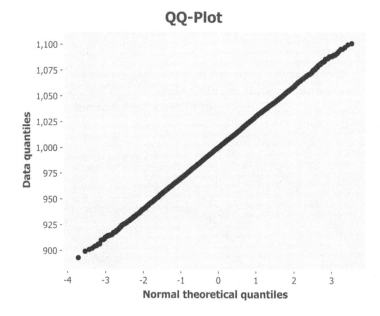

The Q-Q plot for the honest baker is shown earlier. The dishonest baker's plot is next:

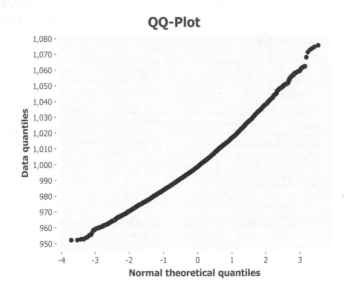

The fact that the line is curved indicates that the data is positively skewed; a curve in the other direction would indicate negative skew. In fact, Q-Q plots make it easier to discern a wide variety of deviations from the standard normal distribution, as shown in the following diagram:

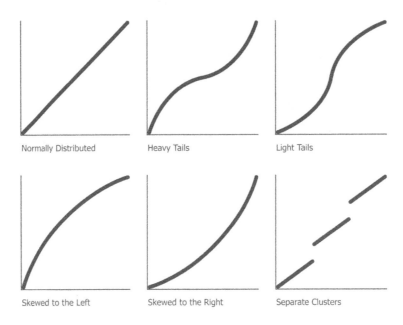

Q-Q plots compare the distribution of the honest and dishonest baker against the theoretical normal distribution. In the next section, we'll compare several alternative ways of visually comparing two (or more) measured sequences of values with each other.

Comparative visualizations

Q-Q plots provide a great way to compare a measured, empirical distribution to a theoretical normal distribution. If we'd like to compare two or more empirical distributions with each other, we can't use Incanter's Q-Q plot charts. We have a variety of other options, though, as shown in the next two sections.

Box plots

Box plots, or **box and whisker plots**, are a way to visualize the descriptive statistics of median and variance visually. We can generate them using the following code:

```
(defn ex-1-22 []
  (-> (c/box-plot (->> (honest-baker 1000 30)
                       (take 10000))
                  :legend true
                  :y-label "Loaf weight (g)"
                  :series-label "Honest baker")
      (c/add-box-plot (->> (dishonest-baker 950 30)
                           (take 10000))
                      :series-label "Dishonest baker")
      (i/view)))
```

This creates the following plot:

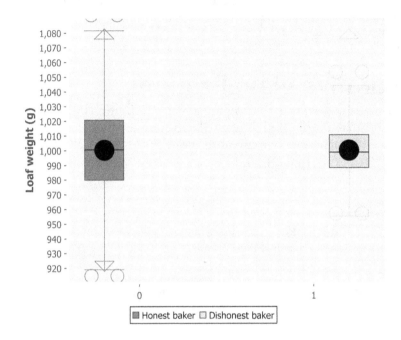

The boxes in the center of the plot represent the **interquartile range**. The median is the line across the middle of the box, and the mean is the large black dot. For the honest baker, the median passes through the centre of the circle, indicating the mean and median are about the same. For the dishonest baker, the mean is offset from the median, indicating a skew.

The whiskers indicate the range of the data and outliers are represented by hollow circles. In just one chart, we're more clearly able to see the difference between the two distributions than we were on either the histograms or the Q-Q plots independently.

Cumulative distribution functions

Cumulative distribution functions, also known as **CDFs**, describe the probability that a value drawn from a distribution will have a value less than x. Like all probability distributions, they value between 0 and 1, with 0 representing impossibility and 1 representing certainty. For example, imagine that I'm about to throw a six-sided die. What's the probability that I'll roll less than a six?

For a fair die, the probability I'll row a five or lower is $\frac{5}{6}$. Conversely, the probability I'll roll a one is only $\frac{1}{6}$. Three or lower corresponds to even odds—a probability of 50 percent.

The CDF of die rolls follows the same pattern as all CDFs—for numbers at the lower end of the range, the CDF is close to zero, corresponding to a low probability of selecting numbers in this range or below. At the high end of the range, the CDF is close to one, since most values drawn from the sequence will be lower.

 The CDF and quantiles are closely related to each other—the CDF is the inverse of the quantile function. If the 0.5 quantile corresponds to a value of 1,000, then the CDF for 1,000 is 0.5.

Just as Incanter's s/quantile function allows us to sample values from a distribution at specific points, the s/cdf-empirical function allows us to input a value from the sequence and return a value between zero and one. It is a higher-order function—one that will accept the value (in this case, a sequence of values) and return a function. The returned function can then be called as often as necessary with different input values, returning the CDF for each of them.

 Higher-order functions are functions that accept or return functions.

Let's plot the CDF of both the honest and dishonest bakers side by side. We can use Incanter's c/xy-plot for visualizing the CDF by plotting the source data—the samples from our honest and dishonest bakers—against the probabilities calculated against the empirical CDF. The c/xy-plot function expects the x values and the y values to be supplied as two separate sequences of values.

To plot both distributions on the same chart, we need to be able to provide multiple series to our xy-plot. Incanter offers functions for many of its charts to add additional series. In the case of an xy-plot, we can use the function c/add-lines, which accepts the chart as the first argument, and the x series and the y series of data as the next two arguments respectively. You can also pass an optional series label. We do this in the following code so we can tell the two series apart on the finished chart:

```
(defn ex-1-23 []
  (let [sample-honest    (->> (honest-baker 1000 30)
                              (take 1000))
        sample-dishonest (->> (dishonest-baker 950 30)
                              (take 1000))
```

```
      ecdf-honest     (s/cdf-empirical sample-honest)
      ecdf-dishonest (s/cdf-empirical sample-dishonest)]
  (-> (c/xy-plot sample-honest (map ecdf-honest sample-honest)
              :x-label "Loaf Weight"
              :y-label "Probability"
              :legend true
              :series-label "Honest baker")
      (c/add-lines sample-dishonest
              (map ecdf-dishonest sample-dishonest)
              :series-label "Dishonest baker")
      (i/view))))
```

The preceding code generates the following chart:

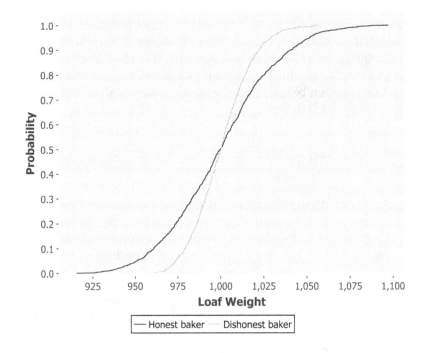

Although it looks very different, this chart shows essentially the same information as the box and whisker plot. We can see that the two lines cross at approximately the median of 0.5, corresponding to 1,000g. The dishonest line is truncated at the lower tail and longer on the upper tail, corresponding to a skewed distribution.

The importance of visualizations

Simple visualizations like those earlier are succinct ways of conveying a large quantity of information. They complement the summary statistics we calculated earlier in the chapter, and it's important that we use them. Statistics such as the mean and standard deviation necessarily conceal a lot of information as they reduce a sequence down to just a single number.

The statistician Francis Anscombe devised a collection of four scatter plots, known as **Anscombe's Quartet**, that have nearly identical statistical properties (including the mean, variance, and standard deviation). In spite of this, it's visually apparent that the distribution of *x*s and *y*s are all very different:

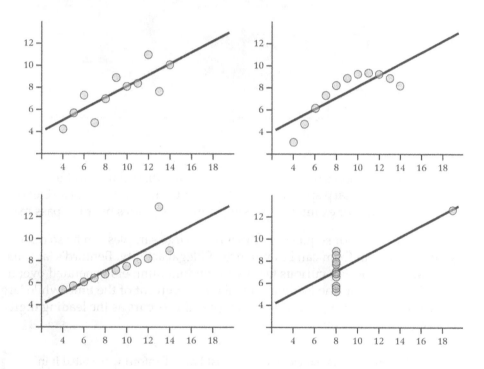

Datasets don't have to be contrived to reveal valuable insights when graphed. Take for example this histogram of the marks earned by candidates in Poland's national Matura exam in 2013:

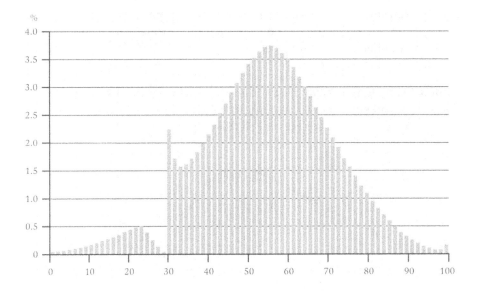

We might expect the abilities of students to be normally distributed and indeed — with the exception of a sharp spike around 30 percent — it is. What we can clearly see is the very human effect of examiners nudging student's grades over the pass mark.

In fact, the distributions for sequences drawn from large samples can be so reliable that any deviation from them can be evidence of illegal activity. Benford's law, also called the first-digit law, is a curious feature of random numbers generated over a large range. One occurs as the leading digit about 30 percent of the time, while larger digits occur less and less frequently. For example, nine occurs as the leading digit less than 5 percent of the time.

Benford's law is named after physicist Frank Benford who stated it in 1938 and showed its consistency across a wide variety of data sources. It had been previously observed by Simon Newcomb over 50 years earlier, who noticed that the pages of his books of logarithm tables were more battered for numbers beginning with the digit one.

Benford showed that the law applied to data as diverse as electricity bills, street addresses, stock prices, population numbers, death rates, and lengths of rivers. The law is so consistent for data sets covering large ranges of values that deviation from it has been accepted as evidence in trials for financial fraud.

Visualizing electorate data

Let's return to the election data and compare the electorate sequence we created earlier against the theoretical normal distribution CDF. We can use Incanter's `s/cdf-normal` function to generate a normal CDF from a sequence of values. The default mean is 0 and standard deviation is 1, so we'll need to provide the measured mean and standard deviation from the electorate data. These values for our electorate data are 70,150 and 7,679, respectively.

We generated an empirical CDF earlier in the chapter. The following example simply generates each of the two CDFs and plots them on a single `c/xy-plot`:

```
(defn ex-1-24 []
  (let [electorate (->> (load-data :uk-scrubbed)
                        (i/$ "Electorate"))
        ecdf    (s/cdf-empirical electorate)
        fitted (s/cdf-normal electorate
                             :mean (s/mean electorate)
                             :sd   (s/sd electorate))]
    (-> (c/xy-plot electorate fitted
                   :x-label "Electorate"
                   :y-label "Probability"
                   :series-label "Fitted"
                   :legend true)
        (c/add-lines electorate (map ecdf electorate)
                     :series-label "Empirical")
        (i/view))))
```

The preceding example generates the following plot:

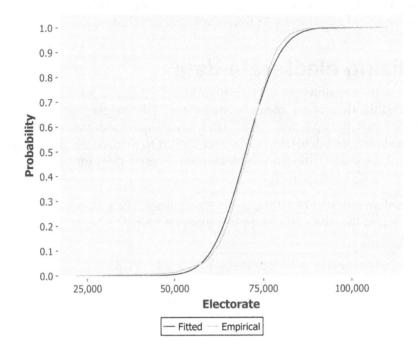

You can see from the proximity of the two lines to each other how closely this data resembles normality, although a slight skew is evident. The skew is in the opposite direction to the dishonest baker CDF we plotted previously, so our electorate data is slightly skewed to the left.

As we're comparing our distribution against the theoretical normal distribution, let's use a Q-Q plot, which will do this by default:

```
(defn ex-1-25 []
  (->> (load-data :uk-scrubbed)
       (i/$ "Electorate")
       (c/qq-plot)
       (i/view)))
```

The following Q-Q plot does an even better job of highlighting the left skew evident in the data:

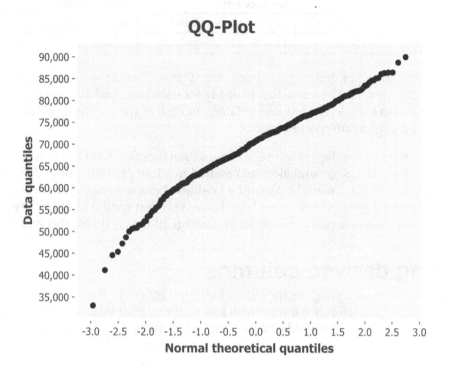

As we expected, the curve bows in the opposite direction to the dishonest baker Q-Q plot earlier in the chapter. This indicates that there is a greater number of constituencies that are smaller than we would expect if the data were more closely normally distributed.

Adding columns

So far this chapter, we've reduced the size of our dataset by filtering both rows and columns. Often we'll want to add rows to a dataset instead, and Incanter supports this in several ways.

Firstly, we can choose whether to replace an existing column within the dataset or append an additional column to the dataset. Secondly, we can choose whether to supply the new column values to replace the existing column values directly, or whether to calculate the new values by applying a function to each row of the data.

The following chart lists our options and the corresponding Incanter function to use:

	Replace data	Append data
By providing a sequence	`i/replace-column`	`i/add-column`
By applying a function	`i/transform-column`	`i/add-derived-column`

When transforming or deriving a column based on a function, we pass the name of the new column to create, a function to apply for each row, and also a sequence of existing column names. The values contained in each of these existing columns will comprise the arguments to our function.

Let's show how to use the `i/add-derived-column` function with reference to a real example. The 2010 UK general election resulted in a hung parliament with no single party commanding an overall majority. A coalition between the Conservative and Liberal Democrat parties was formed. In the next section we'll find out how many people voted for either party, and what percentage of the total vote this was.

Adding derived columns

To find out what percentage of the electorate voted for either the Conservative or Liberal Democrat parties, we'll want to calculate the sum of votes for either party. Since we're creating a new field of data based on a function of the existing data, we'll want to use the `i/add-derived-column` function.

```
(defn ex-1-26 []
  (->> (load-data :uk-scrubbed)
       (i/add-derived-column :victors [:Con :LD] +)))
```

If we run this now, however, an exception will be generated:

```
ClassCastException java.lang.String cannot be cast to java.lang.Number
clojure.lang.Numbers.add (Numbers.java:126)
```

Unfortunately Clojure is complaining that we're trying to add a `java.lang.String`. Clearly either (or both) the `Con` or the `LD` columns contain string values, but which? We can use frequencies again to see the extent of the problem:

```
(->> (load-data :uk-scrubbed)
     ($ "Con")
     (map type)
     (frequencies))

;; {java.lang.Double 631, java.lang.String 19}

(->> (load-data :uk-scrubbed)
```

```
       ($ "LD")
       (map type)
       (frequencies))

  ;; {java.lang.Double 631, java.lang.String 19}
```

Let's use the `i/$where` function we encountered earlier in the chapter to inspect just these rows:

```
(defn ex-1-27 []
  (->> (load-data :uk-scrubbed)
       (i/$where #(not-any? number? [(% "Con") (% "LD")]))
       (i/$ [:Region :Electorate :Con :LD])))

;; |                  Region | Electorate | Con | LD |
;; |-------------------------+------------+-----+----|
;; | Northern Ireland |          60204.0 |     |    |
;; | Northern Ireland |          73338.0 |     |    |
;; | Northern Ireland |          63054.0 |     |    |
;; ...
```

This bit of exploration should be enough to convince us that the reason for these fields being blank is that candidates were not put forward in the corresponding constituencies. Should they be filtered out or assumed to be zero? This is an interesting question. Let's filter them out, since it wasn't even possible for voters to choose a Liberal Democrat or Conservative candidate in these constituencies. If instead we assumed a zero, we would artificially lower the mean number of people who—given the choice—voted for either of these parties.

Now that we know how to filter the problematic rows, let's add the derived columns for the victor and the victor's share of the vote, along with election turnout. We filter the rows to show only those where both a Conservative and Liberal Democrat candidate were put forward:

```
(defmethod load-data :uk-victors [_]
  (->> (load-data :uk-scrubbed)
       (i/$where {:Con {:$fn number?} :LD {:$fn number?}})
       (i/add-derived-column :victors [:Con :LD] +)
       (i/add-derived-column :victors-share [:victors :Votes] /)
       (i/add-derived-column :turnout [:Votes :Electorate] /)))
```

As a result, we now have three additional columns in our dataset: `:victors`, `:victors-share`, and `:turnout`. Let's plot the victor's share of the vote as a Q-Q plot to see how it compares against the theoretical normal distribution:

```
(defn ex-1-28 []
  (->> (load-data :uk-victors)
       (i/$ :victors-share)
       (c/qq-plot)
       (i/view)))
```

The preceding code generates the following plot:

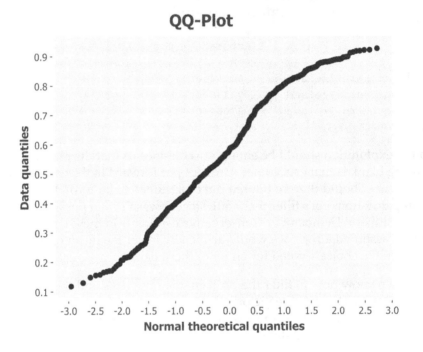

Referring back to the diagram of various Q-Q plot shapes earlier in the chapter reveals that the victor's share of the vote has "light tails" compared to the normal distribution. This means that more of the data is closer to the mean than we might expect from truly normally distributed data.

Comparative visualizations of electorate data

Let's look now at a dataset from another general election, this time from Russia in 2011. Russia is a much larger country, and its election data is much larger too. We'll be loading two large Excel files into the memory, which may exceed your default JVM heap size.

To expand the amount of memory available to Incanter, we can adjust the JVM settings in the project's `profile.clj`. The a vector of configuration flags for the JVM can be provided with the key `:jvm-opts`. Here we're using Java's `Xmx` flag to increase the heap size to 1GB. This should be more than enough.

```
:jvm-opts ["-Xmx1G"]
```

Russia's data is available in two data files. Fortunately the columns are the same in each, so they can be concatenated together end-to-end. Incanter's function `i/conj-rows` exists for precisely this purpose:

```
(defmethod load-data :ru [_]
  (i/conj-rows (-> (io/resource "Russia2011_1of2.xls")
                   (str)
                   (xls/read-xls))
               (-> (io/resource "Russia2011_2of2.xls")
                   (str)
                   (xls/read-xls))))
```

In the preceding code, we define a third implementation of the `load-data` multimethod to load and combine both Russia files.

 In addition to `conj-rows`, Incanter-core also defines `conj-columns` that will merge the columns of datasets provided they have the same number of rows.

Let's see what the Russia data column names are:

```
(defn ex-1-29 []
  (-> (load-data :ru)
      (i/col-names)))

;; ["Code for district"
;; "Number of the polling district (unique to state, not overall)"
;; "Name of district" "Number of voters included in voters list"
;; "The number of ballots received by the precinct election
;; commission" ...]
```

The column names in the Russia dataset are very descriptive, but perhaps longer than we want to type out. Also, it would be convenient if columns that represent the same attributes as we've already seen in the UK election data (the victor's share and turnout for example) were labeled the same in both datasets. Let's rename them accordingly.

Along with a dataset, the i/rename-cols function expects to receive a map whose keys are the current column names with values corresponding to the desired new column name. If we combine this with the i/add-derived-column data we have already seen, we arrive at the following:

```
(defmethod load-data :ru-victors [_]
  (->> (load-data :ru)
       (i/rename-cols
        {"Number of voters included in voters list" :electorate
         "Number of valid ballots" :valid-ballots
         "United Russia" :victors})
       (i/add-derived-column :victors-share
                             [:victors :valid-ballots] i/safe-div)
       (i/add-derived-column :turnout
                             [:valid-ballots :electorate] /)))
```

The i/safe-div function is identical to / but will protect against division by zero. Rather than raising an exception, it returns the value Infinity, which will be ignored by Incanter's statistical and charting functions.

Visualizing the Russian election data

We previously saw that a histogram of the UK election turnout was approximately normal (albeit with light tails). Now that we've loaded and transformed the Russian election data, let's see how it compares:

```
(defn ex-1-30 []
  (-> (i/$ :turnout (load-data :ru-victors))
      (c/histogram :x-label "Russia turnout"
                   :nbins 20)
      (i/view)))
```

The preceding example generates the following histogram:

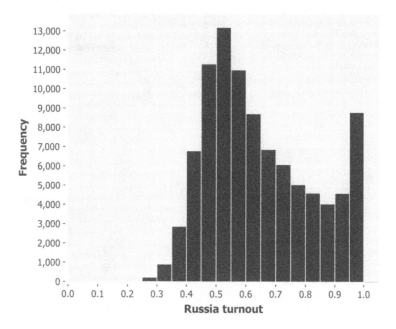

This histogram doesn't look at all like the classic bell-shaped curves we've seen so far. There's a pronounced positive skew, and the voter turnout actually increases from 80 percent towards 100 percent—the opposite of what we would expect from normally-distributed data.

Given the expectations set by the UK data and by the central limit theorem, this is a curious result. Let's visualize the data with a Q-Q plot instead:

```
(defn ex-1-31 []
  (->> (load-data :ru-victors)
       (i/$ :turnout)
       (c/qq-plot)
       (i/view)))
```

This returns the following plot:

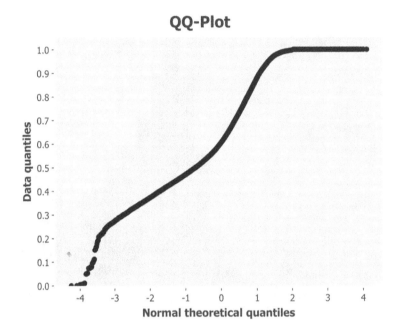

This Q-Q plot is neither a straight line nor a particularly S-shaped curve. In fact, the Q-Q plot suggests a light tail at the top end of the distribution and a heavy tail at the bottom. This is almost the opposite of what we see on the histogram, which clearly indicates an extremely heavy right tail.

In fact, it's precisely because the tail is so heavy that the Q-Q plot is misleading: the density of points between 0.5 and 1.0 on the histogram suggests that the peak should be around 0.7 with a right tail continuing beyond 1.0. It's clearly illogical that we would have a percentage exceeding 100 percent but the Q-Q plot doesn't account for this (it doesn't know we're plotting percentages), so the sudden absence of data beyond 1.0 is interpreted as a clipped right tail.

Given the central limit theorem, and what we've observed with the UK election data, the tendency towards 100 percent voter turnout is curious. Let's compare the UK and Russia datasets side-by-side.

Comparative visualizations

Let's suppose we'd like to compare the distributions of electorate data between the UK and Russia. We've already seen in this chapter how to make use of CDFs and box plots, so let's investigate an alternative that's similar to a histogram.

We could try and plot both datasets on a histogram but this would be a bad idea. We wouldn't be able to interpret the results for two reasons:

- The sizes of the voting districts, and therefore the means of the distributions, are very different
- The number of voting districts overall is so different, so the histograms bars will have different heights

An alternative to the histogram that addresses both of these issues is the **probability mass function (PMF)**.

Probability mass functions

The probability mass function, or PMF, has a lot in common with a histogram. Instead of plotting the counts of values falling into bins, though, it instead plots the probability that a number drawn from a distribution will be exactly equal to a given value. As the function assigns a probability to every value that can possibly be returned by the distribution, and because probabilities are measured on a scale from zero to one, (with one corresponding to certainty), the area under the probability mass function is equal to one.

Thus, the PMF ensures that the area under our plots will be comparable between datasets. However, we still have the issue that the sizes of the voting districts—and therefore the means of the distributions—can't be compared. This can be addressed by a separate technique—normalization.

> Normalizing the data isn't related to the normal distribution. It's the name given to the general task of bringing one or more sequences of values into alignment. Depending on the context, it could mean simply adjusting the values so they fall within the same range, or more sophisticated procedures to ensure that the distributions of data are the same. In general, the goal of normalization is to facilitate the comparison of two or more series of data.

There are innumerable ways to normalize data, but one of the most basic is to ensure that each series is in the range zero to one. None of our values decrease below zero, so we can accomplish this normalization by simply dividing by the largest value:

```
(defn as-pmf [bins]
  (let [histogram (frequencies bins)
        total     (reduce + (vals histogram))]
    (->> histogram
         (map (fn [[k v]]
                [k (/ v total)]))
         (into {})))))
```

With the preceding function in place, we can normalize both the UK and Russia data and plot it side by side on the same axes:

```
(defn ex-1-32 []
  (let [n-bins 40
        uk (->> (load-data :uk-victors)
                (i/$ :turnout)
                (bin n-bins)
                (as-pmf))
        ru (->> (load-data :ru-victors)
                (i/$ :turnout)
                (bin n-bins)
                (as-pmf))]
    (-> (c/xy-plot (keys uk) (vals uk)
                   :series-label "UK"
                   :legend true
                   :x-label "Turnout Bins"
                   :y-label "Probability")
        (c/add-lines (keys ru) (vals ru)
                     :series-label "Russia")
        (i/view))))
```

The preceding example generates the following chart:

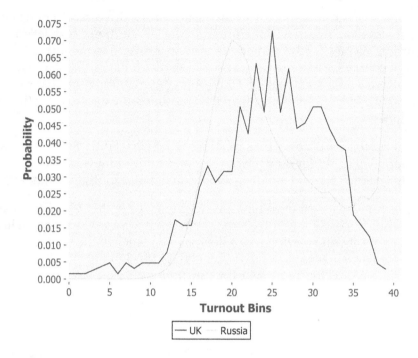

After normalization, the two distributions can be compared more readily. It's clearly apparent how — in spite of having a lower mean turnout than the UK — the Russia election had a massive uplift towards 100-percent turnout. Insofar as it represents the combined effect of many independent choices, we would expect election results to conform to the central limit theorem and be approximately normally distributed. In fact, election results from around the world generally conform to this expectation.

Although not quite as high as the modal peak in the center of the distribution — corresponding to approximately 50 percent turnout — the Russian election data presents a very anomalous result. Researcher Peter Klimek and his colleagues at the Medical University of Vienna have gone as far as to suggest that this is a clear signature of ballot-rigging.

Scatter plots

We've observed the curious results for the turnout at the Russian election and identified that it has a different signature from the UK election. Next, let's see how the proportion of votes for the winning candidate is related to the turnout. After all, if the unexpectedly high turnout really is a sign of foul play by the incumbent government, we'd anticipate that they'll be voting for themselves rather than anyone else. Thus we'd expect most, if not all, of these additional votes to be for the ultimate election winners.

Chapter 3, Correlation, will cover the statistics behind correlating two variables in much more detail, but for now it would be interesting simply to visualize the relationship between turnout and the proportion of votes for the winning party.

The final visualization we'll introduce this chapter is the scatter plot. Scatter plots are very useful for visualizing correlations between two variables: where a linear correlation exists, it will be evident as a diagonal tendency in the scatter plot. Incanter contains the `c/scatter-plot` function for this kind of chart with arguments the same as for the `c/xy-plot` function.

```
(defn ex-1-33 []
  (let [data (load-data :uk-victors)]
    (-> (c/scatter-plot (i/$ :turnout data)
                        (i/$ :victors-share data)
                        :x-label "Turnout"
                        :y-label "Victor's Share")
        (i/view))))
```

The preceding code generates the following chart:

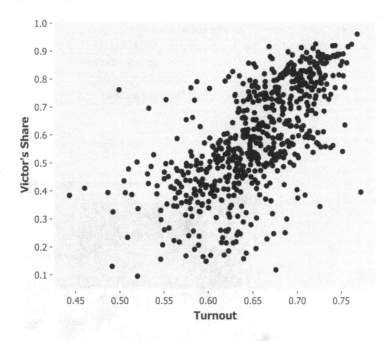

Although the points are arranged broadly in a fuzzy ellipse, a diagonal tendency towards the top right of the scatter plot is clearly apparent. This indicates an interesting result—turnout is correlated with the proportion of votes for the ultimate election winners. We might have expected the reverse: voter complacency leading to a lower turnout where there was a clear victor in the running.

As mentioned earlier, the UK election of 2010 was far from ordinary, resulting in a hung parliament and a coalition government. In fact, the "winners" in this case represent two parties who had, up until election day, been opponents. A vote for either counts as a vote for the winners.

Next, we'll create the same scatter plot for the Russia election:

```
(defn ex-1-34 []
  (let [data (load-data :ru-victors)]
    (-> (c/scatter-plot (i/$ :turnout data)
                        (i/$ :victors-share data)
                        :x-label "Turnout"
                        :y-label "Victor's Share")
        (i/view))))
```

This generates the following plot:

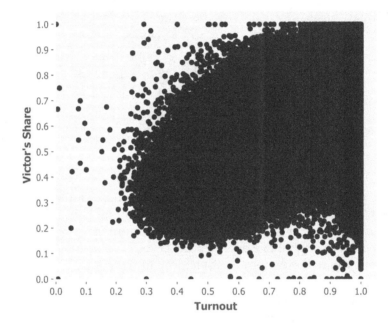

Although a diagonal tendency in the Russia data is clearly evident from the outline of the points, the sheer volume of data obscures the internal structure. In the last section of this chapter, we'll show a simple technique for extracting structure from a chart such as the earlier one using opacity.

Scatter transparency

In situations such as the preceding one where a scatter plot is overwhelmed by the volume of points, transparency can help to visualize the structure of the data. Since translucent points that overlap will be more opaque, and areas with fewer points will be more transparent, a scatter plot with semi-transparent points can show the density of the data much better than solid points can.

We can set the alpha transparency of points plotted on an Incanter chart with the `c/set-alpha` function. It accepts two arguments: the chart and a number between zero and one. One signifies fully opaque and zero fully transparent.

```
(defn ex-1-35 []
  (let [data (-> (load-data :ru-victors)
                 (s/sample :size 10000))]
    (-> (c/scatter-plot (i/$ :turnout data)
                        (i/$ :victors-share data)
                        :x-label "Turnout"
                        :y-label "Victor Share")
        (c/set-alpha 0.05)
        (i/view))))
```

The preceding example generates the following chart:

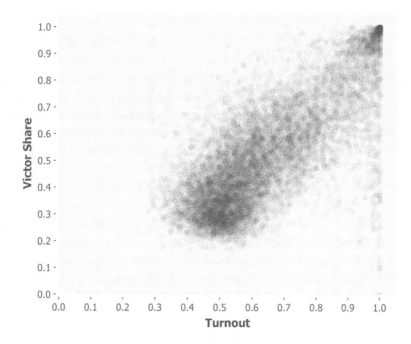

The preceding scatter plot shows the general tendency of the victor's share and the turnout to vary together. We can see a correlation between the two values, and a "hot spot" in the top right corner of the chart corresponding to close to 100-percent turnout and 100-percent votes for the winning party. This in particular is the sign that the researchers at the Medial University of Vienna have highlighted as being the signature of electoral fraud. It's evident in the results of other disputed elections around the world, such as those of the 2011 Ugandan presidential election, too.

The district-level results for many other elections around the world are available at http://www.complex-systems.meduniwien.ac.at/ elections/election.html. Visit the site for links to the research paper and to download other datasets on which to practice what you've learned in this chapter about scrubbing and transforming real data.

We'll cover correlation in more detail in *Chapter 3, Correlation*, when we'll learn how to quantify the strength of the relationship between two values and build a predictive model based on it. We'll also revisit this data in *Chapter 10, Visualization* when we implement a custom two-dimensional histogram to visualize the relationship between turnout and the winner's proportion of the vote even more clearly.

Summary

In this first chapter, we've learned about summary statistics and the value of distributions. We've seen how even a simple analysis can provide evidence of potentially fraudulent activity.

In particular, we've encountered the central limit theorem and seen why it goes such a long way towards explaining the ubiquity of the normal distribution throughout data science. An appropriate distribution can represent the essence of a large sequence of numbers in just a few statistics and we've implemented several of them using pure Clojure functions in this chapter. We've also introduced the Incanter library and used it to load, transform, and visually compare several datasets. We haven't been able to do much more than note a curious difference between two distributions, however.

In the next chapter, we'll extend what we've learned about descriptive statistics to cover inferential statistics. These will allow us to quantify a measured difference between two or more distributions and decide whether a difference is statistically significant. We'll also learn about hypothesis testing—a framework for conducting robust experiments that allow us to draw conclusions from data.

2
Inference

"I can see nothing," said I, handing it back to my friend.

"On the contrary, Watson, you can see everything. You fail, however, to reason from what you see. You are too timid in drawing your inferences."

– Sir Arthur Conan Doyle, The Adventure of the Blue Carbuncle

In the previous chapter, we introduced a variety of numerical and visual approaches to understand the normal distribution. We discussed descriptive statistics, such as the mean and standard deviation, and how they can be used to summarize large amounts of data succinctly.

A dataset is usually a sample of some larger population. Sometimes, this population is too large to be measured in its entirety. Sometimes, it is intrinsically unmeasurable, either because it is infinite in size or it otherwise cannot be accessed directly. In either case, we are forced to generalize from the data that we have.

In this chapter, we consider statistical inference: how we can go beyond simply describing the samples of data and instead describe the population from which they were sampled. We'll look in detail at how confident we can be about the inferences we make from the samples of data. We'll cover hypothesis testing: a robust approach to data analysis that puts the science in data science. We'll also implement an interactive web page with ClojureScript to simulate the relationship between samples and the population from which they are taken.

To help illustrate the principles, we'll invent a fictional company, AcmeContent, that has recently hired us as a data scientist.

Introducing AcmeContent

To help illustrate the concepts in this chapter, let's imagine that we've recently been appointed for the data scientist role at AcmeContent. The company runs a website that lets visitors share video clips that they've enjoyed online.

One of the metrics AcmeContent tracks through its web analytics is **dwell time**. This is a measure of how long a visitor stays on the site. Clearly, visitors who spend a long time on the site are enjoying themselves and AcmeContent wants its visitors to stay as long as possible. If the mean dwell time increases, our CEO will be very happy.

> Dwell time is the length of time between the time a visitor first arrives at a website and the time they make their last request to your site.
>
> A **bounce** is a visitor who makes only one request—their dwell time is zero.

As the company's new data scientist, it falls to us to analyze the dwell time reported by the website's analytics and measure the success of AcmeContent's site.

Download the sample code

The code for this chapter is available at `https://github.com/clojuredatascience/ch2-inference` or from the Packt Publishing's website.

The example data has been generated specifically for this chapter. It's small enough that it has been included with the book's sample code inside the data directory. Consult the book's wiki at `http://wiki.clojuredatascience.com` for links to further read about dwell time analysis.

Load and inspect the data

In the previous chapter, we used Incanter to load Excel spreadsheets with the `incanter.excel/load-xls` function. In this chapter, we will load a dataset from a tab-separated text file. For this, we'll make use of `incanter.io/read-dataset` that expects to receive either a URL object or a file path represented as a string.

The file has been helpfully reformatted by AcmeContent's web team to contain just two columns—the date of the request and the dwell time in seconds. There are column headings in the first row, so we pass `:header true` to `read-dataset`:

```
(defn load-data [file]
  (-> (io/resource file)
```

```
          (iio/read-dataset :header true :delim \tab)))

(defn ex-2-1 []
  (-> (load-data "dwell-times.tsv")
      (i/view)))
```

If you run this code (either in the REPL or on the command line with `lein run -e 2.1`), you should see an output similar to the following:

:date	:dwell-time
2015-01-01T00:03:43Z	74
2015-01-01T00:32:12Z	109
2015-01-01T01:52:18Z	88
2015-01-01T01:54:30Z	17
2015-01-01T02:09:24Z	11
2015-01-01T02:16:00Z	170
2015-01-01T02:27:48Z	149
2015-01-01T03:25:32Z	193
2015-01-01T03:35:29Z	26
2015-01-01T03:42:30Z	39
2015-01-01T03:43:19Z	20
2015-01-01T03:51:12Z	43
2015-01-01T04:11:35Z	212

Let's see what the dwell times look like as a histogram.

Visualizing the dwell times

We can plot a histogram of dwell times by simply extracting the `:dwell-time` column with `i/$`:

```
(defn ex-2-2 []
  (-> (i/$ :dwell-time (load-data "dwell-times.tsv"))
      (c/histogram :x-label "Dwell time (s)"
                   :nbins 50)
      (i/view)))
```

The earlier code generates the following histogram:

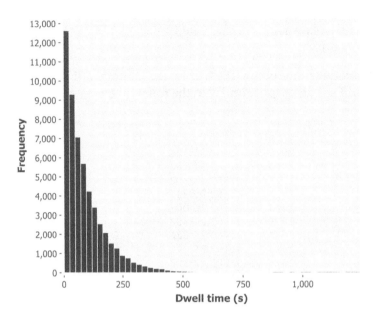

This is clearly not a normally distributed data, nor even a very skewed normal distribution. There is no tail to the left of the peak (a visitor clearly can't be on our site for less than zero seconds). While the data tails off steeply to the right at first, it extends much further along the *x* axis than we would expect from normally distributed data.

When confronted with distributions like this, where values are mostly small but occasionally extreme, it can be useful to plot the *y* axis as a **log scale**. Log scales are used to represent events that cover a very large range. Chart axes are ordinarily linear and they partition a range into equally sized steps like the "number line" we learned at school. Log scales partition the range into steps that get larger and larger as they go further away from the origin.

Some systems of measurement for natural phenomena that cover a very large range are represented on a log scale. For example, the Richter magnitude scale for earthquakes is a base-10 logarithmic scale, which means that an earthquake measuring 5 on the Richter scale is 10 times the magnitude of an earthquake measuring 4. The decibel scale is also a logarithmic scale with a different base — a sound wave of 30 decibels has 10 times the magnitude of a sound wave of 20 decibels. In each case, the principle is the same — the use of a log scale allows a very large range of values to be compressed into a much smaller range.

Plotting our y axis on `log-axis` is simple with Incanter with `c/set-axis`:

```
(defn ex-2-3 []
  (-> (i/$ :dwell-time (load-data "dwell-times.tsv"))
      (c/histogram :x-label "Dwell time (s)"
                   :nbins 20)
      (c/set-axis :y (c/log-axis :label "Log Frequency"))
      (i/view)))
```

By default Incanter will use a base-10 log scale, meaning that each tick on the axis represents a range that is 10 times the previous step. A chart like this — where only one axis is shown on a log scale — is called **log-linear**. Unsurprisingly, a chart showing two log axes is called a **log-log chart**.

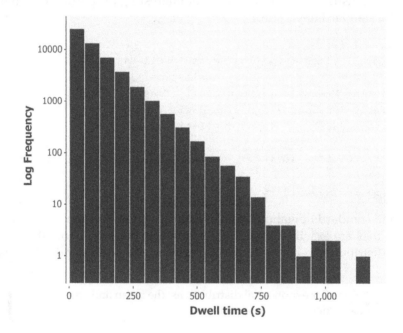

Plotting dwell times on a log-linear plot shows hidden consistency in the data — there is a linear relationship between the dwell time and the logarithm of the frequency. The clarity of the relationship breaks down to the right of the plot where there are fewer than 10 visitors but, aside from this, the relationship is remarkably consistent.

A straight line on a log-linear plot is a clear indicator of an exponential distribution.

The exponential distribution

The exponential distribution occurs frequently when considering situations where there are many small positive quantities and much fewer larger quantities. Given what we have learned about the Richter scale, it won't be a surprise to learn that the magnitude of earthquakes follows an exponential distribution.

The distribution also frequently occurs in waiting times—the time until the next earthquake of any magnitude roughly follows an exponential distribution as well. The distribution is often used to model failure rates, which is essentially the waiting time until a machine breaks down. Our exponential distribution models a process similar to failure—the waiting time until a visitor gets bored and leaves our site.

The exponential distribution has a number of interesting properties. One relates to the mean and standard deviation:

```
(defn ex-2-4 []
  (let [dwell-times (->> (load-data "dwell-times.tsv")
                         (i/$ :dwell-time))]
    (println "Mean:   " (s/mean dwell-times))
    (println "Median:" (s/median dwell-times))
    (println "SD:     " (s/sd dwell-times))))
```

```
Mean:    93.2014074074074
Median:  64.0
SD:      93.96972402519796
```

The mean and standard deviations are very similar. In fact, for an ideal exponential distribution, they are exactly the same. This property holds true for all the exponential distributions—as the mean increases, so does the standard deviation.

 For exponential distributions, the mean and standard deviations are equal.

A second property of the exponential distribution is that it is **memoryless**. This is a counterintuitive property best illustrated by an example. We expect that as a visitor continues to browse our site, the probability of them getting bored and leaving increases. Since the mean dwell time is 93 seconds, it might appear that beyond 93 seconds, they are less and less likely to continue browsing.

The memoryless property of exponential distributions tells us that the probability of a visitor staying on our site for another 93 seconds is exactly the same whether they have already been browsing the site for 93 seconds, 5 minutes, an hour, or they have just arrived.

For a memoryless distribution, the probability of continuing for an additional *x* minutes is not affected by how much time has already elapsed.

The memoryless property of exponential distributions goes some way towards explaining why it is so difficult to predict when an earthquake will occur next. We must rely on other evidence (such as a disturbance in geomagnetism) rather than the elapsed time.

Since the median dwell time is 64 seconds, about half of our visitors are staying on the site for only around a minute. A mean of 93 seconds shows that some visitors are staying much longer than that. These statistics have been calculated on all the visitors over the last 6 months. It might be interesting to see how these statistics vary per day. Let's calculate this now.

The distribution of daily means

The file provided by the web team includes the timestamp of the visit. In order to aggregate by day, it's necessary to remove the time portion from the date. While we could do this with string manipulation, a more flexible approach would be to use a date and time library such as clj-time (https://github.com/clj-time/clj-time) to parse the string. This will allow us to not only remove the time, but also perform arbitrarily complex filters (such as filtering to particular days of the week or the first or last day of the month, for example).

The clj-time.predicates namespace contains a variety of useful predicates and the clj-time.format namespace contains parsing functions that will attempt to convert the string to a date-time object using predefined standard formats. If our timestamp wasn't already in a standard format, we could use the same namespace to build a custom formatter. Consult the clj-time documentation for more information and many usage examples:

```
(defn with-parsed-date [data]
  (i/transform-col data :date (comp tc/to-local-date f/parse)))

(defn filter-weekdays [data]
  (i/$where {:date {:$fn p/weekday?}} data))

(defn mean-dwell-times-by-date [data]
  (i/$rollup :mean :dwell-time :date data))

(defn daily-mean-dwell-times [data]
  (->> (with-parsed-date data)
       (filter-weekdays)
       (mean-dwell-times-by-date)))
```

Combining the previous functions allows us to calculate the mean, median, and standard deviation for the daily mean dwell times:

```
(defn ex-2-5 []
  (let [means (->> (load-data "dwell-times.tsv")
                   (daily-mean-dwell-times)
                   (i/$ :dwell-time))]
    (println "Mean:   " (s/mean means))
    (println "Median: " (s/median means))
    (println "SD:     " (s/sd means))))


;; Mean:     90.210428650562
;; Median:   90.13661202185791
;; SD:       3.722342905320035
```

The mean value of our daily means is 90.2 seconds. This is close to the mean value we calculated previously on the whole dataset, including weekends. The standard deviation is much lower though, just 3.7 seconds. In other words, the distribution of daily means has a much lower standard deviation than the entire dataset. Let's plot the daily mean dwell times on a chart:

```
(defn ex-2-6 []
  (let [means (->> (load-data "dwell-times.tsv")
                   (daily-mean-dwell-times)
                   (i/$ :dwell-time))]
    (-> (c/histogram means
                     :x-label "Daily mean dwell time (s)"
                     :nbins 20)
        (i/view))))
```

This code generates the following histogram:

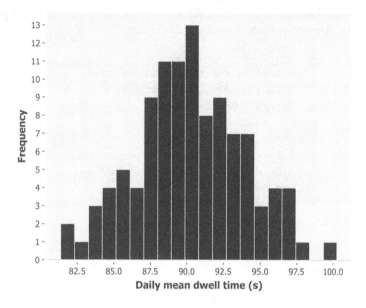

The distribution of sample means is distributed symmetrically around the overall grand mean value of 90 seconds with a standard deviation of 3.7 seconds. Unlike the distribution from which these means were sampled – the exponential distribution – the distribution of sample means is normally distributed.

The central limit theorem

We encountered the central limit theorem in the previous chapter when we took samples from a uniform distribution and averaged them. In fact, the central limit theorem works for any distribution of values, provided the distribution has a finite standard deviation.

[The central limit theorem states that the distribution of sample means will be normally distributed irrespective of the distribution from which they were calculated.]

It doesn't matter that the underlying distribution is exponential – the central limit theorem shows that the mean of random samples taken from any distribution will closely approximate a normal distribution. Let's plot a normal curve over our histogram to see how closely it matches.

To plot a normal curve over our histogram, we have to plot our histogram as a density histogram. This plots the proportion of all the points that have been put in each bucket rather than the frequency. We can then overlay the normal probability density with the same mean and standard deviation:

```
(defn ex-2-7 []
  (let [means (->> (load-data "dwell-times.tsv")
                   (daily-mean-dwell-times)
                   (i/$ :dwell-time))
        mean (s/mean means)
        sd   (s/sd means)
        pdf  (fn [x]
               (s/pdf-normal x :mean mean :sd sd))]
    (-> (c/histogram means
                     :x-label "Daily mean dwell time (s)"
                     :nbins 20
                     :density true)
        (c/add-function pdf 80 100)
        (i/view))))
```

This code generates the following chart:

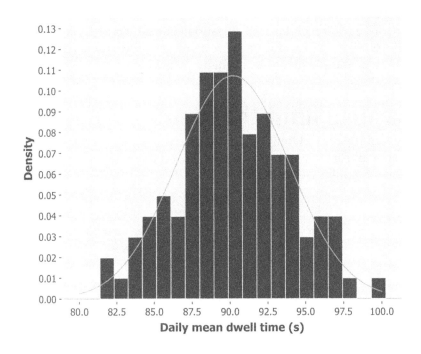

The normal curve plotted over the histogram has a standard deviation of approximately 3.7 seconds. In other words, this quantifies the variation of each daily mean being relative to the grand mean of 90 seconds. We can think of each day's mean as a sample from the overall population with the earlier curve representing the distribution of the sample means. Because 3.7 seconds is the amount that the sample's mean differs from the grand mean, it's referred to as the **standard error**.

Standard error

While the standard deviation measures the amount of variation there is within a sample, the standard error measures the amount of variation there is between the means of samples taken from the same population.

 The standard error is the standard deviation of the distribution of the sample means.

We have calculated the standard error of dwell time empirically by looking at the previous 6 months of data. But there is an equation that allows us to calculate it from only a single sample:

$$SE = \frac{\sigma_x}{\sqrt{n}}$$

Here, σ_x is the standard deviation and n is the sample size. This is unlike the descriptive statistics that we studied in the previous chapter. While they described a single sample, the standard error attempts to describe a property of samples in general—the amount of variation in the sample means that variations can be expected for samples of a given size:

```
(defn standard-deviation [xs]
  (Math/sqrt (variance xs)))

(defn standard-error [xs]
  (/ (standard-deviation xs)
     (Math/sqrt (count xs))))
```

The standard error of the mean is thus related to two factors:

- The size of the sample
- The population standard deviation

The size of the sample has the largest impact on the standard error. Since we take the square root of the sample size, we have to increase the size of the sample by four to halve the size of the standard error.

It may seem curious that the proportion of the population sampled has no effect on the size of the standard error. This is just as well, since some populations could be infinite in size.

Samples and populations

The words "sample" and "population" mean something very particular to statisticians. A population is the entire collection of entities that a researcher wishes to understand or draw conclusions about. For example, in the second half of the 19th century, Gregor Johann Mendel, the originator of genetics, recorded observations about pea plants. Although he was studying specific plants in a laboratory, his objective was to understand the underlying mechanisms behind heredity in all possible pea plants.

 Statisticians refer to the group of entities from which a sample is drawn as the population, whether or not the objects being studied are people.

Since populations may be large—or in the case of Mendel's pea plants, infinite—we must study representative samples and draw inferences about the population from them. To distinguish the measurable attributes of our samples from the inaccessible attributes of the population, we use the word *statistics* to refer to the *sample* attributes and parameters to refer to the population attributes.

 Statistics are the attributes we can measure from our samples. Parameters are the attributes of the population we are trying to infer.

In fact, statistics and parameters are distinguished through the use of different symbols in mathematical formulae:

Measure	Sample statistic	Population parameter
Number of items	n	N
Mean	$\bar{x}$	μ_x
Standard deviation	S_x	σ_x
Standard error	$S_{\bar{x}}$	

Here, $\overline{x}$ is pronounced as "x-bar," μ_x is pronounced as "mu x," and σ_x is pronounced as "sigma x."

If you refer back to the equation for the standard error, you'll notice that it is calculated from the population standard deviation σ_x, not the sample standard deviation S_x. This presents us with a paradox — we can't calculate the sample statistic using population parameters when the population parameters are precisely the values we are trying to infer. In practice, though, the sample and population standard deviations are assumed to be the same above a sample size of about 30.

Let's calculate the standard error from a particular day's means. For example, let's take a particular day, say May 1:

```
(defn ex-2-8 []
  (let [may-1 (f/parse-local-date "2015-05-01")]
    (->> (load-data "dwell-times.tsv")
         (with-parsed-date)
         (filtered-times {:date {:$eq may-1}})
         (standard-error))))


;; 3.627
```

Although we have only taken a sample from one day, the standard error we calculate is very close to the standard deviation of all the sample means — 3.6 compared to 3.7s. It's as if, like a cell containing DNA, each sample encodes information about the entire population within it.

Confidence intervals

Since the standard error of our sample measures how closely we expect our sample mean to match the population mean, we could also consider the inverse — the standard error measures how closely we expect the population mean to match our measured sample mean. In other words, based on our standard error, we can infer that the population mean lies within some expected range of the sample mean with a certain degree of confidence.

Taken together, the "degree of confidence" and the "expected range" define a **confidence interval**. While stating confidence intervals, it is fairly standard to state the 95 percent interval—we are 95 percent sure that the population parameter lies within the interval. Of course, there remains a 5 percent possibility that it does not.

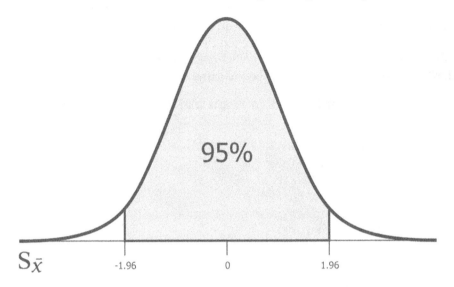

Whatever the standard error, 95 percent of the population mean will lie between -1.96 and 1.96 standard deviations of the sample mean. 1.96 is therefore the *critical z-value* for a 95 percent confidence interval.

> The name z-value comes from the fact that the normal distribution is also called the z-distribution.

The number 1.96 is so commonly used that it's a number worth remembering, but we can also calculate the critical value using the s/quantile-normal function. Our confidence-interval function that follows expects a value for p between zero and one. This will be 0.95 for our 95 percent confidence interval. We need to subtract it from one and divide it by two to calculate the site of each of the two tails (2.5 percent for the 95 percent confidence interval):

```
(defn confidence-interval [p xs]
  (let [x-bar  (s/mean xs)
        se     (standard-error xs)
        z-crit (s/quantile-normal (- 1 (/ (- 1 p) 2)))]
    [(- x-bar (* se z-crit))
```

```
        (+ x-bar (* se z-crit))])))

(defn ex-2-9 []
  (let [may-1 (f/parse-local-date "2015-05-01")]
    (->> (load-data "dwell-times.tsv")
        (with-parsed-date)
        (filtered-times {:date {:$eq may-1}})
        (confidence-interval 0.95))))

;; [83.53415272762004 97.75306531749274]
```

The result tells us that we can be 95 percent confident that the population mean lies between 83.53 and 97.75 seconds. Indeed, the population mean we calculated previously lies well within this range.

Sample comparisons

After a viral marketing campaign, the web team at AcmeContent take a sample of dwell times for us to analyze from a single day. They'd like to know whether their latest campaign has brought more engaged visitors to the site. Confidence intervals provide us with an intuitive way to compare the two samples.

We load the dwell times from the campaign as we did earlier and summarize them in the same way:

```
(defn ex-2-10 []
  (let [times (->> (load-data "campaign-sample.tsv")
                   (i/$ :dwell-time))]
    (println "n:       " (count times))
    (println "Mean:    " (s/mean times))
    (println "Median:  " (s/median times))
    (println "SD:      " (s/sd times))
    (println "SE:      " (standard-error times))))

;; n:       300
;; Mean:    130.22
;; Median:  84.0
;; SD:      136.13370714388046
;; SE:      7.846572839994115
```

The mean seems to be much larger than the means we have been looking at previously—130s compared to 90s. It could be that there is some significant difference here, although the standard error is over twice the size of our previous one day sample, owing to a smaller sample size and larger standard deviation. We can calculate the 95 percent confidence interval for the population mean based on this data using the same `confidence-interval` function like before:

```
(defn ex-2-11 []
  (->> (load-data "campaign-sample.tsv")
       (i/$ :dwell-time)
       (confidence-interval 0.95)))


;; [114.84099983154137 145.59900016845864]
```

The 95 percent confidence interval for the population mean is 114.8s to 145.6s. This doesn't overlap with the 90s population mean we calculated previously at all. There appears to be a large underlying population difference that is unlikely to have occurred just through a sampling error alone. Our task now is to find out why.

Bias

A sample should be representative of the population from which it is drawn. In other words, it should avoid bias that would result in certain kinds of population members being systematically excluded (or included) over others.

A famous example of sample bias is the 1936 Literary Digest poll for the US Presidential Election. It was one of the largest and most expensive polls ever conducted with 2.4 million people being surveyed by mail. The results were decisive—Republican governor of Kansas Alfred Landon would defeat Franklin D. Roosevelt, taking 57 percent of the vote. In the event, Roosevelt won the election with 62 percent of the vote.

The primary cause of the magazine's huge sampling error was sample selection bias. In their attempt to gather as many voter addresses as possible, the Literary Digest scoured telephone directories, magazine subscription lists, and club membership lists. In an era when telephones were more of a luxury item, this process was guaranteed to be biased in favor of upper- and middle-class voters and was not representative of the electorate as a whole. A secondary cause of bias was **nonresponse bias**—less than a quarter of those who were approached actually responded to the survey. This is a kind of selection bias that favors only those respondents who actually wish to participate.

A common way to avoid sample selection bias is to ensure that the sampling is randomized in some way. Introducing chance into the process makes it less likely that experimental factors will unfairly influence the quality of the sample. The Literary Digest poll was focused on getting the largest sample possible, but an unbiased small sample is much more useful than a badly chosen large sample.

If we open up the `campaign-sample.tsv` file, we'll discover that our sample has come exclusively from June 6, 2015. This was a weekend, a fact we can easily confirm with `clj-time`:

```
(p/weekend? (t/date-time 2015 6 6))
;; true
```

Our summary statistics so far have all been based on the data we filtered just to include weekdays. This is a bias in our sample, and if the weekend visitor behavior turns out to be different from the weekday behavior—a very likely scenario—then we would say that the samples represent two different populations.

Visualizing different populations

Let's remove the filter for weekdays and plot the daily mean dwell time for both week days and weekends:

```
(defn ex-2-12 []
  (let [means (->> (load-data "dwell-times.tsv")
                   (with-parsed-date)
                   (mean-dwell-times-by-date)
                   (i/$ :dwell-time))]
    (-> (c/histogram means
                     :x-label "Daily mean dwell time unfiltered (s)"
                     :nbins 20)
        (i/view))))
```

The code generates the following histogram:

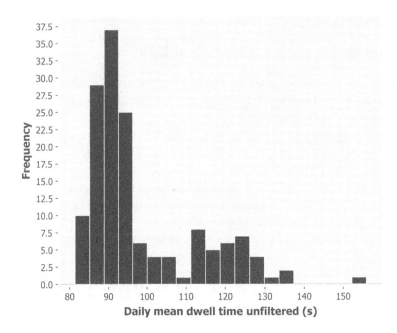

The distribution is no longer a normal distribution. In fact, the distribution is **bimodal** — there are two peaks. The second smaller peak, which corresponds to the newly added weekend data, is lower both because there are not as many weekend days as weekdays and because the distribution has a larger standard error.

In general, distributions with more than one peak are referred to as **multimodal**. They can be an indicator that two or more normal distributions have been combined, and therefore, that two or more populations may have been combined. A classic example of bimodality is the distribution of people's heights, since the modal height for men is larger than that for women.

The weekend data has different characteristics than the weekday data. We should make sure that we're comparing like with like. Let's filter our original dataset just to weekends:

```
(defn ex-2-13 []
  (let [weekend-times (->> (load-data "dwell-times.tsv")
                           (with-parsed-date)
                           (i/$where {:date {:$fn p/weekend?}})
                           (i/$ :dwell-time))]
```

```
    (println "n:        " (count weekend-times))
    (println "Mean:     " (s/mean weekend-times))
    (println "Median:   " (s/median weekend-times))
    (println "SD:       " (s/sd weekend-times))
    (println "SE:       " (standard-error weekend-times))))

;; n:       5860
;; Mean:    117.78686006825939
;; Median:  81.0
;; SD:      120.65234077179436
;; SE:      1.5759770362547665
```

The grand mean value at weekends (based on 6 months of data) is 117.8s, which falls within the 95 percent confidence interval of the marketing sample. In other words, although 130s is a high mean dwell time, even for a weekend, the difference is not so big that it couldn't simply be attributed to chance variation within the sample.

The approach we have just taken to establish a genuine difference in populations (between the visitors to our site on weekends compared to the visitors during the week) is not the way statistical testing would conventionally proceed. A more usual approach is to begin with a theory, and then to test that theory against the data. The statistical method defines a rigorous approach for this called **hypothesis testing**.

Hypothesis testing

Hypothesis testing is a formal process for statisticians and data scientists. The standard approach to hypothesis testing is to define an area of research, decide which variables are necessary to measure what is being studied, and then to set out two competing hypotheses. In order to avoid only looking at the data that confirms our biases, researchers will state their hypothesis clearly ahead of time. Statistics can then be used to confirm or refute this hypothesis, based on the data.

In order to help retain our visitors, designers go to work on a variation of our home page that uses all the latest techniques to keep the attention of our audience. We'd like to be sure that our effort isn't in vain, so we will look for an increase in dwell time on the new site.

Therefore, our research question is "does the new site cause the visitor's dwell time to increase"? We decide that this should be tested with reference to the mean dwell time. Now, we need to set out our two hypotheses. By convention, the data is assumed not to contain what the researcher is looking for. The conservative opinion is that the data would not show anything unusual. This is called the **null hypothesis** and is normally denoted H_0.

Hypothesis testing assumes that the null hypothesis is true until the weight of the evidence makes this proposition unlikely. This "back to front" way of looking for proof is driven partly by the simple psychological fact that when people go looking for something, they tend to find it.

The researcher then forms an alternate hypothesis, denoted by H_1. This could simply be that the population mean is different from the baseline. Or, it could be that the population mean is greater or lesser than the baseline, or even greater or lesser by some specified value. We'd like to test whether the new site increases dwell time, so these will be our null and alternate hypotheses:

- H_0: The dwell time for the new site is no different than the dwell time of the existing site
- H_1: The dwell time is greater for the new site compared to the existing site

Our conservative assumption is that the new site has no effect on the dwell time of users. The null hypothesis doesn't have to be nil hypothesis (that there is no effect), but in this case, we have no reasonable justification to assume otherwise. If the sample data does not support the null hypothesis (if the data differs from its prediction by a margin too large to be by chance alone), then we will reject the null hypothesis and propose the alternative hypothesis as the best alternative explanation.

Having set out the null and alternative hypotheses, we must set a significance level at which we are looking for an effect.

Significance

Significance testing was originally developed independent of hypothesis testing, but the two approaches are now very often used in concert together. The purpose of significance testing is to set the threshold beyond which we determine that the observed data no longer supports the null hypothesis.

There are therefore two risks:

- We may accept a difference as significant when in fact, it arose by chance
- We may attribute a difference to chance when, in fact, it indicates a true population difference

These two possibilities are respectively referred to as Type I and Type II errors:

	H_0 **false**	H_0 **true**
Reject H_0	True negative	Type I error
Accept H_0	Type II error	True positive

The more we reduce our risk of making Type I errors, the more we increase our risk of making Type II errors. In other words, the more confident we wish to be to not claim a real difference when there is none, the bigger the difference we'll demand between our samples to claim statistical significance. This increases the probability that we'll disregard a genuine difference when we encounter it.

Two significance thresholds are commonly used by statisticians. These are the 5 percent and 1 percent levels. A difference at 5 percent is commonly called *significant* and at 1 percent is called *highly significant*. The choice of threshold is often referred to in formulae by the Greek letter alpha, α. Since finding no effect might be regarded as a failure (either of the experiment or of the new site), we might be tempted to adjust α until we find an effect. Because of this, the textbook approach to significance testing requires us to set a significance level before we look at our data. A level of 5 percent is often chosen, so let's go with it.

Testing a new site design

The web team at AcmeContent have been hard at work, developing a new site to encourage visitors to stick around for an extended period of time. They've used all the latest techniques and, as a result, we're pretty confident that the site will show a marked improvement in dwell time.

Rather than launching it to all users at once, AcmeContent would like to test the site on a small sample of visitors first. We've educated them about sample bias, and as a result, the web team diverts a random 5 percent of the site traffic to the new site for one day. The result is provided to us as a single text file containing all the day's traffic. Each row shows the dwell time for a visitor who is given a value of either "0" if they used the original site design, or "1" if they saw the new (and hopefully improved) site.

Performing a z-test

While testing with the confidence intervals previously, we had a single population mean to compare to.

With *z*-testing, we have the option of comparing two samples. The people who saw the new site were randomized, and the data for both groups was collected on the same day to rule out other time-dependent factors.

Since we have two samples, we also have two standard errors. The *z*-test is performed against the pooled standard error, which is simply the square root of the sum of the variances divided by the sample sizes. This is the same as the result we would get if we took the standard error of the samples combined:

$$\sigma_{\overline{ab}} = \sqrt{\frac{\sigma_a^2}{n_a} + \frac{\sigma_b^2}{n_b}}$$

Here, σ_a^2 is the variance of sample *a* and σ_b^2 is the variance of sample *b*. n_a and n_b are the sample sizes of *a* and *b*, respectively. The pooled standard error can be calculated in Clojure like this:

```
(defn pooled-standard-error [a b]
    (i/sqrt (+ (/ (i/sq (standard-deviation a)) (count a))
              (/ (i/sq (standard-deviation b)) (count b)))))
```

To determine if the difference we're seeing is unexpectedly large, we can take the ratio of the observed difference between the means over the pooled standard error. This quantity is given the variable name *z*:

$$z = \frac{\overline{a} - \overline{b}}{\sigma_{\overline{ab}}}$$

Using our `pooled-standard-error` function, the *z*-statistic can be calculated like this:

```
(defn z-stat [a b]
    (-> (- (mean a)
           (mean b))
        (/ (pooled-standard-error a b))))
```

The ratio *z* captures how much the means differ relative to the amount we would expect given the standard error. The *z*-statistic therefore tells us how many standard errors apart the means are. Since the standard error has a normal probability distribution, we can associate this difference with a probability by looking up the *z*-statistic in the normal CDF:

```
(defn z-test [a b]
    (s/cdf-normal (z-stat a b)))
```

The following example uses the *z*-test to compare the performance of the two sites. We do this by grouping the rows by site, returning a map that indexes the site to the collection of rows for the site. We call `map-vals` with `(partial map :dwell-time)` to convert the collection of rows into a collection of dwell times. `map-vals` is a function defined in Medley (`https://github.com/weavejester/medley`), a library of lightweight utility functions:

```
(defn ex-2-14 []
    (let [data (->> (load-data "new-site.tsv")
                    (:rows)
                    (group-by :site)
                    (map-vals (partial map :dwell-time)))
          a (get data 0)
          b (get data 1)]
      (println "a n:" (count a))
      (println "b n:" (count b))
      (println "z-stat: " (z-stat a b))
      (println "p-value:" (z-test a b))))

;; a n: 284
;; b n: 16
;; z-stat:  -1.6467438180091214
;; p-value: 0.049805356789022426
```

Setting a significance level of 5 percent is much like setting a confidence interval of 95 percent. In essence, we're looking to see if the observed difference falls outside the 95 percent confidence interval. If it does, we can claim to have found a result that's significant at the 5 percent level.

The *p*-value is the probability of making a Type I error by wrongly rejecting the null hypothesis if it is, in fact, true. The smaller the *p*-value, the more certainty we have that the null hypothesis is false, and that we have found a genuine effect.

This code returns a value of 0.0498, equating to 4.98 percent. As it is just less than our significance threshold of 5 percent, we can claim to have found something significant.

Let's remind ourselves of the null and alternative hypotheses:

- H_0: The dwell time for the new site is no different from the dwell time of the existing site
- H_1: The dwell time is greater for the new site compared to the existing site

Our alternate hypothesis is that the dwell time is greater for the new site.

We are ready to claim statistical significance, and that the dwell time is greater for the new site compared to the existing site, but we have a problem — with a smaller sample, there is an increased uncertainty that the sample standard deviation matches the population standard deviation. Our new site sample has only 16 visitors, as shown in the output of the previous example. Samples as small as this invalidate the assumption that the standard error is normally distributed.

Fortunately, there is a statistical test and an associated distribution which models the increased uncertainty of standard errors for smaller sample sizes.

Student's t-distribution

The *t*-distribution was popularized by William Sealy Gossett, a chemist working for the Guinness Brewery in Ireland, who incorporated it into his analysis of Stout.

 William Gosset published the test in Biometrika in 1908, but was forced to use a pen name by his employer, who regarded the fact that they were using statistics as a trade secret. The pen name he chose was "Student".

While the normal distribution is completely described by two parameters — the mean and standard deviation, the *t*-distribution is described by only one parameter called the **degrees of freedom**. The larger the degrees of freedom, the closer the *t*-distribution resembles the normal distribution with a mean of zero and a standard deviation of one. As the degrees of freedom decreases, the distribution becomes wider with tails that are fatter than the normal distribution.

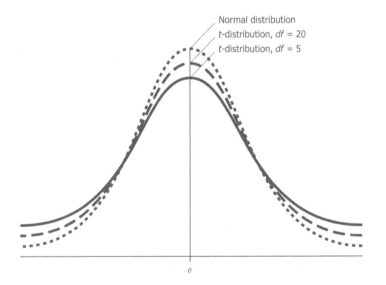

The earlier chart shows how the *t*-distribution varies with respect to the normal distribution for different degrees of freedom. Fatter tails for smaller sample sizes correspond to an increased chance of observing larger deviations from the mean.

Degrees of freedom

The degrees of freedom, often abbreviated to *df*, is closely related to the sample size. It is a useful statistic and an intuitive property of the series that can be demonstrated simply by example.

If you were told that the mean of two values is 10 and that one of the values is 8, you would not need any additional information to be able to infer that the other value is 12. In other words, for a sample size of two and a given mean, one of the values is constrained if the other is known.

If instead you're told that the mean of three values is 10 and the first value is also 10, you would not be able to deduce what the remaining two values are. Since there are an infinite number of sets of three numbers beginning with 10 whose mean is 10, the second value must also be specified before you can infer the value of the third.

For any set of three numbers, the constraint is simple: you can freely pick the first two numbers, but the final number is constrained. The degrees of freedom can thus be generalized in the following way: for any single sample, the degrees of freedom is one less than the sample size.

When comparing two samples of data, the degrees of freedom is two less than the sum of the sample sizes, which is the same as the sum of their individual degrees of freedom.

The t-statistic

While using the *t*-distribution, we look up the *t*-statistic. Like the *z*-statistic, this value quantifies how unlikely a particular observed deviation is. For a dual sample *t*-test, the *t*-statistic is calculated in the following way:

$$t = \frac{\bar{a} - \bar{b}}{S_{\bar{ab}}}$$

Here, $S_{\overline{ab}}$ is the pooled standard error. We could calculate the pooled standard error in the same way as we did earlier:

$$\sigma_{\overline{ab}} = \sqrt{\frac{\sigma_a^2}{n_a} + \frac{\sigma_b^2}{n_b}}$$

However, the equation assumes knowledge of the population parameters σ_a and σ_b, which can only be approximated from large samples. The *t*-test is designed for small samples and does not require us to make assumptions about population variance.

As a result, for the *t*-test, we write the pooled standard error as the square root of the sum of the standard errors:

$$S_{\overline{ab}} = \sqrt{S_{\overline{a}}^2 + S_{\overline{b}}^2}$$

In practice, the earlier two equations for the pooled standard error yield identical results, given the same input sequences. The difference in notation just serves to illustrate that with the *t*-test, we depend only on sample statistics as input. The pooled standard error $S_{\overline{ab}}$ can be calculated in the following way:

```
(defn pooled-standard-error [a b]
  (i/sqrt (+ (i/sq (standard-error a))
             (i/sq (standard-error b)))))
```

Although they are represented differently in mathematical notation, in practice, the calculation of *t*-statistic is identical to *z*-statistic:

```
(def t-stat z-stat)

(defn ex-2-15 []
  (let [data (->> (load-data "new-site.tsv")
                  (:rows)
                  (group-by :site)
                  (map-vals (partial map :dwell-time)))
        a (get data 0)
        b (get data 1)]
    (t-stat a b)))

;; -1.647
```

The difference between the two statistics is conceptual rather than algorithmic – the z-statistic is only applicable when the samples follow a normal distribution.

Performing the t-test

The difference in the way *t*-test works stems from the probability distribution from which our *p*-value is calculated. Having calculated our *t*-statistic, we need to look up the value in the *t*-distribution parameterized by the degrees of freedom of our data:

```
(defn t-test [a b]
  (let [df (+ (count a) (count b) -2)]
    (- 1 (s/cdf-t (i/abs (t-stat a b)) :df df))))
```

The degrees of freedom are two less than the sizes of the samples combined, which is 298 for our samples.

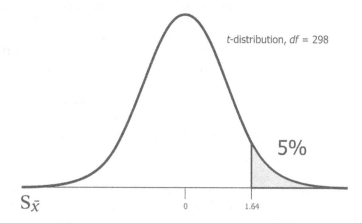

t-distribution, df = 298

$S_{\bar{x}}$ 0   1.64

5%

Recall that we are performing a hypothesis test. So, let's state our null and alternate hypotheses:

- H_0: This sample is drawn from a population with a supplied mean
- H_1: This sample is drawn from a population with a greater mean

Let's run the example:

```
(defn ex-2-16 []
  (let [data (->> (load-data "new-site.tsv")
                  (:rows)
                  (group-by :site)
                  (map-vals (partial map :dwell-time)))
        a (get data 0)
```

```
        b (get data 1)]
    (t-test a b)))
```

```
;; 0.0503
```

This returns a *p*-value of over 0.05. Since this is greater than the α of 5% we set for our hypothesis test, we are not able to reject the null hypothesis. Our test for the difference between the means has not discovered a significant difference using the *t*-test. Our barely significant result of the *z*-test was therefore partly due to it having such a small sample.

Two-tailed tests

There has been an implicit assumption in our alternate hypothesis that the new site would perform better than the previous site. The process of hypothesis testing goes to great lengths to ensure that we don't encode hidden assumptions while looking for statistical significance.

Tests where we look only for a significant increase or decrease in quantity are called **one-tailed tests** and are generally frowned upon, except in the case where a change in the opposite direction would be impossible. The name comes from the fact that a one-tailed test allocates all of the α to a single tail of the distribution. By not testing in the other direction, the test has more power to reject the null hypothesis in a particular direction and, in essence, lowers the threshold by which we would judge a result as significant.

 Statistical power is the probability of correctly accepting the alternative hypothesis. This can be thought of as the ability of the test to detect an effect, where there is an effect to be detected.

While higher statistical power sounds desirable, it comes at the cost of there being a greater probability of making a Type I error. A more correct approach would be to entertain the possibility that the new site could realistically be worse than the existing site. This allocates our α equally to both tails of the distribution and ensures a significant outcome that is not biased by a prior assumption of improvement.

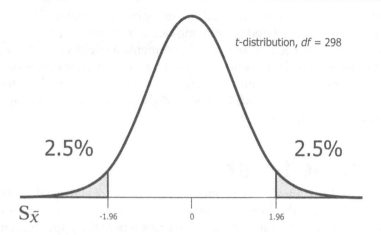

In fact, Incanter already provides functions to perform two-sample *t*-tests with the s/t-test function. We provide a sample of data as the first argument and a sample to compare against with the :y keyword argument. Incanter will assume that we want to perform a two-tailed test, unless we pass the :alternative keyword with a value of :greater or :lower, in which case a one-tailed test will be performed.

```
(defn ex-2-17 []
  (let [data (->> (load-data "new-site.tsv")
                  (:rows)
                  (group-by :site)
                  (map-vals (partial map :dwell-time)))
        a (get data 0)
        b (get data 1)]
    (clojure.pprint/print (s/t-test a :y b))))

;; {:p-value 0.12756432502462456,
;;    :df 17.7613823496861,
;;    :n2 16,
;;    :x-mean 87.95070422535211,
;;    :y-mean 122.0,
;;    :x-var 10463.941024237305,
;;    :conf-int [-78.9894629402365 10.890871390940724],
;;    :y-var 6669.866666666667,
;;    :t-stat -1.5985205593851322,
;;    :n1 284}
```

Incanter's *t*-test returns a lot of information, including the *p*-value. The *p*-value is around twice what we calculated for the one-tailed test. In fact, the only reason it's not exactly double is because Incanter implements a slight variant of the *t*-test called **Welch's t-test**, which is slightly more robust when two samples have different standard deviations. Since we know that, for exponential distributions, the mean and the variance are intimately related, the test is slightly more rigorous to apply and returns an even lower significance.

One-sample t-test

Independent samples of *t*-tests are the most common sort of statistical analysis, which provide a very flexible and generic way of comparing whether two samples represent the same or different population. However, in cases where the population mean is already known, there is an even simpler test represented by s/simple-t-test.

We pass a sample and a population mean to test against with the :mu keyword. So, if we simply want to see whether our new site is significantly different from the previous population mean dwell time of 90s, we can run a test like this:

```
(defn ex-2-18 []
  (let [data (->> (load-data "new-site.tsv")
                  (:rows)
                  (group-by :site)
                  (map-vals (partial map :dwell-time)))
        b (get data 1)]
    (clojure.pprint/pprint (s/t-test b :mu 90))))

;; {:p-value 0.13789520958229406,
;;  :df 15,
;;  :n2 nil,
;;  :x-mean 122.0,
;;  :y-mean nil,
;;  :x-var 6669.866666666667,
;;  :conf-int [78.48152745280898 165.51847254719104],
;;  :y-var nil,
;;  :t-stat 1.5672973291495713,
;;  :n1 16}
```

The simple-t-test function returns not only the *p*-value for the test, but also the confidence interval for the population mean. It is wide, running from 78.5s to 165.5s, certainly overlapping with the 90s of our test. This explains why we were not able to reject the null hypothesis.

Resampling

To develop an intuition as to how the *t*-test can confirm and calculate these statistics from so little data, we can apply an approach called **resampling**. Resampling is based on the premise that each sample is just one of an infinite number of possible samples from a population. We can gain an insight into the nature of what these other samples could have been, and therefore have a better understanding of the underlying population, by taking many new samples from our existing sample.

There are actually several resampling techniques, and we'll discuss one of the simplest — bootstrapping. In bootstrapping, we generate a new sample by repeatedly taking a random value from the original sample with replacement until we generate a sample that is of the same size as the original. Because these values are replaced between each random selection, the same source value can appear multiple times in the new sample. It is as if we were drawing a random card from a deck of playing cards repeatedly, but replacing the card after each draw. Occasionally, we will pick a card that we have previously selected.

We can bootstrap our sample easily in Incanter to generate many resamples with the bootstrap function. The bootstrap function takes two arguments — the original sample and a summary statistic to be calculated on the bootstrapped samples as well as the number of optional arguments — :size (the number of bootstrapped samples to be calculated on, each sample being the size of the original sample), :smooth (whether to smooth the output of discrete statistics such as the median), :smooth-sd, and :replacement, which defaults to true:

```
(defn ex-2-19 []
  (let [data (->> (load-data "new-site.tsv")
                  (i/$where {:site {:$eq 1}})
                  (i/$ :dwell-time ))]
    (-> (s/bootstrap data s/mean :size 10000)
        (c/histogram :nbins 20
                     :x-label "Bootstrapped mean dwell times (s)")
        (i/view))))
```

Let's visualize the output in a histogram:

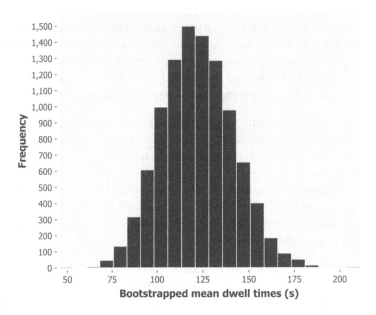

The histogram shows how the values of the mean value have changed with repeated (re) samples of the new site dwell times. Although the input was just a single sample of 16 visitors, the bootstrapped samples have simulated the standard error of our original sample very clearly and visualized the confidence interval (78s to 165s) calculated earlier by our single sample *t*-test.

Through bootstrapping, we simulated by taking multiple samples, even though we only had one sample as our input. It's a generally useful technique to estimate parameters that we cannot or do not know to calculate analytically.

Testing multiple designs

It's been disappointing to discover that there is no statistical significance behind the increased dwell time of users on the new site design. Better that we discovered this on a small sample of users before we rolled it out to the world though.

Not to be discouraged, AcmeContent's web team works overtime and devises a suite of alternative site designs. Taking the best elements from the other designs, they devise 19 variations to be tested. Together with our original site, which will act as a control, there are 20 different sites to direct visitors to.

Calculating sample means

The web team deploys the 19 new site designs alongside the original site. As mentioned earlier, each receives a random 5 percent of the visitors. We let the test run for 24 hours.

The next day, we receive a file that shows the dwell times for visitors to each of the site designs. Each has been labeled with a number, with site 0 corresponding to the original unaltered design, and numbers 1 to 19 representing the other designs:

```
(defn ex-2-20 []
  (->> (i/transform-col (load-data "multiple-sites.tsv")
                        :dwell-time float)
       (i/$rollup :mean :dwell-time :site)
       (i/$order :dwell-time :desc)
       (i/view)))
```

This code generates the following table:

:site	:dwell-time
6	144.19298245614036
10	129.95238095238096
7	123.36734693877551
15	119.34782608695652
1	106.0
5	102.33333333333333
3	97.47916666666667
11	96.98214285714286
18	94.81481481481481
8	94.34693877551021
4	94.33333333333333
13	90.73770491803279
9	89.82
19	89.28070175438596
2	88.22916666666667
16	86.74418604651163
12	80.95081967213115
0	79.85106382978724
17	77.8913043478261
14	74.76470588235294

We would like to test out each of the site designs to see if any generate a statistically significant result. To do so, we could compare the sites with each other as follows:

```
(defn ex-2-21 []
  (let [data (->> (load-data "multiple-sites.tsv")
                  (:rows)
                  (group-by :site)
                  (map-vals (partial map :dwell-time)))
        alpha 0.05]
    (doseq [[site-a times-a] data
            [site-b times-b] data
            :when (> site-a site-b)
```

```
                    :let [p-val (-> (s/t-test times-a :y times-b)
                                    (:p-value))]]
        (when (< p-val alpha)
          (println site-b "and" site-a
                   "are significantly different:"
                   (format "%.3f" p-val))))))
```

However, this would be a bad idea. We are very likely to see a statistical difference between the pages that performed particularly well against the pages that performed particularly poorly, even if these differences were by chance. If you run the earlier example, you'll see that many of the pages are statistically different from each other.

Alternatively, we could compare each site against our current baseline—the mean dwell time of 90 seconds currently measured for our site:

```
(defn ex-2-22 []
  (let [data (->> (load-data "multiple-sites.tsv")
                  (:rows)
                  (group-by :site)
                  (map-vals (partial map :dwell-time)))
        baseline (get data 0)
        alpha 0.05]
    (doseq [[site-a times-a] data
            :let [p-val (-> (s/t-test times-a :y baseline)
                            (:p-value))]]
      (when (< p-val alpha)
        (println site-a
                 "is significantly different from baseline:"
                 (format "%.3f" p-val))))))
```

This test determines two sites as being significantly different from the baseline:

```
;; 6 is significantly different from baseline: 0.007
;; 10 is significantly different from baseline: 0.006
```

The small *p*-values (smaller than 1 percent) indicate that there is a very statistically significant difference. This looks very promising, but we have an issue. We have performed a *t*-test on 20 samples of data with an α of 0.05. The definition of α is that it is the probability of wrongly rejecting the null hypothesis. By running a *t*-test 20 times, it actually becomes probable that we would wrongly reject the null hypothesis for at least one of the pages.

By comparing multiple pages at once like this, we invalidate the results of the *t*-test. There exist a variety of alternative techniques to address the problem of making multiple comparisons in statistical tests, which we'll introduce in a later section.

Multiple comparisons

The fact that with repeated trials, we increase the probability of discovering a significant effect is called the multiple comparisons problem. In general, the solution to the problem is to demand more significant effects when comparing many samples. There is no straightforward solution to this issue though; even with an α of 0.01, we will make a Type I error on an average of 1 percent of the time.

To develop our intuition about how multiple comparisons and statistical significance relate to each other, let's build an interactive web page to simulate the effect of taking multiple samples. It's one of the advantages of using a powerful and general-purpose programming language like Clojure for data analysis that we can run our data processing code in a diverse array of environments.

The code we've written and run so far for this chapter has been compiled for the Java Virtual Machine. But since 2013, there has been an alternative target environment for our compiled code: the web browser. ClojureScript extends the reach of Clojure even further to any computer that has a JavaScript-enabled web browser.

Introducing the simulation

To help visualize the problems associated with multiple significance testing, we'll use ClojureScript to build an interactive simulation, looking for statistically significant differences between the samples drawn at random from two exponential distributions. To see how other factors relate to our hypothesis testing, our simulation will allow us to change the underlying population mean for each of the two distributions, as well as set the sample size and desired confidence level.

If you have downloaded the sample code for this chapter, you will see, in the resources directory, an `index.html` file. If you open this code in a web browser, you should see a message prompting you to compile the JavaScript. We can do this with the Leiningen plugin called `cljsbuild`.

Compile the simulation

`cljsbuild` is a Leiningen plugin that compiles ClojureScript to JavaScript. To use it, we simply have to let the compiler know where we would like to output the JavaScript file. While Clojure code outputs to a `.jar` file (short for Java Archive), ClojureScript outputs to a single `.js` file. We specify the name of the output file and the compiler settings to use with the `:cljsbuilds` section of `project.clj`.

The plugin is accessible on the command line as `lein cljsbuild`. In the root of the project directory, run the following command:

```
lein cljsbuild once
```

This command will compile a JavaScript file for us. An alternative command is as follows:

```
lein cljsbuild auto
```

The preceding will compile the code, but will remain active, monitoring changes to the source files. If any of these files are updated, the output will be recompiled.

Open the file `resources/index.html` in a web browser now to see the effect of the JavaScript.

The browser simulation

An HTML page has been supplied in the resources directory of the sample project. Open the page in any modern browser and you should see something similar to the following image:

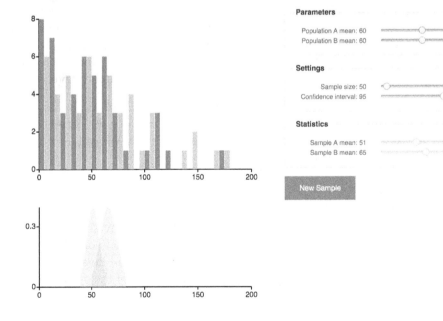

The left of the page shows a dual histogram with the distribution of two samples, both taken from an exponential distribution. The means of the populations from which the samples are generated are controlled by the sliders at the top right corner of the web page in the box marked as **Parameters**. Underneath the histogram is a plot showing the two probability densities for the population means based on the samples. These are calculated using the *t*-distribution, parameterized by the degrees of freedom of the sample. Below these sliders, in a box marked as **Settings**, are another pair of sliders that set the sample size and confidence intervals for the test. Adjusting the confidence intervals will crop the tails of the *t*-distributions; at the 95 percent confidence interval, only the central 95 percent of the probability distributions are displayed. Finally, in a box marked as **Statistics**, are the sliders that show the mean of both the samples. These cannot be changed; their values are measured from the samples. A button marked as **New Sample** can be used to generate two new random samples. Observe how the sample means fluctuate with each new pair of samples being generated. Keep generating samples and you'll occasionally observe significant differences between sample means, even when the underlying population means are identical.

While we explore the effects of changing the sample size and the confidence for different population means, let's look at how the simulation was constructed with the libraries `jStat`, `Reagent`, and `B1`.

jStat

As ClojureScript compiles to JavaScript, we can't make use of the libraries that have Java dependencies. Incanter is heavily reliant on several underlying Java libraries, so we have to find an alternative to Incanter for our browser-based statistical analysis.

 While building ClojureScript applications, we can't make use of the libraries that depend on Java libraries, as they won't be available in the JavaScript engine which executes our code.

`jStat` (`https://github.com/jstat/jstat`) is a JavaScript statistical library. It provides functions to generate sequences according to specific distributions, including the exponential and *t*-distributions.

To use it, we have to make sure it's available on our webpage. We can do this either by linking it to a remote **content distribution network (CDN)** or by hosting the file ourselves. The advantage of linking it to a CDN is that visitors, who previously downloaded `jStat` for another website, can make use of their cached version. However, since our simulation is for local use, we've included the file so that the page works even when our browser is offline.

The `jstat.min.js` file has been downloaded in the `resources/js/vendor` directory. The file is loaded in the main body of `index.html` with a standard HTML tag.

To make use of jStat's distribution generating functions, we have to interact with the JavaScript library from ClojureScript. As with the Java interop, Clojure provides pragmatic syntax to interact with the libraries written in the host language.

`jStat` provides a variety of distributions documented at `https://jstat.github.io/distributions.html`. To generate samples from an exponential distribution, we'd like to call the `jStat.exponential.sample(lambda)` function. The JavaScript interop for it is very straightforward; we prefix the expression with `js/` to ensure that we access JavaScript's namespace and move the position of the brackets:

```
(defn randexp [lambda]
  (js/jStat.exponential.sample lambda))
```

Once we have the ability to generate samples from an exponential distribution, creating a lazy sequence of samples will be as simple as calling the function repeatedly:

```
(defn exponential-distribution [lambda]
  (repeatedly #(randexp lambda)))
```

ClojureScript exposes almost all of Clojure, including lazy sequences. Refer to the book's wiki at `http://wiki.clojuredatascience.com` for links to resources on the JavaScript interop.

B1

Now that we can generate samples of data in ClojureScript, we'd like to be able to plot them on a histogram. We need a pure Clojure alternative to Incanter that will draw histograms in a web-accessible format; the B1 library (`https://github.com/henrygarner/b1`) provides just this functionality. The name is derived from the fact that it is adapted and simplified from the ClojureScript library C2, which in turn is a simplification of the popular JavaScript data visualization framework D3.

We'll be using B1's simple utility functions in `b1.charts` to build histograms out of our data in ClojureScript. B1 does not mandate a particular display format; we could use it to draw on a canvas element or even to build diagrams directly out of the HTML elements. However, B1 does contain functions to convert charts to SVG in `b1.svg` and these can be displayed in all modern web browsers.

Scalable Vector Graphics

SVG stands for Scalable Vector Graphics and defines a set of tags that represent drawing instructions. The advantage of SVG is that results can be rendered at any size without the blurring associated with raster (pixel-based) graphics that are scaled up. An additional benefit is that modern browsers know how to render SVG drawing instructions to produce images directly in the web page and can style and animate the images with CSS.

Although a detailed discussion of SVG and CSS is beyond the scope of this book, B1 does provide syntax that is very much like Incanter's to build simple charts and graphs using SVG. Given a sequence of values, we call the `c/histogram` function to convert it into an internal representation of the data structure. We can add additional histograms with the `c/add-histogram` function and call `svg/as-svg` to render the chart to an SVG representation:

```
(defn sample-histograms [sample-a sample-b]
  (-> (c/histogram sample-a :x-axis [0 200] :bins 20)
      (c/add-histogram sample-b)
      (svg/as-svg :width 550 :height 400)))
```

Unlike Incanter, when we choose to render our histogram, we must also specify the desired width and height of the chart.

Plotting probability densities

In addition to using jStat to generate samples from the exponential distribution, we'll also use it to calculate the probability density for the *t*-distribution. We can construct a simple function to wrap the `jStat.studentt.pdf(t, df)` function, providing the correct *t*-statistic and degrees of freedom to parameterize the distribution:

```
(defn pdf-t [t & {:keys [df]}]
  (js/jStat.studentt.pdf t df))
```

An advantage of using ClojureScript is that we have already written the code to calculate the *t*-statistic from a sample. The code, which worked in Clojure, can be compiled to ClojureScript with no changes whatsoever:

```
(defn t-statistic [test {:keys [mean n sd]}]
  (/ (- mean test)
     (/ sd (Math/sqrt n))))
```

To render the probability density, we can use B1's `c/function-area-plot`. This will generate an area plot from the line described by a function. The provided function simply needs to accept an *x* and return the corresponding *y*.

A slight complication is that the value of *y* we return will be different for different samples. This is because t-pdf will be highest at the sample mean (corresponding to a *t*-statistic of zero). Because of this, we'll need to generate a different function for each sample to be passed to function-area-plot. This is accomplished by the probability-density function, as follows:

```
(defn probability-density [sample alpha]
  (let [mu (mean sample)
        sd (standard-deviation sample)
        n  (count sample)]
    (fn [x]
      (let [df      (dec (count sample))
            t-crit (threshold-t 2 df alpha)
            t-stat (t-statistic x {:mean mu
                                   :sd sd
                                   :n n})]
        (if (< (Math/abs t-stat) t-crit)
          (pdf-t t-stat :df df)
          0)))))
```

Here, we're defining a higher-order function called probability-density that accepts a single value, sample. We calculate some simple summary statistics and then return an anonymous function that calculates the probability density for a given value in the distribution.

This anonymous function is what will be passed to function-area-plot. It accepts an *x* and calculates a *t*-statistic for the given sample from it. The *y* value returned is the probability of the *t*-distribution associated with the *t*-statistic:

```
(defn sample-means [sample-a sample-b alpha]
  (-> (c/function-area-plot (probability-density sample-a alpha)
                            :x-axis [0 200])
      (c/add-function (probability-density sample-b alpha))
      (svg/as-svg :width 550 :height 250)))
```

As with histograms, generating multiple plots is as straightforward as calling add-function with the chart, and the new function we'd like to add.

State and Reagent

State in ClojureScript is managed in the same way as Clojure applications — through the use of atoms, refs, or agents. Atoms provide uncoordinated, synchronous access to a single identity and are an excellent choice for storing the application state. Using an atom ensures that the application always sees a single, consistent view of the data.

Reagent is a ClojureScript library that provides a mechanism to update the content of a web page in response to changing the value of an atom. Markup and state are bound together, so that markup is regenerated whenever the application state is updated.

Reagent also provides syntax to render HTML in an idiomatic way using Clojure data structures. This means that both the content and the interactivity of the page can be handled in one language.

Updating state

With data held in a Reagent atom, updating the state is achieved by calling the swap! function with two arguments — the atom we wish to update and a function to transform the state of the atom. The provided function needs to accept the current state of the atom and return the new state. The exclamation mark indicates that the function has side effects and, in this case, the side effects are desirable; in addition to updating the atom, Reagent will ensure that relevant sections of our HTML page are updated.

The exponential distribution has a single parameter — the rate symbolized by lambda, λ. The rate of an exponential distribution is the reciprocal of the mean, so we calculate (/ 1 mean-a) to pass it as the argument to the exponential distribution function:

```
(defn update-sample [{:keys [mean-a mean-b sample-size]
                       :as state}]
  (let [sample-a (->> (float (/ 1 mean-a))
                      (exponential-distribution)
                      (take sample-size))
        sample-b (->> (float (/ 1 mean-b))
                      (exponential-distribution)
                      (take sample-size))]
    (-> state
        (assoc :sample-a sample-a)
        (assoc :sample-b sample-b)
        (assoc :sample-mean-a (int (mean sample-a)))
        (assoc :sample-mean-b (int (mean sample-b))))))

(defn update-sample! [state]
  (swap! state update-sample))
```

In the preceding code, we have defined an `update-sample` function that accepts a map containing `:sample-size`, `:mean-a`, and `:mean-b`, and returns a new map with the associated new samples and sample means.

The `update-sample` function is pure in the sense that it doesn't have side effects, which makes it easier to test. The `update-sample!` function wraps it with a call to `swap!`. Reagent ensures that any code that depends on the value contained in this atom will be executed when the value in the atom changes. This causes our interface to be re-rendered in response to the new samples.

Binding the interface

To bind the interface to the state, Reagent defines a `render-component` function. This links a particular function (in this case, our `layout-interface` function) with a particular HTML node (the element with the ID `root` on our page):

```
(defn layout-interface []
  (let [sample-a (get @state :sample-a)
        sample-b (get @state :sample-b)
        alpha (/ (get @state :alpha) 100)]
    [:div
     [:div.row
      [:div.large-12.columns
       [:h1 "Parameters & Statistics"]]]
     [:div.row
      [:div.large-5.large-push-7.columns
       [controllers state]]
      [:div.large-7.large-pull-5.columns {:role :content}
       [sample-histograms sample-a sample-b]
       [sample-means sample-a sample-b alpha]]]]))

(defn run []
  (r/render-component
   [layout-interface]
   (.getElementById js/document "root")))
```

Our `layout-interface` function contains an HTML markup expressed as nested Clojure data structures. Amongst the calls to `:div` and `:h1`, elements are calls to our two `sample-histograms` and `sample-means` functions. They will be substituted with their return values — the SVG representations of the histograms and the probability densities of the means.

For the sake of brevity, we have omitted the implementation of the `controllers` function, which handles the rendering of the sliders and the **New Sample** button. Consult the `cljds.ch2.app` namespace in the sample code to see how this is implemented.

Simulating multiple tests

Each time the **New Sample** button is pressed, a pair of new samples from an exponential distribution with population means taken from the sliders are generated. The samples are plotted on a histogram and, underneath, a probability density function is drawn showing the standard error for the sample. As the confidence intervals are changed, observe how the acceptable deviation of the standard error changes as well.

Each time the button is pressed, we could think of it as a significance test with an alpha set to the complement of the confidence interval. In other words, if the probability distributions for the sample means overlap at the 95 percent confidence interval, we cannot reject the null hypothesis at the 5 percent significance level.

Observe how, even when the population means are identical, occasional large deviations in the means will occur. Where samples differ by more than our standard error, we can accept the alternate hypothesis. With a confidence level of 95 percent, we will discover a significant result around one in 20 trials, even when the population means of the distributions are identical. When this happens, we are making a Type 1 error in mistaking a sampling error for a real population difference.

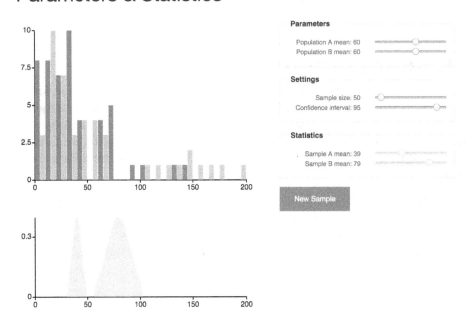

Despite the identical population parameters, large sample differences are occasionally observed.

The Bonferroni correction

We therefore require an alternative approach while conducting multiple tests that will account for an increased probability of discovering a significant effect through repeated trials. The Bonferroni correction is a very simple adjustment that ensures we are unlikely to make Type I errors. It does this by adjusting the alpha for our tests.

The adjustment is a simple one—the Bonferroni correction simply divides our desired alpha by the number of tests we are performing. For example, if we had k site designs to test and an experimental alpha of *0.05*, the Bonferroni correction is expressed as:

$$\alpha = \frac{0.05}{k}$$

This is a safe way to mitigate the increased probability of making a Type I error in multiple testing. The following example is identical to `ex-2-22`, except the alpha value has been divided by the number of groups:

```
(defn ex-2-23 []
  (let [data (->> (load-data "multiple-sites.tsv")
                  (:rows)
                  (group-by :site)
                  (map-vals (partial map :dwell-time)))
        alpha (/ 0.05 (count data))]
    (doseq [[site-a times-a] data
            [site-b times-b] data
            :when (> site-a site-b)
            :let [p-val (-> (s/t-test times-a :y times-b)
                            (:p-value))]]
      (when (< p-val alpha)
        (println site-b "and" site-a
                 "are significantly different:"
                 (format "%.3f" p-val))))))
```

If you run the preceding example, you'll see that none of the pages count as statistically significant any longer using the Bonferroni correction.

Significance testing is a balancing act—the lower our chances of making a Type I error, the greater our risk of making a Type II error. The Bonferroni correction is very conservative and it's possible that we're missing a genuine difference due to being so cautious.

In the final part of this chapter, we'll investigate an alternative approach to significance testing that strikes a balance between making Type I and Type II errors while allowing us to test all the 20 pages simultaneously.

Analysis of variance

Analysis of variance, often shortened to **ANOVA**, is a series of statistical methods used to measure the statistical significance of the difference between groups. It was developed by Ronald Fisher, an extremely gifted statistician, who also popularized significance testing through his work on biological testing.

Our tests, using the z-statistic and t-statistic, have focused on sample means as the primary mechanism to draw a distinction between the two samples. In each case, we looked for a difference in the means divided by the level of difference we could reasonably expect and quantified by the standard error.

The mean isn't the only statistic that might indicate a difference between samples. In fact, it is also possible to use the sample variance as an indicator of statistical difference.

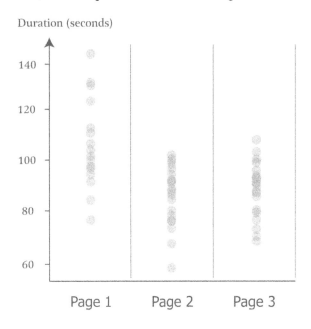

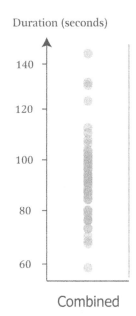

To illustrate how this might work, consider the preceding diagram. Each of the three groups on the left could represent samples of dwell times for a specific page with its own mean and standard deviation. If the dwell times for all the three groups are combined into one, the variance is larger than the average variance for the groups taken individually.

The statistical significance of an ANOVA test is derived from the ratio of two variances — the variance *between* the groups of interest and the variance *within* the groups of interest. If there is a significant difference between the groups that is not reflected within the groups, then those groupings help explain some of the variance between the groups. Conversely, if the variance within the groups is identical to the variance between the groups, the groups are not statistically different from one another.

The F-distribution

The F-distribution is parameterized by two degrees of freedom — those of the sample size and those of the number of groups.

The first degree of freedom is the count of groups less one and the second degree of freedom is the size of the sample less the number of groups. If k represents the number of groups, and n represents the sample size:

$$df1 = k - 1$$

$$df2 = n - k$$

We can visualize different *F*-distributions with an Incanter function plot:

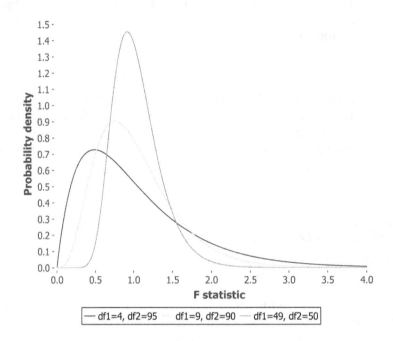

The lines of the preceding diagram show various *F*-distributions for a sample of 100 points split into 5, 10, and 50 groups.

The F-statistic

The test statistic that represents the ratio of the variance within and between the groups is called the *F*-statistic. The closer *F*-statistic is to one, the more alike the two variances are. The *F*-statistic is calculated very simply as follows:

$$F = \frac{S_b^2}{S_w^2}$$

Here, S_b^2 is the *variance between* the groups and S_w^2 is the *variance within* the groups.

As the ratio *F* gets larger, the larger the variance between the groups is compared to the variance within the groups. This implies that the grouping is doing a good job in explaining the variance observed in the sample as a whole. Where this ratio exceeds a critical threshold, we can say that the difference is statistically significant.

The *F*-test is always a one-tailed test, because any variance among the groups tends to make *F* large. It is impossible for *F* to decrease below zero.

The *variance within* for an *F*-test is calculated as the mean squared deviation from the mean. We calculate this as the sum of squared deviations from the mean divided by the first degree of freedom. For example, if there are k groups, each with a mean of $\overline{x}_k$, we could calculate the variance within like this:

$$S_w^2 = \frac{SSW}{df1} = \frac{\sum_{jk}\left(x_{jk} - \overline{x}_k\right)^2}{(k-1)}$$

Here, *SSW* represents the *sum of squares within* and x_{jk} represents the value of the jth element in group k.

The preceding formula for calculating the *SSW* looks intimidating. But, in fact, Incanter defines a useful `s/sum-of-square-devs-from-mean` function that makes calculating the sum of squares within as trivial as:

```
(defn ssw [groups]
  (->> (map s/sum-of-square-devs-from-mean groups)
       (reduce +)))
```

The *variance between* for an *F*-test has a similar formula:

$$S_b^2 = \frac{SST - SSW}{df1}$$

Here, *SST* is the *total sum of squares* and *SSW* is the value we just calculated. The total sum of the squares is the sum of squared differences from the "grand" mean that can be calculated like this:

$$SST = \sum_{i=1}^{n}\left(x_i - \overline{x}\right)^2$$

Thus, *SST* is simply the overall sum of the squares without any grouping. We can calculate both the SST and SSW in Clojure, like this:

```
(defn sst [groups]
  (->> (apply concat groups)
       (s/sum-of-square-devs-from-mean)))

(defn ssb [groups]
  (- (sst groups)
     (ssw groups)))
```

The *F*-statistic is calculated as the ratio of the variance between and the variance within the groups. Combining both our `ssb` and `ssw` functions defined previously and the two degrees of freedom, we can calculate the *F*-statistic in Clojure as follows.

Thus, we can calculate the *F*-statistic from our groups and our two degrees of freedom as follows:

```
(defn f-stat [groups df1 df2]
  (let [msb (/ (ssb groups) df1)
        msw (/ (ssw groups) df2)]
    (/ msbmsw)))
```

Now that we can calculate the *F*-statistic from our groups, we're ready to use it in an *F*-test.

The F-test

As with all of the hypothesis tests we have looked at in this chapter, once we have a statistic and a distribution, we simply need to pick a value of α and see if our data has exceeded the critical value for the test.

Incanter provides an `s/f-test` function, but this only measures the variance between and within the two groups. To run an *F*-test on our 20 different groups, we will need to implement our own *F*-test function. Fortunately, we've already done the hard work in the previous sections by calculating an appropriate *F*-statistic. We can perform the *F*-test by looking up the *F*-statistic in an *F*-distribution parameterized with the correct degrees of freedom. In the following code, we will write an `f-test` function, which uses this to perform the test on an arbitrary number of groups:

```
(defn f-test [groups]
  (let [n (count (apply concat groups))
        m (count groups)
        df1 (- m 1)
```

```
        df2 (- n m)
        f-stat (f-stat groups df1 df2)]
    (s/cdf-f f-stat :df1 df1 :df2 df2 :lower-tail? false)))
```

In the last line of the preceding function, we convert the value of the *F*-statistic into a *p*-value using Incanter's `s/cdf-f` function parameterized by the correct degrees of freedom. This *p*-value is a measure of the whole model, how well the different pages explain the variance of the dwell times overall. All that remains for us to do is to choose a significance level and run the test. Let's stick with a 5 percent significance level:

```
(defn ex-2-24 []
  (let [grouped (->> (load-data "multiple-sites.tsv")
                     (:rows)
                     (group-by :site)
                     (vals)
                     (map (partial map :dwell-time)))]
    (f-test grouped)))
```

```
;; 0.014
```

The test returns a *p*-value of 0.014, which is a significant result. The different pages indeed have different variances that cannot simply be explained away by random sampling error alone.

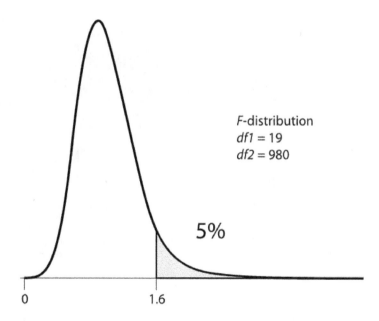

F-distribution
df1 = 19
df2 = 980

5%

0   1.6

We could use a box plot to visualize the distributions of each site together in one chart to compare them side by side:

```
(defn ex-2-25 []
  (let [grouped (->> (load-data "multiple-sites.tsv")
                     (:rows)
                     (group-by :site)
                     (sort-by first)
                     (map second)
                     (map (partial map :dwell-time)))
        box-plot (c/box-plot (first grouped)
                             :x-label "Site number"
                             :y-label "Dwell time (s)")
        add-box (fn [chart dwell-times]
                  (c/add-box-plot chart dwell-times))]
    (-> (reduce add-box box-plot (rest grouped))
        (i/view))))
```

In the preceding code, we reduce over the groups, calling `c/add-box-plot` for each group. The groups are sorted by their site ID before plotting, so our original page 0 is to the extreme left of the chart.

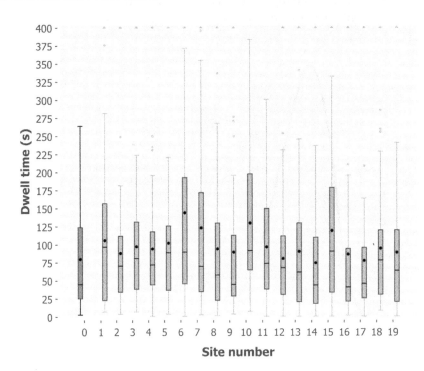

It might appear that site ID 10 has the longest dwell times, since its interquartile range extends furthest up the chart. However, if you look closely, you'll see its mean value is lower than site 6, having a mean dwell time of over 144 seconds:

```
(defn ex-2-26 []
  (let [data (load-data "multiple-sites.tsv")
        site-0 (->> (i/$where {:site {:$eq 0}} data)
                    (i/$ :dwell-time))
        site-10 (->> (i/$where {:site {:$eq 10}} data)
                     (i/$ :dwell-time))]
    (s/t-test site-10 :y site-0)))

;; 0.0069
```

Now that we have confirmed a statistically significant effect using the *F*-test, we're justified in claiming that site ID 6 is statistically different from the baseline:

```
(defn ex-2-27 []
  (let [data (load-data "multiple-sites.tsv")
        site-0 (->> (i/$where {:site {:$eq 0}} data)
                    (i/$ :dwell-time))
        site-6 (->> (i/$where {:site {:$eq 6}} data)
                    (i/$ :dwell-time))]
    (s/t-test site-6 :y site-0)))

;; 0.007
```

Finally, we have evidence to suggest that page ID 6 is a genuine improvement over the current site. As a result of our analysis, the AcmeContent CEO authorizes the launch of a new look website. The web team is delighted!

Effect size

In this chapter, we focused on statistical significance—the methods employed by statisticians to ensure a difference is discovered, which cannot be easily explained as chance variation. We must always remember that finding a significant effect isn't the same as finding a large effect. With very large samples, even a tiny difference in sample means will count as significant. To get a better sense of whether our discovery is both significant and important, we should state the effect size as well.

Cohen's d

Cohen's d is an adjustment that can be applied to see whether the difference we have observed is not just statistically significant, but actually large. Like the Bonferroni correction, the adjustment is a straightforward one:

$$d = \frac{\bar{a} - \bar{b}}{S_{ab}}$$

Here, S_{ab} is the pooled standard deviation (not the pooled standard error) of the samples. It can be calculated in a way similar to the pooled standard error:

```
(defn pooled-standard-deviation [a b]
  (i/sqrt (+ (i/sq (standard-deviation a))
             (i/sq (standard-deviation b)))))
```

Thus, we can calculate Cohen's d for our page 6, as follows:

```
(defn ex-2-28 []
  (let [data (load-data "multiple-sites.tsv")
        a (->> (i/$where {:site {:$eq 0}} data)
               (i/$ :dwell-time))
        b (->> (i/$where {:site {:$eq 6}} data)
               (i/$ :dwell-time))]
    (/ (- (s/mean b)
          (s/mean a))
       (pooled-standard-deviation a b))))

;; 0.389
```

In contrast with the *p*-values, there is no absolute threshold for Cohen's d. Whether an effect can be considered large is partly dependent on the context, but it does provide a useful, normalized measure of the effect size. Values above 0.5 are typically considered large, so 0.38 is a moderate effect. It certainly represents a meaningful increase in the dwell time on our site and is certainly worth the effort of a site upgrade.

Summary

In this chapter, we've learned about the difference between descriptive and inferential statistics. Once again, we've seen the importance of normal distribution and the central limit theorem, and learned how to quantify population differences with z-tests, t-tests, and F-tests.

We've learned about how the techniques of inferential statistics analyze the samples themselves to make claims about the population that was sampled. We've seen a variety of techniques — confidence intervals, bootstrapping, and significance tests — that can yield insight into the underlying population parameters. By simulating repeated tests with ClojureScript, we've also gained an insight into the difficulty of significance testing with multiple comparisons and seen how the F-test attempts to address the issue and strike a balance between Type I and Type II errors.

In the next chapter, we'll apply the lessons we've learned on variance and F-testing to single samples. We'll introduce the technique of regression analysis and use it to find correlations among variables within a sample of Olympic athletes.

3
Correlation

"The more I learn about people, the better I like my dog."

– *Mark Twain*

In previous chapters, we've considered how to describe samples in terms of summary statistics and how population parameters can be inferred from them. Such analysis tells us something about a population in general and a sample in particular, but it doesn't allow us to make very precise statements about individual elements. This is because so much information has been lost by reducing the data to just two statistics: the mean and standard deviation.

We often want to go further and establish a relationship between two or more variables or to predict one variable given another. This takes us into the study of correlation and regression. Correlation concerns the strength and direction of the relationship between two or more variables. Regression determines the nature of this relationship and enables us to make predictions from it.

Linear regression is our first machine learning algorithm. Given a sample of data, our model will learn a linear equation that allows it to make predictions about new, unseen data. To do this, we'll return to Incanter and study the relationship between height and weight for Olympic athletes. We'll introduce the concept of matrices and show how Incanter can be used to manipulate them.

About the data

This chapter will make use of data on athletes in the London 2012 Olympic Games, courtesy of Guardian News and Media Ltd. The data was originally sourced from the Guardian's excellent data blog at http://www.theguardian.com/data.

Download the example code for this chapter from the publisher's website or from `https://github.com/clojuredatascience/ch3-correlation`.

Consult the `Readme` file in this chapter's sample code or the book's wiki at `http://wiki.clojuredatascience.com` for more information on the data.

Inspecting the data

The first task when confronted with a new dataset is to study it to ensure that we understand what it contains.

The `all-london-2012-athletes.xlsx` file is small enough that it's been provided with the sample code for this chapter. We can inspect the data with Incanter, as we did in *Chapter 1, Statistics* using the `incanter.excel/read-xls` and `incanter.core/view` functions:

```
(ns cljds.ch3.examples
  (:require [incanter.charts :as c]
            [incanter.core :as i]
            [incanter.excel :as xls]
            [incanter.stats :as s]))

(defn athlete-data []
  (-> (io/resource "all-london-2012-athletes.xlsx")
      (str)
      (xls/read-xls)))

(defn ex-3-1 []
  (i/view (athlete-data)))
```

If you run this code (either in the REPL or on the command line with `lein run -e 3.1`), you should see the following output:

Name	Country	Age	Height, cm	Weight	Sex	Date of birth	Place of birth	Gold	Silver	Bronze	Total	Sport	Event
Lamusi A	People's Repu...	23.0	170.0	60.0	M	Fri Jun 02 0...	NEIMONGG...	0.0	0.0	0.0	0.0	Judo	Men's -60kg
A G Kruger	United States ...	33.0	193.0	125.0	M	Sun Feb 18 ...	Sheldon (USA)	0.0	0.0	0.0	0.0	Athletics	Men's Hammer Throw
Jamale Aarrass	France	30.0	187.0	76.0	M	Sun Nov 15 ...	BEZONS (FRA)	0.0	0.0	0.0	0.0	Athletics	Men's 1500m
Abdelhak Aata...	Morocco	24.0			M	Tue Feb 09 ...	AIN SEBAA (...	0.0	0.0	0.0	0.0	Boxing	Men's Light Welter (...
Maria Abakum...	Russian Feder...	26.0	178.0	85.0	F	Wed Jan 15 ...	STAVROPO...	0.0	0.0	0.0	0.0	Athletics	Women's Javelin Thr...
Luc Abalo	France	27.0	182.0	80.0	M	Thu Sep 06 ...		0.0	0.0	0.0	0.0	Handball	Men's Handball
Maria Laura Ab...	Argentina	30.0	182.0	73.0	F	Mon Aug 17 ...		0.0	0.0	0.0	0.0	Rowing	Women's Pair
Mohamed Aba...	Morocco	23.0	187.0	75.0	M	Wed May 03...		0.0	0.0	0.0	0.0	Football	Men's Football
Emanuele Abate	Italy	27.0	190.0	80.0	M	Mon Jul 08 0...	Genova (ITA)	0.0	0.0	0.0	0.0	Athletics	Men's 110m Hurdles
Ilyas Abbadi	Algeria	19.0	170.0		M	Wed Oct 21 ...	MEDEA (ALG)	0.0	0.0	0.0	0.0	Boxing	Men's Welter (69kg)
Sohail Abbas	Pakistan	37.0			M	Mon Jun 09 ...		0.0	0.0	0.0	0.0	Hockey	Men's Hockey
Shakeel Abbasi	Pakistan	28.0			M	Thu Jan 05 ...		0.0	0.0	0.0	0.0	Hockey	Men's Hockey
Soulmaz Abba...	Islamic Repub...	28.0	173.0	60.0	F	Thu Jan 19 ...		0.0	0.0	0.0	0.0	Rowing	Women's Single Sculls
Simona Abbate	Italy	28.0	171.0	64.0	F	Mon Aug 22 ...	FONDI (ITA)	0.0	0.0	0.0	0.0	Water Polo	Women's Water Polo
Ahmed Abd El...	Egypt	22.0	171.0	62.0	M	Mon Jul 30 0...		0.0	0.0	0.0	0.0	Football	Men's Football
Reem Abdalaz...	Egypt	19.0	167.0		F	Wed Nov 25 ...	GIZA (EGY)	0.0	0.0	0.0	0.0	Synchronis...	Women's Teams
Mohamed Faw...	United Arab E...	22.0	175.0	63.0	M	Thu Feb 22 ...		0.0	0.0	0.0	0.0	Football	Men's Football
Mohamed Abd...	Egypt	25.0	162.0	69.0	M	Sat Jul 18 00...	FAYOUM	0.0	0.0	0.0	0.0	Weightlifting	Men's 69kg
Hesham Abdel...	Egypt	18.0	167.0		M	Sun Sep 05 ...	ELDAKAHLI...	0.0	0.0	0.0	0.0	Boxing	Men's Fly (52kg)
Tarek Abdelazim	Egypt	25.0	171.0	85.0	M	Mon May 18 ...	ELMENIA	0.0	0.0	0.0	0.0	Weightlifting	Men's 85kg
Shaza Abdelra...	Egypt	19.0	170.0		F	Wed Dec 23 ...	Cairo (EGY)	0.0	0.0	0.0	0.0	Synchronis...	Women's Duets, Wo...
Mouni Abderra...	Algeria	26.0	171.0	60.0	F	Tue Nov 19 ...		0.0	0.0	0.0	0.0	Volleyball	Women's Volleyball

We're fortunate that the data is clearly labeled in the columns and contains the following information:

- Name of the athlete
- Country for which they are competing
- Age in years
- Height in centimeters
- Weight in kilograms
- Sex as the string "M" or "F"
- Date of birth as a string
- Place of birth as a string (with country)
- Gold medals won
- Silver medals won
- Bronze medals won
- Total gold, silver, and bronze medals won
- Sport in which they competed
- Event as a comma-separated list

Even though the data is clearly labeled, gaps are evident in the data for height, weight, and place of birth. We'll have to be careful to make sure these don't trip us up.

Visualizing the data

First, we'll consider the spread of the heights of the London 2012 athletes. Let's plot our height values as a histogram to see how the data is distributed, remembering to filter the nil values first:

```
(defn ex-3-2 []
  (-> (remove nil? (i/$ "Height, cm" (athlete-data)))
      (c/histogram :nbins 20
                   :x-label "Height, cm"
                   :y-label "Frequency")
      (i/view)))
```

This code generates the following histogram:

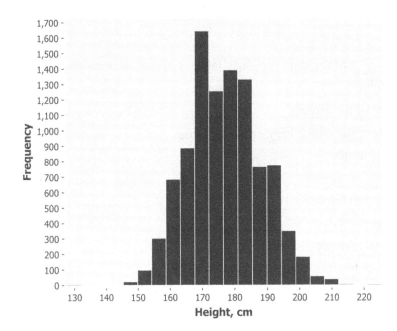

The data is approximately normally distributed, as we have come to expect. The mean height of our athletes is around 177 cm. Let's take a look at the distribution of weights of swimmers from the 2012 Olympics:

```
(defn ex-3-3 []
  (-> (remove nil? (i/$ "Weight" (athlete-data)))
      (c/histogram :nbins 20
                   :x-label "Weight"
                   :y-label "Frequency")
      (i/view)))
```

This code generates the following histogram:

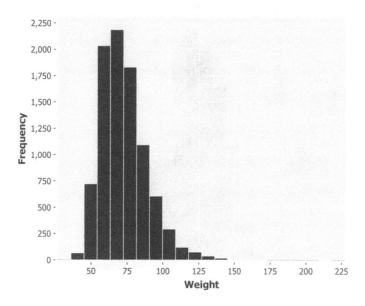

This data shows a pronounced skew. The tail is much longer to the right of the peak than to the left, so we say the skew is positive. We can quantify the skewness of the data with Incanter's `incanter.stats/skewness` function:

```
(defn ex-3-4 []
  (->> (swimmer-data)
       (i/$ "Weight")
       (remove nil?)
       (s/skewness)))
;; 0.238
```

Fortunately, this skew can be effectively mitigated by taking the logarithm of the weight using Incanter's `incanter.core/log` function:

```
(defn ex-3-5 []
  (-> (remove nil? (i/$ "Weight" (athlete-data)))
      (i/log)
      (c/histogram :nbins 20
                   :x-label "log(Weight)"
                   :y-label "Frequency")
      (i/view)))
```

This code results in the following histogram:

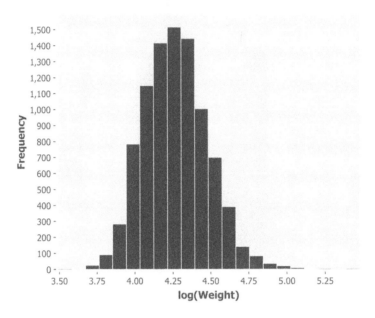

This is much closer to the normal distribution. This suggests that weight is distributed according to a **log-normal distribution**.

The log-normal distribution

The log-normal distribution is simply the distribution of a set of values whose logarithm is normally distributed. The base of the logarithm can be any positive number except for one. Like the normal distribution, the log-normal distribution is important in the description of many naturally occurring phenomena.

A logarithm represents the power to which a fixed number (the base) must be raised to produce a given number. By plotting the logarithms as a histogram, we've shown that these powers are approximately normally distributed. Logarithms are usually taken to base 10 or base e: the transcendental number that's equal to approximately 2.718. Incanter's log function and its inverse exp both use base e. log_e is also called the **natural logarithm** or *ln*, because of the properties that make it particularly suitable in calculus.

The log-normal distribution tends to occur in processes of growth where the growth rate is independent of size. This is known as *Gibrat's law* and was formally defined in 1931 by Robert Gibrat, who noticed that it applied to the growth of firms. Since the growth rate is a proportion of the size, larger firms tend to grow more quickly than smaller firms.

 The normal distribution occurs in situations where many small variations have an additive effect, whereas the log-normal distribution occurs in situations where many small variations have a multiplicative effect.

Gibrat's law has since been found to be applicable to lots of situations, including the sizes of cities and, according to Wolfram MathWorld, the numbers of words in sentences by George Bernard Shaw.

For the rest of this chapter, we'll be using the natural logarithm of the weight data so that our data is approximately normally distributed. We'll choose a population of athletes with roughly similar body types, say Olympic swimmers.

Visualizing correlation

One of the quickest and simplest ways of determining if two variables are correlated is to view them on a scatter plot. We'll filter our data to select only swimmers and then plot the heights against the weights:

```
(defn swimmer-data []
  (->> (athlete-data)
       (i/$where {"Height, cm" {:$ne nil} "Weight" {:$ne nil}
                  "Sport" {:$eq "Swimming"}})))
(defn ex-3-6 []
  (let [data (swimmer-data)
        heights (i/$ "Height, cm" data)
        weights (i/log (i/$ "Weight" data))]
    (-> (c/scatter-plot heights weights
                        :x-label "Height, cm"
                        :y-label "Weight")
        (i/view))))
```

This code yields the following plot:

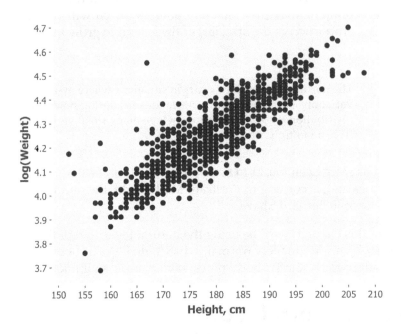

The output clearly shows a relationship between the two variables. The chart has the characteristically skewed elliptical shape of two correlated, normally distributed variables centered on the means. The following diagram compares the scatter plot against probability distributions of the height and log weight:

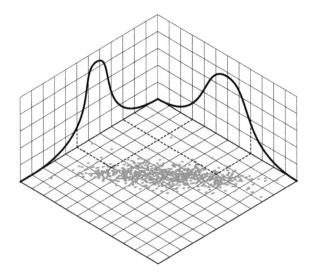

Points close to the tail of one distribution also tend to be close to the same tail of the other distribution, and vice versa. Thus, there is a relationship between the two distributions that we'll show how to quantify over the next several sections. If we look closely at the previous scatter plot though, we'll see that the points are packed into columns and rows due to the measurements being rounded (to centimeters and kilograms for height and weight, respectively). Where this occurs, it is sometimes preferable to *jitter* the data to make the strength of the relationship clearer. Without jittering, it could be that what appears to be one point is actually many points that share exactly the same pair of values. Introducing some random noise makes this possibility less likely.

Jittering

Since each value is rounded to the nearest centimeter, a value captured as 180 could actually have been anywhere between 179.5 cm and 180.5 cm. To unwind this effect, we can add random noise in the -0.5 to 0.5 range to each of the height data points.

The weight data point was captured to the nearest kilogram, so a value of 80 could actually have been anywhere between 79.5 kg and 80.5 kg. We can add random noise in the same range to unwind this effect (though clearly, this must be done before we take the logarithm):

```
(defn jitter [limit]
  (fn [x]
    (let [amount (- (rand (* 2 limit)) limit)]
      (+ x amount))))

(defn ex-3-7 []
  (let [data (swimmer-data)
        heights (->> (i/$ "Height, cm" data)
                     (map (jitter 0.5)))
        weights (->> (i/$ "Weight" data)
                     (map (jitter 0.5))
                     (i/log))]
    (-> (c/scatter-plot heights weights
                        :x-label "Height, cm"
                        :y-label "Weight")
        (i/view))))
```

The jittered graph appears as follows:

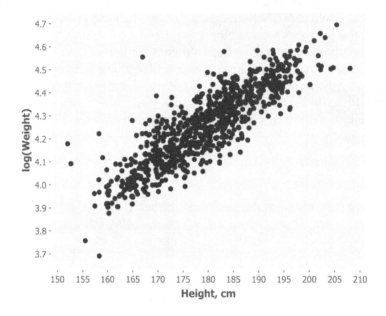

As with introducing transparency to the scatter plot in *Chapter 1, Statistics*, jittering is a mechanism to ensure that we don't let incidental factors — such as data volume or rounding artifacts — obscure our ability to see patterns in the data.

Covariance

One way of quantifying the strength of the relationship between two variables is their covariance. This measures the tendency of two variables to change together.

If we have two series, X and Y, their deviations from the mean are:

$$dx_i = x_i - \overline{x}$$

$$dy_i = y_i - \overline{y}$$

Where x_i is the value of X at index i, y_i is the value of Y at index i, $\bar{x}$ is the mean of X, and $\bar{y}$ is the mean of Y. If X and Y tend to vary together, their deviations from the mean tend to have the same sign: negative if they're less than the mean, positive if they're greater. If we multiply them together, the product is positive when they have the same sign and negative when they have different signs. Adding up the products gives a measure of the tendency of the two variables to deviate from the mean in the same direction for each given sample.

Covariance is defined as the mean of these products:

$$\text{cov}(X,Y) = \frac{1}{n}\sum_{i=1}^{n} dx_i dy_i$$

Covariance can be calculated in Clojure using the following code:

```
(defn covariance [xs ys]
  (let [x-bar (s/mean xs)
        y-bar (s/mean xs)
        dx (map (fn [x] (- x x-bar)) xs)
        dy (map (fn [y] (- y y-bar)) ys)]
    (s/mean (map * dx dy))))
```

Alternatively, we could use the `incanter.stats/covariance` function. The covariance of height and log-weight for our Olympic swimmers is `1.354`, but this is a hard number to interpret. The units are the product of the units of the inputs.

Because of this, covariance is rarely reported as a summary statistic on its own. A solution to make the number more comprehensible is to divide the deviations by the product of the standard deviations. This transforms the units to standard scores and constrains the output to a number between `-1` and `+1`. The result is called **Pearson's correlation**.

Pearson's correlation

Pearson's correlation is often given the variable name r and is calculated in the following way, where dx_i and dy_i are calculated as before:

$$r = \frac{1}{n}\sum_{i=1}^{n} \frac{dx_i}{\sigma_x} \frac{dy_i}{\sigma_y}$$

Since the standard deviations are constant values for the variables X and Y the equation can be simplified to the following, where σ_x and σ_y are the standard deviations of X and Y respectively:

$$r = \frac{\text{cov}(X,Y)}{\sigma_x \sigma_y}$$

This is sometimes referred to as Pearson's product-moment correlation coefficient or simply just the *correlation coefficient* and is usually denoted by the letter *r*.

We have previously written functions to calculate the standard deviation. Combining with our function to calculate covariance yields the following implementation of Pearson's correlation:

```
(defn correlation [x y]
  (/ (covariance x y)
     (* (standard-deviation x)
        (standard-deviation y)))))
```

Alternately, we can make use of the `incanter.stats/correlation` function.

Because standard scores are dimensionless, so is *r*. If *r* is -1.0 or 1.0, the variables are perfectly negatively or perfectly positively correlated.

If *r* is zero though, it doesn't necessarily follow that the variables are uncorrelated. Pearson's correlation only measures linear relationships. There could still be some nonlinear relationship between variables that isn't captured by *r*, as demonstrated by the following plots:

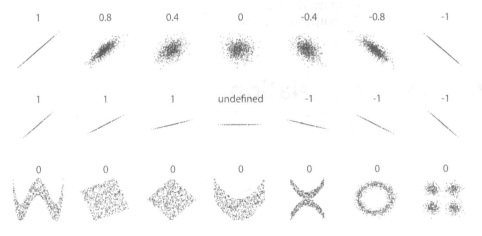

Note that the correlation of the central example is undefined because the standard deviation of y is zero. Since our equation for r would involve dividing the covariance by zero, the result is meaningless. In this case, there can't be any correlation between the variables; the value for y is always the mean. A simple inspection of standard deviations would confirm this.

The correlation coefficient can be calculated for the height and log-weight data for our swimmers:

```
(defn ex-3-8 []
  (let [data (swimmer-data)
        heights (i/$ "Height, cm" data)
        weights (i/log (i/$ "Weight" data))]
    (correlation heights weights)))
```

This yields the answer `0.867`, which quantifies the strong, positive correlation we already observed on the scatter plot.

Sample r and population rho

Like the mean or standard deviation, the correlation coefficient is a statistic. It describes a sample; in this case, a sample of paired values: height and weight. While our known sample correlation coefficient is given the letter r, the unknown population correlation coefficient is given the Greek letter rho: ρ.

As we discovered in the last chapter, we should not assume that what we measured in our sample applies to the population as a whole. In this case, our population might be all swimmers from all recent Olympic Games. It would not be appropriate to generalize, for example, to other Olympic sports such as weightlifting or to noncompetitive swimmers.

Even within an appropriate population—such as swimmers from the recent Olympic Games—our sample is just one of many potential samples of different correlation coefficients. How far we can trust our r as an estimate of ρ will depend on two factors:

- The size of the sample
- The magnitude of r

Clearly, for a fair sample, the larger it is the more we can trust it to be a representative of the population as a whole. It may not be intuitively obvious to you that the magnitude of r also affects how confident we can be of it representing ρ. The reason is that large coefficients are less likely to have arisen by chance or by random sampling error.

Hypothesis testing

In the previous chapter, we introduced hypothesis testing as a means to quantify the probability that a given hypothesis (such as that the two samples were from a single population) is true. We will use the same process to quantify the probability that a correlation exists in the wider population based on our sample.

First, we must formulate two hypotheses, a null hypothesis and an alternate hypothesis:

$$H_0 : \rho = 0$$

$$H_1 : \rho \neq 0$$

H_0 is the hypothesis that the population correlation is zero. In other words, our conservative view is that the measured correlation is purely due to chance sampling error.

H_1 is the alternative possibility that the population correlation is not zero. Notice that we don't specify the direction of the correlation, only that there is one. This means we are performing a two-tailed test.

The standard error of the sample r is given by:

$$SEr = \sqrt{\frac{1-p^2}{n-p^2}}$$

This formula is only accurate when ρ is close to zero (recall that the magnitude of r influences our confidence), but fortunately, this is exactly what we're assuming under our null hypothesis.

Once again, we can make use of the t-distribution and calculate our t-statistic:

$$t = r\sqrt{\frac{df}{1-r^2}}$$

The term *df* is the degree of freedom of our data. For correlation testing, the degree of freedom is *n* - 2 where *n* is the size of the sample. Putting this value into the formula, we obtain:

$$t = r\sqrt{\frac{df}{1-r^2}} = 0.867\sqrt{\frac{857}{1-(0.867)^2}}$$

This gives us a *t*-value of `102.21`. To convert this into a *p* value, we need to refer to the *t*-distribution. Incanter provides the **cumulative distribution function (CDF)** for the *t*-distribution with the `incanter.stats/cdf-t` function. The value of the CDF corresponds to the *p*-value for a one-tailed test. We multiply the value by two because we're performing a two-tailed test:

```
(defn t-statistic [x y]
  (let [r (correlation x y)
        r-square (* r r)
        df (- (count x) 2)]
    (/ (* r df)
       (i/sqrt (- 1 r-square)))))

(defn ex-3-9 []
  (let [data (swimmer-data)
        heights (i/$ "Height, cm" data)
        weights (i/log (i/$ "Weight" data))
        t-value (t-statistic heights weights)
        df (- (count heights) 2)
        p  (* 2 (s/cdf-t t-value :df df :lower-tail? false))]
    (println "t-value" t-value)
    (println "p value " p)))
```

The *p*-value is so small as to be essentially zero, meaning that the chances of the null hypothesis being true is essentially non-existent. We are forced to accept the alternate hypothesis.

Confidence intervals

Having established that there certainly is a correlation in the wider population, we might want to quantify the range of values we expect ρ to lie within by calculating a confidence interval. As in the previous chapter with the mean, the confidence interval of *r* expresses the probability (expressed as a percentage) that the population parameter ρ lies between two specific values.

However, a complication arises when trying to calculate the standard error of the correlation coefficient that didn't exist for the mean. Because the absolute value of *r* cannot exceed **1**, the distribution of possible samples of *r* is skewed as *r* approaches the limit of its range.

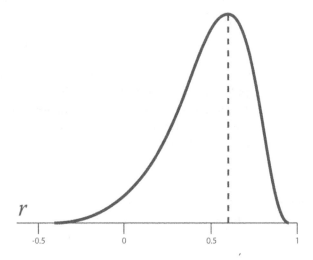

The previous graph shows the negatively skewed distribution of *r* samples for a ρ of 0.6.

Fortunately, a transformation called the **Fisher z-transformation** will stabilize the variance of *r* throughout its range. This is analogous to how our weight data became normally distributed when we took the logarithm.

The equation for the *z*-transformation is:

$$z_r = \frac{1}{2}\ln\left(\frac{1+r}{1-r}\right)$$

The standard error of *z* is:

$$SE_z = \frac{1}{\sqrt{n-3}}$$

Thus, the process to calculate confidence intervals is to convert *r* to *z* using the *z*-transformation, compute a confidence interval in terms of SE_z, and then convert the confidence interval back to *r*.

To calculate a confidence interval in terms of SE_z, we can take the number of standard deviations away from the mean that gives us the desired confidence. 1.96 is a common number to use, because it is the number of standard deviations away from the mean that contains 95 percent of the area. In other words, 1.96 standard errors from the mean of the sample r contains the true population correlation ρ with 95 percent certainty.

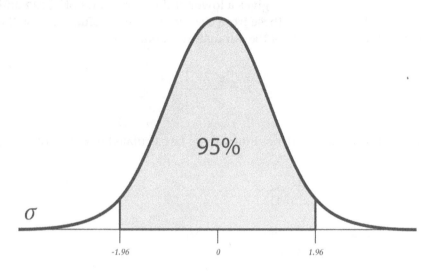

We can verify this using Incanter's `incanter.stats/quantile-normal` function. This will return the standard score associated with a given cumulative probability, assuming a one-tailed test.

However, as shown in the previous diagram, we'd like to subtract the same amount— 2.5 percent—from each tail, so that the 95 percent confidence interval is centered on zero. A simple translation is to halve the difference to 100 percent while performing a two-tailed test. So, a desired confidence of 95 percent means we look up the critical value of 97.5 percent:

```
(defn critical-value [confidence ntails]
  (let [lookup (- 1 (/ (- 1 confidence) ntails))]
    (s/quantile-normal lookup)))

(critical-value 0.95 2)
=> 1.96
```

So, our 95 percent confidence interval in z-space for ρ is given by:

$$z_{range} = z_r \pm \left(\text{critical-value}\right) SEz$$

Substituting our formulae for z_r and SE_z gives:

$$z_{range} = \frac{1}{2}\ln\left(\frac{1+r}{1-r}\right) \pm (1.96)\frac{1}{\sqrt{n-3}}$$

For r = 0.867 and n = 859, this gives a lower and upper bound of 1.137 and 1.722, respectively. To convert these from z-scores back to r-values, we use the following equation, the inverse of the z-transformation:

$$r = \frac{e^{2z} - 1}{e^{2z} + 1}$$

The transformations and confidence interval can be calculated with the following code:

```
(defn z->r [z]
  (/ (- (i/exp (* 2 z)) 1)
     (+ (i/exp (* 2 z)) 1)))

(defn r-confidence-interval [crit x y]
  (let [r   (correlation x y)
        n   (count x)
        zr  (* 0.5 (i/log (/ (+ 1 r)
                             (- 1 r))))
        sez (/ 1 (i/sqrt (- n 3)))]
    [(z->r (- zr (* crit sez)))
     (z->r (+ zr (* crit sez)))]))

(defn ex-3-10 []
  (let [data (swimmer-data)
        heights (i/$ "Height, cm" data)
        weights (i/log (i/$ "Weight" data))
        interval (r-confidence-interval 1.96 heights weights)]
    (println "Confidence Interval (95%): " interval)))
```

This gives a 95 percent confidence interval for ρ being between 0.850 and 0.883. We can be very confident that there is a strong positive correlation between the height and weight in the wider population of Olympic-class swimmers.

Regression

While it may be useful to know that two variables are correlated, we can't use this information alone to predict the weights of Olympic swimmers given their height or vice versa. In establishing a correlation, we have measured the strength and sign of a relationship, but not the slope. Knowing the expected rate of change for one variable given a unit change in the other is required in order to make predictions.

What we'd like to determine is an equation that relates the specific value of one variable, called the **independent variable**, to the expected value of the other, the **dependent variable**. For example, if our linear equation predicts the weight given the height, then the height is our independent variable and the weight is our dependent variable.

The lines described by these equations are called **regression lines**. The term was introduced by the 19th century British polymath Sir Francis Galton. He and his student Karl Pearson (who defined the correlation coefficient) developed a variety of methods to study linear relationships in the 19th century and these collectively became known as regression techniques.

Remember that correlation does not imply causation and there is no implied causation by the terms dependent and independent — they're just the names for mathematical inputs and outputs. A classic example is the highly positive correlation between the number of fire engines sent to a fire and the damage done by the fire. Clearly, sending fire engines to a fire does not itself cause damage. No one would recommend reducing the number of engines sent to a fire as a way of reducing damage. In situations like these, we should look for an additional variable, which is causally connected with the other variables, and explains the correlation between them. In the previous example, this might be the *size of fire*. Such hidden causes are called **confounding variables**, because they confound our ability to determine the relationship between their dependent variables.

Linear equations

Two variables, which we can signify as x and y, may be related to each other exactly or inexactly. The simplest relationship between an independent variable labeled x and a dependent variable labeled y is a straight line expressed in the formula:

$$y = a + bx$$

Here, the values of the parameters a and b determine respectively the precise height and steepness of the line. The parameter a is referred to as the intercept or constant and b as the gradient or slope. For example, in the mapping between Celsius and Fahrenheit temperature scales, $a = 32$ and $b = 1.8$. Substituting these values of a and b into our equation yields:

$$y = 32 + 1.8x$$

To calculate 10 degrees Celsius in Fahrenheit, we substitute 10 for x:

$$y = 32 + 1.8(10) = 50$$

Thus, our equation tells us that 10 degrees Celsius is 50 degrees Fahrenheit, which is indeed the case. Using Incanter, we can easily write a function that maps Celsius to Fahrenheit and plot it as a graph using `incanter.charts/function-plot`:

```
(defn celsius->fahrenheit [x]
  (+ 32 (* 1.8 x)))

(defn ex-3-11 []
  (-> (c/function-plot celsius->fahrenheit -10 40
                       :x-label "Celsius"
                       :y-label "Fahrenheit")
      (i/view)))
```

This code yields the following line graph:

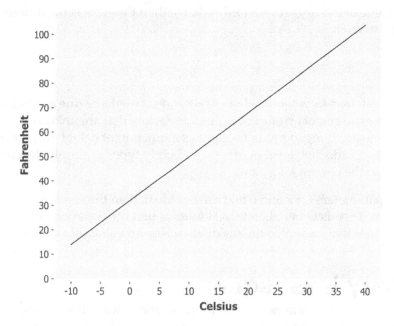

Notice how the red line crosses zero on the Celsius scale at 32 on the Fahrenheit scale. The intercept a is the value of y, where x is zero.

The slope of the line is determined by b; it is close to 2 for this equation. See how the range of the Fahrenheit scale is almost double the range of the Celsius scale. In other words, the line sweeps almost twice as fast vertically as it does horizontally.

Residuals

Unfortunately few relationships we will study are as tidy as the mapping between Celsius and Fahrenheit. The straight-line equation rarely allows us to specify y exactly in terms of x. There will ordinarily be an error, thus:

$$y = a + bx + \varepsilon$$

Here, ε is an error term standing for the difference between the value calculated by the parameters a and b for a given value of x and the actual value of y. If our predicted value of y is $\hat{y}$ (pronounced "y-hat"), then the error is the difference between the two:

$$\varepsilon = y - \hat{y}$$

This error is referred to as the residual. The residual might be due to random factors like measurement error or non-random factors that are unknown. For example, if we are trying to predict weight as a function of height, unknown factors might include diet, level of fitness, and body type (or simply the effect of rounding to the nearest kilogram).

If we select parameters for a and b that are not ideal, then the residual for each x will be larger than it needs to be. Therefore, it follows that the parameters we'd like to find are the ones that minimize the residuals across all values of x and y.

Ordinary least squares

In order to optimize the parameters of our linear model, we'd like to devise a cost function, also called a **loss function**, that quantifies how closely our predictions fit the data. We cannot simply sum up the residuals, positive and negative, because even large residuals will cancel each other out if their signs are in opposite directions.

We could square the values before calculating the sum so that positive and negative residuals both count towards the cost. This also has the effect of penalizing large errors more than smaller errors, but not so much that the largest residual always dominates.

Expressed as an optimization problem, we seek to identify the coefficients that minimize the sum of the residual squares. This is called **Ordinary Least Squares (OLS)**, and the formula to calculate the slope of the regression line using OLS is:

$$b = \frac{\sum_{i=1}^{n}\left(x_i - \overline{x}\right)\left(y_i - \overline{y}\right)}{\sum_{i=1}^{n}\left(x_i - \overline{x}\right)^2}$$

Although this looks more complicated than the previous equations, it's really just the sum of squared residuals divided by the sum of squared differences from the mean. This shares a number of terms from the equations we have already looked at and can be simplified to:

$$b = \frac{\text{cov}(X,Y)}{\text{var}(X)}$$

The intercept is the term that allows a line of this slope to pass through the mean of both X and Y:

$$a = \overline{y} - b\overline{x}$$

These values of a and b are the coefficients of our least squares estimates.

Slope and intercept

We've already written the covariance, variance, and mean functions we need to calculate the slope and intercept for the swimming height and weight data. Therefore, the slope and intercept calculations are trivial:

```
(defn slope [x y]
  (/ (covariance x y)
     (variance x)))

(defn intercept [x y]
  (- (s/mean y)
     (* (s/mean x)
        (slope x y))))

(defn ex-3-12 []
  (let [data (swimmer-data)
        heights (i/$ "Height, cm" data)
        weights (i/log (i/$ "Weight" data))
        a (intercept heights weights)
        b (slope heights weights)]
    (println "Intercept: " a)
    (println "Slope: " b)))
```

The output gives a slope of approximately `0.0143` and an intercept of approximately `1.6910`.

Interpretation

The **intercept value** is the value of the dependent variable (log weight) when the independent variable (height) is zero. To find out what this value equates to in kilograms, we can use the incanter.core/exp function, which performs the inverse of the incanter.core/log function. Our model seems to suggest that the best guess for the weight of an Olympic swimmer of zero height is 5.42 kg. This is meaningless, and it is unwise to extrapolate beyond the bounds of your training data.

The slope value shows how much y changes for each unit change in x. Our model suggests that each additional centimeter of height adds on an average of 1.014 kg to the weight of our Olympic swimmers. Since our model is based on all Olympic swimmers, this is the average effect of a unit increase in height without taking into account any other factor, such as age, gender, or body type.

Visualization

We can visualize the output of our linear equation with incanter.charts/function-plot and a simple function of x that calculates $\hat{y}$ based on the coefficients a and b.

```
(defn regression-line [a b]
  (fn [x]
    (+ a (* b x))))

(defn ex-3-13 []
  (let [data (swimmer-data)
        heights (->> (i/$ "Height, cm" data)
                     (map (jitter 0.5)))
        weights (i/log (i/$ "Weight" data))
        a (intercept heights weights)
        b (slope heights weights)]
    (-> (c/scatter-plot heights weights
                        :x-label "Height, cm"
                        :y-label "log(Weight)")
        (c/add-function (regression-line a b) 150 210)
        (i/view)))))
```

The regression-line function returns a function of x that calculates $a + bx$.

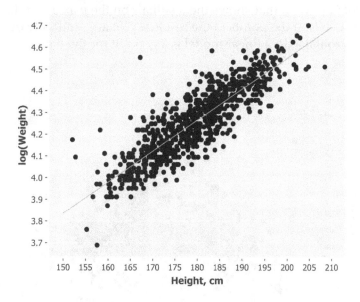

We can also use the `regression-line` function to calculate each residual, showing how far our estimate $\hat{y}$ deviates from each measured y.

```
(defn residuals [a b x y]
  (let [estimate (regression-line a b)
        residual (fn [x y]
                    (- y (estimate x)))]
    (map residual x y)))


(defn ex-3-14 []
  (let [data (swimmer-data)
        heights (->> (i/$ "Height, cm" data)
                     (map (jitter 0.5)))
        weights (i/log (i/$ "Weight" data))
        a (intercept heights weights)
        b (slope heights weights)]
    (-> (c/scatter-plot heights (residuals a b heights weights)
                        :x-label "Height, cm"
                        :y-label "Residuals")
        (c/add-function (constantly 0) 150 210)
        (i/view))))
```

A **residual plot** is a graph that shows the residuals on the *y*-axis and the independent variable on the *x*-axis. If the points in the residual plot are randomly dispersed around the horizontal axis, a linear model is a good fit for the data:

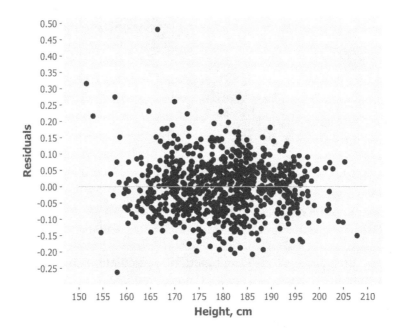

With the exception of some outliers on the left side of the chart, the residual plot appears to indicate that a linear model is a good fit for the data. Plotting the residuals is important to verify that the linear model is appropriate. There are certain assumptions that a linear model makes about your data that will, if violated, invalidate models you build.

Assumptions

Obviously, the primary assumption of linear regression is that there is a linear relationship between the dependent and independent variable. In addition, the residuals must not be correlated with each other or with the independent variable. In other words, we expect the errors to have a zero mean and constant variance versus the dependent and independent variable. A residual plot allows us to quickly determine if this is the case.

The left side of our residual plot has greater residuals than the right side. This corresponds to greater variance of weight amongst shorter athletes. The variables are said to be **heteroscedastic** when the variance of one variable changes with respect to another. This is a concern in regression analysis, because it invalidates the assumption that modeling errors are uncorrelated and normally distributed and that their variances do not vary with the effects being modeled.

The heteroscedasticity of our residuals are fairly small and should not influence the quality of our model very much. If the variance on the left side of the graph were more pronounced, it would cause the least squares estimate of variance to be incorrect, which in turn would affect inferences we make based on the standard error.

Goodness-of-fit and R-square

Although we can see from the residual plot that a linear model is a good fit for our data, it would be desirable to quantify just how good it is. Also called the **coefficient of determination**, R^2 varies between zero and one and indicates the explanatory power of the linear regression model. It calculates the proportion of variation in the dependent variable explained, or accounted for, by the independent variable.

Generally, the closer R^2 is to 1, the better the regression line fits the points and the more the variation in Y is explained by X. R^2 can be calculated using the following formula:

$$R^2 = 1 - \frac{\text{var}(\varepsilon)}{\text{var}(Y)}$$

Here, $var(\varepsilon)$ is the variance of the residuals and $var(Y)$ is the variance in Y. To understand what this means, let's suppose you're trying to guess someone's weight. If you don't know anything else about them, your best strategy would be to guess the mean of the weights within the population in general. This way, the mean squared error of your guess compared to their true weight would be $var(Y)$ or the variance of the weights in the population.

But if I told you their height, you would guess $a + bx$ as per the regression model. In this case, your mean squared error would be $var(\varepsilon)$ or the variance of the residuals of the model.

The term $var(\varepsilon)/var(Y)$ is the ratio of mean squared error with and without the explanatory variable, which is the fraction of variability left unexplained by the model. The complement R^2 is the fraction of variability explained by the model.

As with r, a low R^2 does not mean that the two variables are uncorrelated. It might simply be that their relationship is not linear.

The R^2 value describes how well the line fits the data. The line of *best fit* is the line that minimizes the value of R^2. As the coefficients increase or decrease away from their optimum values, R^2 will always increase.

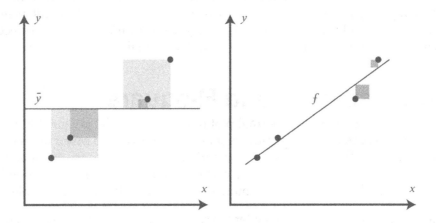

The left graph shows the variance for a model that always guesses the mean of y and the right one shows smaller squares associated with the residuals left unexplained by the model f. In purely geometric terms, you can see the how the model has explained most of the variance in y. The following code calculates R^2 by dividing the variance of the residuals with the variance of the y values:

```
(defn r-squared [a b x y]
  (let [r-var (variance (residuals a b x y))
        y-var (variance y)]
    (- 1 (/ r-var y-var))))

(defn ex-3-15 []
  (let [data (swimmer-data)
        heights (i/$ "Height, cm" data)
        weights (i/log (i/$ "Weight" data))
        a (intercept heights weights)
        b (slope heights weights)]
    (r-squared a b heights weights)))
```

This gives a value of `0.753`. In other words, over 75 percent of the variance of the weight of 2012 Olympic swimmers can be explained by the height.

In the case of a simple regression model (with a single independent variable), the relationship between the coefficient of determination R^2 and the correlation coefficient r is a straightforward one:

$$R^2 = r^2$$

A correlation coefficient of 0.5 might suggest that half the variability in Y is explained by X, but actually, R^2 would be 0.5^2 or 0.25.

Multiple linear regression

We've seen so far in this chapter how to build a regression line with one independent variable. However, it is often desirable to build a model with several independent variables. This is called **multiple linear regression**.

Each independent variable is going to need its own coefficient. Rather than working our way through the alphabet to represent each one, let's designate a new variable β, pronounced "beta", to hold all of our coefficients:

$$y = \beta_1 x_1 + \beta_2 x_2$$

This model is equivalent to our **bivariate linear regression** model, where $\beta_1 = a$ and $\beta_2 = b$ so long as we ensure that x_1 is always equal to one. This ensures that β_1 is always a constant factor representing our intercept. x_1 is called the **bias term**.

Having generalized the linear equation in terms of beta, easy to extend to as many coefficients as we'd like:

$$y = \beta_1 x_1 + \beta_2 x_2 + \cdots + \beta_n x_n$$

Each of the values of x_1 up to x_n correspond to an independent variable that might help explain the value of y. Each of the values of β_1 up to β_n correspond to a coefficient that determines the relative contribution of this independent variable.

Our simple linear regression aimed to explain weight only in terms of height, but many other factors help to explain someone's weight: their age, gender, diet, and body type. We know the ages of our Olympic swimmers, so we could build a model that incorporates this additional data too.

We've been providing the independent variable as a single sequence of values, but with multiple parameters, we'll need to provide several values for each x. We can use Incanter's i/$ function to select multiple columns and manipulate each x as a Clojure vector, but there is a better way: matrices.

Matrices

A matrix is a two-dimensional grid of numbers. The dimensions are expressed as the number of rows and columns in the matrix.

For example, A is a matrix with four rows and two columns:

$$A = \begin{bmatrix} 1402 & 191 \\ 1371 & 821 \\ 949 & 1427 \\ 147 & 1448 \end{bmatrix}$$

In mathematical notation, a matrix will usually be assigned to a variable with an upper-case letter to distinguish it from other variables in an equation.

We can construct a matrix from our dataset using Incanter's incanter.core/to-matrix function:

```
(defn ex-3-16 []
  (->> (swimmer-data)
       (i/$ ["Height, cm" "Weight"])
       (i/to-matrix)))
```

Incanter also defines the incanter.core/matrix function that will take a sequence of scalar values or a sequence of sequences and convert them into a matrix if it can:

```
(defn ex-3-17 []
  (->> (swimmer-data)
       (i/$ "Height, cm")
       (i/matrix)))
```

If you run this in the REPL, the output will be a summary of the contents of the matrix:

```
 A 859x1 matrix
 ---------------
1.66e+02
1.92e+02
1.73e+02
```

```
. . .
1.88e+02
1.87e+02
1.83e+02
```

Incanter returns a representation exactly as shown in the preceding example, presenting only the top and bottom three rows of the matrix. Matrices can often become very large and Incanter takes care not to inundate the REPL with information.

Dimensions

The element in the ith row j^{th} column is referred to as A_{ij}. Therefore, in our earlier example:

$$A_{31} = 2$$

One of the most fundamental attributes of a matrix is its size. Incanter provides the `incanter.core/dim, ncol`, and `nrow` functions to query matrices dimensions.

Vectors

A vector is a special case of matrix with only one column. The number of rows in the vector are referred to as its dimension:

$$y = \begin{bmatrix} 460 \\ 232 \\ 315 \\ 178 \end{bmatrix}$$

Here, y is a four-dimensional vector. The ith element is referred to as y_i.

Vectors in mathematical literature are one-indexed unless otherwise specified. So, y_1 refers to the first element, not the second. Vectors are generally assigned to lowercase variables in equations. Incanter's API doesn't distinguish between vectors and single column matrices and we can create a vector by passing a single sequence to the `incanter.core/matrix` function.

Construction

As we've seen, it's possible to build matrices out of Clojure sequences and Incanter datasets. It's also possible to build matrices out of smaller building blocks, provided the dimensions are compatible. Incanter provides the `incanter.core/bind-columns` and `incanter.core/bind-rows` functions to stack matrices above one another or side by side.

For example, we could add a column of 1s to the front of another matrix in the following way:

```
(defn add-bias [x]
  (i/bind-columns (repeat (i/nrow x) 1) x))
```

In fact, we'll want to do this for our bias term. Recall that β_1 will represent a constant value, so we must ensure that our corresponding x_1 is constant too. Without the bias term, y would have to be zero when the values of x are zero.

Addition and scalar multiplication

A scalar is a name for a simple number. When we add a scalar to a matrix, it's as if we added the number to each element of the matrix, individually. Incanter provides the `incanter.core/plus` function to add scalars and matrices together.

Matrix-matrix addition works by adding the elements in each corresponding position. Only matrices of the same dimensions can be added together. If the matrices are of the same dimensions, they are said to be compatible.

$$\begin{bmatrix} 1 & 0 \\ 2 & 5 \\ 3 & 1 \end{bmatrix} + \begin{bmatrix} 4 & 0.5 \\ 2 & 5 \\ 0 & 1 \end{bmatrix} = \begin{bmatrix} 5 & 0.5 \\ 4 & 10 \\ 3 & 2 \end{bmatrix}$$

The `plus` function will also add compatible matrices. The `minus` function will subtract scalars or compatible matrices. Multiplying a matrix by a scalar results in each of the elements in the matrix being multiplied by the scalar.

$$3 \times \begin{bmatrix} 1 & 0 \\ 2 & 5 \\ 3 & 1 \end{bmatrix} = \begin{bmatrix} 3 & 0 \\ 6 & 15 \\ 9 & 3 \end{bmatrix}$$

The `incanter.core/mult` performs matrix-scalar multiplication, while `incanter.core/div` performs the inverse.

We can also use `mult` and `div` on compatible matrices, but this element-wise method of multiplying and dividing is not what we normally intend to do when we speak of matrix multiplication.

Matrix-vector multiplication

The standard way to multiply matrices is handled by the `incanter.core/mmult` function, which applies the complex matrix multiplication algorithm. For example, the result of multiplying a 3 x 2 matrix with a 2 x 1 matrix is a 3 x 1 matrix. The number of columns on the left has to match the number of rows on the right of the multiplication:

$$A = \begin{bmatrix} 1 & 3 \\ 0 & 4 \\ 2 & 1 \end{bmatrix}$$

$$x = \begin{bmatrix} 1 \\ 5 \end{bmatrix}$$

$$Ax = \begin{bmatrix} 1 & 3 \\ 0 & 4 \\ 2 & 1 \end{bmatrix} \begin{bmatrix} 1 \\ 5 \end{bmatrix} = \begin{bmatrix} 1 \times 1 + 3 \times 5 \\ 0 \times 1 + 4 \times 5 \\ 2 \times 1 + 1 \times 5 \end{bmatrix} = \begin{bmatrix} 16 \\ 20 \\ 7 \end{bmatrix}$$

To get Ax, multiply each row of A element-by-element with the corresponding element of x and sum the results. For example, the first row of matrix A contains the elements 1 and 3. These are multiplied pairwise by the elements in vector x: 1 and 5. Then, the products are added together to produce 16. This is called the **dot product** and is what is commonly intended by matrix multiplication.

Matrix-matrix multiplication

Matrix-matrix multiplication proceeds very similarly to matrix-vector multiplication. The sum of the products is taken pairwise, row by row and column by column, from the corresponding elements of matrices A and B.

$$A = \begin{bmatrix} 1 & 3 \\ 0 & 4 \\ 2 & 1 \end{bmatrix}$$

$$B = \begin{bmatrix} 1 & 0 \\ 5 & 6 \end{bmatrix}$$

$$AB = \begin{bmatrix} 1 & 3 \\ 0 & 4 \\ 2 & 1 \end{bmatrix} \begin{bmatrix} 1 & 0 \\ 5 & 6 \end{bmatrix} = \begin{bmatrix} 1\times1+3\times5 & 1\times0+3\times6 \\ 0\times1+4\times5 & 0\times0+4\times6 \\ 2\times1+1\times5 & 2\times0+1\times6 \end{bmatrix} = \begin{bmatrix} 16 & 18 \\ 20 & 24 \\ 7 & 6 \end{bmatrix}$$

As before, we can only multiply matrices together when the number of columns in the first matrix is equal to the number of rows in the second matrix. If the first matrix A is of dimensions $m_A \times n_A$ and the second matrix B is of dimensions $m_B \times n_B$, n_A and m_B must be equal if the matrices are to be multiplied.

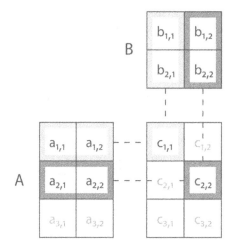

In the previous visual example:

$$a_{1,1}b_{1,1} + a_{1,2}b_{2,1} = c_{1,1}$$

$$a_{2,1}b_{1,2} + a_{2,2}b_{2,2} = c_{2,2}$$

Luckily, we don't have to remember the process ourselves. Incanter uses very efficient algorithms to perform matrix algebra for us.

Transposition

Transposing a matrix means flipping the matrix over the main diagonal running from the top-left to the bottom-right corner. The transpose of matrix A is represented as A^T:

$$A^T = \begin{bmatrix} 1 & 0 & 2 \\ 3 & 4 & 1 \end{bmatrix}$$

The columns and rows have been changed such that:

$$A_{ij} = A^T_{ji}$$

Therefore, if:

$$A_{31} = 2$$

Then:

$$A^T_{13} = 2$$

Incanter provides the `incanter.core/trans` function to transpose a matrix.

The identity matrix

Certain matrices have special properties and are used regularly in matrix algebra. One of the most important of these is the identity matrix. It's a square matrix with ones along the main diagonal and zeros everywhere else:

$$\begin{bmatrix} 1 & 0 & \cdots & 0 \\ 0 & 1 & \cdots & 0 \\ \vdots & \vdots & \ddots & 0 \\ 0 & 0 & 0 & 1 \end{bmatrix}$$

The identity matrix is the identity for matrix multiplication. As with a scalar multiplication by the number one, a matrix multiplication by the identity matrix has no effect.

Incanter provides the `incanter.core/identity-matrix` function to construct identity matrices. Since they're always square, we only provide a single argument corresponding to both, the width and height.

Inversion

If we have a square matrix A, the inverse of A is denoted as A^{-1} and it will have the following properties, where I is the identity matrix:

$$A \times A^{-1} = A^{-1} \times A = 1$$

The identity matrix is its own inverse. Not all matrices are invertible and noninvertible matrices are also called **singular** or **degenerate** matrices. We can calculate the inverse of a matrix with the `incanter.core/solve` function. `solve` will raise an exception if passed a singular matrix.

The normal equation

Now that we've covered the basics of matrix and vector manipulation we're in a position to study the **normal equation**. This is an equation that uses matrix algebra to calculate the coefficients of our OLS linear regression model:

$$\beta = \left(X^T X \right)^{-1} X^T y$$

We read "to find β, multiply the inverse of X transpose X, by X transpose y" where X is the matrix of independent variables (including the intercept term) for our sample and y is a vector containing the dependent variables for our sample. The result β contains the calculated coefficients. This normal equation is relatively easy to derive from the equation of multiple regression, applying the rules of matrix multiplication, but the mathematics is beyond the scope of this book.

We can implement the normal equation with Incanter using only the functions we have just encountered:

```
(defn normal-equation [x y]
  (let [xtx  (i/mmult (i/trans x) x)
        xtxi (i/solve xtx)
        xty  (i/mmult (i/trans x) y)]
    (i/mmult xtxi xty)))
```

This normal equation expresses the mathematics of least squares linear regression in a very succinct way. We can use it as follows (remembering to add the bias term):

```
(defn ex-3-18 []
  (let [data (swimmer-data)
        x (i/matrix (i/$ "Height, cm" data))
        y (i/matrix (i/log (i/$ "Weight" data)))]
    (normal-equation (add-bias x) y)))
```

This yields the following matrix:

```
A 2x1 matrix
-------------
1.69e+00
1.43e-02
```

These are the values of β_1 and β_2 corresponding to the intercept and slope parameters. Happily, they agree with the values we calculated previously.

More features

Part of the strength of the normal equation is that we've now implemented everything we need in order to support multiple linear regression. Let's write a function to convert the features of interest to a matrix:

```
(defn feature-matrix [col-names dataset]
  (-> (i/$ col-names dataset)
      (i/to-matrix)))
```

This function will allow us to select specific columns as a matrix in one step.

 A feature is a synonym for an independent variable and is popularly used in machine learning. Other synonyms are predictor, regressor, and explanatory variable, or simply input variable.

To start with, let's select height and age as our two features:

```
(defn ex-3-19 []
  (feature-matrix ["Height, cm" "Age"] (swimmer-data)))
```

This returns the following matrix of two columns:

```
A 859x2 matrix
---------------
1.66e+02    2.30e+01
1.92e+02    2.20e+01
```

```
1.73e+02   2.00e+01
...
1.88e+02   2.40e+01
1.87e+02   1.90e+01
1.83e+02   2.20e+01
```

Our normal equation function will accept this new matrix without any further change:

```
(defn ex-3-20 []
  (let [data (swimmer-data)
        x (->> data
               (feature-matrix ["Height, cm" "Age"])
               (add-bias))
        y (->> (i/$ "Weight" data)
               (i/log)
               (i/matrix))]
    (normal-equation x y)))
```

It will return the following coefficients:

```
A 3x1 matrix
------------
1.69e+00
1.40e-02
2.80e-03
```

These three numbers correspond to the intercept, the slope for height, and the slope for age, respectively. To determine whether our model has significantly improved by this new data, we could calculate the R^2 value of our new model and compare it to the earlier one.

Multiple R-squared

While calculating R^2 previously, we saw how it was the amount of variance explained by the model:

$$R^2 = 1 - \frac{\text{var}(\varepsilon)}{\text{var}(y)}$$

Since the variance is the mean squared error, we can multiply both the *var(ε)* and *var(y)* terms by the sample size and arrive at the following alternative equation for R²:

$$R^2 = 1 - \frac{\sum(y - \hat{y})^2}{\sum(y - \hat{y})^2}$$

This is simply the sum of squared residuals over the sum of squared differences from the mean. Incanter contains the `incanter.core/sum-of-squares` function that makes this very simple to express:

```
(defn r-squared [coefs x y]
  (let [fitted      (i/mmult x coefs)
        residuals   (i/minus y fitted)
        differences (i/minus y (s/mean y))
        rss         (i/sum-of-squares residuals)
        ess         (i/sum-of-squares differences)]
    (- 1 (/ rss ess))))
```

We use the variable names `rss` for **residual sum of squares** and `ess` for **explained sum of squares**. We can calculate the matrix R^2 for our new model as follows:

```
(defn ex-3-21 []
  (let [data (swimmer-data)
        x (->> (feature-matrix ["Height, cm" "Age"] data)
               (add-bias))
        y (->> (i/$ "Weight" data)
               (i/log)
               (i/matrix))
        beta (normal-equation x y)]
    (r-squared beta x y)))
```

This yields the value `0.757`. Our R^2 value has increased by a small amount by including the age value. Because we have used multiple independent variables, R^2 is now called the **coefficient of multiple determination**.

Adjusted R-squared

As we add more independent variables to our regression, we might be encouraged by the fact that our R^2 value always increases. Adding a new independent variable isn't going to make it harder to predict the dependent variable — if the new variable has no explanatory power, then its coefficient will simply be zero and the R² will remain the same as it was without the independent variable.

However, this doesn't tell us whether a model has been improved by the addition of a new variable. If we want to know whether our new variable is really helping it to generate a better fit, we can use the adjusted R^2, often written as $\bar{R}^2$ and pronounced as "R-bar squared." Unlike R^2, $\bar{R}^2$ will only increase if the new independent variable increases R^2 more than would be expected due to chance:

```
(defn matrix-adj-r-squared [coefs x y]
  (let [r-squared (matrix-r-squared coefs x y)
        n (count y)
        p (count coefs)]
    (- 1
      (* (- 1 r-squared)
        (/ (dec n)
          (dec (- n p)))))))
```

The adjusted R^2 depends on two additional parameters, n and p, corresponding to the sample size and number of model parameters, respectively:

```
(defn ex-3-22 []
  (let [data (swimmer-data)
        x (->> (feature-matrix ["Height, cm" "Age"] data)
               (add-bias))
        y (->> (i/$ "Weight" data)
               (i/log)
               (i/matrix))
        beta (normal-equation x y)]
    (adj-r-squared beta x y)))
```

This example returns a value of 0.756. This is still greater than the original model, so age certainly carries some explanatory power.

Incanter's linear model

While implementing our own version of the normal equation and R^2 provides a valuable opportunity to introduce matrix algebra, it's important to note that Incanter provides the `incanter.stats/linear-model` function that does everything we've covered and more.

The function expects to be called with y and x (as either sequences or, in the case of multiple regression, matrices). We can also pass in an optional keyword argument— `intercept` with a Boolean value—indicating whether we'd like Incanter to add the intercept term for us. The function will return a map containing the coefficients of the linear model— `:coefs` and the fitted data— `:fitted`, as well as `:residuals`, `:r-square`, and `:adj-r-square`, amongst others.

It will also return significance tests and 95 percent confidence intervals for the coefficients as the `:t-probs` and `:coefs-ci` keys, respectively, as well as the `:f-prob` keys, corresponding to a significance test on the regression model as a whole.

The F-test of model significance

The `:f-prob` key returned by `linear-model` is a significance test of the entire model using an F-test. As we discovered in the previous chapter, an F-test is appropriate when performing multiple significance tests at once. In the case of multiple linear regression, we are testing whether any of the coefficients of the model, except for the intercept term, are statistically indistinguishable from zero.

Our null and alternate hypotheses are therefore:

$$H_0 : \theta_2 = \cdots = \theta_n = 0$$

$$H_1 : \theta_j \neq 0$$

Here, j is some index in the parameter's vector excluding the intercept. The F-statistic we calculate is the ratio of explained variance over the unexplained (residual) variance. This can be expressed as the **mean square model (MSM)** over the **mean square error (MSE)**:

$$F = \frac{MSM}{MSE}$$

The MSM is equal to the **explained sum of squares (ESS)** divided by the model degree of freedom, where the model degree of freedom is the number of parameters in the model excluding the intercept term. The MSE is equal to the **sum of residual squares (RSS)** divided by the residual degree of freedom, where the residual degree of freedom is the size of the sample minus the number of model parameters.

Once we've calculated the F-statistic, we look it up in an F-distribution parameterized by the same two degrees of freedom:

```
(defn f-test [y x]
  (let [coefs        (normal-equation x y)
        fitted       (i/mmult x coefs)
        difference   (i/minus fitted (s/mean y))
        residuals    (i/minus y fitted)
        ess          (i/sum-of-squares difference)
```

```
        rss           (i/sum-of-squares residuals)
        p             (i/ncol x)
        n             (i/nrow y)
        df1           (- p 1)
        df2           (- n p)
        msm           (/ ess df1)
        mse           (/ rss df2)
        f-stat        (/ msm mse)]
    (s/cdf-f f-stat :df1 df1 :df2 df2 :lower-tail? false)))


(defn ex-3-23 []
  (let [data (swimmer-data)
        x (->> (feature-matrix ["Height, cm" "Age"] data)
               (add-bias))
        y (->> (i/$ "Weight" data)
               (i/log))
        beta (:coefs (s/linear-model y x :intercept false))]
    (f-test beta x y)))
```

The test returns a result of `1.11x10e-16`. This is a tiny number; as a result, we can be certain that the model is significant.

Note that with smaller samples of data, the *F*-test quantifies increasing uncertainty that a linear model is appropriate. With a random sample of five, for example, the data sometimes shows barely any linear relationship at all and the *F*-test judges the data insignificant at even a 50 percent confidence interval.

Categorical and dummy variables

We might attempt at this point to include `"Sex"` as a feature in our regression analysis, but we'll encounter a problem. The input is expressed as `"M"` or `"F"` rather than a number. This is an example of a categorical variable: a variable that can take one of a finite set of values that are unordered and (usually) not numeric. Other examples of categorical variables are the sport that the athlete participates in or the particular event in which they are most proficient.

Ordinary least squares relies on a numerical value of residual distance to minimize. What could the numeric distance between swimming and athletics be? This might imply that it is impossible to include categorical variables in our regression equation.

Categorical or nominal variables are distinct from continuous variables, because they don't sit on the number line. Sometimes categories are represented by numbers like for ZIP codes, but we shouldn't assume that numeric categories are necessarily ordered or that the interval between categories are equal.

Fortunately, many categorical variables can be considered dichotomies and, in fact, our sample data contains two categories for sex. These can be included in our regression model provided we transform them into two numbers, for example, zero and one.

When a category such as sport takes on more than two values, we could include an independent variable for each type of sport. We would create a variable for swimming and another for weightlifting, and so on. The value of swimming would be one for swimmers and zero otherwise.

Since sex might be a useful explanatory variable for our regression model, let's convert female to 0 and male to 1. We can add a derived column containing our dummy variable using Incanter's incanter.core/add-derived-column function.

Let's calculate our $\bar{R}^2$ value to see if it has improved:

```
(defn dummy-mf [sex]
  (if (= sex "F")
    0.0 1.0))

(defn ex-3-25 []
  (let [data (->> (swimmer-data)
                  (i/add-derived-column "Dummy MF"
                                        ["Sex"]
                                        dummy-mf))
        x (->> data
               (feature-matrix ["Height, cm"
                                "Age"
                                "Dummy MF"])
               (add-bias))
        y (->> (i/$ "Weight" data)
               (i/log)
               (i/matrix))
        beta (normal-equation x y)]
    (adj-r-squared beta x y)))
```

The code yields the value 0.809. Using the height, age, and gender features, we have successfully explained over 80 percent of the variance in weight of our Olympic swimmers.

Relative power

At this point, it might be useful to ask what is the most important feature to explain the observed weight: is it age, gender, or height? We could make use of our adjusted R^2 and see how much the value changes, but this would require us to re-run the regression for each variable we want to test.

We can't look at the magnitude of the coefficients, because the ranges of the data they apply to are vastly different: height in centimeters, age in years, and gender measured as a dummy variable in the range zero to one.

In order to compare the relative contributions of the coefficients, we can calculate the standardized regression coefficient, or beta weight.

$$\beta_{i(adj)} = \beta_i \frac{\sigma x_i}{\sigma y}$$

To calculate the beta weight we multiply each coefficient by the ratio of the standard deviations for the associated independent variable and the model's dependent variable. This can be accomplished with the following Clojure code:

```
(defn beta-weight [coefs x y]
  (let [sdx (map s/sd (i/trans x))
        sdy (s/sd y)]
    (map #(/ (* %1 %2) sdy) sdx coefs)))


(defn ex-3-26 []
  (let [data (->> (swimmer-data)
                  (i/add-derived-column "Dummy MF"
                                        ["Sex"]
                                        dummy-mf))
        x (->> data
               (feature-matrix ["Height, cm"
                                "Age"
                                "Dummy MF"])
               (add-bias))
        y (->> (i/$ "Weight" data)
               (i/log)
               (i/matrix))
        beta (normal-equation x y)]
    (beta-weight beta x y)))
```

This outputs (rounded to three decimal places):

```
(0.0 0.650 0.058 0.304)
```

This indicates that height is the most important explanatory variable, followed by gender and then age. Transforming it into standardized coefficients tells us that with an increase of one standard deviation in height, the mean weight increases by 0.65 standard deviations.

Collinearity

We might try at this point to keep adding features to our model in an attempt to increase its explanatory power.

For example, we also have a "Date of birth" column and we may be tempted to try and include this too. It is a date, but we could easily convert it into a number suitable for use in regression. We could do this simply by extracting the year from their birth date using the `clj-time` library:

```
(defn to-year [str]
  (-> (coerce/from-date str)
      (time/year)))


(defn ex-3-27 []
  (let [data (->> (swimmer-data)
                  (i/add-derived-column "Dummy MF"
                                        ["Sex"]
                                        dummy-mf)
                  (i/add-derived-column "Year of birth"
                                        ["Date of birth"]
                                        to-year))
        x (->> data
               (feature-matrix ["Height, cm"
                                "Age"
                                "Dummy MF"
                                "Year of birth"])
               (add-bias))
        y (->> (i/$ "Weight" data)
               (i/log)
               (i/matrix))
        beta (normal-equation x y)]
    (beta-weight beta x y)))

;; (-0.0 0.650 0.096 0.304 0.038)
```

The new "Year of Birth" feature has a beta weight of only `0.038`, less than the weight of the age feature we calculated earlier. However, the age weight of the age feature is now showing a value of `0.096`. Its relative importance has increased by over 65 percent since we added `"Year of birth"` as a feature. The fact that the addition of a new feature has altered the importance of an existing feature indicates that we have a problem.

By including the additional `"Year of birth"` parameter, we have inadvertently broken a rule of the regression estimator. Let's see why:

```
(defn ex-3-28 []
  (let [data (->> (swimmer-data)
                  (i/add-derived-column "Year of birth"
                                        ["Date of birth"]
                                        to-year))
        x (->> (i/$ "Age" data)
               (map (jitter 0.5)))
        y (i/$ "Year of birth" data)]
    (-> (c/scatter-plot x y
                        :x-label "Age"
                        :y-label "Year of birth")
        (i/view))))
```

The following scatter plot shows the age of swimmers (with jittering) plotted against their year of birth. As you would expect, the two variables are very closely correlated:

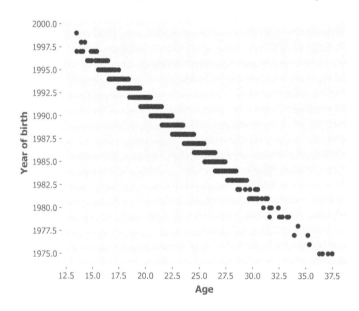

The two features are so highly correlated that the algorithm is unable to determine which of them best explains the observed changes in y. This is an undesirable issue when we deal with multivariate linear regression called **collinearity**.

Multicollinearity

For multiple regression to produce the best coefficient estimates, the underlying data must conform to the same assumptions as simple regression plus one additional assumption— the absence of perfect **multicollinearity**. This means that the independent variables should not be exactly linearly correlated with each other.

> In practice, independent variables are often collinear in some way. Consider, for example, that age and height or gender and height are themselves correlated with each other. It's only when this condition becomes extreme that serious coefficient errors can arise.

If the independent variables are, in fact, not independent, then linear regression can't determine the relative contribution of each independent variable. If two features are so strongly correlated that they always vary together, how can the algorithm distinguish their relative importance? As a result, there may be high variance in the coefficient estimates and a high standard error.

We've already seen one symptom of high multicollinearity: regression coefficients that change significantly when independent variables are added or removed from the equation. Another symptom is when there is an insignificant coefficient in a multiple regression for a particular independent variable, but a substantial R^2 for the simple regression model using the same independent variable.

While these offer clues of multicollinearity, to confirm, we must look directly at the intercorrelation of the independent variables. One way to determine the intercorrelation is to examine the correlation between each of the independent variables, looking for coefficients of 0.8 or more. While this simple approach often works, it may fail to take into account situations where an independent variable has a linear relationship with the other variables taken together.

The surest method to assess multicollinearity is to regress each independent variable on all the other independent variables. When any of the R^2 from these equations is near 1.0, there is high-multicollinearity. In fact, the largest of these R^2 serves as an indicator of the degree of multicollinearity that exists.

Once identified, there are several ways to address multicollinearity:

- Increase the sample size. More data can produce more precise parameter estimates with smaller standard errors.
- Combine the features into one. If you have several features that measure essentially the same attribute, find a way to unify them into a single feature.
- Discard the offending variable(s).
- Limit the equation of prediction. Collinearity affects the coefficients of the model, but the result may still be a good fit for the data.

Since age and year of birth carry essentially the same information, we may as well discard one. We can easily see which of the two contains more explanatory power by calculating the bivariate regression for each feature and the dependent variable.

"Age" R^2 = 0.1049, whereas "Year of birth" R^2 = 0.1050.

As expected, there is virtually no difference between the two features, both explaining around 10 percent of the variance in weight. Since the year of birth marginally explains marginally more of the variance, we'll keep it and discard the age feature.

Prediction

Finally, we arrive at one of the most important uses of linear regression: prediction. We've trained a model capable of predicting the weight of Olympic swimmers given the data about their height, gender, and year of birth.

Mark Spitz is a nine-time Olympic swimming champion, and he won seven gold medals at the 1972 Olympics. He was born in 1950 and, according to his Wikipedia page, is 183cm tall and weighs 73kg. Let's see what our model predicts as his weight.

Our multiple regression model requires these values to be presented as a matrix form. Each of the parameters needs to be provided in the order in which the model learned the features so that the correct coefficient is applied. After the bias term, our feature vector needs to contain height, gender, and year of birth in the same units as our model was trained:

$$x_{spitz} = \begin{bmatrix} 1.0 \\ 183 \\ 1 \\ 1950 \end{bmatrix}$$

Our β matrix contains the coefficients for each of these features:

$$\beta \approx \begin{bmatrix} 6.90 \\ 0.011 \\ 0.097 \\ -0.002 \end{bmatrix}$$

The prediction of our model will be the sum of the products of the β coefficients and features x for each row:

$$\hat{y} = \sum_{i=0}^{n} \beta_i x_i$$

Since matrix multiplication produces each element by adding up the products of the rows and columns of each matrix respectively, producing our result is as simple as multiplying the transpose of β with the x_{spitz} vector.

Recall that the dimensions of the resulting matrix will be the number of rows from the first matrix and the number of columns from the second matrix:

$$\hat{y} = \beta^T x$$

$\beta^T x$ is a product of a $1 \times n$ matrix and an $n \times 1$ matrix. The result is a 1×1 matrix:

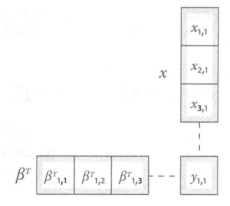

Calculating this in code is very simple:

```
(defn predict [coefs x]
  (-> (i/trans coefs)
      (i/mmult x)
      (first)))
```

We call `first` to return the first (and only) element from the matrix rather than the matrix itself:

```
(defn ex-3-29 []
  (let [data (->> (swimmer-data)
                  (i/add-derived-column "Dummy MF"
                                        ["Sex"]
                                        dummy-mf)
                  (i/add-derived-column "Year of birth"
                                        ["Date of birth"]
                                        to-year))
        x (->> data
               (feature-matrix ["Height, cm"
                                "Dummy MF"
                                "Year of birth"])
               (add-bias))
        y (->> (i/$ "Weight" data)
               (i/log)
               (i/matrix))
        beta (normal-equation x y)
        xspitz (i/matrix [1.0 183 1 1950])]
    (i/exp (predict beta xspitz))))
```

This returns `84.21`, corresponding to a expected weight of 84.21 kg. This is much heavier than Mark Spitz's reported weight of 73 kg. Our model doesn't appear to have performed very well.

The confidence interval of a prediction

We previously calculated confidence intervals for population parameters.
It's also possible to construct confidence intervals for a specific prediction called **prediction interval**. The prediction interval quantifies the amount of uncertainty in the prediction by providing a minimum and a maximum value between which the true value is expected to fall with a certain probability.

The prediction interval for $\hat{y}$ is wider than the confidence interval for a population parameter such as μ, the mean. This is because the confidence interval simply needs to account for our uncertainty in estimating the mean, while the prediction interval must also take into account the variance of y from the mean.

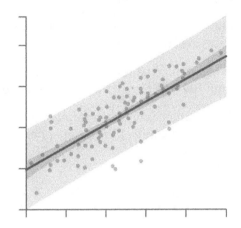

The previous image shows the relationship between the outer prediction interval and the inner confidence interval. We can calculate the prediction interval using the following formula:

$$\hat{y}_p \pm t_{\alpha/2, n-p} \sqrt{\sigma^2 \left(1 + x_p^T \left(X^T X\right)^{-1} x_p\right)}$$

Here, $\hat{y}_p$ is the prediction, plus or minus the interval. We're making use of the t-distribution, where the degree of freedom is $n - p$, the sample size minus the number of parameters. This is the same as we calculated for the F-test previously. While the formula may look intimidating, it's relatively straightforward to translate into the code shown in the following example, which calculates the 95 percent prediction interval:

```
(defn prediction-interval [x y a]
  (let [xtx    (i/mmult (i/trans x) x)
        xtxi   (i/solve xtx)
        xty    (i/mmult (i/trans x) y)
        coefs  (i/mmult xtxi xty)
        fitted (i/mmult x coefs)
        resid  (i/minus y fitted)
        rss    (i/sum-of-squares resid)
        n      (i/nrow y)
        p      (i/ncol x)
```

```
    dfe    (- n p)
    mse    (/ ssr dfe)
    se-y   (first (i/mmult (i/trans a) xtxi a))
    t-stat (i/sqrt (* mse (+ 1 se-y)))]
(* (s/quantile-t 0.975 :df dfe) t-stat)))
```

Since the *t*-statistic is parameterized by the degree of freedom of the error, it takes into account the uncertainty present in the model.

If we'd like to calculate the confidence interval for the mean instead of the prediction interval, we can simply omit the addition of one to `se-y` while calculating `t-stat`.

The preceding code can be used to generate the following chart, showing how the prediction interval varies with the value of the independent variable:

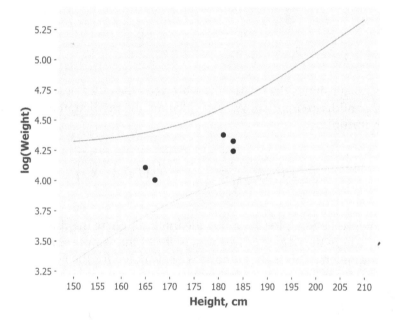

In the preceding graph, a model trained on a sample size of five shows how the 95 percent prediction interval increases as we move further from the mean height. Applying the previous formula to Mark Spitz yields the following:

```
(defn ex-3-30 []
  (let [data (->> (swimmer-data)
                  (i/add-derived-column "Dummy MF"
                                        ["Sex"]
                                        dummy-mf)
```

```
                    (i/add-derived-column "Year of birth"
                                          ["Date of birth"]
                                          to-year))
      x (->> data
             (feature-matrix ["Height, cm"
                              "Dummy MF"
                              "Year of birth"])
             (add-bias))
      y (->> (i/$ "Weight" data)
             (i/log)
             (i/matrix))
      xspitz (i/matrix [1.0 183 1 1950])]
  (i/exp (prediction-interval x y xspitz))))
```

This returns the range from 72.7 kg to 97.4 kg. This range just includes Mark's weight of 73 kg, so our prediction is within the 95 percent prediction interval. It's uncomfortably close to the bounds though.

Model scope

Mark Spitz was born in 1950, decades before even the oldest swimmer in the 2012 Olympic Games. By trying to predict Mark's weight using his year of birth, we're guilty of trying to extrapolate too far beyond our training data. We have exceeded the scope of our model.

There is a second way in which this is problematic. Our data was based entirely on swimmers currently competing at international standard, whereas Mark has not competed for many years. In other words, Mark is now not a part of the population we have trained our model on. To fix both of these problems, we need to look up Mark's details from 1979, when he was a competition swimmer.

According to `http://www.topendsports.com/athletes/swimming/spitz-mark.htm`, in 1972, 22-year-old Mark Spitz was 185 cm tall and he weighed 79 kg.

 Selecting the right features is one of the most important prerequisites to get good results from any predictive algorithm.

You should strive to select features not only on the basis of their predictive power, but also on their relevance to the domain being modeled.

The final model

Although it has a slightly lower R^2, let's retrain our model with age in place of year of birth as a feature. This will allow us to easily predict weights for past and future unseen data, as it models more closely the variable we suspect of having a causal relationship with weight.

This yields β of approximately:

$$\beta \approx \begin{bmatrix} 2.230 \\ 0.011 \\ 0.097 \\ -0.002 \end{bmatrix}$$

Our features for Mark in the 1972 games are:

$$x_{spitz} = \begin{bmatrix} 1.0 \\ 185 \\ 1 \\ 22 \end{bmatrix}$$

We can use them to predict his competitive weight with the following code:

```
(defn ex-3-32 []
  (let [data (->> (swimmer-data)
                  (i/add-derived-column "Dummy MF"
                                        ["Sex"]
                                        dummy-mf))
        x (->> data
               (feature-matrix ["Height, cm"
                                "Dummy MF"
                                "Age"])
               (add-bias))
        y (->> (i/$ "Weight" data)
               (i/log)
               (i/matrix))
        beta (normal-equation x y)
        xspitz (i/matrix [1.0 185 1 22])]
    (i/exp (predict beta xspitz))))
```

This returns `78.47`, corresponding to a prediction of 78.47 kg. This is now very close to Mark's true competition weight of 79 kg.

Summary

In this chapter, we've learned about how to determine whether two or more variables share a linear relationship. We've seen how to express the strength of their correlation with r and how well a linear model explains the variance with R^2 and $\bar{R}^2$. We've also performed hypothesis tests and calculated confidence intervals to infer the range of the true population parameter for correlation, ρ.

Having established a correlation between variables, we were able to build a predictive model using ordinary least squares regression and simple Clojure functions. We then generalized our approach using Incanter's matrix functionality and the normal equation. This simple model demonstrated the principles of machine learning by determining the model parameters β, inferred from our sample data, that could be used to make predictions. Our model was able to predict an expected weight for a new athlete that fell well within the prediction interval of the true value.

In the next chapter, we'll see how similar techniques can be used to classify data into discrete classes. We'll demonstrate a variety of different approaches particular to classification as well as introduce a very general technique for parameter optimization that works for a variety of machine learning models, including linear regression.

4
Classification

"It is a truth universally acknowledged, that a single man in possession of a good fortune, must be in want of a wife."

– Jane Austen, Pride and Prejudice

In the previous chapter, we learned how to make numeric predictions using linear regression. The model we built was able to learn how the features of Olympic swimmers related to their weight and we were able to use the model to make a weight prediction for a new swimmer. As with all regression techniques, our output was a number.

Not all predictions demand a numeric solution, though—sometimes we want our predictions to be items. For example, we may want to predict which candidate a voter will back in an election. Or we may want to know which of several products a customer is likely to buy. In these cases, the outcome is a selection from one of a number of possible discrete options. We call these options classes, and models we'll build in this chapter are classifiers.

We'll learn about several different types of classifier and compare their performance on a sample dataset—the list of passengers from the Titanic. Prediction and classification are intimately connected to theories of probability and information, and so we'll cover these in more detail too. We'll begin the chapter with ways of measuring relative probabilities between groups and move then on to applying statistical significance testing to the groups themselves.

About the data

This chapter will make use of data about the passengers on the Titanic, which famously sank on her maiden voyage in 1912 after hitting an iceberg. The survival rates of passengers were strongly affected by a variety of factors, including class and sex.

The dataset is derived from a painstakingly compiled dataset produced by Michael A. Findlay. For more information about how the data was derived, including links to original sources, consult the book's wiki at http://wiki.clojuredatascience.com.

[The example code for this chapter is available from Packt Publishing's website or from https://github.com/clojuredatascience/ch4-classification.]

The data is small enough to have been included together with the source code in the data directory.

Inspecting the data

We encountered categorical variables in the previous chapter as the dichotomous variable "sex" in the athlete dataset. That dataset also contained many other categorical variables including "sport", "event", and "country".

Let's take a look at the Titanic dataset (using the clojure.java.io library to access the file resource and the incanter.io library to read it in):

```
(defn load-data [file]
  (-> (io/resource file)
      (str)
      (iio/read-dataset :delim \tab :header true)))

(defn ex-4-1 []
  (i/view (load-data :titanic)))
```

The preceding code generates the following table:

:survived	:sex	:age	:pclass	:name	:sibsp	:parch	:ticket	:fare	:cabin	:embarked	:boat	:body	:home.dest
y	female	29	first	Allen, Miss. Elisabeth Walton	0	0	24160	211.3375	B5	S	2		St Louis, MO
y	male		first	Allison, Master. Hudson Trevor	1	2	113781	151.55	C22 C26	S	11		Montreal, PQ / ...
n	female	2	first	Allison, Miss. Helen Loraine	1	2	113781	151.55	C22 C26	S			Montreal, PQ / ...
n	male	30	first	Allison, Mr. Hudson Joshua C...	1	2	113781	151.55	C22 C26	S		135	Montreal, PQ / ...
n	female	25	first	Allison, Mrs. Hudson J C (Bes...	1	2	113781	151.55	C22 C26	S			Montreal, PQ / ...
y	male	48	first	Anderson, Mr. Harry	0	0	19952	26.55	E12	S	3		New York, NY
y	female	63	first	Andrews, Miss. Kornelia The...	1	0	13502	77.9583	D7	S	10		Hudson, NY
n	male	39	first	Andrews, Mr. Thomas Jr	0	0	112050	0	A36	S			Belfast, NI
y	female	53	first	Appleton, Mrs. Edward Dale ...	2	0	11769	51.4792	C101	S	D		Bayside, Queen...
n	male	71	first	Artagaveytia, Mr. Ramon	0	0	PC 17609	49.5042		C		22	Montevideo, Ur...
n	male	47	first	Astor, Col. John Jacob	1	0	PC 17757	227.525	C62 C64	C		124	New York, NY
y	female	18	first	Astor, Mrs. John Jacob (Made...	1	0	PC 17757	227.525	C62 C64	C	4		New York, NY
y	female	24	first	Aubart, Mme. Leontine Pauline	0	0	PC 17477	69.3	B35	C	9		Paris, France
y	female	26	first	Barber, Miss. Ellen "Nellie	0	0	19877	78.85		S	6		
y	male	80	first	Barkworth, Mr. Algernon Hen...	0	0	27042	30	A23	S	B		Hessle, Yorks
n	male		first	Baumann, Mr. John D	0	0	PC 17318	25.925		S			New York, NY
n	male	24	first	Baxter, Mr. Quigg Edmond	0	1	PC 17558	247.5208	B58 B60	C			Montreal, PQ
y	female	50	first	Baxter, Mrs. James (Helene D...	0	1	PC 17558	247.5208	B58 B60	C	6		Montreal, PQ
y	female	32	first	Bazzani, Miss. Albina	0	0	11813	76.2917	D15	C	8		
n	male	36	first	Beattie, Mr. Thomson	0	0	13050	75.2417	C6	C	A		Winnipeg, MN
y	male	37	first	Beckwith, Mr. Richard Leonard	1	1	11751	52.5542	D35	S	5		New York, NY
y	female	47	first	Beckwith, Mrs. Richard Leona...	1	1	11751	52.5542	D35	S	5		New York, NY
y	male	26	first	Behr, Mr. Karl Howell	0	0	111369	30	C148	C	5		New York, NY

The Titanic dataset includes categorical variables too. For example—**:sex**, **:pclass** (the passenger class), and **:embarked** (a letter signifying the port of boarding). These are all string values, taking categories such as **female**, **first**, and **C**, but classes don't always have to be string values. Columns such as **:ticket**, **:boat**, and **:body** can be thought of as containing categorical variables too. Despite having numeric values, they are simply labels that have been applied to things.

A categorical variable is one that can take on only a discrete number of values. This is in contrast to a continuous variable that can take on any value within its range.

Other numbers representing counts are not so easy to define. The field **:sibsp** reports how many companions (spouse or siblings) were traveling with a passenger. These are counts, and their units are people. But they could just as easily represent labels, with **0** standing for "a passenger with no companions" and **1** "a passenger with one companion", and so on. There are only a small set of labels, and so the field's representation as a number is largely convenience. In other words, we could choose to represent **:sibsp** (and **:parch**—a count of related parents and children) as either categorical or numerical features.

Since categorical variables don't make sense on the number line, we can't plot a chart showing how these numbers relate to each other. We can construct a frequency table, though, showing how the counts of passengers in each of the groups are distributed. Since there are two sets of two variables, there are four groups in total.

The data can be summarized using Incanter core's `$rollup` function:

```
(defn frequency-table [sum-column group-columns dataset]
  (->> (i/$ group-columns dataset)
       (i/add-column sum-column (repeat 1))
       (i/$rollup :sum sum-column group-columns)))

(defn ex-4-2 []
  (->> (load-data "titanic.tsv")
       (frequency-table :count [:sex :survived])))
```

Incanter's `$rollup` requires that we provide three arguments—a function with which to "roll up" a group of rows, a column to roll up, and the columns whose unique values define the groups of interest. Any function that reduces a sequence to a single value can be used as a rollup function, but some are so common we can supply the keywords `:min`, `:max`, `:sum`, `:count`, and `:mean` instead.

The example generates the following table:

```
| :survived |   :sex | :count |
|-----------+--------+--------|
|         n |   male |    682 |
|         n | female |    127 |
|         y |   male |    161 |
|         y | female |    339 |
```

This chart represents the frequencies of passengers falling into the various groups "males who perished", "females who survived", and so on. There are several ways of making sense of frequency counts like this; let's start with the most common.

Comparisons with relative risk and odds

The preceding Incanter dataset is an easily comprehensible representation of our data, but to extract the numbers for each of the groups individually we'll want to store the data in a more readily accessible data structure. Let's write a function to convert the dataset to a series of nested maps:

```
(defn frequency-map [sum-column group-cols dataset]
  (let [f (fn [freq-map row]
            (let [groups (map row group-cols)]
              (->> (get row sum-column)
```

```
                     (assoc-in freq-map groups)))))]
  (->> (frequency-table sum-column group-cols dataset)
       (:rows)
       (reduce f {})))))
```

For example, we can use the `frequency-map` function as follows to calculate a nested map of `:sex` and `:survived`:

```
(defn ex-4-3 []
  (->> (load-data "titanic.tsv")
       (frequency-map :count [:sex :survived])))
```

```
;; => {"female" {"y" 339, "n" 127}, "male" {"y" 161, "n" 682}}
```

More generally, given any dataset and sequence of columns, this will make it easier to pull out just the counts we're interested in. We're going to be comparing the survival rates of males and females, so let's use Clojure's `get-in` function to extract the number of fatalities for men and women as well as the overall counts of men and women:

```
(defn fatalities-by-sex [dataset]
  (let [totals (frequency-map :count [:sex] dataset)
        groups (frequency-map :count [:sex :survived] dataset)]
    {:male (/ (get-in groups ["male" "n"])
              (get totals "male"))
     :female (/ (get-in groups ["female" "n"])
                (get totals "female"))}))
```

```
(defn ex-4-4 []
  (-> (load-data "titanic.tsv")
      (fatalities-by-sex)))
```

```
;; {:male 682/843, :female 127/466}
```

From these numbers, we can calculate simple ratios. Relative risk is a ratio of probabilities of an event occurring in two separate groups:

$$RR = \frac{P\left(\text{event in group } A\right)}{P\left(\text{event in group } B\right)}$$

$$RR = \frac{682/843}{127/466} = 2.97$$

Where *P(event)* is the probability of the event occurring. The risk of perishing on the Titanic as a male was *682* divided by *843*; the risk of perishing on the Titanic as a female was *127* divided by *466*:

```
(defn relative-risk [p1 p2]
  (float (/ p1 p2)))

(defn ex-4-5 []
  (let [proportions (-> (load-data "titanic.tsv")
                        (fatalities-by-sex))]
    (relative-risk (get proportions :male)
                   (get proportions :female))))
;; 2.9685
```

In other words, the risk of perishing on the Titanic was almost three times higher if you were a man. The relative risk is often used in healthcare to show how one's chances of developing an illness are affected by some other factor. A relative risk of one means that there is no difference in risk between the groups.

In contrast, the odds ratio can be either positive or negative and measures the extent to which being in a group raises your odds of some other attribute. As with any correlation, no causation is implied. Both attributes could of course be linked by a third property — their mutual cause:

$$OR = \frac{\text{events } y \text{ in group } A \,/\, \text{events } n \text{ in group } A}{\text{events } y \text{ in group } B \,/\, \text{events } n \text{ in group } B}$$

$$OR = \frac{682/161}{127/339} = 11.31$$

The odds of perishing as a male are *682:161* and the odds of perishing as a female are *127:339*. The odds ratio is simply the ratio of the two:

```
(defn odds-ratio [p1 p2]
  (float
    (/ (* p1 (- 1 p2))
       (* p2 (- 1 p1)))))

(defn ex-4-6 []
  (let [proportions (-> (load-data "titanic.tsv")
```

```
                        (fatalities-by-sex))]
        (odds-ratio (get proportions :male)
                    (get proportions :female))))
    ;; 11.3072
```

This example shows how the odds ratio is sensitive to stating relative positions, and can generate much larger numbers.

 When presented with ratios, make sure you're aware whether they're relative-risk or odds ratios. While the two approaches appear similar, they output results over very different ranges.

Compare the two equations for relative risk and odds ratio. The numerators are the same in each case but for risk the denominator is all females, whereas with the odds ratio it is females who survived.

The standard error of a proportion

It's clear that the proportion of women surviving the Titanic is much greater than the proportion of men. But, as with the dwell time differences we encountered in *Chapter 2, Inference*, we should ask ourselves whether these differences could have occurred due to chance alone.

We have seen in previous chapters how to construct confidence intervals around statistics based on the sample's standard error. The standard error is based on the sample's variance, but what is the variance of a proportion? No matter how many samples we take, only one proportion will be generated—the proportion in the overall sample.

Clearly a proportion is still subject to some sort of variance. When we flip a fair coin 10 times we would expect to get roughly five heads, but there's it's not impossible we'd get ten heads in a row.

Estimation using bootstrapping

In *Chapter 2, Inference*, we learned about bootstrapping statistics such as the mean and we saw how bootstrapping can be a useful way of estimating parameters through simulation. Let's use bootstrapping to estimate the standard error of the proportion of female passengers surviving the Titanic.

We can represent the 466 female passengers as a sequence of zeros and ones. Zero could represent a passenger who perished, and one a passenger who survived. This is a convenient representation because it means the sum of the whole sequence equals the total number of passengers who survived. By taking repeated random samples of 466 elements from this sequence of 466 zeros and ones, and taking the sum each time, we can get an estimate of the variance in the proportion:

```
(defn ex-4-7 []
  (let [passengers (concat (repeat 127 0)
                           (repeat 339 1))
        bootstrap (s/bootstrap passengers i/sum :size 10000)]
    (-> (c/histogram bootstrap
                     :x-label "Female Survivors"
                     :nbins 20)
        (i/view))))
```

The preceding code generates the following histogram:

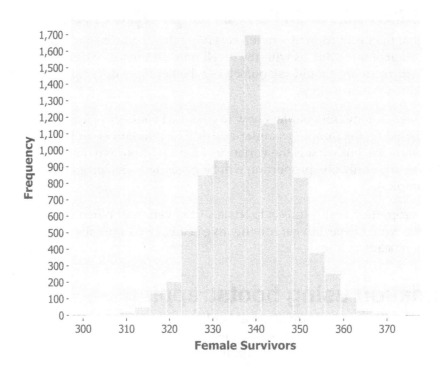

The histogram appears to show a normal distribution with a mean of 339 — the measured number of female survivors. The standard deviation of this distribution is the standard error of the sampled survivors and we can calculate it simply from the bootstrapped samples like so:

```
(defn ex-4-8 []
  (-> (concat (repeat 127 0)
              (repeat 339 1))
      (s/bootstrap i/sum :size 10000)
      (s/sd)))


;; 9.57
```

Your standard deviation may be slightly different, depending on chance variation in the bootstrapped sample. It should be very close, though.

The units of standard deviation are people — female passengers — so to figure out the standard error of the proportion we have to divide this through by the total number of passengers in our sample, 466. This yields a standard error of the proportion of 0.021.

The binomial distribution

The preceding histogram looks a great deal like a normal distribution, but in fact it is a binomial distribution. The two distributions are very similar, but the binomial distribution is used to model cases where we want to determine how many times a binary event is expected to occur.

Let's plot both the binomial and the normal distribution on a histogram to see how they compare:

```
(defn ex-4-9 []
  (let [passengers (concat (repeat 127 0)
                           (repeat 339 1))
        bootstrap (s/bootstrap passengers i/sum :size 10000)
        binomial (fn [x]
                    (s/pdf-binomial x :size 466 :prob (/ 339 466)))
        normal (fn [x]
                    (s/pdf-normal x :mean 339 :sd 9.57))]
    (-> (c/histogram bootstrap
                     :x-label "Female Survivors"
                     :series-label "Bootstrap"
                     :nbins 20
                     :density true
```

```
                          :legend true)
       (c/add-function binomial 300 380
                       :series-label "Biomial")
       (c/add-function normal 300 380
                       :series-label "Normal")
       (i/view))))
```

The preceding code generates the following chart:

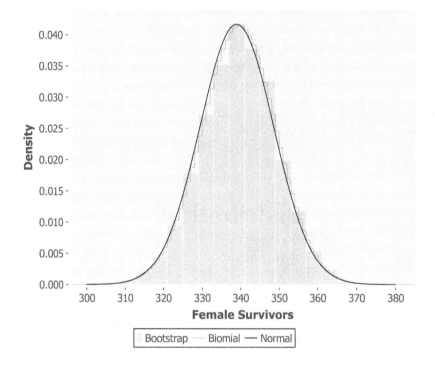

Notice how in the preceding chart the line corresponding to the binomial distribution is jagged—it represents discrete counts of things rather than a continuous value such as the normal distribution.

The standard error of a proportion formula

We have calculated the standard error empirically and found it to equal 0.021, using only the proportion of female survivors and the total number of female passengers. Although it's been instructive to see what the standard error of the proportion is actually measuring, there is a formula that allows us to get there in one step:

$$SE = \sqrt{\frac{p(1-p)}{n}}$$

Substituting in the counts of female survivors gives us the following:

$$SE = \sqrt{\frac{\frac{339}{466} \cdot \frac{127}{466}}{466}} = 0.0206$$

Fortunately, this number closely matches the standard error we calculated through bootstrapping. It's not exact, of course, since our bootstrapping calculation has its own sampling error.

```
(defn standard-error-proportion [p n]
  (-> (- 1 p)
      (* p)
      (/ n)
      (i/sqrt)))

(defn ex-4-10 []
  (let [survived (->> (load-data "titanic.tsv")
                      (frequency-map :count [:sex :survived]))
        n (reduce + (vals (get survived "female")))
        p (/ (get-in survived ["female" "y"]) n)]
    (se-proportion p n)))

;; 0.0206
```

The equation for the standard error of a proportion gives us an important insight—the value of $p(1 - p)$ is greatest when p is close to 0.5. This means that the greatest standard error in a proportion is when the proportion is close to a half.

If this seems surprising to you, consider this—when the proportion is 50 percent, the variation in the sample is greatest. Like a fair coin toss, we have no way of predicting what the next value will be. As the proportion increases (or decreases) within the sample, the data becomes increasingly homogenous. As a result, the variation decreases, and so the standard error decreases accordingly.

Significance testing proportions

Let's return to the question of whether the measured differences in male or female fatality rates could be due to chance alone. As in *Chapter 2, Inference*, our z-test is simply the difference in proportions divided by the pooled standard error:

$$z = \frac{p_1 - p_2}{SE}$$

In the preceding formula, p_1 denotes the proportion of women who survived, that is, *339/466 = 0.73*. And p_2 denotes the proportion of men who survived, that is, *161/843 = 0.19*.

To calculate the z-statistic, we need to pool our standard errors for the two proportions. Our proportions measure the survival rates of males and females respectively, so the pooled standard error is simply the standard error of the males and females combined, or the total survival rate overall, as follows:

$$SE_{pooled} = \sqrt{\frac{\dfrac{500}{1309} \cdot \dfrac{809}{1309}}{1309}} = 0.013$$

Substituting the values into the equation for the z-statistic:

$$z = \frac{0.73 - 0.19}{0.013} = 39.95$$

Using a z-score means we'll use the normal distribution to look up the p-value:

```
(defn ex-4-11 []
  (let [dataset     (load-data "titanic.tsv")
        proportions (fatalities-by-sex dataset)
        survived    (frequency-map :count [:survived] dataset)
        total   (reduce + (vals survived))
        pooled (/ (get survived "n") total)
```

```
      p-diff (- (get proportions :male)
                (get proportions :female))
      z-stat (/ p-diff (se-proportion pooled total))]
   (- 1 (s/cdf-normal (i/abs z-stat)))))))
```

```
;; 0.0
```

As we have a one-tailed test, the *p*-value is the probability that the *z*-score is less than 39.95. The response is zero, corresponding to a very, very significant result. This allows us to reject the null hypothesis and conclude that the difference between survival rates between men and women was certainly not down to chance alone.

Adjusting standard errors for large samples

You may be wondering why we're talking about standard errors at all. The data we have on passengers on the Titanic is not a sample of a wider population. It is the population. There was only one Titanic and only one fateful journey.

While this is true in one sense, there are many ways in which the Titanic disaster could have occurred. If the "women and children first" instructions had not been followed or had been followed more universally, a different set of results would have been obtained. If there had been enough lifeboats for everyone, or the evacuation process had run more smoothly, then this would have been represented in the outcome too.

Standard error and significance testing allows us to treat the disaster as one of an infinite number of potential similar disasters and determine whether the observed differences are likely to have been systemic or purely coincidental.

That said, sometimes we are more interested in how confident we can be that our samples are representative of a finite, quantified population. Where samples begin to measure more than about 10 percent of the population, we can adjust the standard error downwards to account for the decreased uncertainty:

$$SE = \sqrt{\frac{p(1-p)}{n}} \sqrt{\frac{(N-n)}{(N-1)}}$$

This can be written in Clojure as:

```
(defn se-large-proportion [p n N]
  (* (se-proportion p n)
     (i/sqrt (/ (- N n)
                (- n 1)))))
```

Where N is the size of the overall population. As the sample size increases relative to the size of the population, $(N - n)$ tends towards zero. If you sample the entire population, then any difference in proportion—however small—is going to be judged significant.

Chi-squared multiple significance testing

Not all categories are dichotomous (such as male and female, survived and perished). Although we would expect categorical variables to have a finite number of categories, there is no hard upper limit on the number of categories a particular attribute can have.

We could use other categorical variables to separate out the passengers on the Titanic, such as the class in which they were traveling. There were three class levels on the Titanic, and the `frequency-table` function we constructed at the beginning of this chapter is already able to handle multiple classes.

```
(defn ex-4-12 []
  (->> (load-data "titanic.tsv")
       (frequency-table :count [:survived :pclass])))
```

This code generates the following frequency table:

```
| :pclass | :survived | :count |
|---------+-----------+--------|
|   third |         y |    181 |
|   third |         n |    528 |
|  second |         y |    119 |
|  second |         n |    158 |
|   first |         n |    123 |
|   first |         y |    200 |
```

These three classes give us an additional way to cut our data on survival rates. As the number of classes increases, it becomes harder to read patterns in the frequency table, so let's visualize it.

Visualizing the categories

Although they were originally devised to represent proportions, pie charts are generally not a good way to represent parts of a whole. People have a difficult time visually comparing the areas of slices of a circle. Representing quantities linearly, as with a stacked bar chart, is nearly always a better approach. Not only are the areas easier to interpret but they're easier to compare side by side.

We can visualize our data as a stacked bar chart:

```
(defn ex-4-13 []
  (let [data (->> (load-data "titanic.tsv")
                  (frequency-table :count [:survived :pclass]))]
    (-> (c/stacked-bar-chart :pclass :count
                             :group-by :survived
                             :legend true
                             :x-label "Class"
                             :y-label "Passengers"
                             :data data)
        (i/view))))
```

The preceding code generates the following chart:

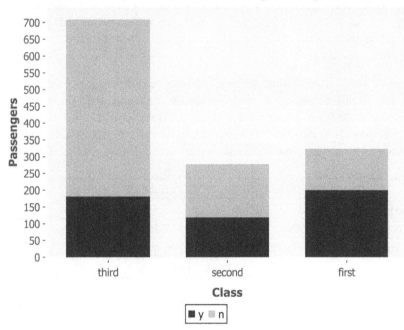

The data clearly shows a difference in both the number of passengers who perished, and the proportion of passengers who perished, most visible between first and third class. We'd like to determine if this difference is significant.

We could perform a *z*-test between each pair of proportions but, as we learned in *Chapter 2, Inference*, this is much more likely to lead to Type I errors and cause us to find a significant result where, in fact, there is none.

The problem of multiple-category significance testing may seem to call for the *F*-test but the *F*-test is based on the ratio of variance of some continuous variable within and between groups. What we'd like, therefore, is a similar test that cares only about the relative proportion between groups. This is the premise on which the X^2 test is based.

The chi-squared test

Pronounced *kai square*, the X^2 test is a statistical test applied to sets of categorical data to evaluate how likely it is that any observed difference between proportions of those categories in the sets arose by chance.

When performing a X^2 test, therefore, our null hypothesis is that the observed difference in proportions between groups is simply the result of chance variation. We can think of this as an independence test between two categorical variables. If category *A* is the passenger class and category *B* is whether they survived or not, the null hypothesis is that passenger class and survival rate are independent of each other. The alternate hypothesis is that the categories are not independent—that the passenger class and survival are related to each other in some way.

The X^2 statistic is calculated by comparing the observed frequency counts from the sample to a table of frequencies calculated under the assumption of independence. This frequency table is an estimation of what the data would have looked like had the categories been independent. We can calculate the frequency table assuming independence in the following way, using the row, column, and grand totals:

	Survived	Perished	Total
First Class	323*500/1309 = 123.4	323*809/1309 = 199.6	323
Second Class	277*500/1309 = 105.8	277*809/1309 = 171.2	277
Third Class	709*500/1309 = 270.8	709*809/1309 = 438.2	709
Total	500	809	1,309

A simple formula calculates each cell value using only the totals for each row and column, and assumes an even distribution amongst cells. This is our table of expected frequencies.

```
(defn expected-frequencies [data]
  (let [as (vals (frequency-map :count [:survived] data))
        bs (vals (frequency-map :count [:pclass] data))
        total (-> data :rows count)]
```

```
    (for [a as
          b bs]
      (* a (/ b total)))))))
```

```
(defn ex-4-14 []
  (-> (load-data "titanic.tsv")
      (expected-frequencies)))
```

```
;; => (354500/1309 138500/1309 9500/77 573581/1309 224093/1309
15371/77)
```

To demonstrate a statistically significant difference between the survival rates by class, we'll need to show that the difference between the frequencies assuming independence and the observed frequencies is unlikely to have arisen through chance alone.

The chi-squared statistic

The X^2 statistic simply measures how far the actual frequencies differ from those calculated under the assumption of independence:

$$\chi^2 = \sum_{ij} \frac{(f_{ij} - F_{ij})^2}{F_{ij}}$$

F_{ij} is the expected frequency assuming independence for categories i and j, and f_{ij} is the observed frequency for categories i and j. We therefore need to fetch the observed frequencies for our data. We can calculate this in Clojure as follows:

```
(defn observed-frequencies [data]
  (let [as (->> (i/$rollup :sum :count :survived data)
                (summary :count [:survived]))
        bs (->> (i/$rollup :sum :count :pclass data)
                (summary :count [:pclass]))
        actual (summary :count [:survived :pclass] data)]
    (for [a (keys as)
          b (keys bs)]
      (get-in actual [a b]))))
```

As with the `expected-frequencies` function earlier, the `observed-frequencies` function returns a sequence of frequency counts for each combination of categories.

```
(defn ex-4-15 []
  (-> (load-data "titanic.tsv")
      (observed-frequencies)))


;; (200 119 181 123 158 528)
```

This sequence—and the sequence of expected values from the previous example—give us all we need to calculate the X^2 statistic:

```
(defn chisq-stat [observed expected]
  (let [f (fn [observed expected]
            (/ (i/sq (- observed expected)) expected))]
    (reduce + (map f observed expected))))

(defn ex-4-16 []
  (let [data (load-data "titanic.tsv")
        observed (observed-frequencies data)
        expected (expected-frequencies data)]
    (float (chisq-stat observed expected))))


;; 127.86
```

Now that we have our test statistic, we'll need to look this up in the relevant distribution to determine if the result is significant. Unsurprisingly, the distribution we refer to is the X^2 distribution.

The chi-squared test

The X^2 distribution is paramaterized by one degree of freedom: the product of each of the category counts less one:

$$df = (a-1)(b-1)$$

Here, a is the number of categories for attribute A and b is the number of categories for attribute B. For our Titanic data, a is 3 and b is 2, so our degrees of freedom parameter is 2.

Our X^2 test simply needs to view our X^2 statistic against the X^2 cumulative distribution function (CDF). Let's do this now:

```
(defn ex-4-17 []
  (let [data (load-data "titanic.tsv")
        observed (observed-frequencies data)
        expected (expected-frequencies data)
        x2-stat  (chisq-stat observed expected)]
    (s/cdf-chisq x2-stat :df 2 :lower-tail? false)))


;; 1.721E-28
```

This is an absolutely tiny number, and is as close to zero as makes no difference so we can comfortably reject the null hypothesis at any significance level. In other words, we can be absolutely certain that the observed difference is not the result of a chance sampling error.

Although it is useful to see the X^2 conducted by hand, the Incanter stats namespace has a function, `chisq-test`, for conducting the X^2 test in one step. To use it we simply need to supply our original table of observations as a matrix:

```
(defn ex-4-18 []
  (let [table     (->> (load-data "titanic.tsv")
                       (frequency-table :count [:pclass :survived])
                       (i/$order [:survived :pclass] :asc))
        frequencies (i/$ :count table)
        matrix      (i/matrix frequencies 3)]
    (println "Observed:"     table)
    (println "Frequencies:"  frequencies)
    (println "Observations:" matrix)
    (println "Chi-Squared test:")
    (-> (s/chisq-test :table matrix)
        (clojure.pprint/pprint))))
```

In preceding the code, we calculated a frequency-table from the Titanic data and then ordered the contents, using `i/$order`, so that we get a table like this:

:survived	:pclass	:count
n	first	123
n	second	158
n	third	528
y	first	200
y	second	119
y	third	181

We take the count column and convert it into a matrix of three columns using `(i/matrix frequencies 3)`:

```
A 2x3 matrix

-------------
1.23e+02  1.58e+02  5.28e+02
2.00e+02  1.19e+02  1.81e+02
```

This matrix is the only input required by Incanter's `s/chisq-test` function. Run the example and you'll see the response is a map containing keys `:X-sq`, the X^2 statistic, and `:p-value`, the result of the test, amongst many others.

We have established that the categories of class and survived, and gender and survived are certainly not independent. This is analogous to discovering a correlation between variables – height, sex, and weight – in the previous chapter.

Now, as then, the next step is to use the dependence between the variables to make predictions. Whereas in the previous chapter our output was a predicted number – the weight – in this chapter our output will be a class – a prediction about whether the passenger survived or not. Assigning items to their expected class based on other attributes is the process of classification.

Classification with logistic regression

In the previous chapter, we saw how linear regression produces a predicted value, $\hat{y}$, from an input vector x and a vector of coefficients β:

$$\hat{y} = \beta^T x$$

Here, $\hat{y}$ can be any real number. Logistic regression proceeds in a very similar way, but adjusts the prediction to guarantee an answer only between zero and one:

$$\hat{y} \in \{0,1\}$$

Zero and one represent two different classes. The change is a simple one; we simply wrap the prediction in a function g that constrains the output between zero and one:

$$\hat{y} = g\left(\beta^T x\right)$$

Where *g* is called the **sigmoid function**. This seemingly minor change is enough to transform linear regression into logistic regression and turn real-valued predictions into classes.

The sigmoid function

The sigmoid function is also referred to as the *logistic function* and is shown next:

$$g(y) = \frac{1}{1+e^{-y}}$$

For positive inputs, the logistic function rises quickly to one while, for negative inputs, it falls quickly to zero. These outputs correspond to the predicted classes. For values close to zero, the logistic function returns values close to **0.5**. This corresponds to increased uncertainty about the correct output class.

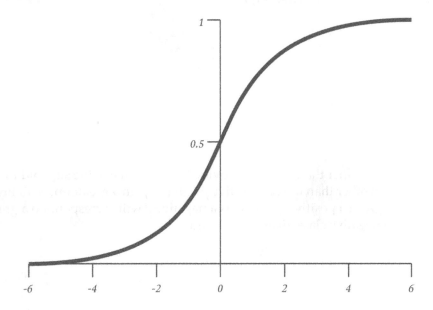

Combining the formulae we have seen already gives rise to the following complete definition of the logistic hypothesis:

$$\hat{y} = \frac{1}{1+e^{-\beta^T x}}$$

As with linear regression, the parameter vector β contains the coefficients that we're seeking to learn, and x is our vector of input features. We can express this in Clojure with the following higher-order function. Given a vector of coefficients, this function returns a function that will calculate $\hat{y}$ for a given x:

```
(defn sigmoid-function [coefs]
  (let [bt (i/trans coefs)
        z  (fn [x] (- (first (i/mmult bt x))))]
    (fn [x]
      (/ 1
         (+ 1
            (i/exp (z x)))))))
```

If the logistic function is given a β of [0], then the feature is discounted as having any predictive power. The function will output 0.5, corresponding to complete uncertainty, for any input x:

```
(let [f (sigmoid-function [0])]
  (f [1])
  ;; => 0.5

  (f [-1])
  ;; => 0.5

  (f [42])
  ;; => 0.5
  )
```

However, if values other than zero are provided as coefficients, the sigmoid function can return values other than 0.5. A positive β will result in a greater probability of a positive class given a positive x, whereas a negative β will correspond to a greater probability of a negative class given a positive x.

```
(let [f (sigmoid-function [0.2])
      g (sigmoid-function [-0.2])]
  (f [5])
  ;; => 0.73

  (g [5])
  ;; => 0.27
  )
```

Since values above 0.5 correspond to a positive class and values less than 0.5 correspond to a negative class, the sigmoid function output can simply be rounded to the nearest integer to get the output class. This would result in values of exactly 0.5 being classified as the positive class.

Now that we have a `sigmoid-function` that can return class predictions, we need to learn the parameters β which yield the best predictions $\hat{y}$. In the previous chapter, we saw two methods for calculating the coefficients for a linear model—calculating the slope and intercept using covariance, and the normal equation using matrices. In both cases the equations were able to find a linear solution that minimized the least-squares estimates of our model.

The squared error was an appropriate function to use for our linear model, but it doesn't translate well to classification where classes are measured only between zero and one. We need an alternative method of determining how incorrect our predictions are.

The logistic regression cost function

As with linear regression, the logistic regression algorithm must learn from data. The `cost` function is a way to let the algorithm know how well, or poorly, it's doing.

The following is the `cost` function for logistic regression, which imposes a different cost depending on whether the output class is supposed to be zero or one. The cost for a single training example is calculated like so:

$$cost(\hat{y}, y) = \begin{cases} -log(\hat{y}) \text{ if } y = 1 \\ -log(1 - \hat{y}) \text{ if } y = 0 \end{cases}$$

This pair of functions captures the intuition that, if $\hat{y} = 0$ but $y = 1$, then the model should be penalized by a very large cost. Symmetrically, the model should also be heavily penalized if $\hat{y} = 1$ and $y = 0$. Where the model closely agrees with the data, the cost falls steeply towards zero.

This is the cost for an individual training point. To combine the individual costs and calculate an overall cost for a given vector of coefficients and a set of training data, we can simply take the average across all the training examples:

$$cost(\beta) = \frac{1}{m} \sum_{i=1}^{m} cost(\hat{y}_i, y_i)$$

This can be represented in Clojure as follows:

```
(defn logistic-cost [ys y-hats]
  (let [cost (fn [y y-hat]
               (if (zero? y)
                 (- (i/log (- 1 y-hat)))
                 (- (i/log y-hat))))]
    (s/mean (map cost ys y-hats))))
```

Now that we have a `cost` function that can quantify how incorrect our predictions are, the next step is to make use of this information to figure out better predictions. The very best classifier will be the one with the lowest overall cost, since by definition its predicted classes will be closest to the true classes. The method by which we can incrementally improve our cost is called **gradient descent**.

Parameter optimization with gradient descent

The cost function, also called the **loss function**, is the function that calculates the error of the model based on our coefficients. Different parameters will generate different costs for the same dataset, and we can visualize how the cost function changes with respect to the parameters on a graph.

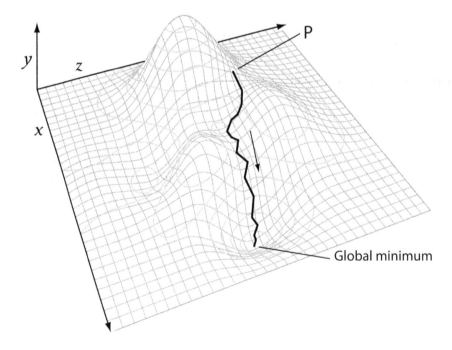

The preceding chart shows a representation of a cost function for a two-parameter model. The cost is plotted on the y axis (higher values correspond to a higher cost) and the two parameters are plotted on the x and z axes, respectively.

The best parameters are the ones that minimize the cost function, corresponding to the parameters at the point identified as the "Global minimum". We don't know ahead of time what these parameters will be, but we can make an initial, arbitrary guess. These parameters are the ones identified by the point "P".

Gradient descent is an algorithm that iteratively improves on the initial condition by following the gradient downhill towards the minimum value. When the algorithm can't descend any further, the minimum cost has been found. The parameters at this point correspond to our best estimate for the parameters that minimize the cost function.

Gradient descent with Incanter

Incanter provides the ability to run gradient descent with the function `minimize` in the `incanter.optimize` namespace. Mathematical optimization is the general term for a series of techniques that aim to find the best available solution to some set of constraints. The `incanter.optimize` namespace contains functions for calculating the parameters that will minimize or maximize the value of any arbitrary function.

For example, the following code finds the minimum value of `f` given a starting position of `10`. Since `f` is x^2, the input that will produce the minimum value is `0`:

```
(defn ex-4-19 []
  (let [f (fn [[x]]
            (i/sq x))
        init [10]]
    (o/minimize f init)))
```

Indeed, if you run the example you should get an answer very close to zero. You are very unlikely to get exactly zero though because gradient descent tends to provide only approximate answers — Incanter's `minimize` function accepts a tolerance argument `:tol` that defaults to 0.00001. If the result differs by less than this amount between iterations, then the equation is said to have converged. The function also accepts a `:max-iter` argument, the maximum number of steps to take before returning an answer, irrespective of convergence.

Convexity

Gradient descent is not always guaranteed to find the lowest possible cost for all equations. For example, the answer may find what is called a "local minimum", which represents the lowest cost in the vicinity of the initial guess but doesn't represent the best overall solution to the problem. This is illustrated in the following illustration:

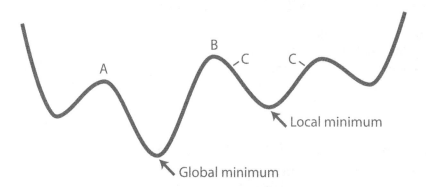

If the initial position corresponds to either of the points labeled **C** on the graph, then the algorithm will converge to a local minimum. Gradient descent will have found a minimum, but it is not the best overall solution. Only initial guesses within the range **A** to **B** will converge on the global minimum.

It is therefore possible that gradient descent will converge to different answers depending on its initialization. For gradient descent to guarantee the optimal solution, the equation to optimize needs to be a convex equation. This means that there is a single global minimum and no local minima.

For example, there is no global minimum of the `sin` function. The result we calculate for the minimum will depend strongly on our starting conditions:

```
(defn ex-4-20 []
  (let [f (fn [[x]]
            (i/sin x))]
    (println (:value (o/minimize f [1])))
    (println (:value (o/minimize f [10])))
    (println (:value (o/minimize f [100])))))

A 1x1 matrix

 ------------
-2.14e+05

 A 1x1 matrix
```

```
------------
1.10e+01

A 1x1 matrix
------------
9.90e+01
```

Fortunately, logistic regression is a convex function. This means that gradient descent will be able to determine the values of our coefficients corresponding to the global minimum irrespective of our starting position.

Implementing logistic regression with Incanter

We can define a logistic regression function with Incanter's `minimize` function as follows:

```
(defn logistic-regression [ys xs]
  (let [cost-fn (fn [coefs]
                  (let [classify (sigmoid-function coefs)
                        y-hats   (map (comp classify i/trans) xs)]
                    (logistic-cost ys y-hats)))
        init-coefs (repeat (i/ncol xs) 0.0)]
    (o/minimize cost-fn init-coefs)))
```

The `cost-fn` accepts a matrix of coefficients. We create a classifier from the coefficients using the `sigmoid-function` previously defined, and a sequence of predictions, `y-hats`, based on the input data. Finally, we can calculate and return the `logistic-cost` value based on the provided coefficients.

To perform logistic regression, we minimize the logistic `cost-fn` by selecting the optimal parameters to the `sigmoid-function`. Since we have to start somewhere, our initial coefficients are simply `0.0` for each parameter.

The `minimize` function expects to receive an input in numeric form. Like the athlete data in the previous chapter, we have to convert our Titanic data into a feature matrix and create dummy variables for our categorical data.

Creating a feature matrix

Let's define a function, add-dummy, that will create a dummy variable for a given column. Where the value in the input column equals a particular value, the dummy column will contain a 1. Where the value in the input column does not contain that value, the dummy column will be 0.

```
(defn add-dummy [column-name from-column value dataset]
  (i/add-derived-column column-name
                        [from-column]
                        #(if (= % value) 1 0)
                        dataset))
```

This simple function makes it very straightforward to convert our Titanic data to a feature matrix:

```
(defn matrix-dataset []
  (->> (load-data "titanic.tsv")
       (add-dummy :dummy-survived :survived "y")
       (i/add-column :bias (repeat 1.0))
       (add-dummy :dummy-mf :sex "male")
       (add-dummy :dummy-1 :pclass "first")
       (add-dummy :dummy-2 :pclass "second")
       (add-dummy :dummy-3 :pclass "third")
       (i/$ [:dummy-survived :bias :dummy-mf
             :dummy-1 :dummy-2 :dummy-3])
       (i/to-matrix)))
```

Our output matrix will entirely consist of zeros and ones. The first element in the feature matrix is the dummy variable determining survival. This is our class label. 0 corresponds to perishing and 1 corresponds to survival. The second is a bias term, which always contains the value 1.0.

With our matrix-dataset and logistic-regression functions defined, running logistic regression is as simple as this:

```
(defn ex-4-21 []
  (let [data (matrix-dataset)
        ys (i/$ 0 data)
        xs (i/$ [:not 0] data)]
    (logistic-regression ys xs)))
```

We're providing 0 to Incanter's i/$ function to select the first column of the matrix (the classes), and [:not 0] to select everything else (the features):

```
;; [0.9308681940090573 -2.5150078795265753 1.1782368822555778
;;  0.29749924127081434 -0.5448679293359383]
```

If you run this example, you'll find that it returns a vector of numbers. This vector corresponds to the best estimates for the coefficients of the logistic model.

Evaluating the logistic regression classifier

The vector calculated in the previous section contains the coefficients of our logistic model. We can make predictions with them by passing them to our `sigmoid-function` like this:

```
(defn ex-4-22 []
  (let [data (matrix-dataset)
        ys (i/$ 0 data)
        xs (i/$ [:not 0] data)
        coefs (logistic-regression ys xs)
        classifier (comp logistic-class
                         (sigmoid-function coefs)
                         i/trans)]
    (println "Observed: " (map int (take 10 ys)))
    (println "Predicted:" (map classifier (take 10 xs)))))

;; Observed:  (1 1 0 0 0 1 1 0 1 0)
;; Predicted: (1 0 1 0 1 0 1 0 1 0)
```

You can see that the classifier is not doing a perfect job—it's confused by some of the classes. In the first ten results, it's getting four classes incorrect, which is only just better than chance. Let's see what proportion of classes was correctly identified over the entire dataset:

```
(defn ex-4-23 []
  (let [data (matrix-dataset)
        ys (i/$ 0 data)
        xs (i/$ [:not 0] data)
        coefs (logistic-regression ys xs)
        classifier (comp logistic-class
                         (sigmoid-function coefs)
                         i/trans)
        y-hats (map classifier xs)]
    (frequencies (map = y-hats (map int ys)))))

;; {true 1021, false 288}
```

In the preceding code we train a classifier as before, and simply map over the entire dataset looking for predictions that equal observed classes. We use Clojure core's `frequencies` function to provide a simple count of the number of times the classes are equal.

Predicting the correct outcome 1,021 times out of 1,309 equates to 78 percent correct. Our classifier is definitely performing better than chance.

The confusion matrix

While percent correct is a simple measure to calculate and comprehend, it's vulnerable to situations where a classifier systematically under- or over-represents a given class. As an extreme example, consider a classifier that always classifies passengers as having perished. On our Titanic dataset such a classifier would appear to be 68 percent correct, but it would perform terribly on an alternative dataset where most of the passengers survived.

A `confusion-matrix` function shows how many misclassified items there are in the training set, split into true positives, true negatives, false positives, and false negatives. The confusion matrix has a row for each category of the input and a column for each category of the model. We can create one like this in Clojure:

```
(defn confusion-matrix [ys y-hats]
  (let [classes    (into #{} (concat ys y-hats))
        confusion (frequencies (map vector ys y-hats))]
    (i/dataset (cons nil classes)
               (for [x classes]
                 (cons x
                       (for [y classes]
                         (get confusion [x y])))))))
```

We can then run our confusion matrix on the results of our logistic regression like so:

```
(defn ex-4-24 []
  (let [data (matrix-dataset)
        ys (i/$ 0 data)
        xs (i/$ [:not 0] data)
        coefs (logistic-regression ys xs)
        classifier (comp logistic-class
                         (sigmoid-function coefs)
                         i/trans)
        y-hats (map classifier xs)]
    (confusion-matrix (map int ys) y-hats)))
```

which returns the following matrix:

```
|   |   0 |   1 |
|---+-----+-----|
| 0 | 682 | 127 |
| 1 | 161 | 339 |
```

We can see how the model returned `682` true negatives and `339` true positives, adding up to the 1,021 correctly predicted results. The confusion matrix for a good model will be dominated by counts along the diagonal, with much smaller numbers in the off-diagonal positions. A perfect classifier would have zero in all off-diagonal cells.

The kappa statistic

The kappa statistic can be used for comparing two pairs of classes to see how well the classes agree. It is more robust that simply looking at percentage agreement because the equation aims to account for the possibility that some of the agreement has occurred simply due to chance alone.

The kappa statistic models how often each class occurs in each sequence and factors this into the calculation. For example, if I correctly guess the result of a coin toss 50 percent of the time, but I always guess heads, the kappa statistic will be zero. This is because the agreement is no more than could be expected by chance.

To calculate the kappa statistic we need to know two things:

- $p(a)$: This is the probability of actual observed agreement
- $p(e)$: This is the probability of expected agreement

The value of $p(a)$ is the percentage agreement we calculated previously to be 78 percent. It's the sum of true positives and true negatives divided by the size of the sample.

To calculate the value of $p(e)$ we need to know both the proportion of negative classes present in the data, and the proportion of negative classes predicted by our model. The proportion of negative classes in our data is $\frac{809}{1309}$, or 62 percent. This is the probability of perishing in the Titanic disaster overall. The proportion of negative classes in our model can be calculated from the confusion matrix as $\frac{843}{1309}$, or 64 percent.

The probability that the data and model might agree by chance, $p(e)$, is the probability that the model and the data both have a negative class $\left(\frac{809}{1309} \cdot \frac{843}{1309}\right)$ plus the probability that both the data and the model have a positive class $\left(\frac{500}{1309} \cdot \frac{466}{1309}\right)$. Therefore the probability of random agreement $p(e)$ is about 53 percent.

The preceding information is all we need to calculate the kappa statistic:

$$k = \frac{p(a) - p(e)}{1 - p(e)}$$

Substituting in the values we just calculated yields:

$$k = \frac{0.78 - 0.53}{1 - 0.53} = 0.53$$

We can calculate this in Clojure as follows:

```
(defn kappa-statistic [ys y-hats]
  (let [n (count ys)
        pa (/ (count (filter true? (map = ys y-hats))) n)
        ey (/ (count (filter zero? ys)) n)
        eyh (/ (count (filter zero? y-hats)) n)
        pe (+ (* ey eyh)
              (* (- 1 ey)
                 (- 1 eyh)))]
    (/ (- pa pe)
       (- 1 pe))))

(defn ex-4-25 []
  (let [data (matrix-dataset)
        ys (i/$ 0 data)
        xs (i/$ [:not 0] data)
        coefs (logistic-regression ys xs)
        classifier (comp logistic-class
                         (sigmoid-function coefs)
                         i/trans)
        y-hats (map classifier xs)]
    (float (kappa-statistic (map int ys) y-hats))))
```

```
;; 0.527
```

Values of kappa range between 0 and 1, with 1 corresponding to complete agreement across both output classes. Complete agreement for only one output class is undefined with kappa – if I guess the result of a coin toss correctly 100 percent of the time, but the coin always comes up heads, there is no way of knowing that the coin was a fair coin.

Probability

We have encountered probability in several guises so far in this book: as *p*-values, confidence intervals, and most recently as the output of logistic regression where the result can be considered as the probability of the output class being positive. The probabilities we calculated for the kappa statistic were the result of adding up counts and dividing by totals. The probability of agreement, for example, was calculated as the number of times the model and the data agreed divided by the number of samples. This way of calculating probabilities is referred to as **frequentist**, because it is concerned with the rates at which things happen.

An output of 1.0 from logistic regression (pre-rounding) corresponds to the certainty that the input is in the positive class; an output of 0.0 corresponds to the certainty that the input isn't in the positive class. An output of 0.5 corresponds to complete uncertainty about the output class. For example, if *ŷ* = 0.7 the probability of *y* = 1 is 70 percent. We can write this in the following way:

$$\hat{y} = P(y = 1 \mid x; \beta)$$

We say *y-hat equals the probability that y equals one given x, parameterized by beta.* This new notation expresses the fact that our prediction, $\hat{y}$, is informed by inputs including *x* and *β*. The values contained in these vectors affect our calculation of the output probability, and correspondingly our prediction for *y*.

An alternative to the frequentist view of probability is **Bayesian view**. The Bayesian conception of probability incorporates a prior belief into the probability calculation. To illustrate the difference, let's look again at the example of tossing a coin.

Let's imagine that a coin is tossed 14 times in a row and comes up as heads 10 times. You're asked to bet whether it will land heads on the next two throws. Would you take the bet?

To a frequentist, the probability of the coin landing heads for two consecutive further throws is $\frac{10}{14} \cdot \frac{10}{14} = \frac{25}{49}$. This is marginally better than 50 percent, so it makes sense to take the bet.

A Bayesian would frame the problem differently. With a prior belief that the coin is fair, how well does the data fit this belief? The standard error of the proportion over 14 throws is 0.12. The difference between $\frac{10}{14}$ and $\frac{1}{2}$ divided by the standard error is approximately 1.77, corresponding to a *p*-value of about 0.08. There's simply not enough evidence to reject the theory that the coin is fair. If the coin were fair, then the probability of getting two consecutive heads is $\frac{1}{2} \cdot \frac{1}{2} = \frac{1}{4}$ and we would likely lose the bet.

In the 18th Century, Pierre-Simon Laplace posited "What is the probability the sun will rise tomorrow?" to illustrate the difficulty of using probability theory to evaluate the plausibility of statements.

The Bayesian view of probability gives rise to a very useful theorem called **Bayes theorem**.

Bayes theorem

The logistic regression equation we presented in the previous section is an example of conditional probability:

$$\hat{y} = P(y = 1 \mid x; \beta)$$

The probability of our prediction $\hat{y}$ is determined by the values x and β. A conditional probability is the likelihood of one thing given another thing we already know about. For example, we have already considered questions such as the "probability of survival given that the passenger was female".

Assuming we are interested in x, y, and z, the basic notation for probability is as follows:

- $P(A)$: This is the probability of A occurring
- $P(A \cap B)$: This is the joint probability of both A and B occurring
- $P(A \cup B)$: This is the probability of A or B occurring
- $P(A \mid B)$: This is the probability of A occurring given B has occurred
- $P(A, B \mid C)$: This is the probability of both A and B occurring given that C has occurred

The relationship between the preceding variables is expressed in the following formula:

$$P(A \mid B)P(B) = P(A \cap B) = P(B \mid A)P(A)$$

Using this, we can solve for $P(A \mid B)$ assuming $P(A) \neq 0$ to get what is called Bayes theorem:

$$P(A \mid B) = \frac{P(B \mid A)P(A)}{P(B)}$$

We read this as "the probability of A given B is equal to the probability of B, given A, times the probability of A all over the probability of B".

$P(A)$ is the prior probability: the initial degree of belief in A.

$P(A|B)$ is the conditional probability — the degree of belief in A having taken B into account.

The quotient $\frac{P(B|A)}{P(B)}$ represents the support that B provides for A.

Bayes theorem can appear intimidating and abstract, so let's see an example of why it's useful. Let's say we're testing for disease that has infected 1 percent of the population. We have a highly sensitive and specific test that is not quite perfect:

- 99 percent of sick patients test positive
- 99 percent of healthy patients test negative

Given that a patient tests positive, what is the probability that the patient is actually sick?

The preceding bullet points appear to imply that a positive test means a 99 percent chance of being sick, but this fails to take into account how rare the disease is in the population. Since the probability of being infected (the prior) is so small, this hugely decreases your chances of actually having the disease even if you test positive.

Let's work through the numbers with 10,000 representative people. That would mean that 100 are sick, but 9,900 are healthy. If we applied the test to all 10,000 people we would find 99 sick people testing sick (true positives), but 99 healthy people, testing sick (false positives) as well. If you test positive, the chances of actually having the disease are $\frac{99}{99}$, or 50 percent:

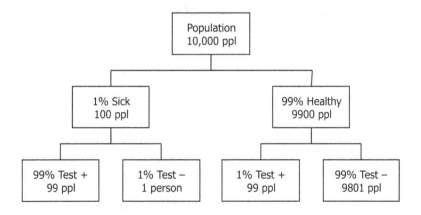

We can calculate the same example using Bayes rule. Let y to refer to "sick" and x refer to the event "+" for a positive result:

$$P(sick \mid +) = \frac{P(+\mid sick)P(sick)}{P(+)} = \frac{0.99 \cdot 0.01}{0.99 \cdot 0.01 + 0.01 \cdot 0.99} = 0.5$$

In other words, although a positive test has vastly increased your chances of having the disease (up from 1 percent in the population), you still only have even odds of actually being sick—nowhere near the 99 percent implied by the test accuracy alone.

The previous example provides neat numbers for us to work through, let's run the example on the Titanic data now.

The probability of surviving given you are female is equal to the probability of being female given you survived multiplied by the probability of surviving all divided by the probability of being a woman on the Titanic:

$$P(survival \mid female) = \frac{P(female \mid survival)P(suvival)}{P(female)}$$

Let's remind ourselves of the contingency table from earlier:

```
| :survived |   :sex  | :count |
|-----------+---------+--------|
|         n |    male |    682 |
|         n |  female |    127 |
|         y |    male |    161 |
|         y |  female |    339 |
```

P(survival | female) is the posterior, the degree of belief in survival given the evidence. This is the value we are trying to calculate.

P(female | survival) is the conditional probability of being female, given survival:

$$P(female \mid survival) = \frac{339}{339 + 161} = \frac{339}{500}$$

P(survival) is the prior, the initial degree of belief in survival:

$$P(survival) = \frac{339 + 161}{1309} = \frac{500}{1309}$$

P(female) is the evidence:

$$P\left(female\right)=\frac{127+339}{1309}=\frac{466}{1309}$$

Substituting these proportions into Bayes rule:

$$P(survival \mid female)=\frac{\frac{339}{500}\cdot\frac{500}{1309}}{\frac{446}{1309}}=\frac{\frac{339}{1309}}{\frac{446}{1309}}=\frac{339}{446}$$

Using Bayes rule we have calculated that the probability of survival, given being female, is $\frac{339}{446}$ or 76 percent.

Notice that we could have calculated this value from the contingency table too, by looking up the proportion of survivors out of the total females: $\frac{339}{339+127}$. The reason for the popularity of Bayes rule is that it gives us a way of calculating this probability where no such contingency table exists.

Bayes theorem with multiple predictors

As an example of how we can use Bayes rule without a full contingency table, let's use the example of a third-class male. What's the probability of survival for third-class male passengers?

Let's write out Bayes rule for this new question:

$$P(survival \mid male \cap third)=\frac{P(male \cap third \mid survival)P\left(suvival\right)}{P\left(male \cap third\right)}$$

Next, we have two contingency tables:

:survived	:pclass	:count
n	first	123
n	second	158
n	third	528
y	first	200
y	second	119

```
|          y |  third |    181 |

| :survived |  :sex | :count |
|-----------+--------+--------|
|         n | female |    127 |
|         n |   male |    682 |
|         y | female |    339 |
|         y |   male |    161 |
```

"Third-class male" is not a category in any of our contingency tables that we can simply look up. However, by using Bayes theorem we can calculate it like this:

The posterior probability we're seeking is *P(survive | male,third)*.

The prior probability of survival is the same as before: $\frac{500}{1309}$ or about 0.38.

The conditional probability is $P(male \cap third \mid survival)$. This is the same as $P(male \mid survive)P(third \mid survive)$. In other words, we can multiply the two probabilities together:

$$P(male \mid survive) \cdot P(third \mid survive) = \frac{161}{161+339} \cdot \frac{181}{181+119+200} = \frac{161}{500} \cdot \frac{181}{500}$$

$$\approx 0.12$$

The evidence is the probability of being both male and in third class $P(male \cap third)$:

$$P(male) \cdot P(third) = \frac{682+161}{1309} \cdot \frac{528+181}{1309} = \frac{843}{1309} \cdot \frac{709}{1309}$$

$$\approx 0.35$$

Putting this all together:

$$P(survival \mid male \cap third) = \frac{0.12 \cdot 0.38}{0.35} = 0.13$$

In actual fact, there were 75 surviving third class males out of 493 in total, giving a true survival rate of 15 percent. Bayes Theorem has allowed us to calculate the true answer very closely, without the use of a complete contingency table.

Naive Bayes classification

The reason that the answer we arrived at using Bayes theorem and the actual result differ slightly is that by using Bayes rule we made an assumption when calculating $P(male \cap third)$ that the probability of being male, and the probability of being in third class, are independent. In the next section, we'll use Bayes theorem to produce a naive Bayes classifier.

 The reason this algorithm is called naive is because it assumes all variables are independent. We know this is often not the case, and there are interaction effects between variables. For example, we might know that combinations of parameters make a certain class very much more likely — for example, being both male and in third class.

Let's look at how we might use Bayes rule for a classifier. The Bayes theorem for two possible classes, survive and perish, are shown as follows for a male in third class:

$$P(survive \mid male \cap third) = \frac{P(male \cap third \mid survive)P(survive)}{P(male \cap third)}$$

$$P(perish \mid male \cap third) = \frac{P(male \cap third \mid perish)P(perish)}{P(male \cap third)}$$

The most likely class will be the one with the greatest posterior probability.

$P(male \cap third)$ appears as the common factor for both classes. If we were to relax the requirements of Bayes theorem a little so that it didn't have to return probabilities, we could remove the common factor to arrive at the following:

$$P(survive \mid male \cap third) \approx P(male \cap third \mid survive)P(survive)$$

$$P(perish \mid male \cap third) \approx P(male \cap third \mid perish)P(perish)$$

We have simply removed the denominator from the right hand side of both equations. Since we are no longer calculating probabilities, the equals sign has become $\approx$, meaning "is proportional to".

Putting the values from our previous table of data into the equations yields:

$$P(survive \,|\, male \cap third) \approx \frac{500}{1309} \cdot \frac{181}{500} \cdot \frac{161}{500} = 0.045$$

$$P(perish \,|\, male \cap third) \approx \frac{809}{1309} \cdot \frac{528}{809} \cdot \frac{682}{809} = 0.340$$

We can instantly see that we are not calculating probabilities because the two classes do not add up to one. This doesn't matter for our classifier since we were only going to select the class associated with the highest value anyway. Unfortunately for our third-class male, our naive Bayes model predicts that he will perish.

Let's do the equivalent calculation for a first class female:

$$P(survive \,|\, female \cap first) \approx \frac{500}{1309} \cdot \frac{200}{500} \cdot \frac{339}{500} = 0.104$$

$$P(perish \,|\, female \cap first) \approx \frac{809}{1309} \cdot \frac{123}{809} \cdot \frac{127}{809} = 0.015$$

Fortunately for our first class female, the model predicts that she will survive.

A Bayes classifier is a combination of the Bayes probability model combined with a decision rule (which class to choose). The decision rule described earlier is the maximum a posteriori rule, or MAP rule.

Implementing a naive Bayes classifier

Fortunately, implementing a naive Bayes model in code is much easier than understanding the mathematics. The first step is simply to calculate the number of examples corresponding to each value of each feature for each class. The following code keeps a count of the number of times each parameter is seen for each class label:

```
(defn inc-class-total [model class]
  (update-in model [class :total] (fnil inc 0)))

(defn inc-predictors-count-fn [row class]
  (fn [model attr]
    (let [val (get row attr)]
```

```
              (update-in model [class attr val] (fnil inc 0)))))))

(defn assoc-row-fn [class-attr predictors]
  (fn [model row]
    (let [class (get row class-attr)]
      (reduce (inc-predictors-count-fn row class)
              (inc-class-total model class)
              predictors)))))

(defn bayes-classifier [data class-attr predictors]
  (reduce (assoc-row-fn class-attr predictors) {} data))
```

The label is the attribute corresponding to the class (for example, in our Titanic data "survived" is the label corresponding to our classes true and false), and parameters are the sequence of attributes corresponding to the features (sex and class).

It can be used like so:

```
(defn ex-4-26 []
  (->> (load-data "titanic.tsv")
       (:rows)
       (bayes-classifier :survived [:sex :pclass])
       (clojure.pprint/pprint)))
```

This example yields the following Bayes model:

```
{:classes
 {"n"
  {:predictors
   {:pclass {"third" 528, "second" 158, "first" 123},
    :sex {"male" 682, "female" 127}},
   :n 809},
  "y"
  {:predictors
   {:pclass {"third" 181, "second" 119, "first" 200},
    :sex {"male" 161, "female" 339}},
   :n 500}},
 :n 1309}
```

The model is simply a two-level hierarchy implemented as nested maps. At the top level are our two classes— "n" and "y", corresponding to "perished" and "survived", respectively. For each class we have a map of predictors— :pclass and :sex. Each key corresponds to a map of possible values and counts. As well as a map of predictors, each class has a count :n.

Now that we have calculated our Bayes model, we can implement our MAP decision rule. The following is a function that calculates the conditional probability of a provided class. For example, $P(male \cap third \mid survive)P(survive)$:

```
(defn posterior-probability [model test class-attr]
  (let [observed (get-in model [:classes class-attr])
        prior (/ (:n observed)
                 (:n model))]
    (apply * prior
           (for [[predictor value] test]
             (/ (get-in observed [:predictors predictor value])
                (:n observed))))))
```

Given a particular `class-attr`, the preceding code will calculate the posterior probability of the class, given the observations. Having implemented the earlier code, the classifier simply needs to return the class corresponding to the maximum posterior probability:

```
(defn bayes-classify [model test]
  (let [probability (partial posterior-probability model test)
        classes     (keys (:classes model))]
    (apply max-key probability classes)))
```

The preceding code calculates the probability of the test input against each of the model's classes. The returned class is simply the one with the highest posterior probability.

Evaluating the naive Bayes classifier

Now that we have written two complementary functions, `bayes-classifier` and `bayes-classify`, we can use our model to make predictions. Let's train our model on the Titanic dataset and check its predictions for the third-class male and first-class female that we've already calculated:

```
(defn ex-4-27 []
  (let [model (->> (load-data "titanic.tsv")
                   (:rows)
                   (naive-bayes :survived [:sex :pclass]))]
    (println "Third class male:"
             (bayes-classify model {:sex "male" :pclass "third"}))
    (println "First class female:"
             (bayes-classify model {:sex "female" :pclass "first"}))))

;; Third class male: n
;; First class female: y
```

It's a good start—our classifier is in agreement with the outcomes we've calculated by hand. Let's take a look at the percent correct for the naive Bayes classifier:

```
(defn ex-4-28 []
   (let [data (:rows (load-data "titanic.tsv"))
         model (bayes-classifier :survived [:sex :pclass] data)
         test (fn [test]
                 (= (:survived test)
                    (bayes-classify model
                                    (select-keys test [:sex :class]))))
         results (frequencies (map test data))]
      (/ (get results true)
         (apply + (vals results)))))

;; 1021/1309
```

By replicating our test over the entire dataset and comparing outputs, we can see how often our classifier got the correct answer. 78 percent is the same percent correct we got using our logistic regression classifier. For such a simple model, naive Bayes is performing remarkably well.

We can calculate a confusion matrix:

```
(defn ex-4-195 []
    (let [data (:rows (load-data "titanic.tsv"))
          model (bayes-classifier :survived [:sex :pclass] data)
          classify (fn [test]
                     (->> (select-keys test [:sex :pclass])
                          (bayes-classify model)))
          ys       (map :survived data)
          y-hats (map classify data)]
       (confusion-matrix ys y-hats)))
```

The preceding code generates the following matrix:

```
|   |   n |   y |
|---+-----+-----|
| n | 682 | 127 |
| y | 161 | 339 |
```

This confusion matrix is identical to the one we obtained previously from logistic regression. Despite taking very different approaches, they have both been able to classify the dataset to the same degree of accuracy.

Comparing the logistic regression and naive Bayes approaches

Although they have performed equally well on our small Titanic dataset, the two methods of classification are generally suited to different tasks.

In spite of being conceptually a simpler classifier as compared to logistic regression, naive Bayes can often outperform it in cases where either data is scarce or the number of parameters is very large. Because of naive Bayes' ability to deal with a very large number of features, it is often employed for problems such as automatic medical diagnosis or in spam classification. In spam classification, features could run into the tens or hundreds of thousands, with each word representing a feature that can help identify whether the message is spam or not.

However, a drawback of naive Bayes is its assumption of independence—in problem domains where this assumption is not valid, other classifiers can outperform naive Bayes. With a lot of data, logistic regression is able to learn more sophisticated models and classify potentially more accurately than naive Bayes is able to.

There is another method that—while simple and relatively straightforward to model—is able to learn more sophisticated relationships amongst parameters. This method is the decision tree.

Decision trees

The third method of classification we'll look at in this chapter is the decision tree. A decision tree models the process of classification as a series of tests that checks the value of a particular attribute or attributes of the item to be classified. It can be thought of as similar to a flowchart, with each test being a branch in the flow. The process continues, testing and branching, until a leaf node is reached. The leaf node will represent the most likely class for the item.

Decision trees share some similarities with both logistic regression and naive Bayes. Although the classifier can support categorical variables without dummy coding, it is also able to model complex dependencies between variables through repeated branching.

In the old-fashioned parlor game *Twenty Questions*, one person, the "answerer", chooses an object but does not reveal their choice to the others. All other players are "questioners" and take turns to ask questions that aim to guess the object the answerer has thought of. Each question can only be answered with a simple "yes" or "no". The challenge for the questioners is to guess the object the answerer was thinking of in only 20 questions, and to pick questions that reveal the most amount of information about the object the answerer is thinking of. This is not an easy task — ask questions that are too broad and you do not gain much information through the answer. Ask questions that are too specific and you will not reach an answer in only 20 steps.

Unsurprisingly, these concerns also appear in decision tree classification. Information is something that is quantifiable, and decision trees aim to ask questions that are likely to yield the biggest information gain.

Information

Imagine that I pick a random card from a normal deck of 52 playing cards. Your challenge is to guess what card I have picked. But first, I offer to answer one question with a "yes" or a "no". Which question would you rather ask?

- Is it red? (a Heart or a Diamond)
- Is it a picture card? (a Jack, Queen, or King)

We will explore this challenge in detail over the coming pages. Take a moment to consider your question.

There are 26 red cards in a deck, so the probability of a random red card being chosen is $\frac{1}{2}$. There are 12 picture cards in a deck so the probability of a picture card being randomly chosen is $\frac{3}{13}$.

The information I associated with a single event is:

$$I(e) = -log_2 P(e)$$

Incanter has a log2 function that enables us to calculate information like this:

```
(defn information [p]
  (- (i/log2 p)))
```

Here, log2 is the log to base 2. Therefore:

$$I\left(red\right) = -log_2 \frac{1}{2} = 1$$

$$I\left(picture\right) = -log_2 \frac{3}{13} = 2.12$$

Since a picture card has the lower probability, it also carries the highest information value. If we know the card is a picture card, there are only 12 cards it could possibly be. If we know the card is red, then 26 possibilities still remain.

Information is usually measured in bits. The information content of knowing the card is red carries only one bit of information. A computer bit can only represent a zero or a one. One bit is enough to contain a simple 50/50 split. Knowing that the card is a picture card offers two bits of information. This appears to suggest that the best question to ask therefore is "Is it a picture card?". An affirmative answer will carry with it a lot of information.

But look what happens if we find out the answer to the question is "no". What's the information content of finding out that the card I've chosen is not a picture card?

$$I\left(black\right) = -log_2 \frac{1}{2} = 1$$

$$I\left(not\ picture\right) = -log_2 \frac{10}{13} = 0.38$$

It appears that now we could be better off asking whether the card is red, since the information content is greater. Finding out our card is not a picture card still leaves 36 possibilities remaining. We clearly don't know in advance whether the answer will be "yes" or "no", so how can we go about choosing the best question?

Entropy

Entropy is a measure of uncertainty. By calculating the entropy we can strike a balance between information content over all possible responses.

 The concept of entropy was introduced by Rudolf Clausius in the mid-nineteenth century as part of the emerging science of thermodynamics to help explain how part of the functional energy of combustion engines was lost due to heat dissipation. In this chapter we talk about Shannon Entropy, which comes from Claude Shannon's work on information theory in the mid-twentieth century. The two concepts are closely related, despite hailing from different corners of science in very different contexts.

Entropy, *H*, can be calculated in the following way:

$$H(X) = \sum_i P(x_i) I(P(x_i))$$

Here, *P(x)* is the probability of *x* occurring and *I(P(x))* is the information content of *x*.

For example, let's compare the entropy of a pack of cards where each class is simply "red" and "not red". We know the information content of "red" is 1 and the probability is $\frac{1}{2}$. The same is true for "not red", so the entropy is the following sum:

$$1 \cdot \frac{1}{2} + 1 \cdot \frac{1}{2} = 1$$

Splitting the pack in this way yields an entropy of 1. What about splitting the pack into "picture" and "not picture" cards? The information content of "picture" is 2.12 and the probability is $\frac{3}{13}$. The information content of "not picture" is 0.38 and the probability is $\frac{10}{13}$:

$$2.12 \cdot \frac{3}{13} + 0.38 \cdot \frac{10}{13} = 0.78$$

If we imagine the deck of cards as a sequence of classes, positive and negative, we can calculate the entropy for our two decks using Clojure:

```clojure
(defn entropy [xs]
  (let [n (count xs)
        f (fn [x]
            (let [p (/ x n)]
              (* p (information p))))]
    (->> (frequencies xs)
         (vals)
         (map f)
         (reduce +))))

(defn ex-4-30 []
  (let [red-black (concat (repeat 26 1)
                          (repeat 26 0))]
    (entropy red-black)))

;; 1.0

(defn ex-4-202 []
  (let [picture-not-picture (concat (repeat 12 1)
                                    (repeat 40 0))]
    (entropy picture-not-picture)))

;; 0.779
```

Entropy is a measure of uncertainty. The lower entropy by splitting the deck into "picture" and "not picture" groups shows us that asking whether or not the card is a picture is the best question to ask. It remains the best question to have asked even if we discover that my card is not a picture card, because the amount of uncertainty remaining in the deck is lower. Entropy does not just apply to sequences of numbers, but to any sequence.

```clojure
(entropy "mississippi")
;; 1.82
```

is lower than

```clojure
(entropy "yellowstone")
;; 2.91
```

This in spite of their equal length, because there is more consistency amongst the letters.

Information gain

Entropy has indicated to us that the best question to ask—the one that will decrease the entropy of our deck of cards most—is whether or not the card is a picture card.

In general, we can use entropy to tell us whether a grouping is a good grouping or not using the theory of information gain. To illustrate this, let's return to our Titanic survivors. Let's assume that I've picked a passenger at random and you have to guess whether or not they survived. This time, before you answer, I offer to tell you one of two things:

- Their sex (male or female)
- The class they were traveling in (first, second, or third)

Which would you rather know?

It might appear at first that the best question to ask is which class they were travelling in. This will divide the passengers into three groups and, as we saw with the playing cards, smaller groups are better. Don't forget, though, that the objective is to guess the survival of the passenger. To determine the best question to ask we need to know which question gives us the highest information gain.

Information gain is measured as the difference between entropy before and after we learn the new information. Let's calculate the information gain when we learn that the passenger is male. First, let's calculate the baseline entropy of the survival rates for all passengers.

We can use our existing entropy calculation and pass it the sequence of survival classes:

```
(defn ex-4-32 []
  (->> (load-data "titanic.tsv")
       (:rows)
       (map :survived)
       (entropy)))
```

```
;; 0.959
```

This is a high entropy. We already know that an entropy of 1.0 indicates a 50/50 split, yet we also know that survival on the Titanic was around 38 percent. The reason for this apparent discrepancy is that entropy does not change linearly, but rises quickly towards 1 as illustrated in the following graph:

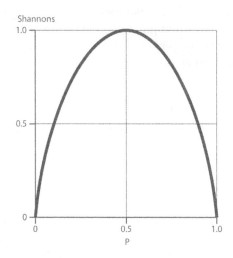

Next, let's consider the entropy of survival when split by sex. Now we have two groups to calculate entropy for: males and females. The combined entropy is the weighted average of the two groups. We can calculate the weighted average for an arbitrary number of groups in Clojure by using the following function:

```
(defn weighted-entropy [groups]
  (let [n (count (apply concat groups))
        e (fn [group]
            (* (entropy group)
               (/ (count group) n)))]
    (->> (map e groups)
         (reduce +))))

(defn ex-4-33 []
  (->> (load-data "titanic.tsv")
       (:rows)
       (group-by :sex)
       (vals)
       (map (partial map :survived))
       (weighted-entropy)))

;; 0.754
```

We can see that the weighted entropy for the survival classes that have been grouped by sex is lower than the 0.96 we obtained from the passengers as a whole. Therefore our information gain is *0.96 - 0.75 = 0.21* bits.

We can easily express the gain as a Clojure function based on the `entropy` and `weighted-entropy` functions that we've just defined:

```
(defn information-gain [groups]
  (- (entropy (apply concat groups))
     (weighted-entropy groups)))
```

Let's use this to calculate the gain if we group the passengers by their class, instead:

```
(defn ex-4-205 []
  (->> (load-data "titanic.tsv")
       (:rows)
       (group-by :pclass)
       (vals)
       (map (partial map :survived))
       (information-gain)))
```

```
;; 0.07
```

The information gain for passenger class is 0.07, and for sex is 0.21. Therefore, when classifying survival rates, knowing the passenger's sex is much more useful than the class they were traveling in.

Using information gain to identify the best predictor

Using the functions we have just defined, we can construct an effective tree classifier. We'll want a general purpose way to calculate the information gain for a specific predictor attribute, given an output class. In the preceding example, the predictor was `:pclass` and the class attribute was `:survived`, but we can make a generic function that will accept these keywords as the arguments `class-attr` and `predictor`:

```
(defn gain-for-predictor [class-attr xs predictor]
  (let [grouped-classes (->> (group-by predictor xs)
                             (vals)
                             (map (partial map class-attr)))]
    (information-gain grouped-classes)))
```

Next, we'll want a way to calculate the best predictor for a given set of rows. We can simply map the preceding function over all the desired predictors and return the predictor corresponding to the highest gain:

```
(defn best-predictor [class-attr xs predictors]
  (let [gain (partial gain-for-predictor class-attr xs)]
    (when (seq predictors)
      (apply max-key gain predictors))))
```

Let's test this function by asking which of the predictors :sex and :pclass is the best predictor:

```
(defn ex-4-35 []
  (->> (load-data "titanic.tsv")
       (:rows)
       (best-predictor :survived [:sex :pclass])))

;; :sex
```

Reassuringly, we're getting the same answer as before. Decision trees allow us to apply this logic recursively to build a tree structure that chooses the best question to ask at each branch, based solely on the data in that branch.

Recursively building a decision tree

By applying the functions we have written recursively to the data, we can build up a data structure that represents the best category split at each level of the tree. First, let's define a function that will return the **modal** (most common) class, given a sequence of data. When our decision tree reaches a point at which it can't split the data any more (either because the entropy is zero or because there are no remaining predictors left on which to split), we'll return the modal class.

```
(defn modal-class [classes]
  (->> (frequencies classes)
       (apply max-key val)
       (key)))
```

With that simple function in place, we're ready to construct the decision tree. This is implemented as a recursive function. Given a class attribute, a sequence of predictors, and a sequence of values, we build a sequence of available classes by mapping the class-attr over our xs. If the entropy is zero, then all the classes are the same, so we simply return the first.

If the classes are not identical in our group, then we need to pick a predictor to branch on. We use our `best-predictor` function to select the predictor associated with the highest information gain. We remove this from our list of predictors (there's no point in trying to use the same predictor twice), and construct a `tree-branch` function. This is a partial recursive call to `decision-tree` with the remaining predictors.

Finally, we group our data on the `best-predictor`, and call our partially applied `tree-branch` function on each group. This causes the whole process to repeat again, but this time only on the subset of data defined by `group-by`. The return value is wrapped in a vector, together with the predictor:

```
(defn decision-tree [class-attr predictors xs]
  (let [classes (map class-attr xs)]
    (if (zero? (entropy classes))
      (first classes)
      (if-let [predictor (best-predictor class-attr
                                         predictors xs)]
        (let [predictors  (remove #{predictor} predictors)
              tree-branch (partial decision-tree
                                   class-attr predictors)]
          (->> (group-by predictor xs)
               (map-vals tree-branch)
               (vector predictor)))
        (modal-class classes)))))
```

Let's visualize the output of this function for the predictors `:sex` and `:pclass`.

```
(defn ex-4-36 []
  (->> (load-data "titanic.tsv")
       (:rows)
       (decision-tree :survived [:pclass :sex])
       (clojure.pprint/pprint)))

;; [:sex
;;  {"female" [:pclass {"first" "y", "second" "y", "third" "n"}],
;;   "male" [:pclass {"first" "n", "second" "n", "third" "n"}]}]
```

We can see how the decision tree is represented as a vector. The first element of the vector is the predictor that's being used to branch the tree. The second element is a map containing the attributes of this predictor as keys `"male"` and `"female"` with values corresponding to a further branch on `:pclass`.

To see how we can build up arbitrarily deep trees using this function, let's add a further predictor :age. Unfortunately, the tree classifier we've built is only able to deal with categorical data, so let's split the age continuous variable into three simple categories: unknown, child, and adult.

```
(defn age-categories [age]
  (cond
    (nil? age) "unknown"
    (< age 13) "child"
    :default   "adult"))
```

```
(defn ex-4-37 []
  (let [data (load-data "titanic.tsv")]
    (->> (i/transform-col data :age age-categories)
         (:rows)
         (decision-tree :survived [:pclass :sex :age])
         (clojure.pprint/pprint))))
```

This code yields the following tree:

```
[:sex
 {"female"
  [:pclass
   {"first" [:age {"adult" "y", "child" "n", "unknown" "y"}],
    "second" [:age {"adult" "y", "child" "y", "unknown" "y"}],
    "third" [:age {"adult" "n", "child" "n", "unknown" "y"}]}],
  "male"
  [:age
   {"unknown" [:pclass {"first" "n", "second" "n", "third" "n"}],
    "adult" [:pclass {"first" "n", "second" "n", "third" "n"}],
    "child" [:pclass {"first" "y", "second" "y", "third" "n"}]}]}]
```

Notice how the best overall predictor is still the sex of the passenger, as before. However, if the sex is male, age is the next most informative predictor. On the other hand, if the sex is female, passenger class is the most informative predictor. Because of the recursive nature of the tree, each branch is able to determine the best predictor only for the data in that particular branch of the tree.

Using the decision tree for classification

With the data structure returned from the decision-tree function, we have all the information we require to classify passengers into their most likely class. Our classifier will also be implemented recursively. If a vector has been passed in as the model, we know it will contain two elements — the predictor and the branches. We destructure the predictor and branches from the model and then determine the branch our test is on. To do this, we simply get the value of the predictor from the test with `(get test predictor)`. The branch we want will be the one corresponding to this value.

Once we have the branch, we need to call `tree-classify` again on the branch. Because we're in the tail position (no further logic is applied after the `if`) we can call `recur`, allowing the Clojure compiler to optimize our recursive function call:

```
(defn tree-classify [model test]
  (if (vector? model)
    (let [[predictor branches] model
          branch (get branches (get test predictor))]
      (recur branch test))
    model))
```

We continue to call tree-classify recursively until `(vector? model)` returns false. At this point we will have traversed the full depth of the decision tree and reached a leaf node. At this point the `model` argument contains the predicted class, so we simply return it.

```
(defn ex-4-38 []
  (let [data (load-data "titanic.tsv")
        tree (->> (i/transform-col data :age age-categories)
                  (:rows)
                  (decision-tree :survived [:pclass :sex :age]))
        test {:sex "male" :pclass "second" :age "child"}]
    (tree-classify tree test)))

;; "y"
```

The decision tree predicts that the young male from second class will survive.

Evaluating the decision tree classifier

As before, we can calculate our confusion matrix and kappa statistic:

```
(defn ex-4-39 []
  (let [data (-> (load-data "titanic.tsv")
                 (i/transform-col :age age-categories)
                 (:rows))
        tree (decision-tree :survived [:pclass :sex :age] data)]
    (confusion-matrix (map :survived data)
                      (map (partial tree-classify tree) data))))
```

The confusion matrix looks like this:

```
|   |   n |   y |
|---+-----+-----|
| n | 763 |  46 |
| y | 219 | 281 |
```

We can immediately see that the classifier is generating a lot of false negatives: 219. Let's calculate the kappa statistic:

```
(defn ex-4-40 []
  (let [data (-> (load-data "titanic.tsv")
                 (i/transform-col :age age-categories)
                 (:rows))
        tree (decision-tree :survived [:pclass :sex :age] data)
        ys      (map :survived data)
        y-hats (map (partial tree-classify tree) data)]
    (float (kappa-statistic ys y-hats))))
```

```
;; 0.541
```

Our tree classifier isn't performing nearly as well as others we have tried. One way we could try to improve the accuracy is to increase the number of predictors we're using. Rather than use crude categories for age, let's use the actual data for age as a feature. This will allow our classifier to better distinguish between our passengers. While we're at it, let's add the fare too:

```
(defn ex-4-41 []
  (let [data (-> (load-data "titanic.tsv")
                 (:rows))
        tree (decision-tree :survived
                            [:pclass :sex :age :fare] data)
        ys      (map :survived data)
```

```
        y-hats (map (partial tree-classify tree) data)]
    (float (kappa-statistic ys y-hats))))
```

```
;; 0.925
```

Great! We've made fantastic progress; our new model is the best yet. By adding more granular predictors, we've built a model that's able to predict with a very high degree of accuracy.

Before we celebrate too much, though, we should think carefully about how general our model is. The purpose of building a classifier is usually to make predictions about new data. This means that it should perform well on data that it's never seen before. The model we've just built has a significant problem. To understand what it is, we'll turn to the library clj-ml, which contains a variety of functions for training and testing classifiers.

Classification with clj-ml

While building our own versions of logistic regression, naive Bayes, and decision trees has provided a valuable opportunity to talk about the theory behind them, Clojure gives us several libraries for building classifiers. One of the better supported is the clj-ml library.

The clj-ml library is currently maintained by Josua Eckroth and is documented on his GitHub page at `https://github.com/joshuaeckroth/clj-ml`. The library provides Clojure interfaces for running linear regression described in the previous chapter, as well as classification with logistic regression, naive Bayes, decision trees, and other algorithms.

 The underlying implementation for most machine learning functionality in clj-ml is provided by the Java machine learning library Weka. **Waikato Environment for Knowledge Analysis (Weka)**, an open source machine learning project released and maintained primarily by the Machine Learning Group at the University of Waikato, New Zealand (`http://www.cs.waikato.ac.nz/ml/`).

Loading data with clj-ml

Because of its specialized support for machine learning algorithms, clj-ml provides functions for creating datasets that identify the classes and attributes of a dataset. The function `clj-ml.data/make-dataset` allows us to create a dataset that can be passed to Weka's classifiers. In the following code, we include `clj-ml.data` as `mld`:

```
(defn to-weka [dataset]
  (let [attributes [{:survived ["y" "n"]}
                    {:pclass ["first" "second" "third"]}
                    {:sex ["male" "female"]}
                    :age
                    :fare]
        vectors (->> dataset
                     (i/$ [:survived :pclass :sex :age :fare])
                     (i/to-vect))]
    (mld/make-dataset :titanic-weka attributes vectors
                      {:class :survived})))
```

`mld/make-dataset` expects to receive the name of the dataset, a vector of attributes, a dataset as a sequence of row vectors, and an optional map of further settings. The attributes identify the column names and, in the case of categorical variables, also enumerate all the possible categories. Categorical variables, for example `:survived`, are passed as a map `{:survived ["y" "n"]}`, whereas continuous variables such as `:age` and `:fare` are passed as straightforward keywords. The dataset must be provided as a sequence of row vectors. To construct this, we're simply using Incanter's `i/$` function and calling `i/to-vect` on the results.

> While `make-dataset` is a flexible way to create datasets from arbitrary data sources, `clj-ml.io` provides a `load-instances` function that loads data from a variety of sources such as CSV or Attribute-Relation File Format (ARFF) files and the MongoDB database.

With our dataset in a format that clj-ml understands, it's time to train a classifier.

Building a decision tree in clj-ml

Clj-ml implements a large variety of classifiers, and all are accessible through the `cl/make-classifier` function. We pass two keyword arguments to the constructor: the classifier type and an algorithm to use. For example, let's look at the `:decision-tree`, `:c45` algorithm. The **C4.5 algorithm** was devised by Ross Quinlan and builds a tree classifier based on information entropy in the same way as our very own `tree-classifier` function from earlier in the chapter. C4.5 extends the classifier we built in a couple of ways:

- Where none of the predictors provide any information gain, C4.5 creates a decision node higher up the tree using the expected value of the class

- If a previously-unseen class is encountered, C4.5 will create a decision node higher up the tree with the expected value of the class

We can create a decision tree in clj-ml with the following code:

```
(defn ex-4-42 []
    (let [dataset (to-weka (load-data "titanic.tsv"))
          classifier (-> (cl/make-classifier :decision-tree :c45)
                         (cl/classifier-train dataset))
          classify (partial cl/classifier-classify classifier)
          ys       (map str  (mld/dataset-class-values dataset))
          y-hats (map name (map classify dataset))]
      (println "Confusion:" (confusion-matrix ys y-hats))
      (println "Kappa:" (kappa-statistic ys y-hats)))))
```

The preceding code returns the following information:

```
;; Confusion:
;; |     |   n |   y |
;; |---+-----+-----|
;; | n | 712 |  97 |
;; | y | 153 | 347 |
;;
;; Kappa: 0.587
```

Notice how we don't need to explicitly provide the class and predictor attributes while training our classifier or using it for prediction. The Weka dataset already contains the information about the class attribute of each instance, and the classifier will use all the attributes it can to arrive at a prediction. In spite of this, the results still aren't as good as we were getting before. The reason is that Weka's implementation of decision trees is refusing to over-fit the data.

Bias and variance

Overfitting is a problem that occurs with machine learning algorithms that are able to generate very accurate results on a training dataset but fail to generalize very well from what they've learned. We say that models which have overfit the data have very high variance. When we trained our decision tree on data that included the numeric age of passengers, we were overfitting the data.

Conversely, certain models may have very high bias. This is a situation where the model has a strong tendency towards a certain outcome irrespective of the training examples to the contrary. Recall our example of a classifier that always predicts that a survivor will perish. This classifier would perform well on dataset with low survivor rates, but very poorly otherwise.

In the case of high bias, the model is unlikely to perform well on diverse inputs at the training stage. In the case of high variance, the model is unlikely to perform well on data that differs from that which it was trained on.

 Like the balance to be struck between Type I and Type II errors in hypothesis testing, balancing bias and variance is critical for producing good results from machine learning.

If we have too many features, the learned hypothesis may fit the training set very well but fail to generalize to new examples very well.

Overfitting

The secret to identifying overfitting, then, is to test the classifier on examples that it has not been trained on. If the classifier performs poorly on these examples then there is a possibility that the model is overfitting.

The usual approach is to divide the dataset into two groups: a training set and a test set. The training set is used to train the classifier, and the test set is used to determine whether the classifier is able to generalize well from what it has learned.

The test set should be large enough that it will be a representative sample from the dataset, but should still leave the majority of records for training. Test sets are often around 10-30 percent of the overall dataset. Let's use `clj-ml.data/do-split-dataset` to return two sets of instances. The smaller will be our test set and the larger will be our training set:

```
(defn ex-4-43 []
  (let [[test-set train-set] (-> (load-data "titanic.tsv")
```

```
                                    (to-weka)
                                    (mld/do-split-dataset :percentage
                                                           30))
              classifier (-> (cl/make-classifier :decision-tree :c45)
                             (cl/classifier-train train-set))
              classify (partial cl/classifier-classify classifier)
              ys      (map str  (mld/dataset-class-values test-set))
              y-hats (map name (map classify test-set))]
        (println "Confusion:" (confusion-matrix ys y-hats))
        (println "Kappa:" (kappa-statistic ys y-hats))))

;; Confusion:
;; |   |  n  |  y  |
;; |---+-----+-----|
;; | n | 152 |   9 |
;; | y |  65 | 167 |
;;
;; Kappa: 0.630
```

If you compare this kappa statistic to the previous one, you'll see that actually our accuracy has improved on unseen data. Whilst this appears to suggest our classifier is not overfitting our training set, it doesn't seem very realistic that our classifier should be able to make better predictions for new data than the data we've actually told it about.

This suggests that we may have been fortunate with the values that were returned in our test set. Perhaps this just happened to contain some of the easier-to-classify passengers compared to the training set. Let's see what happens if we take the test set from the final 30 percent instead:

```
(defn ex-4-44 []
  (let [[train-set test-set] (-> (load-data "titanic.tsv")
                                 (to-weka)
                                 (mld/do-split-dataset :percentage
                                                        70))
              classifier (-> (cl/make-classifier :decision-tree :c45)
                             (cl/classifier-train train-set))
              classify (partial cl/classifier-classify classifier)
              ys      (map str  (mld/dataset-class-values test-set))
              y-hats (map name (map classify test-set))]
        (println "Kappa:" (kappa-statistic ys y-hats))))

;; Kappa: 0.092
```

The classifier is struggling on test data from the final 30 percent of the dataset. To get a fair reflection of the actual performance of the classifier overall, therefore, we'll want to make sure we test it on several random subsets of the data to even out the classifier's performance.

Cross-validation

The process of splitting a dataset into complementary subsets of training and test data is called cross-validation. To reduce the variability in output we've just seen, with a lower error rate on the test set compared to the training set, it's usual to run multiple rounds of cross-validation on different partitions of the data. By averaging the results of all runs we get a much more accurate picture of the model's true accuracy. This is such a common practice that clj-ml includes a function for just this purpose:

```
(defn ex-4-45 []
  (let [dataset (-> (load-data "titanic.tsv")
                    (to-weka))
        classifier (-> (cl/make-classifier :decision-tree :c45)
                       (cl/classifier-train dataset))
        evaluation (cl/classifier-evaluate classifier
                                           :cross-validation
                                           dataset 10)]
    (println (:confusion-matrix evaluation))
    (println (:summary evaluation))))
```

In the preceding code, we make use of `cl/classifier-evaluate` to run 10 cross-validations on our dataset. The result is returned as a map with useful information about the model performance—for example, a confusion matrix and a list of summary statistics—including the kappa statistic we've been tracking so far. We print out the confusion matrix and the summary string that clj-ml provides, as follows:

```
;; === Confusion Matrix ===
;;
;;    a    b    <-- classified as
;;  338  162  |    a = y
;;   99  710  |    b = n
;;
;;
;; Correctly Classified Instances      1048        80.0611 %
;; Incorrectly Classified Instances     261        19.9389 %
;; Kappa statistic                     0.5673
;; Mean absolute error                 0.284
;; Root mean squared error             0.3798
```

```
;; Relative absolute error                60.1444 %
;; Root relative squared error            78.171  %
;; Coverage of cases (0.95 level)         99.3888 %
;; Mean rel. region size (0.95 level)     94.2704 %
;; Total Number of Instances              1309
```

The kappa after 10 cross-validations is 0.56, only slightly lower than our model validated against the training data. This seems about as high as we will be able to get.

Addressing high bias

Whereas overfitting can be caused by including too many features in our model — such as when we included age as a categorical variable in our decision tree — high bias can be caused by other factors including not having enough data.

One simple way of increasing the accuracy of the model is to ensure that there are no missing values in the training set. Missing values are necessarily discarded by the model, limiting the number of training examples from which the model can learn. With a relatively small dataset such as this, each example can have a material effect on the outcome, and there are numerous age values and one fare value missing from the dataset.

We could simply substitute the mean value for a missing value in numeric columns. This is a reasonable default value and a fair tradeoff — in return for slightly lowering the variance of the field, we are potentially gaining several more training examples.

Clj-ml contains numerous filters in the `clj-ml.filters` namespace that are able to alter the dataset in some way. A useful filter is `:replace-missing-values`, which will substitute any missing numeric values with the means from the dataset. For categorical data, the modal category is substituted.

```
(defn ex-4-46 []
  (let [dataset (->> (load-data "titanic.tsv")
                     (to-weka)
                     (mlf/make-apply-filter
                       :replace-missing-values {}))
        classifier (-> (cl/make-classifier :decision-tree :c45)
                       (cl/classifier-train dataset))
        evaluation (cl/classifier-evaluate classifier
                                           :cross-validation
                                           dataset 10)]
    (println (:kappa evaluation))))

;; 0.576
```

Simply plugging the missing values in the age column has nudged our kappa statistic upwards. Our model is currently struggling to distinguish between passengers with different survival outcomes and more information may help the algorithm determine the correct class. Whilst we could return to the data and pull in all of the remaining fields, it's also possible to construct new features out of existing features.

For numeric values, another way of increasing the number of parameters is to include polynomial versions of the values as features. For example we could create features for age^2 and age^3 simply by squaring or cubing the existing age value. While these may appear to add no new information to the model, polynomials scale differently and provide alternative features for the model to learn from.

The final way we'll look at for balancing bias and variance is to combine the output from multiple models.

Ensemble learning and random forests

Ensemble learning combines the output from multiple models to obtain a better prediction than could be obtained with any of the models individually. The principle is that the combined accuracy of many weak learners is greater than any of the weak learners taken individually.

Random forests is an ensemble learning algorithm devised and trademarked by Leo Breiman and Adele Cutler. It combines multiple decision trees into one large forest learner. Each tree is trained on the data using a subset of the available features, meaning that each tree will have a slightly different view of the data and is capable of generating a different prediction from that of its peers.

Creating a Random Forest in clj-ml simply requires that we alter the arguments to `cl/make-classifier` to `:decision-tree, :random-forest`.

Bagging and boosting

Bagging and boosting are two opposing techniques for creating ensemble models. Boosting is the name for a general technique of building an ensemble by training each new model to emphasize correct the classification of training examples that previous models weren't able to correctly classify. It is a **meta-algorithm**.

One of the most popular boosting algorithms is **AdaBoost**, a portmanteau of "adaptive boosting". As long as each model performs slightly better than random guessing, the combined output can be shown to converge to a strong learner.

Bagging is a portmanteau of "bootstrap aggregating" and is the name of another meta-algorithm that is usually applied to decision tree learners but can be applied to other learners too. In cases where a single tree might overfit the training data, bagging helps reduce the variance of the combined model. It does this by sampling the training data with replacement, just as with our bootstrapped standard error at the beginning of the chapter. As a result, each model in the ensemble has a differently incomplete view of the world, making it less likely that the combined model will learn an overly specific hypothesis on the training data. Random forests is an example of a bagging algorithm.

```
(defn ex-4-47 []
  (let [dataset (->> (load-data "titanic.tsv")
                     (to-weka)
                     (mlf/make-apply-filter
                       :replace-missing-values {}))
        classifier (cl/make-classifier :decision-tree
                                       :random-forest)
        evaluation (cl/classifier-evaluate classifier
                                           :cross-validation
                                           dataset 10)]
    (println (:confusion-matrix evaluation))
    (println (:summary evaluation))))
```

With the random forests classifier, you should observe a kappa of around 0.55, slightly lower than the decision tree we have been optimizing. The random forest implementation has sacrificed some of the variance of the model.

Whilst this might seem disappointing, it is actually part of the reason for random forests' appeal. Their ability to strike a balance between bias and variance makes them flexible and general-purpose classifiers suitable for a wide variety of problems.

Saving the classifier to a file

Finally, we can write out our classifier to a file using `clj-ml.utils/serialize-to-file`:

```
(defn ex-4-48 []
  (let [dataset (->> (load-data "titanic.tsv")
                     (to-weka)
                     (mlf/make-apply-filter
                       :replace-missing-values {}))
        classifier (cl/make-classifier :decision-tree
                                       :random-forest)
        file (io/file (io/resource "classifier.bin"))]
    (clu/serialize-to-file classifier file)))
```

At some point later, we can load up our trained classifier using the `clj-ml.utils/deserialize-from-file` and immediately begin classifying new data.

Summary

In this chapter, we've learned about how to make use of categorical variables to group data into classes.

We've seen how quantify the difference between groups using the odds ratio and relative risk, and how to perform statistical significance tests on groups using the X^2 test. We've learned about how to build machine learning models suitable for the task of classification with a variety of techniques: logistic regression, naive Bayes, decision trees, and random forests, and several methods of evaluating them; the confusion matrix and the kappa statistic. We also learned about the opposing dangers of high bias and of overfitting in machine learning, and how to ensure that your model is not overfitting by making use of cross-validation. Finally, we've seen how the clj-ml library can help to prepare data and to build many different types of classifiers and save them for future use.

In the next chapter, we'll learn about how to adapt some of the techniques we've learned about so far to the task of processing very large datasets that exceed the storage and processing capabilities of any single computer—so-called **Big Data**. We'll see how one of the techniques we encountered in this chapter, gradient descent, turns out to be particularly amenable to parameter optimization on a very large scale.

5
Big Data

"More is different."

- Philip Warren Anderson

In the previous chapters, we've used regression techniques to fit models to the data. In *Chapter 3, Correlation*, for example, we built a linear model that used ordinary least squares and the normal equation to fit a straight line through the athletes' heights and log weights. In *Chapter 4, Classification*, we used Incanter's optimize namespace to minimize the logistic cost function and build a classifier of Titanic's passengers. In this chapter, we'll apply similar analysis in a way that's suitable for much larger quantities of data.

We'll be working with a relatively modest dataset of only 100,000 records. This isn't big data (at 100 MB, it will fit comfortably in the memory of one machine), but it's large enough to demonstrate the common techniques of large-scale data processing. Using Hadoop (the popular framework for distributed computation) as its case study, this chapter will focus on how to scale algorithms to very large volumes of data through parallelism. We'll cover two libraries that Clojure offers to work with Hadoop—**Tesser** and **Parkour**.

Before we get to Hadoop and distributed data processing though, we'll see how some of the same principles that enable Hadoop to be effective at a very large scale can also be applied to data processing on a single machine, by taking advantage of the parallel capacity available in all modern computers.

Downloading the code and data

This chapter makes use of data on individual income by the zip code provided by the U.S. Internal Revenue Service (IRS). The data contains selected income and tax items classified by state, zip code, and income classes.

It's 100 MB in size and can be downloaded from http://www.irs.gov/pub/irs-soi/12zpallagi.csv to the example code's data directory. Since the file contains the IRS Statistics of Income (SoI), we've renamed the file to soi.csv for the examples.

 The example code for this chapter is available from the Packt Publishing's website or https://github.com/clojuredatascience/ch5-big-data.

As usual, a script has been provided to download and rename the data for you. It can be run on the command line from within the project directory with:

```
script/download-data.sh
```

If you run this, the file will be downloaded and renamed automatically.

Inspecting the data

Once you've downloaded the data, take a look at the column headings in the first line of the file. One way to access the first line of the file is to load the file into memory, split on newline characters, and take the first result. The Clojure core library's function slurp will return the whole file as a string:

```
(defn ex-5-1 []
  (-> (slurp "data/soi.csv")
      (str/split #"\n")
      (first)))
```

The file is around 100 MB in size on disk. When loaded into memory and converted into object representations, the data will occupy more space in memory. This is particularly wasteful when we're only interested in the first row.

Fortunately, we don't have to load the whole file into memory if we take advantage of Clojure's lazy sequences. Instead of returning a string representation of the contents of the whole file, we could return a reference to the file and then step through it one line at a time:

```
(defn ex-5-2 []
  (-> (io/reader "data/soi.csv")
      (line-seq)
      (first)))
```

In the preceding code, we're using `clojure.java.io/reader` to return a reference to the file. Also, we're using the `clojure.core` function `line-seq` to return a lazy sequence of lines from the file. In this way, we can read files even larger than the available memory.

The result of the previous function is as follows:

```
"STATEFIPS,STATE,zipcode,AGI_STUB,N1,MARS1,MARS2,MARS4,PREP,N2,NUMDEP,
A00100,N00200,A00200,N00300,A00300,N00600,A00600,N00650,A00650,N00900,
A00900,SCHF,N01000,A01000,N01400,A01400,N01700,A01700,N02300,A02300,N0
2500,A02500,N03300,A03300,N00101,A00101,N04470,A04470,N18425,A18425,N1
8450,A18450,N18500,A18500,N18300,A18300,N19300,A19300,N19700,A19700,N0
4800,A04800,N07100,A07100,N07220,A07220,N07180,A07180,N07260,A07260,N5
9660,A59660,N59720,A59720,N11070,A11070,N09600,A09600,N06500,A06500,N1
0300,A10300,N11901,A11901,N11902,A11902"
```

There are 77 fields in the file, so we won't identify them all. The first four fields are:

- `STATEFIPS`: This is the Federal Information Processing System (FIPS) code.
- `STATE`: This is the two-letter code for the State.
- `zipcode`: This is the 5-digit zip code.
- `AGI_STUB`: This is the side of the adjusted gross income, binned in the following way:
    1. $1 under $25,000
    2. $25,000 under $50,000
    3. $50,000 under $75,000
    4. $75,000 under $100,000
    5. $100,000 under $200,000
    6. $200,000 or more

The other fields that we're interested in are as follows:

- `N1`: The number of returns submitted
- `MARS2`: The number of joint returns submitted
- `NUMDEP`: The number of dependents
- `N00200`: The number of returns with salaries and wages
- `N02300`: The number of returns with unemployment compensation

If you're curious, the full list of column definitions is available in the IRS data definition document at `http://www.irs.gov/pub/irs-soi/12zpdoc.doc`.

Counting the records

Our file is certainly wide, but is it tall? We'd like to determine the total number of rows in the file. Having created a lazy sequence, this is simply a matter of counting the length of the sequence:

```
(defn ex-5-3 []
  (-> (io/reader "data/soi.csv")
      (line-seq)
      (count)))
```

The preceding example returns 166,905, including the header row, so we know there are actually 166,904 rows in the file.

The count function is the simplest way to count the number of elements in a sequence. For vectors (and other types implementing the counted interface), this is also the most efficient one, since the collection already knows how many elements it contains and therefore it doesn't need to recalculate it. For a lazy sequence however, the only way to determine how many elements are contained in the sequence is to step through it from the beginning to the end.

Clojure's implementation of count is written in Java, but the Clojure equivalent would be a reduce over the sequence like this:

```
(defn ex-5-4 []
  (->> (io/reader "data/soi.csv")
       (line-seq)
       (reduce (fn [i x]
                 (inc i)) 0)))
```

The preceding function we pass to reduce accepts a counter i and the next element from the sequence x. For each x, we simply increment the counter i. The reduce function accepts an initial value of zero, which represents the concept of nothing. If there are no lines to reduce over, zero will be returned.

As of version 1.5, Clojure offers the reducers library (http://clojure.org/reducers), which provides an alternative way to perform reductions that trades memory efficiency for speed.

The reducers library

The `count` operation we implemented previously is a sequential algorithm. Each line is processed one at a time until the sequence is exhausted. But there is nothing about the operation that demands that it must be done in this way.

We could split the number of lines into two sequences (ideally of roughly equal length) and reduce over each sequence independently. When we're done, we would just add together the total number of lines from each sequence to get the total number of lines in the file:

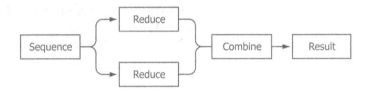

If each **Reduce** ran on its own processing unit, then the two count operations would run in parallel. All the other things being equal, the algorithm would run twice as fast. This is one of the aims of the `clojure.core.reducers` library — to bring the benefit of parallelism to algorithms implemented on a single machine by taking advantage of multiple cores.

Parallel folds with reducers

The parallel implementation of reduce implemented by the reducers library is called **fold**. To make use of a fold, we have to supply a combiner function that will take the results of our reduced sequences (the partial row counts) and return the final result. Since our row counts are numbers, the combiner function is simply +.

 Reducers are a part of Clojure's standard library, they do not need to be added as an external dependency.

The adjusted example, using `clojure.core.reducers` as r, looks like this:

```
(defn ex-5-5 []
  (->> (io/reader "data/soi.csv")
       (line-seq)
       (r/fold + (fn [i x]
                   (inc i)))))
```

The combiner function, +, has been included as the first argument to fold and our unchanged reduce function is supplied as the second argument. We no longer need to pass the initial value of zero— fold will get the initial value by calling the combiner function with no arguments. Our preceding example works because +, called with no arguments, already returns zero:

```
(defn ex-5-6 []
  (+))


;; 0
```

To participate in folding then, it's important that the combiner function have two implementations: one with zero arguments that returns the identity value and another with two arguments that *combines* the arguments. Different folds will, of course, require different combiner functions and identity values. For example, the identity value for multiplication is 1.

We can visualize the process of seeding the computation with an identity value, iteratively reducing over the sequence of xs and combining the reductions into an output value as a tree:

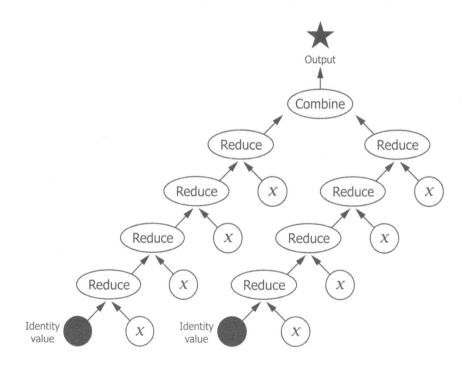

There may be more than two reductions to combine, of course. The default implementation of `fold` will split the input collection into chunks of 512 elements. Our 166,000-element sequence will therefore generate 325 reductions to be combined. We're going to run out of page real estate quite quickly with a tree representation diagram, so let's visualize the process more schematically instead—as a two-step reduce and combine process.

The first step performs a parallel reduce across all the chunks in the collection. The second step performs a serial reduce over the intermediate results to arrive at the final result:

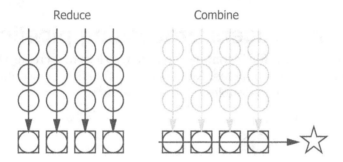

The preceding representation shows reduce over several sequences of `xs`, represented here as circles, into a series of outputs, represented here as squares. The squares are combined serially to produce the final result, represented by a star.

Loading large files with iota

Calling `fold` on a lazy sequence requires Clojure to realize the sequence into memory and then chunk the sequence into groups for parallel execution. For situations where the calculation performed on each row is small, the overhead involved in coordination outweighs the benefit of parallelism. We can improve the situation slightly by using a library called `iota` (`https://github.com/thebusby/iota`).

 The `iota` library loads files directly into the data structures suitable for folding over with reducers that can handle files larger than available memory by making use of memory-mapped files.

With `iota` in the place of our `line-seq` function, our line count simply becomes:

```
(defn ex-5-7 []
  (->> (iota/seq "data/soi.csv")
       (r/fold + (fn [i x]
                   (inc i)))))
```

So far, we've just been working with the sequences of unformatted lines, but if we're going to do anything more than counting the rows, we'll want to parse them into a more useful data structure. This is another area in which Clojure's reducers can help make our code more efficient.

Creating a reducers processing pipeline

We already know that the file is comma-separated, so let's first create a function to turn each row into a vector of fields. All fields except the first two contain numeric data, so let's parse them into doubles while we're at it:

```
(defn parse-double [x]
  (Double/parseDouble x))

(defn parse-line [line]
  (let [[text-fields double-fields] (->> (str/split line #",")
                                         (split-at 2))]
    (concat text-fields
            (map parse-double double-fields))))
```

We're using the reducers version of `map` to apply our `parse-line` function to each of the lines from the file in turn:

```
(defn ex-5-8 []
  (->> (iota/seq "data/soi.csv")
       (r/drop 1)
       (r/map parse-line)
       (r/take 1)
       (into [])))

;; [("01" "AL" 0.0 1.0 889920.0 490850.0 ...)]
```

The final `into` function call converts the reducers' internal representation (a reducible collection) into a Clojure vector. The previous example should return a sequence of 77 fields, representing the first row of the file after the header.

We're just dropping the column names at the moment, but it would be great if we could make use of these to return a map representation of each record, associating the column name with the field value. The keys of the map would be the column headings and the values would be the parsed fields. The `clojure.core` function `zipmap` will create a map out of two sequences—one for the keys and one for the values:

```
(defn parse-columns [line]
  (->> (str/split line #",")
       (map keyword)))

(defn ex-5-9 []
  (let [data (iota/seq "data/soi.csv")
        column-names (parse-columns (first data))]
    (->> (r/drop 1 data)
         (r/map parse-line)
         (r/map (fn [fields]
                  (zipmap column-names fields)))
         (r/take 1)
         (into []))))
```

This function returns a map representation of each row, a much more user-friendly data structure:

```
[{:N2 1505430.0, :A19300 181519.0, :MARS4 256900.0 ...}]
```

A great thing about Clojure's reducers is that in the preceding computation, calls to `r/map`, `r/drop` and `r/take` are composed into a reduction that will be performed in a single pass over the data. This becomes particularly valuable as the number of operations increases.

Let's assume that we'd like to filter out zero ZIP codes. We could extend the reducers pipeline like this:

```
(defn ex-5-10 []
  (let [data (iota/seq "data/soi.csv")
        column-names (parse-columns (first data))]
    (->> (r/drop 1 data)
         (r/map parse-line)
         (r/map (fn [fields]
                  (zipmap column-names fields)))
         (r/remove (fn [record]
                     (zero? (:zipcode record))))
         (r/take 1)
         (into []))))
```

The `r/remove` step is now also being run together with the `r/map`, `r/drop` and `r/take` calls. As the size of the data increases, it becomes increasingly important to avoid making multiple iterations over the data unnecessarily. Using Clojure's reducers ensures that our calculations are compiled into a single pass.

Curried reductions with reducers

To make the process clearer, we can create a **curried** version of each of our previous steps. To parse the lines, create a record from the fields and filter zero ZIP codes. The curried version of the function is a reduction waiting for a collection:

```
(def line-formatter
  (r/map parse-line))

(defn record-formatter [column-names]
  (r/map (fn [fields]
           (zipmap column-names fields))))

(def remove-zero-zip
  (r/remove (fn [record]
              (zero? (:zipcode record)))))
```

In each case, we're calling one of reducers' functions, but without providing a collection. The response is a curried version of the function that can be applied to the collection at a later time. The curried functions can be composed together into a single `parse-file` function using `comp`:

```
(defn load-data [file]
  (let [data (iota/seq file)
        col-names (parse-columns (first data))
        parse-file (comp remove-zero-zip
                         (record-formatter col-names)
                         line-formatter)]
    (parse-file (rest data))))
```

It's only when the `parse-file` function is called with a sequence that the pipeline is actually executed.

Statistical folds with reducers

With the data parsed, it's time to perform some descriptive statistics. Let's assume that we'd like to know the mean *number of returns* (column N1) submitted to the IRS by ZIP code. One way of doing this—the way we've done several times throughout the book—is by adding up the values and dividing it by the count. Our first attempt might look like this:

```
(defn ex-5-11 []
  (let [data (load-data "data/soi.csv")
        xs (into [] (r/map :N1 data))]
   (/ (reduce + xs)
      (count xs))))
```

```
;; 853.37
```

While this works, it's comparatively slow. We iterate over the data once to create xs, a second time to calculate the sum, and a third time to calculate the count. The bigger our dataset gets, the larger the time penalty we'll pay. Ideally, we would be able to calculate the mean value in a single pass over the data, just like our parse-file function previously. It would be even better if we can perform it in parallel too.

Associativity

Before we proceed, it's useful to take a moment to reflect on why the following code wouldn't do what we want:

```
(defn mean
  ([] 0)
  ([x y] (/ (+ x y) 2)))
```

Our mean function is a function of two arities. Without arguments, it returns zero, the identity for the mean computation. With two arguments, it returns their mean:

```
(defn ex-5-12 []
  (->> (load-data "data/soi.csv")
       (r/map :N1)
       (r/fold mean)))
```

```
;; 930.54
```

The preceding example folds over the N1 data with our mean function and produces a different result from the one we obtained previously. If we could expand out the computation for the first three xs, we might see something like the following code:

```
(mean (mean (mean 0 a) b) c)
```

This is a bad idea, because the mean function is not associative. For an associative function, the following holds true:

$$f\big(f(a,b),c\big) = f\big(a, f(b,c)\big)$$

Addition is associative, but multiplication and division are not. So the mean function is not associative either. Contrast the mean function with the following simple addition:

```
(+ 1 (+ 2 3))
```

This yields an identical result to:

```
(+ (+ 1 2) 3)
```

It doesn't matter how the arguments to + are partitioned. Associativity is an important property of functions used to reduce over a set of data because, by definition, the results of a previous calculation are treated as inputs to the next.

The easiest way of converting the mean function into an associative function is to calculate the sum and the count separately. Since the sum and the count are associative, they can be calculated in parallel over the data. The mean function can be calculated simply by dividing one by the other.

Calculating the mean using fold

We'll create a fold using two custom functions, mean-combiner and mean-reducer. This requires defining three entities:

- The identity value for the fold
- The reduce function
- The combine function

We discovered the benefits of associativity in the previous section, and so we'll want to update our intermediate mean by using associative operations only and calculating the sum and count separately. One way of representing the two values is a map of two keys, :count and :sum. The value that represents zero for our mean would be a sum of zero and a count of zero, or a map such as the following: {:count 0 :sum 0}.

The combine function, mean-combiner, provides the seed value when it's called without arguments. The two-argument combiner needs to add together the :count and the :sum for each of the two arguments. We can achieve this by merging the maps with +:

```
(defn mean-combiner
  ([] {:count 0 :sum 0})
  ([a b] (merge-with + a b)))
```

The mean-reducer function needs to accept an accumulated value (either an identity value or the results of a previous reduction) and incorporate the new x. We do this simply by incrementing the :count and adding x to the accumulated :sum:

```
(defn mean-reducer [acc x]
  (-> acc
      (update-in [:count] inc)
      (update-in [:sum] + x)))
```

The preceding two functions are enough to completely specify our mean fold:

```
(defn ex-5-13 []
  (->> (load-data "data/soi.csv")
       (r/map :N1)
       (r/fold mean-combiner
               mean-reducer)))

;; {:count 166598, :sum 1.4216975E8}
```

The result gives us all we need to calculate the mean of N1, which is calculated in only one pass over the data. The final step of the calculation can be performed with the following mean-post-combiner function:

```
(defn mean-post-combiner [{:keys [count sum]}]
  (if (zero? count) 0 (/ sum count)))

(defn ex-5-14 []
  (->> (load-data "data/soi.csv")
       (r/map :N1)
       (r/fold mean-combiner
               mean-reducer)
       (mean-post-combiner)))

;; 853.37
```

Happily, the values agree with the mean we calculated previously.

Calculating the variance using fold

Next, we'd like to calculate the variance of the N1 values. Remember that the variance is the mean squared difference from the mean:

$$s^2 = \frac{1}{n} \sum_{i=1}^{n} \left(x_i - \bar{x} \right)^2$$

To implement this as a fold, we might write something as follows:

```
(defn ex-5-15 []
   (let [data (->> (load-data "data/soi.csv")
                   (r/map :N1))
         mean-x (->> data
                     (r/fold mean-combiner
                             mean-reducer)
                     (mean-post-combine))
         sq-diff (fn [x] (i/pow (- x mean-x) 2))]
      (->> data
           (r/map sq-diff)
           (r/fold mean-combiner
                   mean-reducer)
           (mean-post-combine)))))
```

```
;; 3144836.86
```

First, we calculate the mean value of the series using the fold we constructed just now. Then, we define a function of x and sq-diff, which calculates the squared difference of x from the mean value. We map it over the squared differences and call our mean fold a second time to arrive at the final variance result.

Thus, we make two complete passes over the data, firstly to calculate the mean, and secondly to calculate the difference of each x from the mean value. It might seem that calculating the variance is necessarily a sequential algorithm: it may not seem possible to reduce the number of steps further and calculate the variance in only a single fold over the data.

In fact, it is possible to express the variance calculation as a single fold. To do so, we need to keep track of three things: the count, the (current) mean, and the sum of squared differences:

```
(defn variance-combiner
  ([] {:count 0 :mean 0 :sum-of-squares 0})
  ([a b]
   (let [count (+ (:count a) (:count b))]
     {:count count
      :mean (/ (+ (* (:count a) (:mean a))
                  (* (:count b) (:mean b)))
               count)
      :sum-of-squares (+ (:sum-of-squares a)
                         (:sum-of-squares b)
                         (/ (* (- (:mean b)
                                  (:mean a))
                               (- (:mean b)
                                  (:mean a))
                               (:count a)
                               (:count b))
                            count))})))
```

Our combiner function is shown in the preceding code. The identity value is a map with all three values set to zero. The zero-arity combiner returns this value.

The two-arity combiner needs to combine the counts, means, and sums-of-squares for both of the supplied values. Combining the counts is easy — we simply add them together. The means is only marginally trickier: we need to calculate the weighted mean of the two means. If one mean is based on fewer records, then it should count for less in the combined mean:

$$\mu_{a,b} = \frac{\mu_a n_a + \mu_b n_b}{n_a + n_b}$$

Combining the sums of squares is the most complicated calculation. While adding the sums of squares, we also need to add a factor to account for the fact that the sum of squares from a and b were likely calculated from differing means:

```
(defn variance-reducer [{:keys [count mean sum-of-squares]} x]
  (let [count' (inc count)
        mean'  (+ mean (/ (- x mean) count'))]
    {:count count'
     :mean mean'
     :sum-of-squares (+ sum-of-squares
                        (* (- x mean') (- x mean)))}))
```

The reducer is much simpler and contains the explanation on how the variance fold is able to calculate the variance in one pass over the data. For each new record, the :mean value is recalculated from the previous mean and current count. We then add to the sum of squares the product of the difference between the means before and after taking account of this new record.

The final result is a map containing the count, mean and total sum-of-squares. Since the variance is just the sum-of-squares divided by the count, our variance-post-combiner function is a relatively simple one:

```
(defn variance-post-combiner [{:keys [count mean sum-of-squares]}]
  (if (zero? count) 0 (/ sum-of-squares count)))
```

Putting the three functions together yields the following:

```
(defn ex-5-16 []
  (->> (load-data "data/soi.csv")
       (r/map :N1)
       (r/fold variance-combiner
               variance-reducer)
       (variance-post-combiner)))


;; 3144836.86
```

Since the standard deviation is simply the square root of the variance, we only need a slightly modified variance-post-combiner function to calculate it as well.

Mathematical folds with Tesser

We should now understand how to use folds to calculate parallel implementations of simple algorithms. Hopefully, we should also have some appreciation for the ingenuity required to find efficient solutions that will perform the minimum number of iterations over the data.

Fortunately, the Clojure library Tesser (https://github.com/aphyr/tesser) includes implementations for common mathematical folds, including the mean, standard deviation, and covariance. To see how to use Tesser, let's consider the covariance of two fields from the IRS dataset: the salaries and wages, A00200, the unemployment compensation, A02300.

Calculating covariance with Tesser

We encountered covariance in *Chapter 3, Correlation,* as a measure of how two sequences of data vary together. The formula is reproduced as follows:

$$\mathrm{cov}(X,Y) = \frac{1}{n}\sum_{i=1}^{n}(x_i - \bar{x})(y_i - \bar{y})$$

A covariance fold is included in `tesser.math`. In the following code, we'll include `tesser.math` as m and `tesser.core` as t:

```
(defn ex-5-17 []
  (let [data (into [] (load-data "data/soi.csv"))]
    (->> (m/covariance :A02300 :A00200)
         (t/tesser (t/chunk 512 data )))))

;; 3.496E7
```

The `m/covariance` function expects to receive two arguments: a function to return the x value and another to return the y value. Since keywords act as functions to extract their corresponding values from a map, we simply pass the keywords as arguments.

Tesser works in a similar way to Clojure's reducers, but with some minor differences. Clojure's `fold` takes care of splitting our data into subsequences for parallel execution. With Tesser however, we must divide our data into chunks explicitly. Since this is something we're going to do repeatedly, let's create a little helper function called `chunks`:

```
(defn chunks [coll]
  (->> (into [] coll)
       (t/chunk 1024)))
```

For the most of the rest of this chapter, we'll be using the `chunks` function to split our input data into groups of 1024 records.

Commutativity

Another difference between Clojure's reducers and Tesser's folds is that Tesser doesn't guarantee that the input order will be preserved. Along with being associative, as we discussed previously, Tesser's functions must be commutative. A commutative function is the one whose result is the same if its arguments are provided in a different order:

$$f(a,b) = f(b,a)$$

Addition and multiplication are commutative, but subtraction and division are not. Commutativity is a useful property of functions intended for distributed data processing, because it lowers the amount of coordination required between subtasks. When Tesser executes a combine function, it's free to do so on whichever reducer functions return their values first. If the order doesn't matter, it doesn't need to wait for the first to complete.

Let's rewrite our `load-data` function into a `prepare-data` function that will return a commutative Tesser fold. It performs the same steps (parsing a line of the text file, formatting the record as a map and removing zero ZIP codes) that our previous reducers-based function did, but it no longer assumes that the column headers will be the first row in the file—*first* is a concept that explicitly requires ordered data:

```
(def column-names
  [:STATEFIPS :STATE :zipcode :AGI_STUB :N1 :MARS1 :MARS2 ...])

(defn prepare-data []
  (->> (t/remove #(.startsWith % "STATEFIPS"))
       (t/map parse-line)
       (t/map (partial format-record column-names))
       (t/remove #(zero? (:zipcode %)))))
```

Now that all the preparation is being done in Tesser, we can pass the result of `iota/seq` directly as input. This will be particularly useful when we come to run our code distributed on Hadoop later in the chapter:

```
(defn ex-5-18 []
  (let [data (iota/seq "data/soi.csv")]
    (->> (prepare-data)
         (m/covariance :A02300 :A00200)
         (t/tesser (chunks data)))))

;; 3.496E7
```

In *Chapter 3, Correlation*, we saw how in the case of simple linear regression with one feature and one response variable, the correlation coefficient is the covariance over the product of standard deviations:

$$r = \frac{\text{cov}(X,Y)}{\sigma_X \sigma_Y}$$

Tesser includes functions to calculate the correlation of a pair of attributes as a fold too:

```
(defn ex-5-19 []
  (let [data (iota/seq "data/soi.csv")]
    (->> (prepare-data)
         (m/correlation :A02300 :A00200)
         (t/tesser (chunks data)))))

;; 0.353
```

There's a modest, positive correlation between these two variables. Let's build a linear model that predicts the value of unemployment compensation, A02300, using salaries and wages, A00200.

Simple linear regression with Tesser

Tesser doesn't currently provide a linear regression fold, but it does give us the tools we need to implement one. We saw in *Chapter 3, Correlation*, how the coefficients for a simple linear regression model, the slope and the intercept, can be calculated as a simple function of the variance, covariance, and means of the two inputs:

$$r = \frac{\text{cov}(X,Y)}{\text{var}(X)}$$

$$a = \overline{y} - b\overline{x}$$

The slope b is the covariance divided by the variance in X. The intercept is the value that ensures the regression line passes through the means of both the series. Ideally, therefore, we'd be able to calculate each of these four variables in a single fold over the data. Tesser provides two fold combinators, t/fuse and t/facet, to build more sophisticated folds out of more basic folds.

In cases where we have one input record and multiple calculations to be run in parallel, we should use t/fuse. For example, in the following example, we're fusing the mean and the standard deviation folds into a single fold that will calculate both values at once:

```
(defn ex-5-20 []
  (let [data (iota/seq "data/soi.csv")]
    (->> (prepare-data)
         (t/map :A00200)
         (t/fuse {:A00200-mean (m/mean)
                  :A00200-sd   (m/standard-deviation)})
         (t/tesser (chunks data)))))

;; {:A00200-sd 89965.99846545042, :A00200-mean 37290.58880658831}
```

Here, we have the same calculation to run on all the fields in the map; therefore, we should use t/facet:

```
(defn ex-5-21 []
  (let [data (iota/seq "data/soi.csv")]
    (->> (prepare-data)
         (t/map #(select-keys % [:A00200 :A02300]))
         (t/facet)
         (m/mean)
         (t/tesser (chunks data)))))

;; {:A02300 419.67862159209596, :A00200 37290.58880658831}
```

In the preceding code, we selected only two values from the record (A00200 and A02300) and calculated the mean value for both of them simultaneously. Returning to the challenge of performing simple linear regression—we have four numbers to calculate, so let's fuse them together:

```
(defn calculate-coefficients [{:keys [covariance variance-x
                                      mean-x mean-y]}]
  (let [slope      (/ covariance variance-x)
        intercept (- mean-y (* mean-x slope))]
    [intercept slope]))

(defn ex-5-22 []
  (let [data (iota/seq "data/soi.csv")
        fx :A00200
        fy :A02300]
    (->> (prepare-data)
         (t/fuse {:covariance (m/covariance fx fy)
                  :variance-x (m/variance (t/map fx))
                  :mean-x (m/mean (t/map fx))
```

```
                :mean-y (m/mean (t/map fx))})
        (t/post-combine calculate-coefficients)
        (t/tesser (chunks data)))))
```

```
;; [37129.529236553506 0.0043190406799462925]
```

fuse very succinctly binds together the calculations we want to perform. In addition, it allows us to specify a post-combine step to be included as part of the fuse. Rather than handing the result off to another function to finalize the output, we can specify it directly as an integral part of the fold. The post-combine step receives the four results and calculates the slope and intercept from them, returning the two coefficients as a vector.

Calculating a correlation matrix

We've only compared two features to see how they are correlated, but Tesser makes it very simple to look at the inter-correlation of a large number of target features. We supply the target features as a map of the feature name to some function of the input record that returns the desired feature. In *Chapter 3, Correlation*, for example, we would have taken the logarithm of the height. Here, we will simply extract each of the features as it is and provide human-readable names for each of them:

```
(defn ex-5-23 []
  (let [data (iota/seq "data/soi.csv")
        attributes {:unemployment-compensation :A02300
                    :salary-amount             :A00200
                    :gross-income              :AGI_STUB
                    :joint-submissions         :MARS2
                    :dependents                :NUMDEP}]
    (->> (prepare-data)
         (m/correlation-matrix attributes)
         (t/tesser (chunks data)))))
```

Tesser will calculate the correlation between each pair of features and return the results in a map. The map is keyed by tuples (vectors of two elements) containing the names of each pair of features, and the associated value is the correlation between them.

If you run the preceding example now, you'll find that there are a high correlations between some of the variables. For example, the correlation between :dependents and :unemployment-compensation is 0.821. Let's build a linear regression model that uses all of these variables as inputs.

Multiple regression with gradient descent

When we ran multiple linear regression in *Chapter 3, Correlation*, we used the normal equation and matrices to quickly arrive at the coefficients for a multiple linear regression model. The normal equation is repeated as follows:

$$\beta = \left(X^T X\right)^{-1} X^T y$$

The normal equation uses matrix algebra to very quickly and efficiently arrive at the least squares estimates. Where all data fits in memory, this is a very convenient and concise equation. Where the data exceeds the memory available to a single machine however, the calculation becomes unwieldy. The reason for this is matrix inversion.

The calculation of $\left(X^T X\right)^{-1}$ is not something that can be accomplished on a fold over the data — each cell in the output matrix depends on many others in the input matrix. These complex relationships require that the matrix be processed in a nonsequential way.

An alternative approach to solve linear regression problems, and many other related machine learning problems, is a technique called **gradient descent**. Gradient descent reframes the problem as the solution to an iterative algorithm — one that does not calculate the answer in one very computationally intensive step, but rather converges towards the correct answer over a series of much smaller steps.

We encountered gradient descent in the previous chapter, when we used Incanter's `minimize` function to calculate the parameters that produced the lowest cost for our logistic regression classifier. As the volume of data increases, Incanter no longer remains a viable solution to run gradient descent. In the next section, we'll see how we can run gradient descent for ourselves using Tesser.

The gradient descent update rule

Gradient descent works by the iterative application of a function that moves the parameters in the direction of their optimum values. To apply this function, we need to know the gradient of the cost function with the current parameters.

Calculating the formula for the gradient involves calculus that's beyond the scope of this book. Fortunately, the resulting formula isn't terribly difficult to interpret:

$$\frac{\delta}{\delta\beta_j} J(\beta) = \left(\hat{y} - y\right) x_j$$

$\dfrac{\delta}{\delta\beta_j}$ is the partial derivative, or the gradient, of our cost function $J(\beta)$ for the parameter at index j. Therefore, we can see that the gradient of the cost function with respect to the parameter at index j is equal to the difference between our prediction and the true value of y multiplied by the value of x at index j.

Since we're seeking to descend the gradient, we want to subtract some proportion of the gradient from the current parameter values. Thus, at each step of gradient descent, we perform the following update:

$$\beta_j := \beta_j - \alpha\left(\hat{y} - y\right)x_j$$

Here, $:=$ is the assigment operator and α is a factor called the **learning rate**. The learning rate controls how large an adjustment we wish make to the parameters at each iteration as a fraction of the gradient. If our prediction $\hat{y}$ nearly matches the actual value of y, then there would be little need to change the parameters. In contrast, a larger error will result in a larger adjustment to the parameters. This rule is called the **Widrow-Hoff learning rule** or the **Delta rule**.

The gradient descent learning rate

As we've seen, gradient descent is an iterative algorithm. The learning rate, usually represented by α, dictates the speed at which the gradient descent converges to the final answer. If the learning rate is too small, convergence will happen very slowly. If it is too large, gradient descent will not find values close to the optimum and may even diverge from the correct answer:

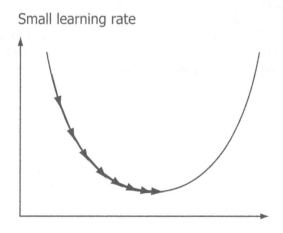

Small learning rate

In the preceding chart, a small learning rate leads to a show convergence over many iterations of the algorithm. While the algorithm does reach the minimum, it does so over many more steps than is ideal and, therefore, may take considerable time. By contrast, in following diagram, we can see the effect of a learning rate that is too large. The parameter estimates are changed so significantly between iterations that they actually overshoot the optimum values and diverge from the minimum value:

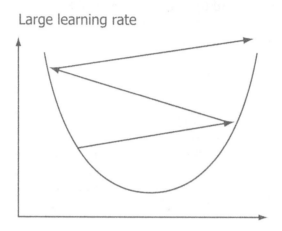

The gradient descent algorithm requires us to iterate repeatedly over our dataset. With the correct version of alpha, each iteration should successively yield better approximations of the ideal parameters. We can choose to terminate the algorithm when either the change between iterations is very small or after a predetermined number of iterations.

Feature scaling

As more features are added to the linear model, it is important to scale features appropriately. Gradient descent will not perform very well if the features have radically different scales, since it won't be possible to pick a learning rate to suit them all.

A simple scaling we can perform is to subtract the mean value from each of the values and divide it by the standard-deviation. This will tend to produce values with zero mean that generally vary between -3 and 3:

```
(defn feature-scales [features]
  (->> (prepare-data)
       (t/map #(select-keys % features))
       (t/facet)
       (t/fuse {:mean (m/mean)
                :sd   (m/standard-deviation)}))))
```

The feature-factors function in the preceding code uses t/facet to calculate the mean value and standard deviation of all the input features:

```
(defn ex-5-24 []
  (let [data (iota/seq "data/soi.csv")
        features [:A02300 :A00200 :AGI_STUB :NUMDEP :MARS2]]
    (->> (feature-scales features)
         (t/tesser (chunks data)))))

;; {:MARS2 {:sd 533.4496892658647, :mean 317.0412009748016}...}
```

If you run the preceding example, you'll see the different means and standard deviations returned by the feature-scales function. Since our feature scales and input records are represented as maps, we can perform the scale across all the features at once using Clojure's merge-with function:

```
(defn scale-features [factors]
  (let [f (fn [x {:keys [mean sd]}]
            (/ (- x mean) sd))]
    (fn [x]
      (merge-with f x factors))))
```

Likewise, we can perform the all-important reversal with unscale-features:

```
(defn unscale-features [factors]
  (let [f (fn [x {:keys [mean sd]}]
            (+ (* x sd) mean))]
    (fn [x]
      (merge-with f x factors))))
```

Let's scale our features and take a look at the very first feature. Tesser won't allow us to execute a fold without a reduce, so we'll temporarily revert to using Clojure's reducers:

```
(defn ex-5-25 []
  (let [data     (iota/seq "data/soi.csv")
        features [:A02300 :A00200 :AGI_STUB :NUMDEP :MARS2]
        factors (->> (feature-scales features)
                     (t/tesser (chunks data)))]
    (->> (load-data "data/soi.csv")
         (r/map #(select-keys % features ))
         (r/map (scale-features factors))
         (into [])
         (first))))

;; {:MARS2 -0.14837567114357617, :NUMDEP 0.30617757526890155,
;;  :AGI_STUB -0.714280814223704, :A00200 -0.5894942801950217,
;;  :A02300 0.031741856083514465}
```

This simple step will help gradient descent perform optimally on our data.

Feature extraction

Although we've used maps to represent our input data in this chapter, it's going to be more convenient when running gradient descent to represent our features as a matrix. Let's write a function to transform our input data into a map of xs and y. The y axis will be a scalar response value and xs will be a matrix of scaled feature values.

As in the previous chapters, we're adding a bias term to the returned matrix of features:

```
(defn feature-matrix [record features]
  (let [xs (map #(% record) features)]
    (i/matrix (cons 1 xs))))

(defn extract-features [fy features]
  (fn [record]
    {:y  (fy record)
     :xs (feature-matrix record features)}))
```

Our `feature-matrix` function simply accepts an input of a record and the features to convert into a matrix. We call this from within `extract-features`, which returns a function that we can call on each input record:

```
(defn ex-5-26 []
  (let [data     (iota/seq "data/soi.csv")
        features [:A02300 :A00200 :AGI_STUB :NUMDEP :MARS2]
        factors (->> (feature-scales features)
                     (t/tesser (chunks data)))]
    (->> (load-data "data/soi.csv")
         (r/map (scale-features factors))
         (r/map (extract-features :A02300 features))
         (into [])
         (first))))

;; {:y 433.0, :xs  A 5x1 matrix
;;  -------------
;;   1.00e+00
;;  -5.89e-01
;;  -7.14e-01
;;   3.06e-01
;;  -1.48e-01
;; }
```

The preceding example shows the data converted into a format suitable to perform gradient descent: a map containing the y response variable and a matrix of values, including the bias term.

Creating a custom Tesser fold

Each iteration of gradient descent adjusts the coefficients by an amount determined by the cost function. The cost function is calculated by summing over the errors for each parameter in the dataset, so it will be useful to have a fold that sums the values of the matrices element-wise.

Whereas Clojure represents a fold with a reducer, a combiner, and an identity value obtained from the combiner, Tesser folds are expressed as six collaborative functions. The implementation of Tesser's m/mean fold is as follows:

```
{:reducer-identity  (constantly [0 0])
 :reducer           (fn reducer [[s c] x]
                      [(+ s x) (inc c)])
 :post-reducer      identity
 :combiner-identity (constantly [0 0])
 :combiner          (fn combiner [x y] (map + x y))
 :post-combiner     (fn post-combiner [x]
                      (double (/ (first x)
                        (max 1 (last x)))))}
```

Tesser chooses to represent the reducer identity separately from the combiner function, and includes three other functions as well; the combiner-identity, post-reducer, and post-combiner functions. Tesser's mean fold represents the pair of numbers (the count and the accumulated sum) as a vector of two numbers but, in other respects, it's similar to our own.

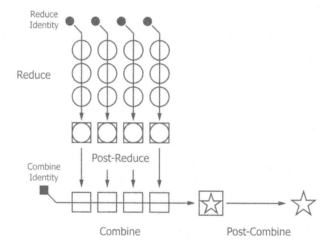

We've already seen how to make use of a post-combiner function with our mean-post-combiner and variance-post-combiner functions earlier in the chapter.

Creating a matrix-sum fold

To create a custom matrix-sum fold, we'll need an identity value. We encountered the identity matrix in *Chapter 3, Correlation*, but this is the identity for matrix multiplication not addition. If the identity value for + is zero (because adding zero to a number doesn't change it), it follows that the identity matrix for matrix addition is simply a matrix of zeros.

We have to make sure that the matrix is the same size as the matrices we want to add. So, let's parameterize our `matrix-sum` fold with the number rows and columns for the matrix. We can't know in advance how large this needs to be, because the identity function is called before anything else in the fold:

```
(defn matrix-sum [nrows ncols]
  (let [zeros-matrix (i/matrix 0 nrows ncols)]
    {:reducer-identity (constantly zeros-matrix)
     :reducer i/plus
     :combiner-identity (constantly zeros-matrix)
     :combiner i/plus}))
```

The preceding example is the completed `matrix-sum` fold definition. We don't provide the `post-combiner` and `post-reducer` functions; since, if omitted, these are assumed to be the identity function, which is what we want. We can use our new fold to calculate a sum of all the features in our input like this:

```
(defn ex-5-27 []
  (let [columns [:A02300 :A00200 :AGI_STUB :NUMDEP :MARS2]
        data    (iota/seq "data/soi.csv")]
    (->> (prepare-data)
         (t/map (extract-features :A02300 columns))
         (t/map :xs)
         (t/fold (matrix-sum (inc (count columns)) 1))
         (t/tesser (chunks data)))))

;; A 6x1 matrix
;; -------------
;; 1.67e+05
;; 6.99e+07
;; 6.21e+09
;; ...
;; 5.83e+05
;; 9.69e+07
;; 5.28e+07
```

Calculating the sum of a matrix gets us closer to being able to perform gradient descent. Let's use our new fold to calculate the total model error, given some initial coefficients.

Calculating the total model error

Let's take a look again at the delta rule for gradient descent:

$$\beta_j := \beta_j - \alpha \frac{1}{m} \sum_{i=1}^{m} (\hat{y} - y) x$$

For each parameter j, we adjust the parameter by some proportion of the overall prediction error, $\hat{y}$ - y, multiplied by the feature. Larger features, therefore, get a larger share of the cost than smaller features and are adjusted by a correspondingly larger amount. To implement this in the code, we need to calculate:

$$\sum_{i=1}^{m} (\hat{y} - y) x$$

This is the sum of the prediction error multiplied by the feature across all the input records. As we did earlier, our predicted value of y will be calculated using the following formula for each input record x:

$$\hat{y} = \beta^T x$$

The coefficients β will be the same across all our input records, so let's create a `calculate-error` function. Given the transposed coefficients β^T, we return a function that will calculate $(\hat{y} - y) x$. Since x is a matrix and $\hat{y}$ - y is a scalar, the result will be a matrix:

```
(defn calculate-error [coefs-t]
  (fn [{:keys [y xs]}]
    (let [y-hat (first (i/mmult coefs-t xs))
          error (- y-hat y)]
      (i/mult xs error))))
```

To calculate the sum of the error for the entire dataset, we can simply chain our previously defined `matrix-sum` function after the `calculate-error` step:

```
(defn ex-5-28 []
  (let [columns [:A02300 :A00200 :AGI_STUB :NUMDEP :MARS2]
        fcount  (inc (count columns))
        coefs   (vec (replicate fcount 0))
        data    (iota/seq "data/soi.csv")]
    (->> (prepare-data)
```

```
        (t/map (extract-features :A02300 columns))
        (t/map (calculate-error (i/trans coefs)))
        (t/fold (matrix-sum fcount 1))
        (t/tesser (chunks data)))))

;; A 6x1 matrix
;; -------------
;; -6.99e+07
;; -2.30e+11
;; -8.43e+12
;; ...
;; -1.59e+08
;; -2.37e+11
;; -8.10e+10
```

Notice how the gradient is negative for all the features. This means that in order to descend the gradient and produce better estimates of the model coefficients, parameters must be increased.

Creating a matrix-mean fold

The update rule defined in the previous code actually calls for the mean of the cost to be assigned to each of the features. This means that we need both `sum` and `count` to be calculated. We don't want to perform two separate passes over the data. So, as we did previously, we `fuse` the two folds into one:

```
(defn ex-5-29 []
  (let [columns [:A02300 :A00200 :AGI_STUB :NUMDEP :MARS2]
        fcount  (inc (count columns))
        coefs   (vec (replicate fcount 0))
        data    (iota/seq "data/soi.csv")]
    (->> (prepare-data)
         (t/map (extract-features :A02300 columns))
         (t/map (calculate-error (i/trans coefs)))
         (t/fuse {:sum   (t/fold (matrix-sum fcount 1))
                  :count (t/count)})
         (t/post-combine (fn [{:keys [sum count]}]
                           (i/div sum count)))
         (t/tesser (chunks data)))))
```

The `fuse` function will return a map of `:sum` and `:count`, so we'll call `post-combine` on the result. The `post-combine` function specifies a function to be run at the end of our fold which simply divides the sum by the count.

Alternatively, we could create another custom fold to return the mean instead of the sum of a sequence of matrices. It has a lot in common with the `matrix-sum` fold defined previously but, like the `mean` fold we calculated earlier in the chapter, we will also keep track of the count of records processed:

```
(defn matrix-mean [nrows ncols]
  (let [zeros-matrix (i/matrix 0 nrows ncols)]
    {:reducer-identity  (constantly [zeros-matrix 0])
     :reducer           (fn [[sum counter] x]
                          [(i/plus sum x) (inc counter)])
     :combiner-identity (constantly [zeros-matrix 0])
     :combiner          (fn [[sum-a count-a] [sum-b count-b]]
                          [(i/plus sum-a sum-b)
                           (+ count-a count-b)])
     :post-combiner     (fn [[sum count]]
                          (i/div sum count))}))
```

The reducer identity is a vector containing `[zeros-matrix 0]`. Each reduction adds to the matrix total and increments the counter by one. Each combine step sums the two matrices—and both the counts—to yield a total sum and count over all the partitions. Finally, in the `post-combiner` step, the mean is calculated as the ratio of sum and count.

Although the code for the custom fold is more lengthy than our fused sum and count solution, we now have a general way of computing the means of matrices. It leads to more concise and readable examples and we can use it in our error-calculating code like this:

```
(defn ex-5-30 []
  (let [features [:A02300 :A00200 :AGI_STUB :NUMDEP :MARS2]
        fcount   (inc (count features))
        coefs    (vec (replicate fcount 0))
        data     (iota/seq "data/soi.csv")]
    (->> (prepare-data)
         (t/map (extract-features :A02300 features))
         (t/map (calculate-error (i/trans coefs)))
         (t/fold (matrix-mean fcount 1))
         (t/tesser (chunks data)))))

;;   A 5x1 matrix
;;   -------------
;;   4.20e+01
;;   3.89e+01
;;  -3.02e+01
;;   9.02e+01
;;   6.62e+01
```

The small extra effort of creating a custom fold has made the intention of the calling code a little easier to follow.

Applying a single step of gradient descent

The objective of calculating the cost is to determine the amount by which to adjust each of the coefficients. Once we've calculated the average cost, as we did previously, we need to update the estimate of our coefficients β. Together, these steps represent a single iteration of gradient descent:

$$\beta_j := \beta_j - \alpha \frac{1}{m} \sum_{i=1}^{m} (\hat{y} - y) x$$

We can return the updated coefficients in a post-combiner step that makes use of the average cost, the value of alpha, and the previous coefficients. Let's create a utility function update-coefficients, which will receive the coefficients and alpha and return a function that will calculate the new coefficients, given a total model cost:

```
(defn update-coefficients [coefs alpha]
  (fn [cost]
    (->> (i/mult cost alpha)
         (i/minus coefs))))
```

With the preceding function in place, we have everything we need to package up a batch gradient descent update rule:

```
(defn gradient-descent-fold [{:keys [fy features factors
                                     coefs alpha]}]
  (let [zeros-matrix (i/matrix 0 (count features) 1)]
    (->> (prepare-data)
         (t/map (scale-features factors))
         (t/map (extract-features fy features))
         (t/map (calculate-error (i/trans coefs)))
         (t/fold (matrix-mean (inc (count features)) 1))
         (t/post-combine (update-coefficients coefs alpha)))))

(defn ex-5-31 []
  (let [features [:A00200 :AGI_STUB :NUMDEP :MARS2]
        fcount   (inc (count features))
        coefs    (vec (replicate fcount 0))
        data     (chunks (iota/seq "data/soi.csv"))
```

```
            factors  (->> (feature-scales features)
                          (t/tesser data))
            options {:fy :A02300 :features features
                     :factors factors :coefs coefs :alpha 0.1}]
        (->> (gradient-descent-fold options)
             (t/tesser data)))))

;; A 6x1 matrix
;; ------------
;; -4.20e+02
;; -1.38e+06
;; -5.06e+07
;; -9.53e+02
;; -1.42e+06
;; -4.86e+05
```

The resulting matrix represents the values of the coefficients after the first iteration of gradient descent.

Running iterative gradient descent

Gradient descent is an iterative algorithm, and we will usually need to run it many times to convergence. With a large dataset, this can be very time-consuming.

To save time, we've included a random sample of soi.csv in the data directory called soi-sample.csv. The smaller size allows us to run iterative gradient descent in a reasonable timescale. The following code runs gradient descent for 100 iterations, plotting the values of the parameters between each iteration on an xy-plot:

```
(defn descend [options data]
  (fn [coefs]
    (->> (gradient-descent-fold (assoc options :coefs coefs))
         (t/tesser data))))

(defn ex-5-32 []
  (let [features [:A00200 :AGI_STUB :NUMDEP :MARS2]
        fcount   (inc (count features))
        coefs    (vec (replicate fcount 0))
        data     (chunks (iota/seq "data/soi-sample.csv"))
        factors  (->> (feature-scales features)
                      (t/tesser data))
        options  {:fy :A02300 :features features
                  :factors factors :coefs coefs :alpha 0.1}
        iterations 100
```

```
           xs (range iterations)
           ys (->> (iterate (descend options data) coefs)
                   (take iterations))]
  (-> (c/xy-plot xs (map first ys)
                 :x-label "Iterations"
                 :y-label "Coefficient")
      (c/add-lines xs (map second ys))
      (c/add-lines xs (map #(nth % 2) ys))
      (c/add-lines xs (map #(nth % 3) ys))
      (c/add-lines xs (map #(nth % 4) ys))
      (i/view))))
```

If you run the example, you should see a chart similar to the following:

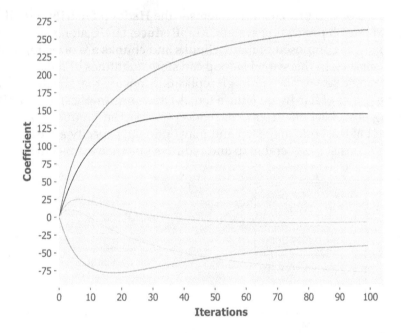

In the preceding chart, you can see how the parameters converge to relatively stable the values over the course of 100 iterations.

Scaling gradient descent with Hadoop

The length of time each iteration of batch gradient descent takes to run is determined by the size of your data and by how many processors your computer has. Although several chunks of data are processed in parallel, the dataset is large and the processors are finite. We've achieved a speed gain by performing calculations in parallel, but if we double the size of the dataset, the runtime will double as well.

Hadoop is one of several systems that has emerged in the last decade which aims to parallelize work that exceeds the capabilities of a single machine. Rather than running code across multiple processors, Hadoop takes care of running a calculation across many servers. In fact, Hadoop clusters can, and some do, consist of many thousands of servers.

Hadoop consists of two primary subsystems— the **Hadoop Distributed File System (HDFS)**—and the job processing system, **MapReduce**. HDFS stores files in chunks. A given file may be composed of many chunks and chunks are often replicated across many servers. In this way, Hadoop can store quantities of data much too large for any single server and, through replication, ensure that the data is stored reliably in the event of hardware failure too. As the name implies, the MapReduce programming model is built around the concept of map and reduce steps. Each job is composed of at least one map step and may optionally specify a reduce step. An entire job may consist of several map and reduce steps chained together.

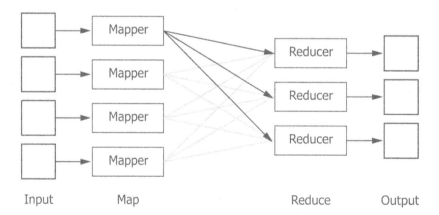

| Input | Map | | Reduce | Output |

In the respect that reduce steps are optional, Hadoop has a slightly more flexible approach to distributed calculation than Tesser. Later in this chapter and in the future chapters, we'll explore more of the capabilities that Hadoop has to offer. Tesser does enable us to convert our folds into Hadoop jobs, so let's do this next.

Gradient descent on Hadoop with Tesser and Parkour

Tesser's Hadoop capabilities are available in the `tesser.hadoop` namespace, which we're including as `h`. The primary public API function in the Hadoop namespace is `h/fold`.

The `fold` function expects to receive at least four arguments, representing the configuration of the Hadoop job, the input file we want to process, a working directory for Hadoop to store its intermediate files, and the fold we want to run, referenced as a Clojure var. Any additional arguments supplied will be passed as arguments to the fold when it is executed.

The reason for using a var to represent our fold is that the function call initiating the fold may happen on a completely different computer than the one that actually executes it. In a distributed setting, the var and arguments must entirely specify the behavior of the function. We can't, in general, rely on other mutable local state (for example, the value of an atom, or the value of variables closing over the function) to provide any additional context.

Parkour distributed sources and sinks

The data which we want our Hadoop job to process may exist on multiple machines too, stored distributed in chunks on HDFS. Tesser makes use of a library called **Parkour** (`https://github.com/damballa/parkour/`) to handle accessing potentially distributed data sources. We'll study Parkour in more detail later this and the next chapter but, for now, we'll just be using the `parkour.io.text` namespace to reference input and output text files.

Although Hadoop is designed to be run and distributed across many servers, it can also run in *local mode*. Local mode is suitable for testing and enables us to interact with the local filesystem as if it were HDFS. Another namespace we'll be using from Parkour is the `parkour.conf` namespace. This will allow us to create a default Hadoop configuration and operate it in local mode:

```
(defn ex-5-33 []
  (->> (text/dseq "data/soi.csv")
       (r/take 2)
       (into [])))
```

In the preceding example, we use Parkour's `text/dseq` function to create a representation of the IRS input data. The return value implements Clojure's reducers protocol, so we can use `r/take` on the result.

Running a feature scale fold with Hadoop

Hadoop needs a location to write its temporary files while working on a task, and will complain if we try to overwrite an existing directory. Since we'll be executing several jobs over the course of the next few examples, let's create a little utility function that returns a new file with a randomly-generated name.

```
(defn rand-file [path]
  (io/file path (str (long (rand 0x100000000)))))
```

```
(defn ex-5-34 []
  (let [conf      (conf/ig)
        input     (text/dseq "data/soi.csv")
        workdir   (rand-file "tmp")
        features [:A00200 :AGI_STUB :NUMDEP :MARS2]]
    (h/fold conf input workdir #'feature-scales features)))
```

Parkour provides a default Hadoop configuration object with the shorthand (conf/ig). This will return an empty configuration. The default value is enough, we don't need to supply any custom configuration.

 All of our Hadoop jobs will write their temporary files to a random directory inside the project's tmp directory. Remember to delete this folder later, if you're concerned about preserving disk space.

If you run the preceding example now, you should get an output similar to the following:

```
;; {:MARS2 317.0412009748016, :NUMDEP 581.8504423822615,
;; :AGI_STUB 3.499939975269811, :A00200 37290.58880658831}
```

Although the return value is identical to the values we got previously, we're now making use of Hadoop behind the scenes to process our data. In spite of this, notice that Tesser will return the response from our fold as a single Clojure data structure.

Running gradient descent with Hadoop

Since tesser.hadoop folds return Clojure data structures just like tesser.core folds, defining a gradient descent function that makes use of our scaled features is very simple:

```
(defn hadoop-gradient-descent [conf input-file workdir]
  (let [features [:A00200 :AGI_STUB :NUMDEP :MARS2]
        fcount   (inc (count features))
        coefs    (vec (replicate fcount 0))
```

```
input   (text/dseq input-file)
options {:column-names column-names
          :features features
          :coefs coefs
          :fy :A02300
          :alpha 1e-3}
factors (h/fold conf input (rand-file workdir)
                  #'feature-scales
                  features)
descend (fn [coefs]
            (h/fold conf input (rand-file workdir)
                    #'gradient-descent-fold
                    (merge options {:coefs coefs
                                    :factors factors})))]
    (take 5 (iterate descend coefs)))))
```

The preceding code defines a `hadoop-gradient-descent` function that iterates a `descend` function 5 times. Each iteration of descend calculates the improved coefficients based on the `gradient-descent-fold` function. The final return value is a vector of coefficients after 5 iterations of a gradient descent.

We run the job on the full IRS data in the following example:

```
(defn ex-5-35 []
  (let [workdir  "tmp"
        out-file (rand-file workdir)]
    (hadoop-gradient-descent (conf/ig) "data/soi.csv" workdir)))
```

After several iterations, you should see an output similar to the following:

```
;; ([0 0 0 0 0]
;; (20.9839310796048 46.87214911003046 -7.363493937722712
;;   101.46736841329326 55.67860863427868)
;; (40.918665605227744 56.55169901254631 -13.771345753228694
;;   162.1908841131747 81.23969785586247)
;; (59.85666340457121 50.559130068258995 -19.463888245285332
;;   202.32407094149158 92.77424653758085)
;; (77.8477613139478 38.67088624825574 -24.585818946408523
;;   231.42399118694212 97.75201693843269))
```

We've seen how we're able to calculate gradient descent using distributed techniques locally. Now, let's see how we can run this on a cluster of our own.

Preparing our code for a Hadoop cluster

Hadoop's Java API defines `Tool` and the associated `ToolRunner` classes that are intended to help execute jobs on a Hadoop cluster. A `Tool` class is Hadoop's name for a generic command-line application that interacts with the Hadoop framework. By creating our own tool, we create a command-line application that can be submitted to a Hadoop cluster.

Since it's a Java framework, Hadoop expects to interact with class representations of our code. So, the namespace defining our tool needs to contain the `:gen-class` declaration, which instructs the Clojure compiler to create a class from our namespace:

```
(ns cljds.ch5.hadoop
  (:gen-class)
  ...)
```

By default, `:gen-class` will expect the namespace to define a main function called `-main`. This will be the function that Hadoop will call with our arguments, so we can simply delegate the call to a function that will actually execute our job:

```
(defn -main [& args]
  (tool/run hadoop-gradient-descent args))
```

Parkour provides a Clojure interface to many of Hadoop's classes. In this case, `parkour.tool/run` contains all we need to run our distributed gradient descent function on Hadoop. With the preceding example in place, we need to instruct the Clojure compiler to ahead-of-time (AOT) compile our namespace and specify the class we'd like our project's main class to be. We can achieve it by adding the `:aot` and `:main` declarations to the `project.clj` function like this:

```
{:main cljds.ch5.hadoop
 :aot [cljds.ch5.hadoop]}
```

In the example code, we have specified these as a part of the `:uberjar` profile, since our last step, before sending the job to the cluster, would be to package it up as an uberjar file.

Building an uberjar

A JAR contains executable java code. An uberjar contains executable java code, plus all the dependencies required to run it. An uberjar provides a convenient way to package up code to be run in a distributed environment, because the job can be sent from machine to machine while carrying its dependencies with it. Although it makes for large job payloads, it avoids the need to ensure that job-specific dependencies are preinstalled on all the machines in the cluster. To create an uberjar file with **Leiningen**, execute the following command line within the project directory:

```
lein uberjar
```

Once you do this, two files will be created in the target directory. One file, `ch5-0.1.0.jar`, contains the project's compiled code. This is the same file as the one that would be generated with `lein jar`. In addition, uberjar generates the `ch5-0.1.0-standalone.jar` file. This contains the AOT-compiled project code in addition to the project's dependencies. The resulting file is large, but it contains everything the Hadoop job will need in order to run.

Submitting the uberjar to Hadoop

Once we've created an uberjar file, we're ready to submit it to Hadoop. Having a working local Hadoop installation is not a prerequisite to follow along with the examples in this chapter, and we won't describe the steps required to install it here.

 Links to Hadoop installation guides are provided on this book's wiki at http://wiki.clojuredatascience.com.

However, if you already have Hadoop installed and configured in local mode, you can run the example job on the command line now. Since the tool specified by the main class also accepts two arguments — the work directory and the input file — these will need to be provided too:

```
hadoop jar target/ch5-0.1.0-standalone.jar data/soi.csv tmp
```

If the command runs successfully, you may see logging messages as an output by the Hadoop process. After some time, you should see the final coefficients output by the job.

Although it takes more time to execute at the moment, our Hadoop job has the advantage that it can be distributed on a cluster that can scale indefinitely with the size of the data we have.

Stochastic gradient descent

The method we've just seen of calculating gradient descent is often called **batch gradient descent**, because each update to the coefficients happens inside an iteration over all the data in a *single batch*. With very large amounts of data, each iteration can be time-consuming and waiting for convergence could take a very long time.

An alternative method of gradient descent is called **stochastic gradient descent** or **SGD**. In this method, the estimates of the coefficients are continually updated as the input data is processed. The update method for stochastic gradient descent looks like this:

$$\beta_j := \beta_j - \alpha \frac{1}{m} \sum_{i=1}^{m} (\hat{y} - y) x$$

In fact, this is identical to batch gradient descent. The difference in application is purely that expression $(\hat{y} - y)x$ is calculated over a *mini-batch* — a random smaller subset of the overall data. The mini-batch size should be large enough to represent a fair sample of the input records — for our data, a reasonable mini-batch size might be about 250.

Stochastic gradient descent arrives at the best estimates by splitting the entire dataset into mini-batches and processing each of them in turn. Since the output of each mini-batch is the coefficient we would like to use for the next mini-batch (in order to incrementally improve the estimates), the algorithm is inherently sequential.

The advantage stochastic gradient descent offers over batch gradient descent is that it can arrive at good estimates in just one iteration over the dataset. For very large datasets, it may not even be necessary to process all the mini-batches before good convergence has been achieved.

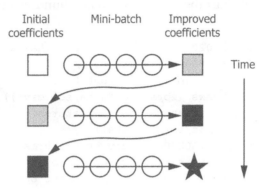

We could implement SGD with Tesser by taking advantage of the fact that the combiner is applied serially, and treat each chunk as a mini-batch from which the coefficients could be calculated. This would mean that our reduce step was the identity function—we have no reduction to perform.

Instead, let's use this as an opportunity to learn more on how to construct a Hadoop job in Parkour. Before delving more into Parkour, let's see how stochastic gradient descent could be implemented using what we already know:

```
(defn stochastic-gradient-descent [options data]
  (let [batches (->> (into [] data)
                     (shuffle)
                     (partition 250))
        descend (fn [coefs batch]
                  (->> (gradient-descent-fold
                        (assoc options :coefs coefs))
                       (t/tesser (chunks batch))))]
    (reductions descend (:coefs options) batches)))
```

The preceding code groups the input collection into smaller groups of 250 elements. Gradient descent is run on each of these mini-batches and the coefficients are updated. The next iteration of gradient descent will use the new coefficients on the next batch and, for an appropriate value of alpha, produce improved recommendations.

The following code will chart the output over many hundreds of batches:

```
(defn ex-5-36 []
  (let [features [:A00200 :AGI_STUB :NUMDEP :MARS2]
        fcount   (inc (count features))
        coefs    (vec (replicate fcount 0))
        data     (chunks (iota/seq "data/soi.csv"))
        factors  (->> (feature-scales features)
                      (t/tesser data))
        options  {:fy :A02300 :features features
                  :factors factors :coefs coefs :alpha 1e-3}
        ys       (stochastic-gradient-descent options data)
        xs       (range (count ys))]
    (-> (c/xy-plot xs (map first ys)
                   :x-label "Iterations"
                   :y-label "Coefficient")
        (c/add-lines xs (map #(nth % 1) ys))
        (c/add-lines xs (map #(nth % 2) ys))
        (c/add-lines xs (map #(nth % 3) ys))
        (c/add-lines xs (map #(nth % 4) ys))
        (i/view))))
```

We're supplying a learning rate over 100 times smaller than the value for batch gradient descent. This will help ensure that mini-batches containing outliers don't pull the parameters too far away from their optimal values. Because of the variance inherent in each of the mini-batches, the output of stochastic gradient descent will not converge exactly to the most optimal parameters, but will instead oscillate around the minimum.

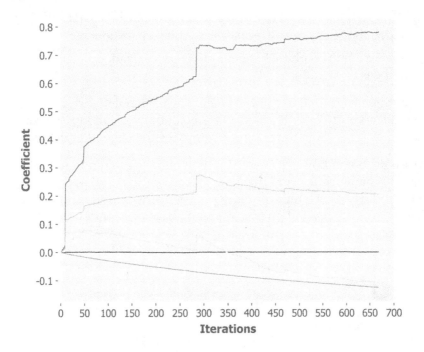

The preceding image shows the more random effect of stochastic gradient descent; in particular, the effect of variance among the mini-batches on the parameter estimates. In spite of the much lower learning rate, we can see spikes corresponding to the batches with the data containing outliers.

Stochastic gradient descent with Parkour

For the rest of this chapter, we're going to build a Hadoop job directly with Parkour. Parkour exposes more of Hadoop's underlying capabilities than Tesser does, and this is a mixed blessing. While Tesser makes it very easy to write folds and apply them to large datasets in Hadoop, Parkour will require us to understand more about Hadoop's computation model.

Although Hadoop's approach to MapReduce embodies many of the principles we've encountered so far this chapter, it differs from Tesser's abstractions in several critical ways:

- Hadoop assumes that the data to be processed are key/value pairs
- Hadoop does not require a reduce stage following a map
- Tesser folds over the whole sequence of inputs, Hadoop reduces over groups
- Hadoop's groups of values are defined by a partitioner
- Tesser's combine phase happens *after* reduce, Hadoop's combine stage happens *before* reduce

The last of these is particularly unfortunate. The terminology we've learned for Clojure reducers and Tesser is reversed for Hadoop: for Hadoop, the combiners aggregate the output from the mappers before the data is sent to the reducers.

We can see the broad flow represented in the following diagram with the output of the mappers combined into intermediate representations and sorted before being sent to the reducers. Each reducer reduces over a subset of the entire data. The combine step is optional and, in fact, we won't need one for our stochastic gradient descent jobs:

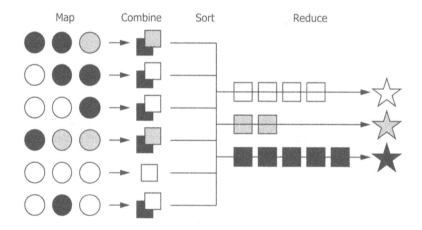

With or without a combining step, the data is sorted into groups before being sent to the reducers and the grouping strategy is defined by a partitioner. The default partitioning scheme is to partition by the key of your key/value pair (different keys are represented by different shades of gray in the preceding diagram). In fact, any custom partitioning scheme can be used.

As you can see, Parkour and Hadoop do not assume that the output is a single result. Since the groups that Hadoop reduces over are by default defined by the grouping key, the result of a reduce can be a dataset of many records. In the preceding diagram, we illustrated the case for three different results, one for each of the keys in our data.

Defining a mapper

The first component of the Hadoop job we'll define is the **mapper**. The mapper's role is usually to take a chunk of input records and transform them in some way. It's possible to specify a Hadoop job with no reducers; in this case, the output of the mappers is also the output of the whole job.

Parkour allows us to define the action of a mapper as a Clojure function. The only requirement of the function is that it accepts the input data (either from a source file or the output of a previous MapReduce step) as the final argument. Additional arguments can be provided if necessary, so long as the input is the final argument:

```
(defn parse-m
  {::mr/source-as :vals
   ::mr/sink-as   :vals}
  [fy features factors lines]
  (->> (skip-header lines)
       (r/map parse-line)
       (r/map (partial format-record column-names))
       (r/map (scale-features factors))
       (r/map (extract-features fy features))
       (into [])
       (shuffle)
       (partition 250)))
```

The map function in the preceding example, parse-m (by convention, Parkour mappers have the suffix -m), is responsible for taking a single line of the input and converting it into a feature representation. We're reusing many of the functions we defined earlier in the chapter: parse-line, format-record, scale-features, and extract-features. Parkour will provide input to the mapper function as a reducible collection, so we will chain the functions together with r/map.

Stochastic gradient descent expects to process data in mini-batches, so our mapper is responsible for partitioning the data into groups of 250 rows. We shuffle before calling partition to ensure that the ordering of the data is random.

Parkour shaping functions

We're also supplying metadata to the `parse-m` function in the form of the `{::mr/source-as :vals ::mr/sink-as :vals}` map. These are two namespaced keywords referencing `parkour.mapreduce/source-as` and `parkour.mapreduce/sink-as`, and are instructions to Parkour on how the data should be shaped before providing it to the function and what shape of data it can expect in return.

Valid options for a Parkour mapper are `:keyvals`, `:keys`, and `:vals`. The preceding diagram shows the effect for a short sequence of three key/value pairs. By requesting to source our data as `:vals`, we get a sequence containing only the value portion of the key/value pair.

Defining a reducer

Defining a reducer in Parkour is the same as defining a mapper. Again, the last argument must be the input (now, the input from a prior map step), but additional arguments can be provided. Our Parkour reducer for stochastic gradient descent looks like this:

```
(defn sum-r
  {::mr/source-as :vals
   ::mr/sink-as   :vals}
  [fcount alpha batches]
  (let [initial-coefs (vec (replicate fcount 0))
        descend-batch (fn [coefs batch]
                        (->> (t/map (calculate-error
                                      (i/trans coefs)))
                             (t/fold (matrix-mean fcount 1))
                             (t/post-combine
                              (update-coefficients coefs alpha))
                             (t/tesser (chunks batch))))]
    (r/reduce descend-batch initial-coefs batches)))
```

Our input is provided as a reducible collection like before, so we use the Clojure's reducers library to iterate over it. We're using `r/reduce` rather than `r/fold`, because we don't want to perform our reduction in parallel over the data. In fact, the reason for using Hadoop is that we can control the parallelism of each of the map and reduce phases independently. Now that we have our map and reduce steps defined, we can combine them into a single job by using the functions in the `parkour.graph` namespace.

Specifying Hadoop jobs with Parkour graph

The `graph` namespace is Parkour's main API to define Hadoop jobs. Each job must have at a minimum an input, a mapper, and an output, and we can chain these specifications with Clojure's `->` macro. Let's first define a very simple job, which takes the output from our mappers and writes them immediately to disk:

```
(defn hadoop-extract-features [conf workdir input output]
  (let [fy         :A02300
        features [:A00200 :AGI_STUB :NUMDEP :MARS2]
        fcount   (inc (count features))
        input    (text/dseq input)
        factors  (h/fold conf input (rand-file workdir)
                          #'feature-scales
                          features)
        conf (conf/ig)]
    (-> (pg/input input)
        (pg/map #'parse-m fy features factors)
        (pg/output (text/dsink output))
        (pg/execute conf "extract-features-job"))))

(defn ex-5-37 []
  (let [workdir  "tmp"
        out-file (rand-file workdir)]
    (hadoop-extract-features (conf/ig) "tmp"
                             "data/soi.csv" out-file)
    (str out-file)))

;; "tmp/1935333306"
```

The response from the preceding example should be a directory within the project's `tmp` directory, where Hadoop will have written its files. If you navigate to the directory, you should see several files. On my computer, I see four files—`_SUCCESS`, `part-m-00000`, `part-m-00001`, and `part-m-00002`. The presence of the `_SUCCESS` file indicates that our job is completed successfully. The `part-m-xxxxx` files are chunks of our input file.

The fact that there are three files indicates that Hadoop created three mappers to process our input data. If we were running in distributed mode, these could have been created in parallel. If you open one of the files, you should see a long sequence of `clojure.lang.LazySeq@657d118e`. Since we wrote to a text file, it is a text representation of the output of our mapper data.

Chaining mappers and reducers with Parkour graph

What we really want to do is to its chain our map and reduce steps to happen one after the other. For this, we will have to insert an intermediate step, the **partitioner**, and tell the partitioner how to serialize our `clojure.lang.LazySeqs`.

The latter can be accomplished by borrowing from Tesser, which implements the serialization and deserialization of arbitrary Clojure data structures using **Fressian**. In the next chapter, we'll look closer, at the support Parkour provides to create well-defined schemas for our partitioned data but, for now, it's simply enough for the partitioner to pass the encoded data through.

 Fressian is an extensible binary data format. You can learn more about it from the documentation at `https://github.com/clojure/data.fressian`.

Our keys will be encoded as `FressianWritable`, while our keys are not specified at all (we sink our map data just as `vals`). Hadoop's representation of nil is a `NullWritable` type. We import both in our namespace with:

```
(:import [org.apache.hadoop.io NullWritable]
         [tesser.hadoop_support FressianWritable])
```

With the import in place, we can specify our job in its entirety:

```
(defn hadoop-sgd [conf workdir input-file output]
  (let [kv-classes [NullWritable FressianWritable]
        fy          :A02300
        features [:A00200 :AGI_STUB :NUMDEP :MARS2]
        fcount    (inc (count features))
        input     (text/dseq input-file)
        factors (h/fold conf input (rand-file workdir)
                        #'feature-scales
                        features)
        conf (conf/assoc! conf "mapred.reduce.tasks" 1)]
    (-> (pg/input input)
        (pg/map #'parse-m fy features factors)
```

```
(pg/partition kv-classes)
(pg/reduce #'sum-r fcount 1e-8)
(pg/output (text/dsink output))
(pg/execute conf "sgd-job")))))
```

We need to ensure that we have only one reducer processing our mini-batches (although there are variations of SGD that would permit us to average the results of several stochastic gradient descent runs, we want to arrive at a single set of near-optimal coefficients). We will use Parkour's `conf` namespace to `assoc!` `mapred.reduce.tasks` to 1.

Between the map and reduce steps, we specify the partitioner and pass the `kv-classes` function defined at the top of the function. The final example simply runs this job:

```
(defn ex-5-38 []
  (let [workdir  "tmp"
        out-file (rand-file workdir)]
    (hadoop-sgd (conf/ig) "tmp" "data/soi.csv" out-file)
    (str out-file)))

;; "tmp/4046267961"
```

If you navigate to the directory returned by the job, you should now see a directory containing just two files— _SUCCESS and part-r-00000. One file is the output per reducer, so with one reducer, we ended up with one part-r-xxxxx file. Inside this file will be the coefficients of the linear model calculated with stochastic gradient descent.

Summary

In this chapter, we learned some of the fundamental techniques of distributed data processing and saw how the functions used locally for data processing, map and reduce, are powerful ways of processing even very large quantities of data. We learned how Hadoop can scale unbounded by the capabilities of any single server by running functions on smaller subsets of the data whose outputs are themselves combined to finally produce a result. Once you understand the tradeoffs, this "divide and conquer" approach toward processing data is a simple and very general way of analyzing data on a large scale.

We saw both the power and limitations of simple folds to process data using both Clojure's reducers and Tesser. We've also begun exploring how Parkour exposes more of Hadoop's underlying capabilities.

In the next chapter, we'll see how to use Hadoop and Parkour to address a particular machine learning challenge—clustering a large volume of text documents.

6
Clustering

Things that have a common quality ever quickly seek their kind.

- Marcus Aurelius

In previous chapters, we covered multiple learning algorithms: linear and logistic regression, C4.5, naive Bayes, and random forests. In each case we were required to train the algorithm by providing features and a desired output. In linear regression, for example, the desired output was the weight of an Olympic swimmer, whereas for the other algorithms we provided a class: whether the passenger survived or perished. These are examples of **supervised learning algorithms**: we tell our algorithm the desired output and it will attempt to learn a model that reproduces it.

There is another class of learning algorithm referred to as **unsupervised learning**. Unsupervised algorithms are able to operate on the data without a set of reference answers. We may not even know ourselves what structure lies within the data; the algorithm will attempt to determine the structure for itself.

Clustering is an example of an unsupervised learning algorithm. The results of cluster analysis are groupings of input data that are more similar to each other in some way. The technique is general: any set entities that have a conceptual similarity or distance from each other can be clustered. For example, we could cluster groups of social media accounts by similarity in terms of shared followers, or we could cluster the results of market research by measuring the similarity of respondents' answers to a questionnaire.

One common application of clustering is to identify documents that share similar subject matter. This provides us with an ideal opportunity to talk about text processing, and this chapter will introduce a variety of techniques specific to dealing with text.

Downloading the data

This chapter makes use of the **Reuters-21578** dataset: a venerable collection of articles that were published on the Reuters newswire in 1987. It is one of the most widely used for testing the categorization and classification of text. The copyright for the text of articles and annotations in the Reuters-21578 collection resides with Reuters Ltd. Reuters Ltd. and Carnegie Group, Inc. have agreed to allow the free distribution of this data for research purposes only.

 You can download the example code for this chapter from the Packt Publishing's website or from `https://github.com/clojuredatascience/ch6-clustering`.

As usual, within the sample code is a script to download and unzip the files to the data directory. You can run it from within the project directory with the following command:

```
script/download-data.sh
```

Alternatively, at the time of writing, the Reuters dataset can be downloaded from `http://kdd.ics.uci.edu/databases/reuters21578/reuters21578.tar.gz`. The rest of this chapter will assume that the files have been downloaded and installed to the project's data directory.

Extracting the data

After you run the preceding script, the articles will be unzipped to the directory `data/reuters-sgml`. Each `.sgm` file in the extract contains around 1,000 short articles that have been wrapped in XML-style tags using Standard Generalized Markup Language (SGML). Rather than write our own parser for the format, we can make use of the one already written in the Lucene text indexer.

```clojure
(:import [org.apache.lucene.benchmark.utils ExtractReuters])

(defn sgml->txt [in-path out-path]
  (let [in-file  (clojure.java.io/file in-path)
        out-file (clojure.java.io/file out-path)]
    (.extract (ExtractReuters. in-file out-file))))
```

Here we're making use of Clojure's Java interop to simply call the extract method on Lucene's `ExtractReuters` class. Each article is extracted as its own text file.

This code can be run by executing:

```
lein extract-reuters
```

on the command line within the project directory. The output will be a new directory, `data/reuters-text`, containing over 20,000 individual text files. Each file contains a single Reuters newswire article.

If you're short on disk space you can delete the `reuters-sgml` and `reuters21578.tar.gz` files now: the contents of the `reuters-text` directory are the only files we will be using in this chapter. Let's look at a few now.

Inspecting the data

The year 1987 was the year of "Black Monday". On 19th October stock markets around the world crashed and the Dow Jones Industrial Average declined 508 points to 1738.74. Articles such as the one contained in `reut2-020.sgm-962.txt` describe the event:

```
19-OCT-1987 16:14:37.57

WALL STREET SUFFERS WORST EVER SELLOFF

Wall Street tumbled to its worst point loss ever and the worst
percentage decline since the First World War as a frenzy of stock
selling stunned even the most bearish market participants.
"Everyone is in awe and the word 'crash' is on everyone's mind,"
one trader said.    The Dow Jones industrial average fell 508
points to 1738, a level it has not been at since the Autumn of
1986.    Volume soared to 603 mln shares, almost doubling the
previous record of 338 mln traded just last Friday. Reuter &#3;
```

The structure of this article is representative of the majority of articles in the corpus. The first line is the timestamp indicating when the article was published, followed by a blank line. The article has a headline which is often—but not always—in upper case, and then another blank line. Finally comes the article body text. As is often the case when working with semi-structured text such as this, there are multiple spaces, odd characters, and abbreviations.

Other articles are simply headlines, for example in `reut2-020.sgm-761.txt`:

```
20-OCT-1987 17:09:34.49
REAGAN SAYS HE SEES NO RECESSION
```

These are the files on which we will be performing our cluster analysis.

Clustering text

Clustering is the process of finding groups of objects that are similar to each other. The goal is that objects within a cluster should be more similar to each other than to objects in other clusters. Like classification, it is not a specific algorithm so much as a general class of algorithms that solve a general problem.

Although there are a variety of clustering algorithms, all rely to some extent on a distance measure. For an algorithm to determine whether two objects belong in the same or different clusters it must be able to determine a quantitative measure of the distance (or, if you prefer, the similarity) between them. This calls for a numeric measure of distance: the smaller the distance, the greater the similarity between two objects.

Since clustering is a general technique that can be applied to diverse data types, there are a large number of possible distance measures. Nonetheless, most data can be represented by one of a handful of common abstractions: a set, a point in space, or a vector. For each of these there exists a commonly-used measure.

Set-of-words and the Jaccard index

If your data can be represented as a set of things the Jaccard index, also known as the **Jaccard similarity**, can be used. It's one of the simplest measures conceptually: it is the set intersection divided by the set union, or the number of shared elements in common out of the total unique elements in the sets:

$$J(A, B) = \frac{|A \cap B|}{|A \cup B|}$$

Many things can be represented as sets. Accounts on social networks can be represented as sets of friends or followers, and customers can be represented as sets of products purchased or viewed. For our text documents, a set representation could simply be the set of unique words used.

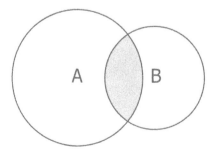

The Jaccard index is very simple to calculate in Clojure:

```
(:require [clojure.set :as set])

(defn jaccard-similarity [a b]
  (let [a (set a)
        b (set b)]
    (/ (count (set/intersection a b))
       (count (set/union a b)))))

(defn ex-6-1 []
  (let [a [1 2 3]
        b [2 3 4]]
    (jaccard a b)))

;; => 1/2
```

It has the advantage that the sets don't have to be of the same cardinality for the distance measure to make sense. In the preceding diagram, **A** is "larger" than **B**, yet the intersection divided by the union is still a fair reflection of their similarity. To apply the Jaccard index to text documents, we need to translate them into sets of words. This is the process of **tokenization**.

Tokenizing the Reuters files

Tokenization is the name for the technique of taking a string of text and splitting it into smaller units for the purpose of analysis. A common approach is to split a text string into individual words. An obvious separator would be whitespace so that `"tokens like these"` become `["tokens" "like" "these"]`.

```
(defn tokenize [s]
  (str/split s #"\W+"))
```

This is convenient and simple, but unfortunately, language is subtle and few simple rules can be applied universally. For example, our tokenizer treats apostrophes as whitespace:

```
(tokenize "doesn't handle apostrophes")
;; ["doesn" "t" "handle" "apostrophes"]
```

Hyphens are treated as whitespace too:

```
(tokenize "good-looking user-generated content")
;; ["good" "looking" "user" "generated" "content"]
```

and removing them rather changes the meaning of the sentence. However, not all hyphens should be preserved:

```
(tokenize "New York-based")
;; ["New" "York" "based"]
```

The terms `"New"`, `"York"`, and `"based"` correctly represent the subject of the phrase, but it would be preferable to group `"New York"` into a single term, since it represents a specific name and really ought to be preserved intact. `York-based`, on the other hand, would be a meaningless token on its own.

In short, text is messy, and parsing meaning reliably from free text is an extremely rich and active area of research. In particular, for extracting names (e.g. `"New York"`) from text, we need to consider the context in which the terms are used. Techniques that label tokens within a sentence by their grammatical function are called **parts-of-speech taggers**.

> For more information on advanced tokenization and parts-of-speech tagging, see the `clojure-opennlp` library at `https://github.com/dakrone/clojure-opennlp`.

In this chapter we have the luxury of a large quantity of documents and so we'll continue to use our simple tokenizer. We'll find that—in spite of its deficiencies—it will perform well enough to extract meaning from the documents.

Let's write a function to return the tokens for a document from its file name:

```
(defn tokenize-reuters [content]
  (-> (str/replace content  #"^.*\n\n" "")
      (str/lower-case)
      (tokenize)))

(defn reuters-terms [file]
  (-> (io/resource file)
      (slurp)
      (tokenize-reuters)))
```

We're removing the timestamp from the top of the file and making the text lower-case before tokenizing. In the next section, we'll see how to measure the similarity between tokenized documents.

Applying the Jaccard index to documents

Having tokenized our input documents, we can simply pass the resulting sequence of tokens to our `jaccard-similarity` function defined previously. Let's compare the similarity of a couple of documents from the Reuters corpus:

```
(defn ex-6-2 []
  (let [a (set (reuters-terms "reut2-020.sgm-761.txt"))
        b (set (reuters-terms "reut2-007.sgm-750.txt"))
        s (jaccard a b)]
    (println "A:" a)
    (println "B:" b)
    (println "Similarity:" s)))
```

```
A: #{recession says reagan sees no he}
B: #{bill transit says highway reagan and will veto he}
Similarity: 1/4
```

The Jaccard index outputs a number between zero and one, so it has judged these documents to be 25 percent similar based on the words in their headlines. Notice how we've lost the order of the words in the headline. Without further tricks that we'll come to shortly, the Jaccard index looks only at the items in common between two sets. Another aspect we've lost is the number of times a term occurs in the document. A document that repeats the same word many times may in some sense regard that word as more important. For example, `reut2-020.sgm-932.txt` has a headline like this:

```
19-OCT-1987 16:41:40.58
NYSE CHAIRMAN JOHN PHELAN SAYS NYSE WILL OPEN TOMORROW ON TIME
```

NYSE appears twice in the headline. We could infer that this headline is especially about the New York Stock Exchange, perhaps more so than a headline that mentioned NYSE only once.

The bag-of-words and Euclidean distance

A possible improvement over the set-of-words approach is the **bag-of-words approach**. This preserves the word count of the terms within the document. The term count can be incorporated by distance measures for a potentially more accurate result.

One of the most common conceptions of distance is the Euclidean distance measure. In geometry, the Euclidean measure is how we calculate the distance between two points in space. In two dimensions, the Euclidean distance is given by the **Pythagoras formula**:

$$d = \sqrt{\left(x_2 - x_1\right)^2 + \left(y_2 - y_1\right)^2}$$

This represents the difference between two points as the length of the straight-line distance between them.

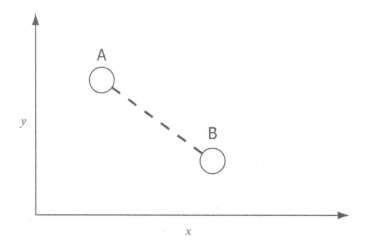

This can be extended to three dimensions:

$$d = \sqrt{\left(x_2 - x_1\right)^2 + \left(y_2 - y_1\right)^2 + \left(z_2 - z_1\right)^2}$$

and generalized to n dimensions:

$$d = \sqrt{\sum_{i=1}^{n}\left(A_i - B_i\right)^2}$$

where A_i and B_i are the values of A or B at dimension i. The distance measure is thus the overall similarity between two documents, having taken into account how many times each word occurs.

```
(defn euclidean-distance [a b]
  (->> (map (comp i/sq -) a b)
       (apply +)
       (i/sqrt)))
```

Since each word now represents a dimension in space, we need to make sure that when we calculate the Euclidean distance measure we are comparing the magnitude in the same dimension of each document. Otherwise, we may literally be comparing "apples" with "oranges".

Representing text as vectors

Unlike the Jaccard index, the Euclidean distance relies on a consistent ordering of words into dimensions. The word count, or term frequency, represents the position of that document in a large multi-dimensional space, and we need to ensure that when we compare values we do so in the correct dimension. Let's represent our documents as term **frequency vectors**.

Imagine all the words that could appear in a document being given a unique number. For example, the word "apple" could be assigned the number 53, the word "orange" could be assigned the number 21,597. If all numbers are unique, they could correspond to the index that a word appears in a term vector.

The dimension of these vectors can be very large. The maximum number of dimensions possible is the cardinality of the vector. The value of the element at the index corresponding to a word is usually the number of occurrences of the word in the document. This is known as the **term frequency (tf)**, weighting.

In order to be able to compare text vectors it's important that the same word always appears at the same index in the vector. This means that we must use the same word/index mapping for each vector that we create. This word/index mapping is our dictionary.

Creating a dictionary

To create a valid dictionary, we need to make sure that the indexes for two words don't clash. One way to do this is to have a monotonically increasing counter which is incremented for each word added to the dictionary. The count at the point the word is added becomes the index of the word. To both add a word to the dictionary and increment a counter in a thread-safe way, we can use an atom:

```
(def dictionary
  (atom {:count 0
         :words {}}))

(defn add-term-to-dict [dict word]
  (if (contains? (:terms dict) word)
    dict
    (-> dict
        (update-in [:terms] assoc word (get dict :count))
        (update-in [:count] inc))))

(defn add-term-to-dict! [dict term]
  (doto dict
    (swap! add-term-to-dict term)))
```

To perform an update to an atom, we have to execute our code in a `swap!` function.

```
(add-term-to-dict! dictionary "love")

;; #<Atom@261d1f0a: {:count 1, :terms {"love" 0}}>
```

Adding another word will cause the count to increase:

```
(add-term-to-dict! dictionary "music")

;; #<Atom@261d1f0a: {:count 2, :terms {"music" 1, "love" 0}}>
```

And adding the same word twice will have no effect:

```
(add-term-to-dict! dictionary "love")

;; #<Atom@261d1f0a: {:count 2, :terms {"music" 1, "love" 0}}>
```

Performing this update inside an atom ensures that each word gets its own index even when the dictionary is being simultaneously updated by multiple threads.

```
(defn build-dictionary! [dict terms]
  (reduce add-term-to-dict! dict terms))
```

Building a whole dictionary is as simple as reducing our `add-term-to-dict!` function over a supplied dictionary atom with a collection of terms.

Creating term frequency vectors

To calculate the Euclidean distance, let's first create a vector from our dictionary and document. This will allow us to easily compare the term frequencies between documents because they will occupy the same index of the vector.

```
(defn term-id [dict term]
  (get-in @dict [:terms term]))

(defn term-frequencies [dict terms]
  (->> (map #(term-id dict %) terms)
       (remove nil?)
       (frequencies)))

(defn map->vector [dictionary id-counts]
  (let [zeros (vec (replicate (:count @dictionary) 0))]
    (-> (reduce #(apply assoc! %1 %2) (transient zeros) id-counts)
        (persistent!))))

(defn tf-vector [dict document]
  (map->vector dict (term-frequencies dict document)))
```

The `term-frequencies` function creates a map of term ID to frequency count for each term in the document. The `map->vector` function simply takes this map and associates the frequency count at the index of the vector given by the term ID. Since there may be many terms, and the vector may be very long, we're using Clojure's `transient!` and `persistent!` functions to temporarily create a mutable vector for efficiency.

Let's print the document, dictionary, and resulting vector for `reut2-020.sgm-742.txt`:

```
(defn ex-6-3 []
  (let [doc  (reuters-terms "reut2-020.sgm-742.txt")
        dict (build-dictionary! dictionary doc)]
    (println "Document:" doc)
    (println "Dictionary:" dict)
    (println "Vector:" (tf-vector dict doc))))
```

The output is shown as follows (the formatting has been adjusted for legibility):

```
;; Document: [nyse s phelan says nyse will continue program
;;            trading curb until volume slows]
;; Dictionary: #<Atom@bb156ec: {:count 12, :terms {s 1, curb 8,
```

```
;;                phelan 2, says 3, trading 7, nyse 0, until 9,
;;                continue 5, volume 10, will 4, slows 11,
;;                program 6}}>
;; Vector: [2 1 1 1 1 1 1 1 1 1 1 1]
```

With 12 terms in the input, there are 12 terms in the dictionary and a vector of 12
elements returned.

```
(defn print-distance [doc-a doc-b measure]
  (let [a-terms (reuters-terms doc-a)
        b-terms (reuters-terms doc-b)
        dict (-> dictionary
                 (build-dictionary! a-terms)
                 (build-dictionary! b-terms))
        a (tf-vector dict a-terms)
        b (tf-vector dict b-terms)]
    (println "A:" a)
    (println "B:" b)
    (println "Distance:" (measure a b))))

(defn ex-6-4 []
  (print-distance "reut2-020.sgm-742.txt"
                  "reut2-020.sgm-932.txt"
                  euclidean-distance))

;; A: [2 1 1 1 1 1 1 1 1 1 1 1 0 0 0 0 0 0]
;; B: [2 0 1 1 1 0 0 0 0 0 0 0 1 1 1 1 1 1]
;; Distance: 3.7416573867739413
```

Like the Jaccard index, the Euclidean distance cannot decrease below zero. Unlike
the Jaccard index, though, the value can grow indefinitely.

The vector space model and cosine distance

The vector space model can be considered a generalization of the set-of-words
and bag-of-words models. Like the bag-of-words model, the vector space model
represents each document as a vector, each element of which represents a term. The
value at each index is a measure of importance of the word, which may or may not
be the term frequency.

If your data conceptually represents a vector (that is to say, a magnitude in a
particular direction), then the cosine distance may be the most appropriate choice.
The cosine distance measure determines the similarity of two elements as the cosine
of the angle between their vector representations.

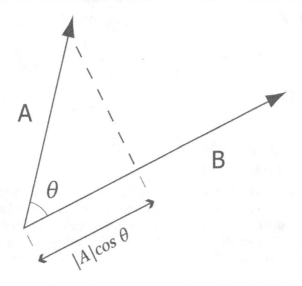

If both vectors point in the same direction, then the angle between them will be zero and the cosine of zero is one. The cosine similarity can be defined in the following way:

$$\cos\left(\theta\right) = \frac{A \cdot B}{\|A\|\|B\|} = \frac{\sum_{i=1}^{n} A_i B_i}{\sqrt{\sum_{i=1}^{n} A_i^2}\sqrt{\sum_{i=1}^{n} B_i^2}}$$

This is a more complicated equation than the ones we've covered previously. It relies on calculating the dot product of the two vectors and the magnitude of each.

```
(defn cosine-similarity [a b]
  (let [dot-product (->> (map * a b)
                         (apply +))
        magnitude (fn [d]
                    (->> (map i/sq d)
                         (apply +)
                         (i/sqrt)))]
    (/ dot-product (* (magnitude a) (magnitude b)))))
```

Examples of the cosine similarity are shown as follows:

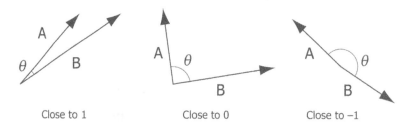

| Close to 1 | Close to 0 | Close to −1 |

The cosine similarity is often used as a similarity measure in high-dimensional spaces where each vector contains a lot of zeros because it can be very efficient to evaluate: only the non-zero dimensions need to be considered. Since most text documents use only a small fraction of all words (and therefore are zero for a large proportion of dimensions), the cosine measure is often used for clustering text.

In the vector space model, we need a consistent strategy for measuring the importance of each term. In the set-of-words model, all terms are counted equally. This is equivalent to setting the value of the vector at that point to one. In the bag-of-words model, the term frequencies were counted. We'll continue to use the term frequency for now, but we'll see shortly how to use a more sophisticated measure of importance, called **term frequency-inverse document frequency (TF-IDF)**.

```
(defn ex-6-5 []
   (print-distance "reut2-020.sgm-742.txt"
                   "reut2-020.sgm-932.txt"
                   cosine-similarity))

;; A: [2 1 1 1 1 1 1 1 1 1 1 1 0 0 0 0 0 0]
;; B: [2 0 1 1 1 0 0 0 0 0 0 0 1 1 1 1 1 1]
;; Distance: 0.5012804118276031
```

The closer the cosine value is to 1, the more similar the two entities are. To convert `cosine-similarity` to a distance measure, we can simply subtract the `cosine-similarity` from 1.

Although all the measures mentioned earlier produce different measures for the same input, they all satisfy the constraint that the distance between *A* and *B* should be the same as the difference between *B* and *A*. Often the same underlying data can be transformed to represent a set (Jaccard), a point in space (Euclidean), or a vector (Cosine). Sometimes the only way to know which is right is to try it and see how good the results are.

The number of unique words that appear in one document is typically small compared to the number of unique words that appear in any document in a collection being processed. As a result, these high-dimensional document vectors are quite sparse.

Removing stop words

Much of the similarity between the headlines has been generated by often-occurring words that don't add a great deal of meaning to the content. Examples are "a", "says", and "and". We should filter these out in order to avoid generating spurious similarities.

Consider the following two idioms:

* `"Music is the food of love"`
* `"War is the locomotive of history"`

We could calculate the cosine similarity between them using the following Clojure code:

```
(defn ex-6-6 []
  (let [a (tokenize "music is the food of love")
        b (tokenize "war is the locomotive of history")]
    (add-documents-to-dictionary! dictionary [a b])
    (cosine-similarity (tf-vector dictionary a)
                       (tf-vector dictionary b))))

;; 0.5
```

The two documents are showing a similarity of 0.5 in spite of the fact that the only words they share in common are is, the, and of. Ideally we'll want to remove these.

Stemming

Now let's consider an alternative phrase:

* `"Music is the food of love"`
* `"It's lovely that you're musical"`

Let's compare their cosine similarity as well:

```
(defn ex-6-7 []
  (let [a (tokenize "music is the food of love")
        b (tokenize "it's lovely that you're musical")]
```

```
    (add-documents-to-dictionary! dictionary [a b])
    (cosine-similarity (tf-vector dictionary a)
                       (tf-vector dictionary b))))
```

```
;; 0.0
```

In spite of the fact that the two sentences refer to music and positive feelings, the two phrases have a cosine similarity of zero: there are no words in common between the two phrases. This makes sense but does not express the behavior we usually want, which is to capture the similarity between "concepts", rather than the precise words that were used.

One way of tackling this problem is to **stem** words, which reduces them to their roots. Words which share a common meaning are more likely to stem to the same root. The Clojure library stemmers (`https://github.com/mattdw/stemmers`) will do this for us, and fortunately they will also remove stop words too.

```
(defn ex-6-8 []
  (let [a (stemmer/stems "music is the food of love")
        b (stemmer/stems "it's lovely that you're musical")]
    (add-documents-to-dictionary! dictionary [a b])
    (cosine-similarity (tf-vector dictionary a)
                       (tf-vector dictionary b))))
```

```
;; 0.8164965809277259
```

Much better. After stemming and stop word removal, the similarity between the phrases has dropped from 0.0 to 0.82. This is a good outcome since, although the sentences used different words, the sentiments they expressed were related.

Clustering with k-means and Incanter

Finally, having tokenized, stemmed, and vectorized our input documents—and with a selection of distance measures to choose from—we're in a position to run clustering on our data. The first clustering algorithm we'll look at is called *k-means clustering*.

k-means is an iterative algorithm that proceeds as follows:

1. Randomly pick *k* cluster centroids.
2. Assign each of the data points to the cluster with the closest centroid.
3. Adjust each cluster centroid to the mean of its assigned data points.
4. Repeat until convergence or the maximum number of iterations reached.

The process is visualized in the following diagram for *k=3* clusters:

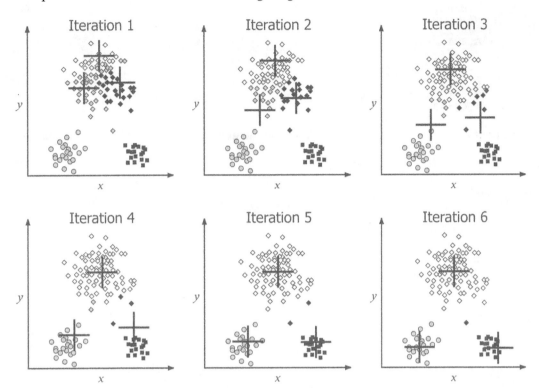

In the preceding figure, we can see that the initial cluster centroids at iteration 1 don't represent the structure of the data well. Although the points are clearly arranged in three groups, the initial centroids (represented by crosses) are all distributed around the top area of the graph. The points are colored according to their closest centroid. As the iterations proceed, we can see how the cluster centroids are moved closer to their "natural" positions in the center of each of the groups of points.

Before we define the main *k*-means function, it's useful to define a couple of utility functions first: a function to calculate the centroid for a cluster, and a function to group the data into their respective clusters.

```
(defn centroid [xs]
  (let [m (i/trans (i/matrix xs))]
    (if (> (i/ncol m) 1)
      (i/matrix (map s/mean m))
      m)))

(defn ex-6-9 []
  (let [m (i/matrix [[1 2 3]
```

```
                              [2 2 5]])]
      (centroid m)))


;; A 3x1 matrix
;;  ------------
;; 1.50e+00
;; 2.00e+00
;; 4.00e+00
```

The `centroid` function simply calculates the mean of each column of the input matrix.

```
(defn clusters [cluster-ids data]
  (->> (map vector cluster-ids data)
       (conj-into {})
       (vals)
       (map i/matrix)))


(defn ex-6-10 []
  (let [m (i/matrix [[1 2 3]
                     [4 5 6]
                     [7 8 9]])]
    (clusters [0 1 0] m)))


;; A 1x3 matrix
;; ------------
;; 4.00e+00  5.00e+00   6.00e+00
;;  A 2x3 matrix
;; ------------
;; 7.00e+00  8.00e+00  9.00e+00
;; 1.00e+00  2.00e+00  3.00e+00
```

The `clusters` function splits a larger matrix up into a sequence of smaller matrices based on the supplied cluster IDs. The cluster IDs are provided as a sequence of elements the same length as the clustered points, listing the cluster ID of the point at that index in the sequence. Items that share a common cluster ID will be grouped together. With these two functions in place, here's the finished `k-means` function:

```
(defn k-means [data k]
  (loop [centroids (s/sample data :size k)
         previous-cluster-ids nil]
    (let [cluster-id (fn [x]
                       (let [distance  #(s/euclidean-distance x %)
                             distances (map distance centroids)]
                         (->> (apply min distances)
                              (index-of distances))))
```

```
             cluster-ids (map cluster-id data)]
      (if (not= cluster-ids previous-cluster-ids)
        (recur (map centroid (clusters cluster-ids data))
               cluster-ids)
        clusters)))))
```

We start by picking k random cluster centroids by sampling the input data.
Then, we use loop/recur to continuously update the cluster centroids until
`previous-cluster-ids` are the same as `cluster-ids`. At this point, no
documents have moved cluster, so the clustering has converged.

Clustering the Reuters documents

Let's use our k-means function to cluster the Reuters documents now. Let's go
easy on our algorithm to start with, and pick a small sample of larger documents.
Larger documents will make it more likely that the algorithm will be able to
determine meaningful similarities between them. Let's set the minimum threshold
at 500 characters. This means that at the very least our input documents will have a
headline and a couple of sentences of body text to work with.

```
(defn ex-6-11 []
  (let [documents (fs/glob "data/reuters-text/*.txt")
        doc-count 100
        k 5
        tokenized (->> (map slurp documents)
                       (remove too-short?)
                       (take doc-count)
                       (map stem-reuters))]
    (add-documents-to-dictionary! dictionary tokenized)
    (-> (map #(tf-vector dictionary %) tokenized)
        (k-means k))))
```

We're using the fs library (https://github.com/Raynes/fs) to create a list of files
to perform our clustering on by calling fs/glob with a pattern that matches all the
text files. We remove those which are too short, tokenize the first 100, and add them
to the dictionary. We create tf vectors for our inputs and then call k-means on them.

If you run the preceding example, you'll receive a list of clustered document vectors,
which isn't very useful. Let's create a summary function that uses the dictionary to
report the most common terms in each of the clusters.

```
(defn cluster-summary [dict clusters top-term-count]
  (for [cluster clusters]
    (let [sum-terms (if (= (i/nrow cluster) 1)
                      cluster
```

```
                    (->> (i/trans cluster)
                         (map i/sum)
                         (i/trans)))
          popular-term-ids (->> (map-indexed vector sum-terms)
                                (sort-by second >)
                                (take top-term-count)
                                (map first))
          top-terms (map #(id->term dict %) popular-term-ids)]
      (println "N:" (i/nrow cluster))
      (println "Terms:" top-terms))))

(defn ex-6-12 []
  (cluster-summary dictionary (ex-6-11) 5))
```

k-means is by its nature a stochastic algorithm, and is sensitive to the starting position for the centroids. I get the following output, but yours will almost certainly differ:

```
;; N: 2
;; Terms: (rocket launch delta satellit first off weather space)
;; N: 4
;; Terms: (said will for system 000 bank debt from bond farm)
;; N: 12
;; Terms: (said reuter for iranian it iraq had new on major)
;; N: 62
;; Terms: (said pct dlr for year mln from reuter with will)
;; N: 20
;; Terms: (said for year it with but dlr mln bank week)
```

Unfortunately, we don't seem to be getting very good results. The first cluster contains two articles about rockets and space, and the third seems to consist of articles about Iran. The most popular word in most of the articles is "said".

Better clustering with TF-IDF

Term Frequency-Inverse Document Frequency (TF-IDF) is a general approach to weighting terms within a document vector so that terms that are popular across the whole dataset are not weighted as highly as terms that are less usual. This captures the intuitive conviction—and what we observed earlier—that words such as "said" are not a strong basis for building clusters.

Zipf's law

Zipf's law states that the frequency of any word is inversely proportional to its rank in the frequency table. Thus, the most frequent word will occur approximately twice as often as the second most frequent word and three times as often as the next most frequent word, and so on. Let's see if this applies across our Reuters corpus:

```
(defn ex-6-13 []
  (let [documents (fs/glob "data/reuters-text/*.txt")
        doc-count 1000
        top-terms 25
        term-frequencies (->> (map slurp documents)
                              (remove too-short?)
                              (take doc-count)
                              (mapcat tokenize-reuters)
                              (frequencies)
                              (vals)
                              (sort >)
                              (take top-terms))]
    (-> (c/xy-plot (range (inc top-terms)) term-frequencies
                   :x-label "Terms"
                   :y-label "Term Frequency")
        (i/view))))
```

Using the preceding code we can calculate the frequency graph of the top 25 most popular terms in the first 1,000 Reuters documents.

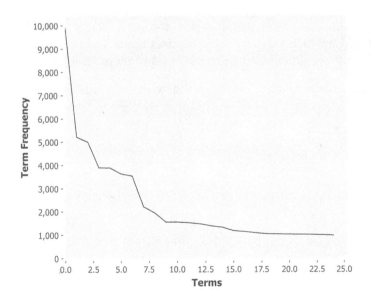

In the first 1,000 documents, the most popular term appears almost 10,000 times. The 25th most popular term appears around 1,000 times overall. In fact, the data is showing that words are appearing more commonly in the Reuters corpus than their placement in the frequency table would suggest. This is most likely due to the bulletin nature of the Reuters corpus, which tends to re-use the same short words repeatedly.

Calculating the TF-IDF weight

Calculating TF-IDF only requires two modifications to the code we've created already. Firstly, we must keep track of how many documents a given term appears in. Secondly, we must weight the term appropriately when building the document vector.

Since we've already created a dictionary of terms, we may as well store the document frequencies for each term there.

```
(defn inc-df! [dictionary term-id]
  (doto dictionary
    (swap! update-in [:df term-id] (fnil inc 0)))))

(defn build-df-dictionary! [dictionary document]
  (let [terms     (distinct document)
        dict      (build-dictionary! dictionary document)
        term-ids  (map #(term-id dictionary %) document)]
    (doseq [term-id term-ids]
      (inc-df! dictionary term-id))
    dict))
```

The `build-df-dictionary` function earlier accepts a dictionary and a sequence of terms. We build the dictionary from the distinct terms and look up the `term-id` for each one. Finally, we iterate over the term IDs and increment the `:df` for each one.

If a document has words $w_1, ..., w_n$, then the inverse document frequency for word w_i is defined as:

$$\text{IDF}(w_i) = \frac{1}{\text{DF}(w_i)}$$

That is, the reciprocal of the number of documents it appears in. If a word occurs commonly across a collection of documents, its *DF* value is large and its *IDF* value is small. With a large number of documents, it's common to normalize the *IDF* value by multiplying it by a constant number, usually the document count *N*, so the *IDF* equation looks like this:

$$\text{IDF}(w_i) = \frac{N}{\text{DF}(w_i)}$$

The TF-IDF weight W_i of word w_i is given by the product of the term frequency and the inverse document frequency:

$$W_i = \text{TF}(w_i) \cdot \text{IDF}(w_i) = \text{TF}(w_i) \frac{N}{\text{DF}(w_i)}$$

However, the *IDF* value in the preceding equation is still not ideal since for large corpora the range of the *IDF* term is usually much greater than the *TF* and can overwhelm its effect. To reduce this problem, and balance the weight of the *TF* and the *IDF* terms, the usual practice is to use the logarithm of the *IDF* value instead:

$$\text{IDF}(w_i) = \log \frac{N}{\text{DF}(w_i)}$$

Thus, the TF-IDF weight W_i for a word w_i becomes:

$$W_i = \text{TF}(w_i) \cdot \log \frac{N}{\text{DF}(w_i)}$$

This is a classic TF-IDF weighting: common words are given a small weight and terms that occur infrequently get a large weight. The important words for determining the topic of a document usually have a high *TF* and a moderately large *IDF*, so the product of the two becomes a large value, thereby giving more importance to these words in the resulting vector.

```
(defn document-frequencies [dict terms]
  (->> (map (partial term-id dict) terms)
       (select-keys (:df @dict)))))

(defn tfidf-vector [dict doc-count terms]
  (let [tf (term-frequencies dict terms)
```

```
      df (document-frequencies dict (distinct terms))
      idf  (fn [df] (i/log (/ doc-count df)))
      tfidf (fn [tf df] (* tf (idf df)))]
  (map->vector dict (merge-with tfidf tf df)))))
```

The preceding code calculates the TF-IDF from `term-frequencies` defined previously and `document-frequencies` extracted from our dictionary.

k-means clustering with TF-IDF

With the preceding adjustments in place, we're in a position to calculate the TF-IDF vectors for the Reuters documents. The following example is a modification of `ex-6-12` using the new `tfidf-vector` function:

```
(defn ex-6-14 []
  (let [documents (fs/glob "data/reuters-text/*.txt")
        doc-count 100
        k 5
        tokenized (->> (map slurp documents)
                       (remove too-short?)
                       (take doc-count)
                       (map stem-reuters))]
    (reduce build-df-dictionary! dictionary tokenized)
    (-> (map #(tfidf-vector dictionary doc-count %) tokenized)
        (k-means k)
        (cluster-summary dictionary 10))))
```

The preceding code is very similar to the previous example, but we have substituted our new `build-df-dictionary` and `tfidf-vector` functions. If you run the example, you should see output that looks a little better than before:

```
N: 5
Terms: (unquot unadjust year-on-year novemb grew sundai labour m-3
ahead 120)
N: 15
Terms: (rumor venezuela azpurua pai fca keat ongpin boren gdp
moder)
N: 16
Terms: (regan drug lng soviet bureau deleg gao dean fdic algerian)
N: 46
Terms: (form complet huski nrc rocket north underwrit card oat
circuit)
N: 18
Terms: (freez cocoa dec brown bean sept seixa telex argentin
brown-forman)
```

Although the top words may be hard to interpret because they have been stemmed, these represent the most unusually common words within each of the clusters. Notice that "said" is no longer the most highly rated word across all clusters.

Better clustering with n-grams

It should be clear from looking at the earlier lists of words how much has been sacrificed by reducing our documents to unordered sequences of terms. Without the context of a sentence, it's very hard to get more than a vague sense of what each cluster might be about.

There is, however, nothing inherent in the vector space model that precludes maintaining the order of our input tokens. We can simply create a new term to represent a combination of words. The combined term, representing perhaps several input words in sequence, is called an *n*-gram.

An example of an *n*-gram might be "new york", or "stock market". In fact, because they contain two terms, these are called **bigrams**. *n*-grams can be of arbitrary length. The longer an *n*-gram, the more context it carries, but also the rarer it is.

n-grams are closely related to the concept of **shingling**. When we shingle our *n*-grams, we're creating overlapping sequences of terms. The term shingling comes from the way the terms overlap like roof shingles.

```
(defn n-grams [n words]
  (->> (partition n 1 words)
       (map (partial str/join " "))))

(defn ex-6-15 []
  (let [terms (reuters-terms "reut2-020.sgm-761.txt")]
    (n-grams 2 terms)))

;; ("reagan says" "says he" "he sees" "sees no" "no recession")
```

Already, using 2-grams would allow us (for example) to distinguish between the following uses of the word "coconut" in the dataset: "coconut oil", "coconut planters", "coconut plantations", "coconut farmers", "coconut association", "coconut authority", "coconut products", "coconut exports", "coconut industry", and the rather pleasing "coconut chief". Each of these pairs of words defines a different concept—sometimes subtly different—that we can capture and compare across documents.

We can get the best of both worlds with *n*-grams and shingling by combining the results of multiple lengths of *n*-gram:

```
(defn multi-grams [n words]
  (->> (range 1 (inc n))
       (mapcat #(n-grams % words))))

(defn ex-6-16 []
  (let [terms (reuters-terms "reut2-020.sgm-761.txt")]
    (multi-grams 4 terms)))

;; ("reagan" "says" "he" "sees" "no" "recession" "reagan says"
;; "says he" "he sees" "sees no" "no recession" "reagan says he"
;; "says he sees" "he sees no" "sees no recession" "reagan says he
;; sees" "says he sees no" "he sees no recession")
```

While stemming and stop word removal had the effect of reducing the size of our dictionary, and using TF-IDF had the effect of improving the utility of the weight for each term in a document, producing *n*-grams has the effect of massively expanding the number of terms we need to accommodate.

This explosion of features is going to immediately overwhelm our implementation of *k*-means in Incanter. Fortunately, there's a machine learning library called **Mahout** that's specifically designed to run algorithms such as *k*-means on very large quantities of data.

Large-scale clustering with Mahout

Mahout (http://mahout.apache.org/) is a machine learning library intended for use in distributed computing environments. Version 0.9 of the library targets Hadoop and is the version we'll be using here.

 At the time of writing, Mahout 0.10 has just been released and also targets Spark. Spark is an alternative distributed computing framework that we'll be introducing in the next chapter.

We saw in the previous chapter that one of Hadoop's abstractions is the sequence file: a binary representation of Java keys and values. Many of Mahout's algorithms expect to operate on sequence files, and we'll need to create one as input to Mahout's *k*-means algorithm. Mahout's *k*-means algorithm also expects to receive its input as a vector, represented by one of Mahout's vector types.

Although Mahout contains classes and utility programs that will extract vectors from text, we'll use this as an opportunity to demonstrate how to use Parkour and Mahout together. Not only will we have finer-grained control over the vectors that are created, but it will allow us to demonstrate more of the capabilities of Parkour for specifying Hadoop jobs.

Converting text documents to a sequence file

We won't define a custom job to convert our text documents into a sequence file representation, though: Mahout already defines a useful `SequenceFilesFromDirectory` class to convert a directory of text files. We'll use this to create a single file representing the entire contents of the `reuters-txt` directory.

Though the sequence file may be physically stored in separate chunks (on HDFS, for example), it is logically one file, representing all the input documents as key/value pairs. The key is the name of the file, and the value is the file's text contents.

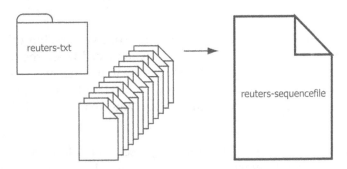

The following code will handle the conversion:

```
(:import [org.apache.mahout.text
           SequenceFilesFromDirectory])

(defn text->sequencefile [in-path out-path]
  (SequenceFilesFromDirectory/main
    (into-array String (vector "-i" in-path
                               "-o" out-path
                               "-xm" "sequential"
                               "-ow"))))

(defn ex-6-17 []
  (text->sequencefile "data/reuters-text"
                      "data/reuters-sequencefile"))
```

`SequenceFilesFromDirectory` is a Mahout utility class, part of a suite of classes designed to be called on the command line.

 Since running the preceding example is a prerequisite for subsequent examples, it's also available on the command line:

`lein create-sequencefile`

We're calling the `main` function directly, passing the arguments we would otherwise pass on the command line as a string array.

Using Parkour to create Mahout vectors

Now that we have a sequence file representation of the Reuters corpus, we need to transform each document (now represented as a single key/value pair) into a vector. We saw how to do this earlier using a shared dictionary modeled as a Clojure atom. The atom ensures that each distinct term gets its own ID even in a multi-threaded environment.

We will be using Parkour and Hadoop to generate our vectors, but this presents a challenge. How can we assign a unique ID to each word when the nature of MapReduce programming is that mappers operate in parallel and share no state? Hadoop doesn't provide the equivalent of a Clojure atom for sharing mutable state across nodes in a cluster, and in fact minimizing shared state is key to scaling distributed applications.

Creating a shared set of unique IDs therefore presents an interesting challenge for our Parkour job: let's see how we can produce unique IDs for our dictionary in a distributed way.

Creating distributed unique IDs

Before we look at Hadoop-specific solutions, though, it's worth noting that one easy way of creating a cluster-wide unique identifier is to create a universally unique identifier, or UUID.

```
(defn uuid []
  (str (java.util.UUID/randomUUID)))
```

This creates a long string of bytes in the form: `3a65c7db-6f41-4087-a2ec-8fe763b5f185` that is virtually guaranteed not to clash with any other UUID generated anywhere else in the world.

While this works for generating unique IDs, the number of possible IDs is astronomically large, and Mahout's sparse vector representation needs to be initialized with the cardinality of the vector expressed as an integer. IDs generated with uuid are simply too big. Besides, it doesn't help us coordinate the creation of IDs: every machine in the cluster will generate different UUIDs to represent the same terms.

One way of getting around this is to use the term itself to generate a unique ID. If we used a consistent hashing function to create an integer from each input term, all machines in the cluster would generate the same ID. Since a good hashing function is likely to produce a unique output for unique input terms, this technique is likely to work well. There will be some hash collisions (where two words hash to the same ID) but this should be a small percentage of the overall.

> The method of hashing the features themselves to create a unique ID is often referred to as the "hashing trick". Although it's commonly used for text vectorization, it can be applied to any problem that involves large numbers of features.

However, the challenge of producing distinct IDs that are unique across the whole cluster gives us the opportunity to talk about a useful feature of Hadoop that Parkour exposes: the distributed cache.

Distributed unique IDs with Hadoop

Let's consider what our Parkour mapper and reducer might look like if we were to calculate unique, cluster-wide IDs. The mapper is easy: we'll want to calculate the document frequency for each term we encounter, so the following mapper simply returns a vector for each unique term: the first element of the vector (the key) is the term itself, and the second element (the value) is 1.

```
(defn document-count-m
  {::mr/source-as :vals}
  [documents]
  (->> documents
       (r/mapcat (comp distinct stemmer/stems))
       (r/map #(vector % 1))))
```

The reducer's job will be to take these key/value pairs of terms to document count and reduce them such that each unique term has a unique ID. A trivial way of doing this would be to ensure that there is only one reducer on the cluster. Since all the terms would all be passed to this single process, the reducer could simply keep an internal counter and assign each term an ID in a similar way to what we did with the Clojure atom earlier. This isn't taking advantage of Hadoop's distributed capabilities, though.

One feature of Parkour that we haven't introduced yet is the runtime context that's accessible from within every mapper and reducer. Parkour binds the `parkour.mapreduce/*context*` dynamic variable to the Hadoop task context of the task within which our mappers and reducers run. The task context contains, amongst other things, the following properties:

Property	Type	Description
`mapred.job.id`	String	The job's ID
`mapred.task.id`	int	The task attempt ID
`mapred.task.partition`	int	The ID of the task within the job

The last of these, the `mapred.task.partition` property, is the number of the task assigned by Hadoop, guaranteed to be a monotonically increasing integer unique across the cluster. This number is our task's global offset. Within each task we can also keep a local offset and output both with each word processed. The two offsets together—global and local—provide a unique identifier for the term across the cluster.

The following diagram visualizes the process for eight terms processed on three separate mappers:

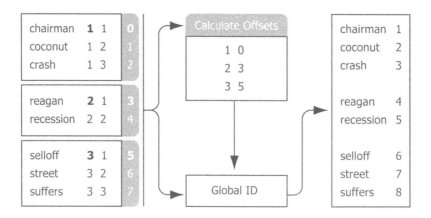

Each mapper is only aware of its own partition number and the term's local offset. However, these two numbers are all that's required to calculate a unique, global ID. The preceding **Calculate Offsets** box determines what the global offset should be for each task partition. Partition **1** has a global offset of **0**. Partition **2** has a global offset of **3**, because partition **1** processed **3** words. Partition **3** has an offset of **5**, because partitions **1** and **2** processed **5** words between them, and so on.

For the preceding approach to work, we need to know three things: the global offset of the mapper, the local offset of the term, and the total number of terms processed by each mapper. These three numbers can be used to define a unique, cluster-wide ID for each term. The reducer that creates these three numbers is defined as follows. It introduces a couple of new concepts that we'll discuss shortly.

```
(defn unique-index-r
  {::mr/source-as :keyvalgroups,
   ::mr/sink-as dux/named-keyvals}
  [coll]
  (let [global-offset (conf/get-long mr/*context*
                                      "mapred.task.partition" -1)]
    (tr/mapcat-state
      (fn [local-offset [word doc-counts]]
        [(inc local-offset)
         (if (identical? ::finished word)
           [[:counts [global-offset local-offset]]]
           [[:data [word [[global-offset local-offset]
                          (apply + doc-counts)]]]])])
      0 (r/mapcat identity [coll [[::finished nil]]]))))
```

The first step the reducer performs is to fetch the `global-offset`, the task partition for this particular reducer. We're using `mapcat-state`, a function defined in the transduce library (`https://github.com/brandonbloom/transduce`) to build up a sequence of tuples in the format `[[:data ["apple" [1 4]] [:data ["orange" [1 5]] ...]` where the vector of numbers `[1 4]` represents the global and local offsets respectively. Finally, when we've reached the end of this reduce task, we append a tuple to the sequence in the format `[:counts [1 5]]`. This represents the final local count, 5, for this particular reducer partition, 1. Thus, a single reducer is calculating all three of the elements we require to calculate all the term IDs.

The keyword provided to `::mr/source-as` is not one we've encountered previously. In the previous chapter, we saw how the shaping options `:keyvals`, `:keys`, and `:vals` let Parkour know how we wanted our data provided, and the structure of the data we'd be providing in return. For reducers, Parkour describes a more comprehensive set of shaping functions that account for the fact that inputs may be grouped. The following diagram illustrates the available options:

Key/value groups	[{○[◇◆]}{●[◇]}]
Key groups	[○●]
Value groups	[[◇◆][◇]]
Key-key/value groups	[{○[{○◇}{○◆}]}{●[{●◇}]}]
Key-key groups	[{○[○○]}{●[●]}]
Keys groups	[[○○][●]]

The option provided to `::mr/sink-as` is not one we've encountered before either. The `parkour.io.dux` namespace provides options for de-multiplexing outputs. In practice this means that, by sinking as `dux/named-keyvals`, a single reducer can write to several different outputs. In other words, we've introduced a fork into our data pipeline: some data is written to one branch, the rest to another.

Having set a sink specification of `dux/named-keyvals`, the first element of our tuple will be interpreted as the destination to write to; the second element of our tuple will be treated as the key/value pair to be written. As a result, we can write out the `:data` (the local and global offset) to one destination and the `:counts` (number of terms processed by each mapper) to another.

The job that makes use of the mapper and reducer that we've defined is presented next. As with the Parkour job we specified in the previous chapter, we chain together an input, map, partition, reduce, and output step.

```
(defn df-j [dseq]
  (-> (pg/input dseq)
      (pg/map #'document-count-m)
      (pg/partition (mra/shuffle [:string :long]))
      (pg/reduce #'unique-index-r)
      (pg/output :data (mra/dsink [:string index-value])
                 :counts (mra/dsink [:long :long])))))
```

There are two primary differences between the preceding code and the job specification we've seen previously. Firstly, our output specifies two named sinks: one for each of the outputs of our reducer. Secondly, we're using the `parkour.io.avro` namespace as `mra` to specify a schema for our data with `(mra/dsink [:string long-pair])`.

In the previous chapter we made use of Tesser's `FressianWritable` to serialize arbitrary Clojure data structures to disk. This worked because the contents of the `FressianWritable` did not need to be interpreted by Hadoop: the value was completely opaque. With Parkour, we have the option to define custom key/value pair types. Since the key and value do need to be interpreted as separate entities by Hadoop (for the purpose of reading, partitioning, and writing sequence files), Parkour allows us to define a "tuple schema" using the `parkour.io.avro` namespace, which explicitly defines the type of the key and the value. `long-pair` is a custom schema used to store both the local and global offset in a single tuple:

```
(def long-pair (avro/tuple-schema [:long :long]))
```

And, since schemas are composable, we can refer to the `long-pair` schema when defining our output schema: `(mra/dsink [:string long-pair])`.

> Parkour uses the library Acbracad to serialize Clojure data structures using Avro. For more information about serialization options consult the documentation for Abracad at `https://github.com/damballa/abracad`.

Let's look at another feature of Hadoop that Parkour exposes which allows our term ID job to be more efficient than it would otherwise be: the distributed cache.

Sharing data with the distributed cache

As we discussed in the previous section, if we know the local offset of each word for a particular mapper, and we know how many records each mapper processed overall, then we're in a position to calculate a unique, contiguous ID for each word.

The diagram that showed the process a few pages ago contained two central boxes each labeled **Calculate Offsets** and a **Global ID**. Those boxes map directly to the functions that we present next:

```
(defn global-id [offsets [global-offset local-offset]]
  (+ local-offset (get offsets global-offset)))

(defn calculate-offsets [dseq]
  (->> (into [] dseq)
```

```
(sort-by first)
(reductions (fn [[_ t] [i n]]
              [(inc i) (+ t n)])
            [0 0])
(into {})))
```

Once we've calculated the map of offsets to use for generating unique IDs, we'd really like them to be available to all of our map and reduce tasks as a shared resource. Having generated the offsets in a distributed fashion, we'd like to consume it in a distributed fashion too.

The distributed cache is Hadoop's way of allowing tasks to access common data. This is a much more efficient way of sharing small quantities of data (data that's small enough to reside in memory) than through potentially costly data joins.

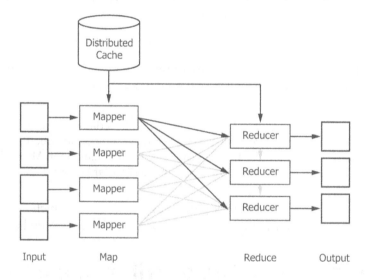

Before reading from the distributed cache, we have to write something to it. This can be achieved with Parkour's `parkour.io.dval` namespace:

```
(defn unique-word-ids [conf df-data df-counts]
  (let [offsets-dval (-> (calculate-offsets df-counts)
                         (dval/edn-dval))]
    (-> (pg/input df-data)
        (pg/map #'word-id-m offsets-dval)
        (pg/output (mra/dsink [word-id]))
        (pg/fexecute conf `word-id)
        (->> (r/map parse-idf)
             (into {}))
        (dval/edn-dval))))
```

Here, we're writing two sets of data to the distributed cache with the `dval/edn-dval` function. The first is the result of the `calculate-offsets` function just defined which is passed to the `word-id-m` mappers for their use. The second set of data written to the distributed cache is their output. We'll see how this is generated in the `word-id-m` function, as follows:

```
(defn word-id-m
  {::mr/sink-as :keys}
  [offsets-dval coll]
  (let [offsets @offsets-dval]
    (r/map
      (fn [[word word-offset]]
        [word (global-id offsets word-offset)])
      coll)))
```

The value returned by `dval/edn-dval` implements the `IDRef` interface. This means that we can use Clojure's `deref` function (or the deref macro character `@`) to retrieve the value that it wraps, just as we do with Clojure's atoms. Dereferencing the distributed value the first time causes the data to be downloaded from the distributed cache to a local mapper cache. Once the data is available locally, Parkour takes care of reconstructing the Clojure data structure (the map of offsets) that we wrote to it in EDN format.

Building Mahout vectors from input documents

In the previous sections, we took a detour to introduce several new Parkour and Hadoop concepts, but we're finally in a position to build text vectors for Mahout using unique IDs for every term. Some further code is omitted for brevity but the whole job is available to view in the `cljds.ch6.vectorizer` example code namespace.

As mentioned previously, Mahout's implementation of *k*-means expects us to provide a vector representation of our input using one of its vector classes. Since our dictionary is large, and most documents use few of these terms, we'll be using a sparse vector representation. The following code makes use of a `dictionary` distributed value to create a `org.apache.mahout.math.RandomAccessSparseVector` for every input document:

```
(defn create-sparse-tfidf-vector [dictionary [id doc]]
  (let [vector (RandomAccessSparseVector. (count dictionary))]
    (doseq [[term tf] (-> doc stemmer/stems frequencies)]
      (let [term-info (get dictionary term)
            id  (:id term-info)
            idf (:idf term-info)]
```

```
            (.setQuick vector id (* tf idf)))))
       [id vector]))

  (defn create-tfidf-vectors-m [dictionary coll]
    (let [dictionary @dictionary]
      (r/map #(create-sparse-tfidf-vector dictionary %) coll)))
```

Finally, we make use of the `create-tfidf-vectors-m` function, which brings everything we've covered together into a single Hadoop job:

```
(defn tfidf [conf dseq dictionary-path vector-path]
  (let [doc-count (->> dseq (into []) count)
        [df-data df-counts] (pg/execute (df-j dseq) conf df)
        dictionary-dval (make-dictionary conf df-data
                                         df-counts doc-count)]
    (write-dictionary dictionary-path dictionary-dval)
    (-> (pg/input dseq)
        (pg/map #'create-tfidf-vectors-m dictionary-dval)
        (pg/output (seqf/dsink [Text VectorWritable] vector-path))
        (pg/fexecute conf `vectorize))))
```

This task handles the creation of the dictionary, writing the dictionary to the distributed cache, and then using the dictionary — with the mapper we just defined — to convert each input document to a Mahout vector. To ensure sequence file compatibility with Mahout, we set the key/value classes of our final output to be `Text` and `VectorWritable`, where the key is the original filename of the document and the value is the Mahout vector representation of the contents.

We can call this job by running:

```
(defn ex-6-18 []
  (let [input-path   "data/reuters-sequencefile"
        output-path "data/reuters-vectors"]
    (vectorizer/tfidf-job (conf/ig) input-path output-path)))
```

The job will write the dictionary out to the `dictionary-path` (we'll be needing it again), and the vectors out to the `vector-path`.

 Since running the preceding example is a prerequisite for subsequent examples, it's also available on the command line:
lein create-vectors

Next, we'll discover how to use these vectors to actually perform clustering with Mahout.

Running k-means clustering with Mahout

Now that we have a sequence file of vectors suitable for consumption by Mahout, it's time to actually run *k*-means clustering on the whole dataset. Unlike our local Incanter version, Mahout won't have any trouble dealing with the full Reuters corpus.

As with the `SequenceFilesFromDirectory` class, we've created a wrapper around another of Mahout's command-line programs, `KMeansDriver`. The Clojure variable names make it easier to see what each command-line argument is for.

```clojure
(defn run-kmeans [in-path clusters-path out-path k]
  (let [distance-measure  "org.apache.mahout.common.distance.
CosineDistanceMeasure"
        max-iterations    100
        convergence-delta 0.001]
    (KMeansDriver/main
      (->> (vector "-i"  in-path
                   "-c"  clusters-path
                   "-o"  out-path
                   "-dm" distance-measure
                   "-x"  max-iterations
                   "-k"  k
                   "-cd" convergence-delta
                   "-ow"
                   "-cl")
           (map str)
           (into-array String)))))
```

We're providing the string `org.apache.mahout.common.distance.`
`CosineDistanceMeasure` to indicate to the driver that we'd like to use Mahout's implementation of the cosine distance measure. Mahout also includes a `EuclideanDistanceMeasure` and a `TanimotoDistanceMeasure` (similar to the Jaccard distance, the complement of the Jaccard index, but one that will operate on vectors rather than sets). Several other distance measures are also defined; consult the Mahout documentation for all the available options.

With the preceding `run-kmeans` function in place, we simply need to let Mahout know where to access our files. As in the previous chapter, we assume Hadoop is running in local mode and all file paths are relative to the project root:

```clojure
(defn ex-6-19 []
  (run-kmeans "data/reuters-vectors/vectors"
              "data/kmeans-clusters/clusters"
              "data/kmeans-clusters"
              10))
```

This example may run for a little while as Mahout iterates over our large dataset.

Viewing k-means clustering results

Once it's finished, we'll want to see a cluster summary for each cluster as we did with our Incanter implementation. Fortunately, Mahout defines a `ClusterDumper` class that will do exactly this for us. We need to provide the location of our clusters, of course, but we'll provide the location of our dictionary, too. Providing the dictionary means that the output can return the top terms for each cluster.

```
(defn run-cluster-dump [in-path dict-path points-dir out-path]
  (let [distance-measure
        "org.apache.mahout.common.distance.CosineDistanceMeasure"]
    (ClusterDumper/main
     (->> (vector "-i" in-path
                  "-o" out-path
                  "-d" dict-path
                  "--pointsDir" points-dir
                  "-dm" distance-measure
                  "-dt" "sequencefile"
                  "-b" "100"
                  "-n" "20"
                  "-sp" "0"
                  "--evaluate")
          (map str)
          (into-array String)))))
```

Next, we define the code that will actually call the `run-cluster-dump` function:

```
(defn path-for [path]
  (-> (fs/glob path)
      (first)
      (.getAbsolutePath)))

(defn ex-6-20 []
  (run-cluster-dump
   (path-for "data/kmeans-clusters/clusters-*-final")
   "data/reuters-vectors/dictionary/part-r-00000"
   "data/kmeans-clusters/clusteredPoints"
   "data/kmeans-clusterdump"))
```

We're making use of the `me.raynes.fs` library once again to determine which directory the final clusters are contained by. Mahout will append `-final` to the directory containing the final clusters, but we don't know ahead of time which directory this will be. The `fs/glob` function will find a directory that matches the pattern `clusters-*-final`, and replace * with whichever iteration number the true directory name contains.

Interpreting the clustered output

If you open the file created by the previous example, `data/kmeans-clusterdump`, in any text editor, you'll see output representing the top terms of the Mahout clusters. The file will be large, but an excerpt is provided next:

```
:VL-11417{n=312 c=[0.01:0.039, 0.02:0.030, 0.07:0.047, 0.1:0.037,
0.10:0.078, 0.11:0.152, 0.12:0.069,
    Top Terms:
        tonnes              =>      2.357810452962533
        department          =>      1.873890568048526
        wheat               =>      1.7797807546762319
        87                  =>      1.6685682321206117
        u.s                 =>      1.634764205186795
        mln                 =>      1.5050923755535712
        agriculture         =>      1.4595903158187866
        ccc                 =>      1.4314624499051998
        usda                =>      1.4069041441648433
        dlrs                =>      1.2770121846443567
```

The first line contains information about the cluster: the ID (in this case `VL-11417`) followed by curly braces containing the size of the cluster and the location of the cluster centroid. Since the text has been converted to weights and numeric IDs, the centroid is impossible to interpret on its own. The top terms beneath the centroid description hint at the contents of the cluster, though; they're the terms around which the cluster has coalesced.

```
VL-12535{n=514 c=[0:0.292, 0.25:0.015, 0.5:0.012, 00:0.137,
00.46:0.018, 00.50:0.036, 00.91:0.018, 0
    Top Terms:
        president           =>      3.330068911559851
        reagan              =>      2.485271333256584
        chief               =>      2.1148699971952327
        senate              =>      1.876725117983985
        officer             =>      1.8531712558019022
        executive           =>      1.7373591731030653
        bill                =>      1.6326750159727461
        chairman            =>      1.6280977206471365
        said                =>      1.6279512813119108
        house               =>      1.5771017798189988
```

The two clusters earlier hint at two clear topics present in the data set, although your clusters may be different due to the stochastic nature of the *k*-means algorithm.

Depending on your initial centroids and how many iterations you let the algorithm run, you may see clusters that appear "better" or "worse" in some respect. This will be based on an instinctive response to how well the clustered terms go together. But often it's not clear simply by looking at the top terms how well clustering has performed. In any case, instinct is not a very reliable way of judging the quality of an unsupervised learning algorithm. What we'd ideally like is some quantitative measure for how well the clustering has performed.

Cluster evaluation measures

At the bottom of the file we looked at in the previous section, you'll see some statistics that suggest how well the data has been clustered:

```
Inter-Cluster Density: 0.6135607681542804
Intra-Cluster Density: 0.6957348405534836
```

These two numbers can be considered as the equivalent to the variance within and the variance between measures we have seen in *Chapter 2, Inference* and *Chapter 3, Correlation*. Ideally, we are seeking a lower variance (or a higher density) within clusters compared to the density between clusters.

Inter-cluster density

Inter-cluster density is the average distance between cluster centroids. Good clusters probably don't have centers that are too close to each other. If they did, it would indicate the clustering is creating groups with similar features, and perhaps drawing distinctions between cluster members that are hard to support.

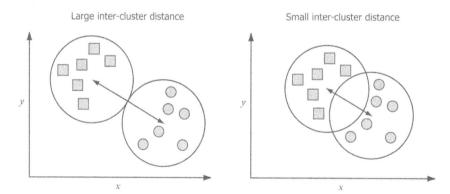

Thus, ideally our clustering will produce clusters with a **large inter-cluster distance**.

Intra-cluster density

By contrast, the intra-cluster density is a measure of how compact the clusters are. Ideally, clustering will identify groups of items that are similar to each other. Compact clusters indicate that all of the items within a cluster are strongly alike.

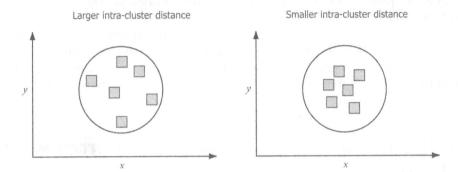

The best clustering outcomes therefore produce compact, distinct clusters with a **high intra-cluster density** and a **low inter-cluster density**.

It is not always clear how many clusters are justified by the data, though. Consider the following that shows the same dataset grouped into varying numbers of clusters. It's hard to say with any degree of confidence what the ideal number of clusters is.

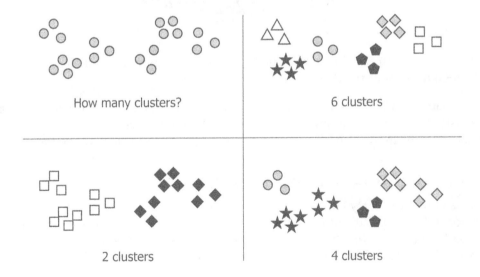

Although the preceding illustration is contrived, it illustrates a general issue with clustering data. There is often no one, clear "best" number of clusters. The most effective clustering will depend to a large degree on the ultimate use of the data.

We can however infer which might be better values of *k* by determining how the value of some quality score varies with the number of clusters. The quality score could be a statistic such as the inter- or intra-cluster density. As the number of clusters approaches its ideal, we would expect the value of this quality score to improve. Conversely, as the number of clusters diverges from its ideal we would expect the quality to decrease. To get a reasonable idea of how many clusters are justified in the dataset, therefore, we should run the algorithm many times for different values of *k*.

Calculating the root mean square error with Parkour

One of the most common measures of cluster quality is the **sum of squared errors (SSE)**. For each point, the error is the measured distance to the nearest cluster centroid. The total clustering SSE is therefore the sum over all clusters for a clustered point to its corresponding centroid:

$$\text{RMSE} = \sqrt{\frac{1}{n} \sum_{i=1}^{k} \sum_{x \in S_i} \|x - \mu_i\|^2}$$

where μ_i is the centroid of points in cluster S_i, k is the total number of clusters and n is the total number of points.

To calculate the *RMSE* in Clojure we therefore need to be able to relate each point in the cluster to its corresponding cluster centroid. Mahout saves cluster centroids and clustered points in two separate files, so in the next section we'll combine them.

Loading clustered points and centroids

Given a parent directory (e.g. `data/reuters-kmeans/kmeans-10`), the following function will load points into vectors stored in a map indexed by cluster ID using Parkour's `seqf/dseq` function to load key/value pairs from a sequence file. In this case, the key is the cluster ID (as an integer) and the value is the TF-IDF vector.

```
(defn load-cluster-points [dir]
  (->> (points-path dir)
       (seqf/dseq)
```

```
(r/reduce
  (fn [accum [k v]]
    (update-in accum [k] conj v)) {}))))
```

The output of the preceding function is a map keyed by cluster ID whose values are sequences of clustered points. Likewise, the following function will convert each cluster into a map, keyed by cluster ID, whose values are maps containing the keys :id and :centroid.

```
(defn load-cluster-centroids [dir]
  (let [to-tuple (fn [^Cluster kluster]
                   (let [id (.getId kluster)]
                     [id  {:id id
                           :centroid (.getCenter kluster)}]))]
    (->> (centroids-path dir)
         (seqf/dseq)
         (r/map (comp to-tuple last))
         (into {})))))
```

Having two maps keyed by cluster ID means that combining the clustered points and cluster centroids is a simple matter of calling merge-with on the maps supplying a custom merging function. In the following code, we merge the clustered points into the map containing the cluster :id and :centroid.

```
(defn assoc-points [cluster points]
  (assoc cluster :points points))

(defn load-clusters [dir]
  (->> (load-cluster-points dir)
       (merge-with assoc-points
                   (load-cluster-centroids dir))
       (vals)))
```

The final output is a single map, keyed by cluster ID, with each value as a map of :id, :centroid and :points. We'll use this map in the next section to calculate the clustering RMSE.

Calculating the cluster RMSE

To calculate the RMSE, we need to be able to establish the distance between every point and its associated cluster centroid. Since we used Mahout's `CosineDistanceMeasure` to perform the initial clustering, we should use the cosine distance to evaluate the clustering as well. In fact, we can simply make use of Mahout's implementation.

```
(def measure
  (CosineDistanceMeasure.))

(defn distance [^DistanceMeasure measure a b]
  (.distance measure a b))

(defn centroid-distances [cluster]
  (let [centroid (:centroid cluster)]
    (->> (:points cluster)
         (map #(distance measure centroid %)))))

(defn squared-errors [cluster]
  (->> (centroid-distances cluster)
       (map i/sq)))

(defn root-mean-square-error [clusters]
  (->> (mapcat squared-errors clusters)
       (s/mean)
       (i/sqrt)))
```

If the RMSE is plotted against the number of clusters, you'll find that it declines as the number of clusters increases. A single cluster will have the highest RMSE error (the variance of the original dataset from the mean), whereas the lowest RMSE will be the degenerate case when every point is in its own cluster (an RMSE of zero). Clearly either of these extremes will provide a poor explanation for the structure of the data. However, the RMSE doesn't decline in a straight line. It declines sharply as the number of clusters is increased from 1, but will fall more slowly once the "natural" number of clusters has been exceeded.

Therefore, one way of judging the ideal number of clusters is to plot how the RMSE changes with respect to the number of clusters. This is called the **elbow method**.

Determining optimal k with the elbow method

In order to determine the value of *k* using the elbow method, we're going to have to re-run *k*-means a number of times. The following code accomplishes this for all *k* between 2 and 21.

```
(defn ex-6-21 []
  (doseq [k (range 2 21)
          :let [dir (str "data/kmeans-clusters-" k)]]
    (println dir)
    (run-kmeans "data/reuters-vectors/vectors"
                (str dir "/clusters")
                dir k)))
```

This will take a little while to run, so it might be time to go and make a hot drink: the `println` statement will log each clustering run to let you know how much progress has been made. On my laptop the whole process takes about 15 minutes.

Once it's complete, you should be able to run the example to generate a scatter plot of the RMSE for each of the clustered values:

```
(defn ex-6-22 []
  (let [ks (range 2 21)
        ys (for [k ks
                 :let [dir (str "data/kmeans-clusters-" k)
                       clusters (load-clusters dir)]]
             (root-mean-square-error clusters))]
    (-> (c/scatter-plot ks ys
                        :x-label "k"
                        :y-label "RMSE")
        (i/view))))
```

This should return a plot similar to the following:

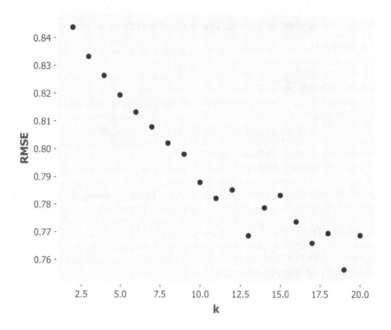

The preceding scatter plot shows the RMSE plotted against the number of clusters. It should be clear how the rate of RMSE change slows as *k* exceeds around 13 clusters and increasing the number of clusters further yields diminishing returns. Therefore, the preceding chart suggests for our Reuters data that around 13 clusters is a good choice.

The elbow method provides an intuitive means to determine the ideal number of clusters, but it is sometimes hard to apply in practice. This is because we must interpret the shape of the curve defined by the RMSE for each *k*. If *k* is small, or the RMSE contains a lot of noise, it may not be apparent where the elbow falls, or if there is an elbow at all.

Since clustering is an unsupervised learning algorithm, we assume here that the internal structure of the clusters is the only means of validating the quality of clustering. If true cluster labels are known then it's possible to use external validation measures (such as entropy) of the kind that we encountered in *Chapter 4, Classification* to validate the success of the model.

Other clustering evaluation schemes aim to provide a clearer means of determining the precise number of clusters. The two we'll cover are the Dunn index and the Davies-Bouldin index. Both are internal evaluation schemes, meaning that they only look at the structure of the clustered data. Each aims to identify the clustering that has produced the most compact, well-separated clusters, in different ways.

Determining optimal k with the Dunn index

The Dunn index offers an alternative way to choose the optimal number of k. Rather than considering the average error remaining in the clustered data, the Dunn index instead considers the ratio of two "worst-case" situations: the minimum distance between two cluster centroids, divided by the maximum cluster diameter. A higher index therefore indicates better clustering since in general we would like large inter-cluster distances and small intra-cluster distances.

For k clusters we can express the Dunn index in the following way:

$$DI_m = \frac{\min\limits_{1 \le i < j \le k} \delta\left(C_i, C_j\right)}{\max\limits_{1 \le m \le k} S_m}$$

where $\delta(C_i, C_j)$ distance between the two clusters C_i and C_j and $\max_{1 \le m \le k} S_m$ represents the size (or scatter) of the largest cluster.

There are several possible ways to calculate the scatter of a cluster. We could take the distance between the furthest two points inside a cluster, or the mean of all the pairwise distances between data points inside the cluster, or the mean of each data point from the cluster centroid itself. In the following code, we calculate the size by taking the median distance from the cluster centroid.

```
(defn cluster-size [cluster]
  (-> cluster
      centroid-distances
      s/median))

(defn dunn-index [clusters]
  (let [min-separation (->> (combinations clusters 2)
                            (map #(apply separation %))
                            (apply min))
        max-cluster-size (->> (map cluster-size clusters)
                              (apply max))]
    (/ min-separation max-cluster-size)))
```

The preceding code makes use of the `combinations` function from `clojure.math.combinatorics` (`https://github.com/clojure/math.combinatorics/`) to produce a lazy sequence of all pairwise combinations of clusters.

```
(defn ex-6-23 []
  (let [ks (range 2 21)
        ys (for [k ks
                 :let [dir (str "data/kmeans-clusters-" k)
                       clusters (load-clusters dir)]]
               (dunn-index clusters))]
    (-> (c/scatter-plot ks ys
                        :x-label "k"
                        :y-label "Dunn Index")
        (i/view))))
```

We use the `dunn-index` function in the preceding code to generate a scatter plot for the clusters from *k=2* to *k=20*:

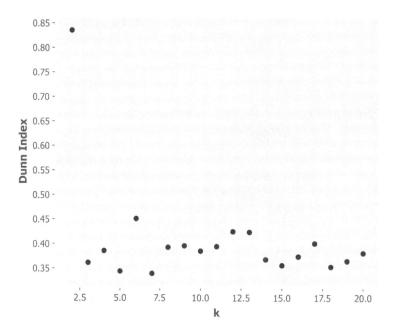

A higher Dunn index indicates a better clustering. Thus, it appears that the best clustering is for *k=2*, followed by *k=6*, with *k=12* and *k=13* following closely behind. Let's try an alternative cluster evaluation scheme and compare the results.

Determining optimal k with the Davies-Bouldin index

The Davies-Bouldin index is an alternative evaluation scheme that measures the mean ratio of size and separation for all values in the cluster. For each cluster, an alternative cluster is found that maximizes the ratio of the sum of cluster sizes divided by the inter-cluster distance. The Davies-Bouldin index is defined as the mean of this value for all clusters in the data:

$$D_i = \max_{i \neq j} \frac{S_i + S_j}{\delta(C_i, C_j)}$$

$$DB = \frac{1}{n} \sum_{i=1}^{n} D_i$$

where $\delta(C_i, C_j)$ is the distance between the two cluster centroids C_i and C_j, and S_i and S_j are the scatter. We can calculate the Davies-Bouldin index using the following code:

```
(defn scatter [cluster]
  (-> (centroid-distances cluster)
      (s/mean)))

(defn assoc-scatter [cluster]
  (assoc cluster :scatter (scatter cluster)))

(defn separation [a b]
  (distance measure (:centroid a) (:centroid b)))

(defn davies-bouldin-ratio [a b]
  (/ (+ (:scatter a)
        (:scatter b))
     (separation a b)))

(defn max-davies-bouldin-ratio [[cluster & clusters]]
  (->> (map #(davies-bouldin-ratio cluster %) clusters)
       (apply max)))

(defn rotations [xs]
  (take (count xs)
        (partition (count xs) 1 (cycle xs))))

(defn davies-bouldin-index [clusters]
```

```
    (let [ds (->> (map assoc-scatter clusters)
                  (rotations)
                  (map max-davies-bouldin-ratio))]
      (s/mean ds)))
```

Let's now plot the Davies-Bouldin on a scatter plot for clusters *k=2* to *k=20*:

```
(defn ex-6-24 []
  (let [ks (range 2 21)
        ys (for [k ks
                 :let [dir (str "data/kmeans-clusters-" k)
                       clusters (load-clusters dir)]]
             (davies-bouldin-index clusters))]
    (-> (c/scatter-plot ks ys
                        :x-label "k"
                        :y-label "Davies-Bouldin Index")
        (i/view)))))
```

This should generate the following plot:

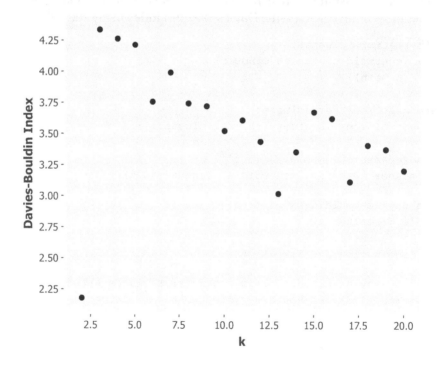

Unlike the Dunn index, the Davies-Bouldin index is minimized for good clustering schemes since in general we seek out clusters that are compact in size and have high inter-cluster distances. The preceding chart suggests that $k=2$ is the ideal cluster size followed by $k=13$.

The drawbacks of k-means

k-means is one of the most popular clustering algorithms due to its relative ease of implementation and the fact that it can be made to scale well to very large datasets. In spite of its popularity, there are several drawbacks.

k-means is stochastic, and does not guarantee to find the global optimum solution for clustering. In fact, the algorithm can be very sensitive to outliers and noisy data: the quality of the final clustering can be highly dependent on the position of the initial cluster centroids. In other words, k-means will regularly discover a local rather than global minimum.

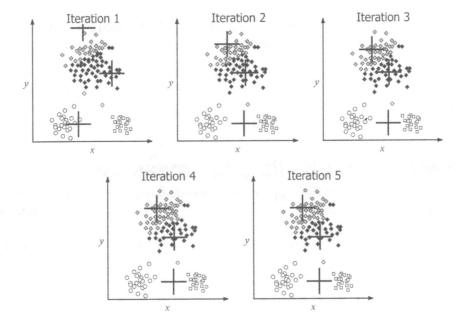

The preceding diagram illustrates how *k*-means may converge to a local minimum based on poor initial cluster centroids. Non-optimal clustering may even occur if the initial cluster centroids are well-placed, since *k*-means prefers clusters with similar sizes and densities. Where clusters are not approximately equal in size and density, *k*-means may fail to converge to the most natural clustering:

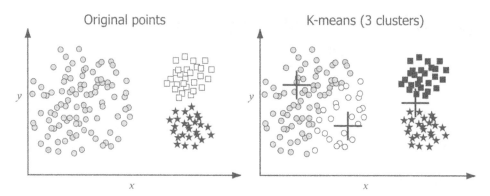

Also, *k*-means strongly prefers clusters that are "globular" in shape. Clusters with more intricate shapes are not well-identified by the *k*-means algorithm.

In the next chapter, we'll see how a variety of dimensionality reduction techniques can help work around these problems. But before we get there, let's develop an intuition for an alternative way of defining distance: as a measure of how far away from a "group" of things an element is.

The Mahalanobis distance measure

We saw at the beginning of the chapter how some distance measures may be more appropriate than others, given your data, by showing how the Jaccard, Euclidean, and cosine measures relate to data representation. Another factor to consider when choosing a distance measure and clustering algorithm is the internal structure of your data. Consider the following scatter plot:

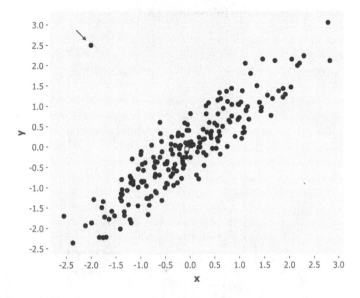

It's "obvious" that the point indicated by the arrow is distinct from the other points. We can clearly see that it's far from the distribution of the others and therefore represents an anomaly. Yet, if we calculate the Euclidean distance of all points from the mean (the "centroid"), the point will be lost amongst the others that are equivalently far, or even further, away:

```
(defn ex-6-25 []
  (let [data (dataset-with-outlier)
        centroid (i/matrix [[0 0]])
        distances (map #(s/euclidean-distance centroid %) data)]
    (-> (c/bar-chart (range 202) distances
                     :x-label "Points"
                     :y-label "Euclidean Distance")
        (i/view))))
```

The preceding code generates the following chart:

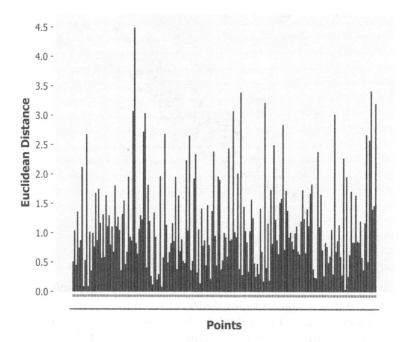

The Mahalanobis distance takes into account the covariance among the variables in calculating distances. In two dimensions, we can imagine the Euclidean distance as a circle growing out from the centroid: all points at the edge of the circle are equidistant from the centroid. The Mahalanobis distance stretches and skews this circle to correct for the respective scales of the different variables, and to account for correlation amongst them. We can see the effect in the following example:

```
(defn ex-6-26 []
  (let [data (dataset-with-outlier)
        distances    (map first (s/mahalanobis-distance data))]
    (-> (c/bar-chart (range 202) distances
                     :x-label "Points"
                     :y-label "Mahalanobis Distance")
        (i/view))))
```

The preceding code uses the function provided by `incanter.stats` to plot the Mahalanobis distance between the same set of points. The result is shown on the following chart:

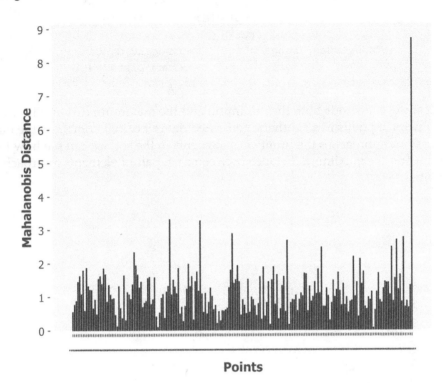

This chart clearly identifies one point in particular as being much more distant than the other points. This matches our perception that this point in particular should be considered as being further away from the others.

The curse of dimensionality

There is one fact that the Mahalanobis distance measure is unable to overcome, though, and this is known as the curse of dimensionality. As the number of dimensions in a dataset rises, every point tends to become equally far from every other point. We can demonstrate this quite simply with the following code:

```
(defn ex-6-27 []
  (let [distances (for [d (range 2 100)
                    :let [data (->> (dataset-of-dimension d)
                                    (s/mahalanobis-distance)
                                    (map first))]]
```

```
                           [(apply min data) (apply max data)])])
    (-> (c/xy-plot (range 2 101) (map first distances)
                   :x-label "Number of Dimensions"
                   :y-label "Distance Between Points"
                   :series-label "Minimum Distance"
                   :legend true)
        (c/add-lines (range 2 101) (map second distances)
                     :series-label "Maximum Distance")
        (i/view)))))
```

The preceding code finds both the minimum and the maximum distance between any two pairs of points in a synthetic generated dataset of 100 points. As the number of dimensions approaches the number of elements in the set, we can see how the minimum and the maximum distance between each pair of elements approach one another:

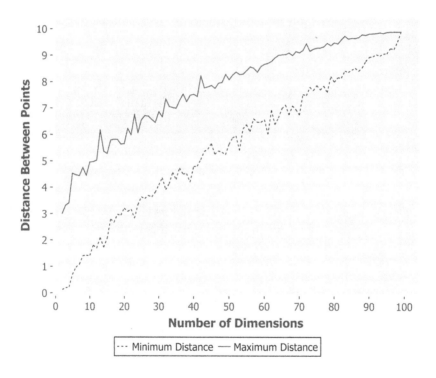

The effect is striking: as the number of dimensions increases, the distance between the closest two points rises too. The distance between the furthest two points rises as well, but at a slower rate. Finally, with 100 dimensions and 100 data points, every point appears to be equally far from every other.

Of course, this is synthetic, randomly generated data. If we're attempting to cluster our data, we implicitly hope that it will have a discernible internal structure that we can tease out. Nonetheless, this structure will become more and more difficult to identify as the number of dimensions rises.

Summary

In this chapter, we've learned about the process of clustering and covered the popular *k*-means clustering algorithm to cluster large numbers of text documents.

This provided an opportunity to cover the specific challenges presented by text processing where data is often messy, ambiguous, and high-dimensional. We saw how both stop words and stemming can help to reduce the number of dimensions and how TF-IDF can help identify the most important dimensions. We also saw how *n*-grams and shingling can help to tease out context for each word at the cost of a vast proliferation of terms.

We've explored Parkour in greater detail and seen how it can be used to write sophisticated, scalable, Hadoop jobs. In particular, we've seen how to make use of the distributed cache and custom tuple schemas to write Hadoop job process data represented as Clojure data structures. We used both of these to implement a method for generating unique, cluster-wide term IDs.

Finally, we witnessed the challenge presented by very high-dimensional spaces: the so-called "curse of dimensionality". In the next chapter, we'll cover this topic in more detail and describe a variety of techniques to combat it. We'll continue to explore the concepts of "similarity" and "difference" as we consider the problem of recommendation: how we can match users and items together.

7
Recommender Systems

"People who like this sort of thing will find this the sort of thing they like."

- attributed to Abraham Lincoln

In the previous chapter, we performed clustering on text documents using the k-means algorithm. This required us to have a measure of similarity between the text documents to be clustered. In this chapter, we'll be investigating recommender systems and we'll use this notion of similarity to suggest items that we think users might like.

We also saw the challenge presented by high-dimensional data—the so-called **curse of dimensionality**. Although it's not a problem specific to recommender systems, this chapter will show a variety of techniques that tackle its effects. In particular, we'll look at the means of establishing the most important dimensions with principle component analysis and singular value decomposition, and probabilistic ways of compressing very high dimensional sets with Bloom filters and MinHash. In addition—because determining the similarity of items with each other involves making many pairwise comparisons—we'll learn how to efficiently precompute groups with the most probable similarity using locality-sensitive hashing.

Finally, we'll introduce Spark, a distributed computation framework, and an associated Clojure library called Sparkling. We'll show how Sparkling can be used with Spark's machine learning library MLlib to build a distributed recommender system.

But first, we'll begin this chapter with a discussion on the basic types of recommender systems and implement one of the simplest in Clojure. Then, we'll demonstrate how Mahout, introduced in the previous chapter, can be used to create a variety of different types of recommender.

Download the code and data

In this chapter, we'll make use of data on film recommendations from the website `https://movielens.org/`. The site is run by GroupLens, a research lab in the Department of Computer Science and Engineering at the University of Minnesota, Twin Cities.

Datasets have been made available in several different sizes at `https://grouplens.org/datasets/movielens/`. In this chapter, we'll be making use of "MovieLens 100k"—a collection of 100,000 ratings from 1,000 users on 1,700 movies. As the data was released in 1998, it's beginning to show its age, but it provides a modest dataset on which we can demonstrate the principles of recommender systems. This chapter will give you the tools you need to process the more recently released "MovieLens 20M" data: 20 million ratings by 138,000 users on 27,000 movies.

> The code for this chapter is available from the Packt Publishing's website or from `https://github.com/clojuredatascience/ch7-recommender-systems`.

As usual, a shell script has been provided that will download and decompress the data to this chapter's `data` directory. You can run it from within the same code directory with:

script/download-data.sh

Once you've run the script, or downloaded an unpacked data manually, you should see a variety of files beginning with the letter "u". The ratings data we'll be mostly using in this chapter is in the `ua.base` file. The `ua.base`, `ua.test`, `ub.base`, and `ub.test` files contain subsets of the data to perform cross-validation. We'll also be using the `u.item` file, which contains information on the movies themselves.

Inspect the data

The ratings files are tab-separated, containing the field's user ID, item ID, rating, and timestamp. The user ID links to a row in the `u.user` file, which provides basic demographic information such as age, sex, and occupation:

```
(defn ex-7-1 []
  (->> (io/resource "ua.base")
       (io/reader)
       (line-seq)
       (first)))

;; "1\t1\t5\t874965758"
```

The string shows a single line from the file—a tab-separated line containing the user ID, item ID, rating (1-5), and timestamp showing when the rating was made. The rating is an integer from 1 to 5 and the timestamp is given as the number of seconds since January 1, 1970. The item ID links to a row in the u.item file.

We'll also want to load the u.item file, so we can determine the names of the items being rated (and the items being predicted in return). The following example shows how data is stored in the u.item file:

```
(defn ex-7-2 []
  (->> (io/resource "u.item")
       (io/reader)
       (line-seq)
       (first)))
```

```
;; "1|Toy Story (1995)|01-Jan-1995||http://us.imdb.com/M/title-
exact?Toy%20Story%20(1995)|0|0|0|1|1|1|0|0|0|0|0|0|0|0|0|0|0|0|0"
```

The first two fields are the item ID and name, respectively. Subsequent fields, not used in this chapter, are the release date, the URL of the movie on IMDB, and a series of flags indicating the genre of the movie.

Parse the data

Since the data will all fit in the main memory for convenience, we'll define several functions that will load the ratings into Clojure data structures. The line->rating function takes a line, splits it into fields where a tab character is found, converts each field to a long datatype, then uses zipmap to convert the sequence into a map with the supplied keys:

```
(defn to-long [s]
  (Long/parseLong s))

(defn line->rating [line]
  (->> (s/split line #"\t")
       (map to-long)
       (zipmap [:user :item :rating])))

(defn load-ratings [file]
  (with-open [rdr (io/reader (io/resource file))]
    (->> (line-seq rdr)
         (map line->rating)
         (into []))))

(defn ex-7-3 []
```

```
(->> (load-ratings "ua.base")
     (first)))

;; {:rating 5, :item 1, :user 1}
```

Let's write a function to parse the u.items file as well, so that we know what the movie names are:

```
(defn line->item-tuple [line]
  (let [[id name] (s/split line #"\|")]
    (vector (to-long id) name)))

(defn load-items [path]
  (with-open [rdr (io/reader (io/resource path))]
    (->> (line-seq rdr)
         (map line->item-tuple)
         (into {}))))
```

The load-items function returns a map of an item ID to a movie name, so that we can look up the names of movies by their ID.

```
(defn ex-7-4 []
  (-> (load-items "u.item")
      (get 1)))

;; "Toy Story (1995)"
```

With these simple functions in place, it's time to learn about the different types of recommender systems.

Types of recommender systems

There are typically two approaches taken to the problem of recommendation. Both make use of the notion of similarity between things, as we encountered it in the previous chapter.

One approach is to start with an item we know the user likes and recommend the other items that have similar attributes. For example, if a user is interested in action adventure movies, we might present to them a list of all the action adventure movies that we can offer. Or, if we have more data available than simply the genre—perhaps a list of tags—then we could recommend movies that have the most tags in common. This approach is called **content-based** filtering, because we're using the attributes of the items themselves to generate recommendations for similar items.

Another approach to recommendation is to take as input some measure of the user's preferences. This may be in the form of numeric ratings for movies, or of movies bought or previously viewed. Once we have this data, we can identify the movies that other users with similar ratings (or purchase history, viewing habits, and so on) have a preference for that the user in question has not already stated a preference for. This approach takes into account the behavior of other users, so it's commonly called **collaborative filtering**. Collaborative filtering is a powerful means of recommendation, because it harnesses the so-called "wisdom of the crowd".

In this chapter, we'll primarily study collaborative filtering approaches. However, by harnessing notions of similarity, we'll provide you with the concepts you'll need to implement content-based recommendation as well.

Collaborative filtering

By taking account only of the users' relationship to items, these techniques require no knowledge of the properties of the items themselves. This makes collaborative filtering a very general technique — the items in question can be anything that can be rated. We can picture collaborative filtering as the act of trying to fill a sparse matrix containing known ratings for users. We'd like to be able to replace the unknowns with predicted ratings and then recommend the predictions with the highest score.

Movies

1	?	?	5	4	?	?	2	1	4
3	?	4	3	?	?	?	?	2	1
4	2	?	2	4	1	?	?	2	2
?	4	4	?	5	4	3	1	?	1

Users

Notice that each question mark sits at the intersection of a row and a column. The rows contain a particular user's preference for all the movies they've rated. The columns contain the ratings for a particular movie from all the users who have rated it. To substitute the question marks in this matrix using only the other numbers in this matrix is the core challenge of collaborative filtering.

Item-based and user-based recommenders

Within the field of collaborative filtering, we can usefully make the distinction between two types of filtering—item-based and user-based recommenders. With item-based recommenders, we take a set of items that a user has already rated highly and look for other items that are similar. The process is visualized in the next diagram:

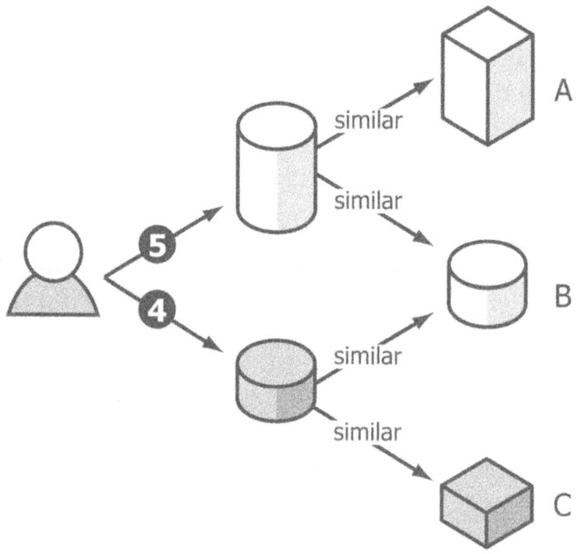

A recommender might recommend item **B**, based on the information presented in the diagram, since it's similar to two items that are already highly rated.

We can contrast this approach to the process of a user-based recommendation shown in the following diagram. A user-based recommendation aims to identify users with similar tastes to the user in question to recommend items that they have rated highly, but which the user has not already rated.

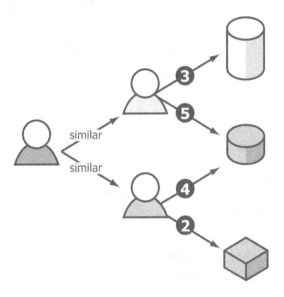

The user-based recommender is likely to recommend item **B**, because it has been rated highly by two other users with similar taste. We'll be implementing both kinds of recommenders in this chapter. Let's start with one of the simplest approaches — **Slope One** predictors for item-based recommendation.

Slope One recommenders

Slope One recommenders are a part of a family of algorithms introduced in a 2005 paper by Daniel Lemire and Anna Maclachlan. In this chapter, we'll introduce the weighted Slope One recommender.

 You can read the paper introducing the Slope One recommender at `http://lemire.me/fr/abstracts/SDM2005.html`.

To illustrate how weighted Slope One recommendation works, let's consider the simple example of four users, labeled **W, X, Y,** and **Z,** who have rated three movies — Amadeus, Braveheart, and Casablanca. The ratings each user has provided are illustrated in the following diagram:

	W	X	Y	Z
Amadeus	4	5	?	5
Braveheart	3	2	3.5	?
Casablanca	4	?	4	3

As with any recommendation problem, we're looking to replace the question marks with some estimate on how the user would rate the movie: the highest predicted ratings can be used to recommend new movies to users.

Weighted Slope One is an algorithm in two steps. Firstly, we must calculate the difference between the ratings for every pair of items. Secondly, we'll use this set of differences to make predictions.

Calculating the item differences

The first step of the Slope One algorithm is to calculate the average difference between each pair of items. The following equation may look intimidating but, in fact, it's simple:

$$\Delta_{i,j} = \sum_{u \in S_{i,j}(X)} \frac{u_i - u_j}{\text{card}\left(S_{i,j}\left(R\right)\right)}$$

The formula calculates $\Delta_{i,j}$, which is the average difference between the ratings for items i and j. It does so by summing over all the u taken from $S_{i,j}(R)$, which is the set of all the users who have rated both the items. The quantity that is summed is $u_i - u_j$, the difference between the user's rating for items i and j divided by $\text{card}\left(S_{i,j}\left(R\right)\right)$, the cardinality of set $S_{i,j}(R)$, or the number of people who have rated both the items.

Let's make this more concrete by applying the algorithm to the ratings in the previous diagram. Let's calculate the difference between the ratings for "Amadeus" and "Braveheart".

There are two users who have rated both the movies, so $\mathrm{card}\left(S_{i,j}(R)\right)$ is two. For each of these users, we take the difference between their ratings for each of the two movies and add them together.

$$\Delta_{amadeus,braveheart} = \frac{(4-3)}{2} + \frac{(5-2)}{2} = \frac{1}{2} + \frac{3}{2} = 2$$

The result is 2, meaning on average, users voted Amadeus two ratings higher than Braveheart. As you might expect, if we calculate the difference in the other direction, between Braveheart and Amadeus, we get -2:

$$\Delta_{braveheart,amadeus} = \frac{(3-4)}{2} + \frac{(2-5)}{2} = \frac{-1}{2} + \frac{-3}{2} = -2$$

We can think of the result as the average difference in the rating between the two movies, as judged by all the people who have rated both the movies. If we perform the calculation several more times, we could end up with the matrix in the following diagram, which shows the average pairwise difference in the rating for each of the three movies:

	Amadeus	Braveheart	Casablanca
Amadeus	0	2	1
Braveheart	-2	0	-0.75
Casablanca	-1	0.75	0

By definition, the values on the main diagonal are zero. Rather than continuing our calculations manually, we can express the computation in the following Clojure code, which will build up a sequence of differences between the pairs of items that every user has rated:

```clojure
(defn conj-item-difference [dict [i j]]
  (let [difference (-  (:rating j) (:rating i))]
    (update-in dict [(:item i) (:item j)] conj difference)))

(defn collect-item-differences [dict items]
  (reduce conj-item-difference dict
          (for [i items
                j items
                :when (not= i j)]
            [i j]))))

(defn item-differences [user-ratings]
  (reduce collect-item-differences {} user-ratings))
```

The following example loads the `ua.base` file into a sequence of ratings using the functions we defined at the beginning of the chapter. The `collect-item-differences` function takes each user's list of ratings and, for each pair of rated items, calculates the difference between the ratings. The `item-differences` function reduces over all the users to build up a sequence of pairwise differences between the items for all the users who have rated both the items:

```clojure
(defn ex-7-5 []
  (->> (load-ratings "ua.base")
       (group-by :user)
       (vals)
       (item-differences)
       (first)))
```

```clojure
;; [893 {558 (-2 4), 453 (-1), 637 (-1), 343 (-2 -2 3 2) ...]
```

We're storing the lists in both directions as values contained within the nested maps, so we can retrieve the differences between any two items using `get-in`:

```clojure
(defn ex-7-6 []
  (let [diffs (->> (load-ratings "ua.base")
                   (group-by :user)
                   (vals)
                   (item-differences))]
    (println "893:343" (get-in diffs [893 343]))))
```

```
        (println "343:893" (get-in diffs [343 893])))))

;; 893:343 (-2 -2 3 2)
;; 343:893 (2 2 -3 -2)
```

To use these differences for prediction, we'll need to summarize them into a mean and keep track of the count of ratings on which the mean was based:

```
(defn summarize-item-differences [related-items]
  (let [f (fn [differences]
            {:mean  (s/mean differences)
             :count (count  differences)})]
    (map-vals f related-items)))

(defn slope-one-recommender [ratings]
  (->> (item-differences ratings)
       (map-vals summarize-item-differences)))

(defn ex-7-7 []
  (let [recommender (->> (load-ratings "ua.base")
                         (group-by :user)
                         (vals)
                         (slope-one-recommender))]
    (get-in recommender [893 343])))

;; {:mean 0.25, :count 4}
```

One of the practical benefits of this method is that we have to perform the earlier step only once. From this point onwards, we can incorporate future user ratings by adjusting the mean difference and count only for the items that the user has already rated. For example, if a user has already rated 10 items, which have been incorporated into the earlier data structure, the eleventh rating only requires that we recalculate the differences for the eleven items. It is not necessary to perform the computationally expensive differencing process from scratch to incorporate new information.

Making recommendations

Now that we have calculated the average differences for each pair of items, we have all we need to recommend new items to users. To see how, let's return to one of our earlier examples.

User **X** has already provided ratings for **Amadeus** and **Braveheart**. We'd like to infer how they would rate the movie **Casablanca** so that we can decide whether or not to recommend it to them.

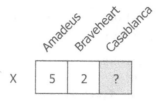

In order to make predictions for a user, we need two things – the matrix of differences we calculated just now and the users' own previous ratings. Given these two things, we can calculate a predicted rating $\hat{r}$ for item j, given user u, using the following formula:

$$c_{j,i} = \mathrm{card}\left(S_{j,i}(R)\right)$$

$$\hat{r}_{j|u} = \frac{\sum_{i \in S(u); i \neq j} \left(\Delta_{i,j} + u_i\right) c_{j,i}}{\sum_{i \in S(u); i \neq j} c_{j,i}}$$

As before, this equation looks more complicated than it is, so let's step through it, starting with the numerator.

The $\sum_{i \in S(u); i \neq j} \cdots$ expression means that we're summing over all the i items that user u has rated (which clearly does not include j, the item for which we're trying to predict a rating). The sum we calculate is over the difference between the users' rating for i and j, plus u's rating for i. We multiply that quantity by $c_{j,i}$ – the number of users that rated both.

The $\sum_{i \in S(u); i \neq j} c_{j,i}$ denominator is simply the sum of all the users who have rated j and any of the movies that user u has rated. It's a constant factor to adjust the size of the numerator downwards to ensure that the output can be interpreted as a rating.

Let's illustrate the previous formula by calculating the predicted rating of user X for "Casablanca" using the table of differences and the ratings provided earlier:

$$\hat{r}_{casablanca|B} = \frac{(-1+5)\times 2 + (0.75+2)\times 2}{4}$$

$$\hat{r}_{casablanca|B} = \frac{13.5}{4} = 3.375$$

So, given the previous ratings, we would predict that user X would rate Casablanca **3.375**. By performing the same process for all the items also rated by the people who rated any of the other items rated by user X, we can arrive at a set of recommendations for user X.

The Clojure code calculates the weighted rating for all such candidates:

```
(defn candidates [recommender {:keys [rating item]}]
  (->> (get recommender item)
       (map (fn [[id {:keys [mean count]}]]
              {:item id
               :rating (+ rating mean)
               :count count})))))

(defn weighted-rating [[id candidates]]
  (let [ratings-count (reduce + (map :count candidates))
        sum-rating (map #(* (:rating %) (:count %)) candidates)
        weighted-rating (/ (reduce + sum-rating) ratings-count)]
    {:item id
     :rating weighted-rating
     :count  ratings-count}))
```

Next, we calculate a weighted rating, which is the weighted average rating for each candidate. The weighted average ensures that the differences generated by large numbers of users count for more than those generated by only a small number of users:

```
(defn slope-one-recommend [recommender rated top-n]
  (let [already-rated  (set (map :item rated))
        already-rated? (fn [{:keys [id]}]
                         (contains? already-rated id))
        recommendations (->> (mapcat #(candidates recommender %)
                                     rated)
                             (group-by :item)
                             (map weighted-rating)
```

```
                               (remove already-rated?)
                               (sort-by :rating >))]
      (take top-n recommendations)))
```

Finally, we remove from the candidate pool any items we have already rated and order the remainder by rating descending: we can take just the highest rated results and present these as our top recommendations. The following example calculates the top ratings for user ID 1:

```
(defn ex-7-8 []
  (let [user-ratings (->> (load-ratings "ua.base")
                          (group-by :user)
                          (vals))
        user-1       (first user-ratings)
        recommender  (->> (rest user-ratings)
                          (slope-one-recommender))
        items        (load-items "u.item")
        item-name (fn [item]
                    (get items (:item item)))]
    (->> (slope-one-recommend recommender user-1 10)
         (map item-name))))
```

The earlier example will take a while to build the Slope One recommender and output the differences. It will take a couple of minutes, but when it's finished, you should see something like the following:

```
;; ("Someone Else's America (1995)" "Aiqing wansui (1994)"
;;  "Great Day in Harlem, A (1994)" "Pather Panchali (1955)"
;;  "Boys, Les (1997)" "Saint of Fort Washington, The (1993)"
;;  "Marlene Dietrich: Shadow and Light (1996) " "Anna (1996)"
;;  "Star Kid (1997)" "Santa with Muscles (1996)")
```

Try running `slope-one-recommender` in the REPL and predicting recommendations for multiple users. You'll find that once the differences have been built, making recommendations is very fast.

Practical considerations for user and item recommenders

As we've seen in the previous section, compiling pairwise differences for all items is a time-consuming job. One of the advantages of item-based recommenders is that pairwise differences between items are likely to remain relatively stable over time. The differences matrix need only be calculated periodically. As we've seen, it's possible to incrementally update very easily too; for a user who has already rated 10 items, if they rate an additional item, we only need to adjust the difference for the 11 items they have now rated. We don't need to calculate the differences from scratch whenever we want to update the matrix.

The runtime of item-based recommenders scales with the number of items they store though. In situations where the number of users is small compared to the number of items, it may be more efficient to implement a user-based recommender. For example content aggregation sites, where items could outnumber users by orders of magnitude, are good candidates for user-based recommendation.

The Mahout library, which we encountered in the previous chapter, contains the tools to create a variety of recommenders, including user-based recommenders. Let's look at these next.

Building a user-based recommender with Mahout

The Mahout library comes with a lot of built-in classes, which are designed to work together to assist in building custom recommendation engines. Mahout's functionality to construct recommenders is in the org.apache.mahout.cf.taste namespace.

 Mahout's recommendation engine capabilities come from the Taste open source project with which it merged in 2008.

In the previous chapter, we discovered how to make use of Mahout to cluster with Clojure's Java interop capabilities. In this chapter, we'll make use of Mahout's recommenders with GenericUserBasedRecommender available in the org.apache.mahout.cf.taste.impl.recommender package.

As with many user-based recommenders, we also need to define a similarity metric to quantify how alike two users are. We'll also define a user neighborhood as each user's set of 10 most similar users.

First, we must load the data. Mahout includes a utility class, `FileDataModel`, to load the MovieLens data in the `org.apache.mahout.cf.taste.impl.model.file` package, which we use next:

```
(defn load-model [path]
  (-> (io/resource path)
      (io/file)
      (FileDataModel.)))
```

Having loaded the data, we can produce recommendations with the following code:

```
(defn ex-7-9 []
  (let [model          (load-model "ua.base")
        similarity     (EuclideanDistanceSimilarity. model)
        neighborhood   (NearestNUserNeighborhood. 10 similarity
                                                     model)
        recommender    (GenericUserBasedRecommender. model
                                                     neighborhood
                                                     similarity)
        items      (load-items "u.item")
        item-name (fn [id] (get items id))]
    (->> (.recommend recommender 1 5)
         (map #(item-name (.getItemID %))))))

;; ("Big Lebowski, The (1998)" "Peacemaker, The (1997)"
;;  "Rainmaker, The (1997)" "Game, The (1997)"
;;  "Cool Hand Luke (1967)")
```

The distance metric that we used in the previous example was the Euclidean distance. This places each user in a high-dimensional space defined by the ratings for the movies they have rated.

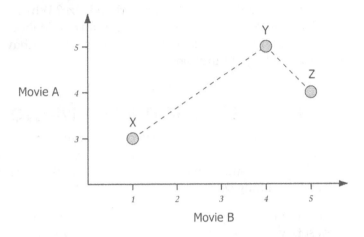

The earlier chart places three users **X**, **Y**, and **Z** on a two-dimensional chart according to their ratings for movies **A** and **B**. We can see that users **Y** and **Z** are more similar to each other, based on these two movies, than they are to user **X**.

If we were trying to produce recommendations for user **Y**, we might reason that other items rated highly by user **X** would be good candidates.

k-nearest neighbors

Our Mahout user-based recommender is making recommendations by looking at the neighborhood of the most similar users. This is commonly called *k*-**nearest neighbors** or *k*-**NN**.

It might appear that a user neighborhood is a lot like the *k*-means clusters we encountered in the previous chapter, but this is not quite the case. This is because each user sits at the center of their own neighborhood. With clustering, we aim to establish a smaller number of groupings, but with *k*-NN, there are as many neighborhoods as there are users; each user is their own neighborhood centroid.

>
> Mahout also defines `ThresholdUserNeighbourhood` that we could use to construct a neighborhood containing only the users that fall within a certain similarity from each other.

The *k*-NN algorithm means that we only generate recommendations based on the taste of the *k* most similar users. This makes intuitive sense; the users with taste most similar to your own are most likely to offer meaningful recommendations.

Two questions naturally arise—what's the best neighborhood size? Which similarity measure should we use? To answer these questions, we can turn to Mahout's recommender evaluation capabilities and see how our recommender behaves against our data for a variety of different configurations.

Recommender evaluation with Mahout

Mahout provides a set of classes to help with the task of evaluating our recommender. Like the cross-validation we performed with the `clj-ml` library in *Chapter 4, Classification*, Mahout's evaluation proceeds by splitting the our ratings into two sets: a test set and a training set.

By training our recommender on the training set and then evaluating its performance on the test set, we can gain an understanding of how well, or poorly, our algorithm is performing against real data. To handle the task of training a model on the training data provided by Mahout's evaluator, we must supply an object conforming to the `RecommenderBuilder` interface. The interface defines just one method: `buildRecommender`. We can create an anonymous `RecommenderBuilder` type using reify:

```
(defn recommender-builder [sim n]
  (reify RecommenderBuilder
    (buildRecommender [this model]
      (let [nhood (NearestNUserNeighborhood. n sim model)]
        (GenericUserBasedRecommender. model nhood sim)))))
```

Mahout provides a variety of evaluators in the `org.apache.mahout.cf.taste.impl.eval` namespace. In the following code, we construct a root-mean-square error evaluator using the `RMSRecommenderEvaluator` class by passing in a recommender builder and the data model that we've loaded:

```
(defn evaluate-rmse [builder model]
  (-> (RMSRecommenderEvaluator.)
      (.evaluate builder nil model 0.7 1.0)))
```

The `nil` value we pass to evaluate in the preceding code indicates that we aren't supplying a custom model builder, which means the `evaluate` function will use the default model builder based on the model we supply. The numbers `0.7` and `1.0` are the proportion of data used for training, and the proportion of the test data to evaluate on. In the earlier code, we're using 70 percent of the data for training and evaluate the model on 100 percent of what's left. The **root mean square error** (**RMSE**) evaluator will calculate the square root of the mean squared error between the predicted rating and the actual rating for each of the test data.

We can use both of the previous functions to evaluate the performance of the user-based recommender using a Euclidean distance and a neighborhood of 10 like this:

```
(defn ex-7-10 []
  (let [model   (load-model "ua.base")
        builder (recommender-builder 10
                  (EuclideanDistanceSimilarity. model))]
    (evaluate-rmse builder model)))


;; 0.352
```

Your result may differ of course, since the evaluation is performed on random subsets of the data.

We defined the Euclidean distance *d* in the previous chapter to be a positive value where zero represents perfect similarity. This could be converted into a similarity measure *s* in the following way:

$$s = \frac{1}{1+d}$$

Unfortunately, the previous measure would bias against users with more rated items in common, since each dimension would provide an opportunity to be further apart. To correct this, Mahout computes the Euclidean similarity as:

$$s = \frac{\sqrt{n}}{1+d}$$

Here, *n* is the number of dimensions. As this formula might result in a similarity which exceeds 1, Mahout clips similarities at 1.

Evaluating distance measures

We encountered a variety of other distance and similarity measures in the previous chapter; in particular, we made use of the Jaccard, Euclidean, and cosine distances. Mahout includes implementations of these as similarity measures in the org.apache.mahout.cf.taste.impl.similarity package as TanimotoCoefficientSimilarity, EuclideanDistanceSimilarity, and UncenteredCosineSimilarity respectively.

We've just evaluated the performance of the Euclidean similarity on our ratings data, so let's see how well the others perform. While we're at it, let's try two other similarity measures that Mahout makes available — PearsonCorrelationSimilarity and SpearmanCorrelationSimilarity.

The Pearson correlation similarity

The Pearson correlation similarity is a similarity measure based on the correlation between users' tastes. The following diagram shows the ratings of two users for three movies **A**, **B**, and **C**.

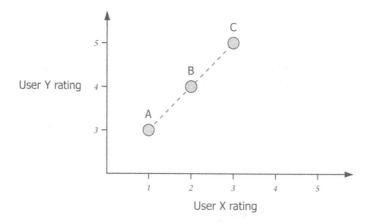

One of the potential drawbacks of the Euclidean distance is that it fails to account for the cases where one user agrees with another precisely in their relative ratings for movies, but tends to be more generous with their rating. Consider the two users in the earlier example. There is perfect correlation between their ratings for movies **A**, **B**, and **C**, but user **Y** rates the movies more highly than user **X**. The Euclidean distance between these two users could be calculated with the following formula:

$$\sqrt{(3-1)^2 + (4-2)^2 + (5-3)^2} = \sqrt{12}$$

Yet, in a sense, they are in complete agreement. Back in *Chapter 3, Correlation* we calculated the Pearson correlation between two series as:

$$r = \frac{1}{n}\sum_{i=1}^{n}\frac{dx_i}{\sigma_x}\frac{dy_i}{\sigma_y}$$

Here, $dx_i = x_i - \overline{x}$ and $dy_i = y_i - \overline{y}$. The example given earlier yields a Pearson correlation of 1.

Let's try making predictions with the Pearson correlation similarity. Mahout implements the Pearson correlation with the `PearsonCorrelationSimilarity` class:

```
(defn ex-7-11 []
  (let [model    (load-model "ua.base")
        builder (recommender-builder
                   10 (PearsonCorrelationSimilarity. model))]
    (evaluate-rmse builder model)))


;; 0.796
```

In fact, the RMSE has increased for the movies data using the Pearson correlation.

The Pearson correlation similarity is mathematically equivalent to the cosine similarity for data which have been centered (data for which the mean is zero). In the example of our two users X and Y illustrated earlier, the means are not identical, so the cosine similarity measure would give a different result to the Pearson correlation similarity. Mahout implements the cosine similarity as `UncenteredCosineSimilarity`.

Although the Pearson method makes intuitive sense, it has some drawbacks in the context of recommendation engines. It doesn't take into account the number of rated items that two users have in common. If they only share one item, then no similarity can be computed. Also, if one user always gives items the same rating, then no correlation can be computed between the user and any other user, even another user who does the same. Perhaps there's simply not enough variety of ratings in the data for the Pearson correlation similarity to work well.

Spearman's rank similarity

Another way in which users may be similar is that the rankings are not particularly closely correlated, but the ordering of the ranks are preserved between users. Consider the following diagram showing the ratings of two users for five different movies:

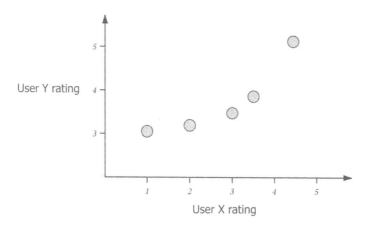

We can see that the linear correlation between users' ratings is not perfect, since their ratings aren't plotted on a straight line. This would result in a moderate Pearson correlation similarity and an even lower cosine similarity. Yet, the ordering between their preferences is identical. If we were to compare a ranked list of users' preferences, they would be exactly the same.

The Spearman's rank correlation coefficient uses this measure to calculate the difference between users. It is defined as the Pearson correlation coefficient between the ranked items:

$$\rho = 1 - \frac{6 \sum d_i^2}{n\left(n^2 - 1\right)}$$

Here, n is the number of ratings and $d_i = x_i - y_i$ is the difference between the ranks for item i. Mahout implements the Spearman's rank correlation similarity with the `SpearmanCorrelationSimilarity` class which we use in the next code. The algorithm has much more work to do, so we evaluate on a much smaller subset, just 10 percent of the test data:

```
(defn ex-7-12 []
  (let [model   (load-model "ua.base")
        builder (recommender-builder
                  10 (SpearmanCorrelationSimilarity. model))]
    (-> (RMSRecommenderEvaluator.)
        (.evaluate builder nil model 0.9 0.1))))


;; 0.907
```

The RMSE evaluation score is even higher than it is for the Pearson correlation similarity. It appears that the best similarity measure so far for the MovieLens data is the Euclidean similarity.

Determining optimum neighborhood size

One aspect we haven't altered in the earlier comparisons is the size of the user neighborhood on which the recommendations are based. Let's see how the RMSE is affected by the neighborhood size:

```
(defn ex-7-13 []
  (let [model (load-model "ua.base")
        sim   (EuclideanDistanceSimilarity. model)
        ns    (range 1 10)
        stats (for [n ns]
                (let [builder (recommender-builder n sim)]
                  (do (println n)
                      (evaluate-rmse builder model))))]
    (-> (c/scatter-plot ns stats
                        :x-label "Neighborhood size"
                        :y-label "RMSE")
        (i/view))))
```

The previous code creates a scatterplot of the RMSE for the Euclidean similarity as the neighborhood increases from 1 to 10.

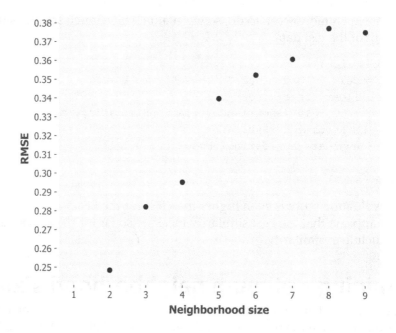

Perhaps surprisingly, as the size of the neighborhood grows, the RMSE of the predicted rating rises. The most accurate predicted ratings are based on a neighborhood of just two people. But, perhaps this should not surprise us: for the Euclidean similarity, the most similar other users are defined as being the users who most closely agree with a user's ratings. The larger the neighborhood, the more diverse a range of ratings we'll observe for the same item.

The earlier RMSE ranges between **0.25** and **0.38**. On this basis alone, it's hard to know if the recommender is performing well or not. Does getting the rating wrong by **0.38** matter much in practice? For example, if we always guess a rating that's exactly **0.38** too high (or too low), we'll be making recommendations of a relative value that precisely agrees with the users' own. Fortunately, Mahout supplies an alternative evaluator that returns a variety of statistics from the field of information retrieval. We'll look at these next.

Information retrieval statistics

One way for us to get a better handle on how to improve our recommendations is to use an evaluator that provides more detail on how well the evaluator is performing in a number of different aspects. The `GenericRecommenderIRStatsEvaluator` function includes several information retrieval statistics that provide this detail.

In many cases, it's not necessary to guess the exact rating that a user would have assigned a movie; presenting an ordered list from best to worst is enough. In fact, even the exact order may not be particularly important either.

 Information retrieval systems are those which return results in response to user queries. Recommender systems can be considered a subset of information retrieval systems where the query is the set of prior ratings associated with the user.

The **Information Retrieval statistics (IR stats)** evaluator treats recommendation evaluation a bit like search engine evaluation. A search engine should strive to return as many of the results that the user is looking for without also returning a lot of unwanted information. These proportions are quantified by the statistics precision and recall.

Precision

The precision of an information retrieval system is the percentage of items it returns that are relevant. If the correct recommendations are the **true positives** and the incorrect recommendations are the **false positives**, then the precision can be measured as the total number of **true positives** returned:

$$\text{precision} = \frac{\text{true positives}}{\text{true positives} + \text{false positives}}$$

Since we return a defined number of recommendations, for example, the top 10, we would talk about the precision at 10. For example, if the model returns 10 recommendations, eight of which were a part of the users' true top 10, the model's precision is 80 percent at 10.

Recall

Recall complements precision and the two measures are often quoted together. Recall measures the fraction of relevant recommendations that are returned:

$$\text{recall} = \frac{\text{true positives}}{\text{true positives} + \text{false negatives}}$$

We could think of this as being the proportion of possible good recommendations the recommender actually made. For example, if the system only recommended five of the user's top 10 movies, then we could say the recall was 50 percent at 10.

Mahout's information retrieval evaluator

The statistics of information retrieval can reframe the recommendation problem as a search problem on a user-by-user basis. Rather than divide the data into test and training sets randomly, GenericRecommenderIRStatsEvaluator evaluates the performance of the recommender for each user. It does this by removing some quantity of the users' top-rated items (say, the top five). The evaluator will then see how many of the users' true top-five rated items were actually recommended by the system.

We implement this as follows:

```
(defn evaluate-ir [builder model]
  (-> (GenericRecommenderIRStatsEvaluator.)
      (.evaluate builder nil model nil 5
        GenericRecommenderIRStatsEvaluator/CHOOSE_THRESHOLD
        1.0)
      (bean)))

(defn ex-7-14 []
  (let [model   (load-model "ua.base")
        builder (recommender-builder
                  10 (EuclideanDistanceSimilarity. model))]
    (evaluate-ir builder model)))
```

The "at" value in the preceding code is 5, which we pass immediately before the GenericRecommenderIRStatsEvaluator/CHOOSE_THRESHOLD that causes Mahout to compute a sensible relevance threshold. The previous code returns the following output:

```
;; {:recall 0.002538071065989847, :reach 1.0,
;;  :precision 0.002538071065989847,
```

```
;;    :normalizedDiscountedCumulativeGain 0.0019637198336778725,
;;    :fallOut 0.0011874376015289575,
;;    :f1Measure 0.002538071065989847,
;;    :class org.apache.mahout.cf.taste.impl.eval.IRStatisticsImpl}
```

The evaluator returns an instance of `org.apache.mahout.cf.taste.eval.IRStatistics`, which we can convert into a map with Clojure's `bean` function. The map contains all the information retrieval statistics calculated by the evaluator. Their meaning is explained in the next section.

F-measure and the harmonic mean

Also called the **F1 measure** or the **balanced F-score**, the F-measure is the weighted harmonic mean of precision and recall:

$$F = \frac{2 \cdot \text{precision} \cdot \text{recall}}{\text{precision} + \text{recall}}$$

The harmonic mean is related to the more common arithmetic mean and, in fact, is one of the three Pythagorean means. It's defined as the reciprocal of the arithmetic mean of the reciprocals and it's particularly useful in situations involving rates and ratios.

For example, consider a vehicle traveling a distance d at a certain speed x, then travelling distance d again at speed y. Speed is measured as a ratio of distance traveled over time taken and therefore the average speed is the harmonic mean of x and y. If x is 60 mph and y is 40 mph, then the average speed is 48 mph, which we can calculate like this:

$$\frac{2}{\frac{1}{60} + \frac{1}{40}} = 48$$

Note that this is lower than the arithmetic mean, which would be 50 mph. If instead d represented a certain amount of time rather than distance, so the vehicle traveled for a certain amount of time at speed x and then the same amount of time at speed y, then its average speed would be the arithmetic mean of x and y, or 50 mph.

The F-Measure can be generalized to the F_β-measure that allows the weight associated with either precision or recall to be adjusted independently:

$$F_\beta = \frac{\left(1 + \beta^2\right) \cdot \text{precision} \cdot \text{recall}}{\beta^2 \cdot \text{precision} + \text{recall}}$$

Common measures are F_2, which weights recall twice as much as precision, and $F_{0.5}$, which weights precision twice as much as recall.

Fall-out

Also called the **false positive** rate, the proportion of nonrelevant recommendations that are retrieved out of all the nonrelevant recommendations:

$$\text{FPR} = \frac{\text{false positives}}{\text{false positives} + \text{true negative}}$$

Unlike the other IR statistics we've seen so far, the lower the fall-out, the better our recommender is doing.

Normalized discounted cumulative gain

The **Discounted Cumulative Gain** (DCG) is a measure of the performance of a recommendation system based on the graded relevance of the recommended entities. It varies between zero and one, with one representing perfect ranking.

The premise of discounted cumulative gain is that highly relevant results appearing lower in a search result list should be penalized as a function of both their relevance and how far down the result list they appear. It can be calculated with the following formula:

$$\text{DCG}_p = \sum_{i=1}^{p} \frac{2^{rel_i} - 1}{\log_2 (i + 1)}$$

Here, rel_i is the relevance of the result at position i and p is the position in the rank. The version presented earlier is a popular formulation that places strong emphasis on retrieving relevant results.

Since the search result lists vary in length depending on the query, we can't consistently compare results using the DCG alone. Instead, we can sort the result by their relevance and calculate the DCG again. Since this will give the best possible cumulative discounted gain for the results (as we sorted them in the order of relevance), the result is called the **Ideal Discounted Cumulative Gain** (IDCG).

Taking the ratio of the DCG and the IDCG gives the normalized discounted cumulative gain:

$$\text{nDCG} = \frac{\text{DCG}}{\text{IDCG}}$$

In a perfect ranking algorithm, the *DCG* will equal the *IDCG* resulting in an *nDCG* of 1.0. Since the *nDCG* provides a result in the range of zero to one, it provides a means to compare the relative performance of different query engines, where each returns different numbers of results.

Plotting the information retrieval results

We can plot the results of the information retrieval evaluation with the following code:

```
(defn plot-ir [xs stats]
  (-> (c/xy-plot xs (map :recall stats)
                 :x-label "Neighbourhood Size"
                 :y-label "IR Statistic"
                 :series-label "Recall"
                 :legend true)
      (c/add-lines xs (map :precision stats)
                   :series-label "Precision")
      (c/add-lines xs
                   (map :normalizedDiscountedCumulativeGain stats)
                   :series-label "NDCG")
      (i/view)))

(defn ex-7-15 []
  (let [model   (load-model "ua.base")
        sim     (EuclideanDistanceSimilarity. model)
        xs      (range 1 10)
        stats   (for [n xs]
                  (let [builder (recommender-builder n sim)]
                    (do (println n)
                        (evaluate-ir builder model))))]
    (plot-ir xs stats)))
```

This generates the following chart:

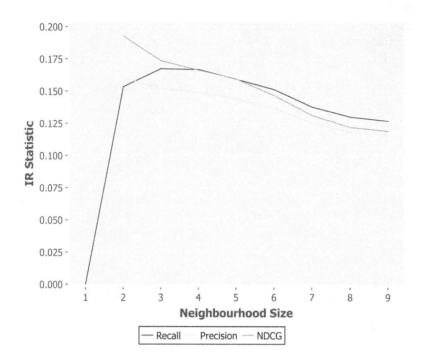

In the previous chart, we can see that the highest precision corresponds to a neighborhood size of two; consulting the most similar user generates the fewest false positives. You may have noticed, though that the values reported for precision and recall are quite low. As the neighborhood grows larger, the recommender will have more candidate recommendations to make. Remember, however, that the information retrieval statistics are calculated at 5, meaning that only the top five recommendations will be counted.

There's a subtle problem concerning these measures in the context of recommenders — the precision is based entirely on *how well we can predict the other items the user has rated*. The recommender will be penalized for making recommendations for rare items that the user has not rated, even if they are brilliant recommendations for items the user would love.

Recommendation with Boolean preferences

There's been an assumption throughout this chapter that the rating a user gives to an item is an important fact. The distance measures we've been looking at so far attempt in different ways to predict the numeric value of a user's future rating.

An alternative distance measure takes the view that the rating a user assigns to an item is much less important than the fact that they rated it at all. In other words, all ratings, even poor ones, could be treated the same. Consider that, for every movie a user rates poorly, there are many more that the user will not even bother to watch— let alone rate. There are many other situations where Boolean preferences are the primary basis on which a recommendation is made; user's likes or favorites on social media, for example.

To use a Boolean similarity measure, we first have to convert our model into a Boolean preferences model, which we can do with the following code:

```
(defn to-boolean-preferences [model]
  (-> (GenericBooleanPrefDataModel/toDataMap model)
      (GenericBooleanPrefDataModel.)))

(defn boolean-recommender-builder [sim n]
  (reify RecommenderBuilder
    (buildRecommender [this model]
      (let [nhood (NearestNUserNeighborhood. n sim model)]
        (GenericBooleanPrefUserBasedRecommender.
         model nhood sim)))))
```

Treating a user's ratings as Boolean values can reduce the user's list of movie ratings to a set representation and, as we saw in the previous chapter, the Jaccard index can be used to determine set similarity. Mahout implements a similarity measure that's closely related to the Jaccard index called the **Tanimoto coefficient**.

 The Tanimoto coefficient applies to vectors where each index represents a feature that can be zero or one, whereas the Jaccard index applies to sets which may contain, or not contain, an element. Which measure to use depends only on your data representation— the two measures are equivalent.

Let's plot the IR statistics for several different neighborhood sizes using Mahout's IR statistics evaluator:

```
(defn ex-7-16 []
  (let [model  (to-boolean-preferences (load-model "ua.base"))
        sim    (TanimotoCoefficientSimilarity. model)
        xs     (range 1 10)
        stats  (for [n xs]
                 (let [builder
                        (boolean-recommender-builder n sim)]
                   (do (println n)
                       (evaluate-ir builder model))))]
    (plot-ir xs stats)))
```

The previous code generates the following chart:

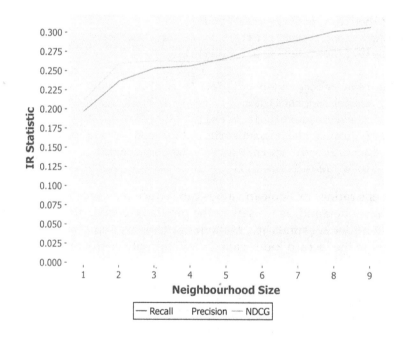

For a Boolean recommender, a larger neighborhood improves the precision score. This is an intriguing result, given what we observed for the Euclidean similarity. Bear in mind though that with Boolean preferences, there is no notion of relative item preference, they are either rated or not rated. The most similar users, and therefore the group forming a neighborhood, will be the ones who have simply rated the same items. The larger this group is, the more chance we will have of predicting the items a user rated.

Also, because there's no relative score for Boolean preferences, the normalized discounted cumulative gain is missing from the earlier chart. The lack of order might make Boolean preferences seem less desirable than the other data, but they can be very useful, as we'll see next.

Implicit versus explicit feedback

In fact, rather than trying to elicit explicit ratings from users on what they like and dislike, a common technique is to simply observe user activity. For example, on an E-commerce site, the set of items viewed could provide an indicator of the sort of products a user is interested in. In the same way, the list of pages a user browses on a website is a strong indicator of the sort of content they're interested in reading.

Using implicit sources such as clicks and page views can vastly increase the amount of information on which to base predictions. It also avoids the so-called "cold start" problem, where a user must provide explicit ratings before you can offer any recommendations at all; the user will begin generating data as soon as they arrive on your site.

In these cases, each page view could be treated as an element in a large set of pages representing the users' preferences, and a Boolean similarity measure could be used to recommend related content. For a popular site, such sets will clearly grow very large very quickly. Unfortunately, Mahout 0.9's recommendation engines are designed to run on a single server in memory. So, they impose a limit on the quantity of data we can process.

Before we look at an alternative recommender that's designed to run on a cluster of machines and scale with the volume of data you have, let's take a detour to look at the ways of performing dimensionality reduction. We'll begin with the ways of probabilistically reducing the size of very large sets.

Probabilistic methods for large sets

Large sets appear in many contexts in data science. We're likely to encounter them while dealing with users' implicit feedback as previously mentioned, but the approaches described next can be applied to any data that can be represented as a set.

Testing set membership with Bloom filters

Bloom filters are data structures that provide a means to compress the size of a set while preserving our ability to tell whether a given item is a member of the set or not. The price of this compression is some uncertainty. A Bloom filter tells us when an item may be in a set, although it will tell us for certain if it isn't. In situations where disk space saving is worth the small sacrifice in certainty, they are a very popular choice for set compression.

The base data structure of a Bloom filter is a bit vector — a sequence of cells that may contain 1 or 0 (or true or false). The level of compression (and the corresponding increase in uncertainty) is configurable with two parameters — **k hash functions** and **m bits**.

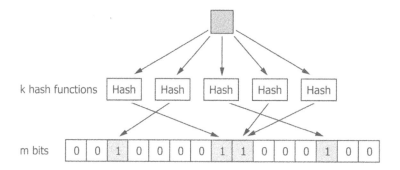

The previous diagram illustrates the process of taking an input item (the top square) and hashing it multiple times. Each hash function outputs an integer, which is used as an index into the bit vector. The elements matching the hash indices are set to 1. The following illustration shows a different element being hashed into a different bit vector, generating a different set of indices that will be assigned the value 1:

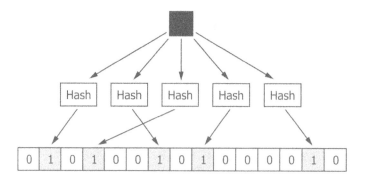

We can implement Bloom filters using the following Clojure. We're using Google's implementation of MurmurHash with different seeds to provide *k* different hash functions:

```clojure
(defn hash-function [m seed]
  (fn [x]
    (-> (Hashing/murmur3_32 seed)
        (.hashUnencodedChars x)
        (.asInt)
        (mod m))))

(defn hash-functions [m k]
  (map (partial hash-function m) (range k)))

(defn indices-fn [m k]
  (let [f (apply juxt (hash-functions m k))]
    (fn [x]
      (f x))))

(defn bloom-filter [m k]
  {:filter     (vec (repeat m false))
   :indices-fn (indices-fn m k)})
```

The earlier code defines a Bloom filter as a map containing a `:filter` (the bit vector) and an `:indices` function. The `indices` function handles the task of applying the *k* hash functions to generate *k* indices. We're representing the 0s as `false` and the 1s as `true`, but the effect is the same. We use the code to create a Bloom filter of length 8 with 5 hash functions in the following example:

```clojure
(defn ex-7-17 []
  (bloom-filter 8 5))

;; {:filter [false false false false false false false false],
;;  :indices-fn #<Bloom_filter$indices_fn$fn__43538
;;  cljds.ch7.Bloom_filter$indices_fn$fn__43538@3da200c>}
```

The response is a map of two keys—the filter itself (a vector of Boolean values, all false), and an indices function, which has been generated from five hash functions. We can bring the earlier code together with a simple `Bloom-assoc` function:

```clojure
(defn set-bit [seq index]
  (assoc seq index true))

(defn set-bits [seq indices]
  (reduce set-bit seq indices))

(defn bloom-assoc [{:keys [indices-fn] :as bloom} element]
  (update-in bloom [:filter] set-bits (indices-fn element)))
```

Given a Bloom filter, we simply call the `indices-fn` function to get the indices we need to set in the Bloom filter:

```
(defn ex-7-18 []
  (-> (bloom-filter 8 5)
      (bloom-assoc "Indiana Jones")
      (:filter)))

;; [true true false true false false false true]
```

To determine whether the Bloom filter contains an item, we simply need to query whether all of the indices that should be true are actually true. If they are, we reason that the item has been added to the filter:

```
(defn bloom-contains? [{:keys [filter indices-fn]} element]
  (->> (indices-fn element)
       (map filter)
       (every? true?)))

(defn ex-7-19 []
  (-> (bloom-filter 8 5)
      (bloom-assoc "Indiana Jones")
      (bloom-contains? "Indiana Jones")))

;; true
```

We add `"Indiana Jones"` to the Bloom filter and find that it contains `"Indiana Jones"`. Let's instead search for another of Harrison Ford's movies `"The Fugitive"`:

```
(defn ex-7-20 []
  (-> (bloom-filter 8 5)
      (bloom-assoc "Indiana Jones")
      (bloom-contains? "The Fugitive")))

;; false
```

So far, so good. But we have traded some accuracy for this huge compression. Let's search for a movie that shouldn't be in the Bloom filter. Perhaps, the 1996 movie `Bogus`:

```
(defn ex-7-21 []
  (-> (bloom-filter 8 5)
      (bloom-assoc "Indiana Jones")
```

```
      (bloom-contains? "Bogus (1996)")))

;; true
```

This is not what we want. The filter claims to contain `"Bogus (1996)"`, even though we haven't associated it into the filter yet. This is the tradeoff that Bloom filters make; although a filter will never claim that an item hasn't been added when it has, it may incorrectly claim that an item has been added when it hasn't.

> In the information retrieval terminology we encountered earlier in the chapter, Bloom filters have 100 percent recall, but their precision is less than 100 percent. How much less is configurable through the values we choose for m and k.

In all, there are 56 movie titles out of the 1,682 titles in the MovieLens dataset that the Bloom filter incorrectly reports on after adding "Indiana Jones" — a 3.3 percent false positive rate. Given that we are only using five hash functions and an eight element filter, you may have expected it to be much higher. Of course, our Bloom filter only contains one element and, as we add more, the probability of obtaining a collision will rise sharply. In fact, the probability of a false positive is approximately:

$$\left(1 - e^{-\frac{kn}{m}}\right)^{k}$$

Here, k and m are the number of hash functions and the length of the filter as it was before, and n is the number of items added to the set. For our earlier singular Bloom, this gives:

$$\left(1 - e^{-\frac{5}{8}}\right)^{5} \approx 0.022$$

So, in fact, the theoretical false positive rate is even lower than what we've observed.

Bloom filters are a very general algorithm, and are very useful when we want to test set membership and don't have the resources to store all the items in the set explicitly. The fact that the precision is configurable through the choice of values for m and k means that it's possible to select the false positive rate you're willing to tolerate. As a result, they're used in a large variety of data-intensive systems.

A drawback of Bloom filters is that it's impossible to retrieve the values you've added to the filter; although we can use the filter to test for set membership, we aren't able to say what that set contains without exhaustive checks. For recommendation systems (and indeed for others too, such as clustering), we're primarily interested in the similarity between two sets rather than their precise contents. But here, the Bloom lets us down; we can't reliably use the compressed filter as a measure of the similarity between two sets of items.

Next, we'll introduce an algorithm that will preserve set similarity as measured by the Jaccard similarity. It does so while also preserving the configurable compression provided by the Bloom filter.

Jaccard similarity for large sets with MinHash

The Bloom filter is a probabilistic data structure to determine whether an item is a member of a set. While comparing user or item similarities, what we are usually interested in is the intersection between sets, as opposed to their precise contents. MinHash is a technique that enables a large set to be compressed in such a way that we can still perform the Jaccard similarity on the compressed representations.

Let's see how it works with a reference to two of the most prolific raters in the MovieLens dataset. Users 405 and 655 have rated 727 and 675 movies respectively. In the following code, we extract their ratings and convert them into sets before passing to Incanter's `jaccard-index` function. Recall that this returns the ratio of movies they've both rated out of all the movies they've rated:

```
(defn rated-items [user-ratings id]
  (->> (get user-ratings id)
       (map :item)))

(defn ex-7-22 []
  (let [ratings      (load-ratings "ua.base")
        user-ratings (group-by :user ratings)
        user-a       (rated-items user-ratings 405)
        user-b       (rated-items user-ratings 655)]
    (println "User 405:" (count user-a))
    (println "User 655:" (count user-b))
    (s/jaccard-index (set user-a) (set user-b))))

;; User 405: 727
;; User 655: 675
;; 158/543
```

There is an approximate similarity of 29 percent between the two large sets of ratings. Let's see how we can reduce the size of these sets while also preserving the similarity between them using MinHash.

The MinHash algorithm shares much in common with the Bloom filter. Our first task is to pick k hash functions. Rather than hashing the set representation itself, these k hash functions are used to hash each element within the set. For each of the k hash functions, the MinHash algorithm stores the minimum value generated by any of the set elements. The output therefore, is a set of k numbers; each equals the minimum hash value for that hash function. The output is referred to as the MinHash signature.

The following diagram illustrates the process for two sets, each containing three elements, being converted into MinHash signatures with a k of 2:

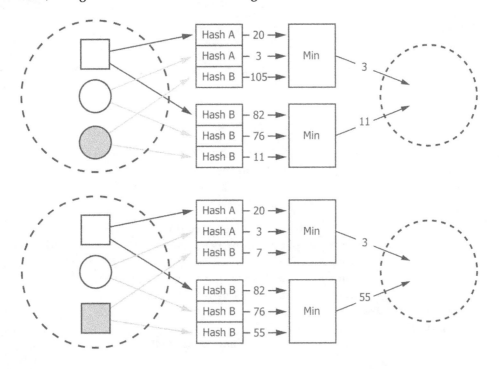

The input sets share two elements out of a total of four unique elements, which equates to Jaccard index of 0.5. The MinHash signatures for the two sets are #{3, 0} and #{3, 55} respectively, which equates to a Jaccard Index of 0.33. Thus, MinHash has reduced the size of our input sets (by just one, in this case), while conserving the approximate similarity between them.

As with the Bloom filter, an appropriate choice of *k* allows you to specify the loss of precision that it is acceptable to tolerate. We can implement the MinHash algorithm using the following Clojure code:

```clojure
(defn hash-function [seed]
  (let [f (Hashing/murmur3_32 seed)]
    (fn [x]
      (-> (.hashUnencodedChars f (str x))
          (.asInt)))))

(defn hash-functions [k]
  (map hash-function (range k)))

(defn pairwise-min [a b]
  (map min a b))

(defn minhasher [k]
  (let [f (apply juxt (hash-functions k))]
    (fn [coll]
      (->> (map f coll)
           (reduce pairwise-min)))))
```

In the following code, we define a `minhasher` function with a *k* of 10 and use it to perform a set test using the Jaccard index on the compressed ratings for users 405 and 655:

```clojure
(defn ex-7-23 []
  (let [ratings      (load-ratings "ua.base")
        user-ratings (group-by :user ratings)
        minhash (minhasher 10)
        user-a  (minhash (rated-items user-ratings 405))
        user-b  (minhash (rated-items user-ratings 655))]
    (println "User 405:" user-a)
    (println "User 655:" user-b)
    (s/jaccard-index (set user-a) (set user-b))))

;; User 405: #{-2147145175 -2141119028 -2143110220 -2143703868 -
;; 2144897714 -2145866799 -2139426844 -2140441272 -2146421577 -
;; 2146662900}
;; User 655: #{-2144975311 -2140926583 -2141119028 -2141275395 -
;; 2145738774 -2143703868 -2147345319 -2147134300 -2146421577 -
;; 2146662900}
;; 1/4
```

The Jaccard index based on our MinHash signatures is remarkably close to that on the original sets—25 percent compared to 29 percent—despite the fact that we compressed the sets down to only 10 elements each.

The benefit of much smaller sets is twofold: clearly storage space is much reduced, but so is the computational complexity required to check the similarity between the two sets as well. It's much less work to check the similarity of the sets that contain only 10 elements than the sets that contain many hundreds. MinHash is, therefore, not just a space-saving algorithm, but also a time-saving algorithm in cases where we need to make a large number of set similarity tests; cases that occur in recommender systems, for example.

If we're trying to establish a user neighborhood for the purposes of recommending items, we'll still need to perform a large number of set tests in order to determine which the most similar users are. In fact, for a large number of users, it may be prohibitively time-consuming to check every other user exhaustively, even after we've calculated MinHash signatures. The final probabilistic technique will look at addressing this specific problem: how to reduce the number of candidates that have to be compared while looking for similar items.

Reducing pair comparisons with locality-sensitive hashing

In the previous chapter, we computed the similarity matrix for a large number of documents. With the 20,000 documents in the Reuters corpus, this was already a time-consuming process. As the size of the dataset doubles, the length of time required to check every pair of items is multiplied by four. It can, therefore, become prohibitively time-consuming to perform this sort of analysis at scale.

For example, suppose we had a million documents and that we computed MinHash signatures of length 250 for each of them. This means we use 1,000 bytes to store each document. As all the signatures can be stored in a Gigabyte, they can all be stored in the main system memory for speed. However, there are $\frac{N^2 - N}{2}$ pairs of documents, or 499,999, 500,000 pairwise combinations to be checked. Even if it takes only a microsecond to compare two signatures, it will still take almost 6 days to compute all the similarities overall.

Locality-sensitive hashing (LSH), addresses this problem by significantly reducing the number of pairwise comparisons that have to be made. It does this by bucketing sets that are likely to have a minimum threshold of similarity together; only the sets that are bucketed together need to be checked for similarity.

Bucketing signatures

We consider any pair of items that hash to the same bucket a candidate pair and check only the candidate pairs for similarity. The aim is that only similar items should become candidate pairs. Dissimilar pairs that happen to hash to the same bucket will be false positives and we seek to minimize these. Similar pairs that hash to different buckets are false negatives and we likewise seek to minimize these too.

If we have computed MinHash signatures for the items, an effective way to bucket them would be to divide the signature matrix into b bands consisting of r elements each. This is illustrated in the following diagram:

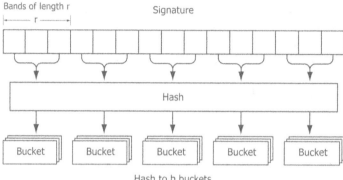

Having already written the code to produce the MinHash signatures in the previous section, performing LSH in Clojure is simply a matter of partitioning the signature into a certain number of bands, each of length r. Each band is hashed (for simplicity, we're using the same hashing function for each band) to a particular bucket:

```
(def lsh-hasher (hash-function 0))

(defn locality-sensitive-hash [r]
  {:r r :bands {}})

(defn buckets-for [r signature]
  (->> (partition-all r signature)
       (map lsh-hasher)
       (map-indexed vector)))

(defn lsh-assoc [{:keys [r] :as lsh} {:keys [id signature]}]
  (let [f (fn [lsh [band bucket]]
            (update-in lsh [:bands band bucket] conj id))]
    (->> (buckets-for r signature)
         (reduce f lsh))))
```

The earlier example defines a locality-sensitive hash simply as a map containing empty bands and some value, *r*. When we come to associate an item into the LSH with lsh-assoc, we split the signature into bands based on the value of *r* and determine the bucket for each band. The item's ID gets added to each of these buckets. Buckets are grouped by the band ID so that items which share a bucket in different bands are not bucketed together:

```
(defn ex-7-24 []
  (let [ratings (load-ratings "ua.base")
        user-ratings (group-by :user ratings)
        minhash (minhasher 27)
        user-a  (minhash (rated-items user-ratings 13))
        lsh     (locality-sensitive-hash 3)]
    (lsh-assoc lsh {:id 13 :signature user-a})))

;; {:r 3, :bands {8 {220825369 (13)}, 7 {-2054093854 (13)},
;; 6 {1177598806 (13)}, 5 {-1809511158 (13)}, 4 {-143738650 (13)},
;; 3 {-704443054 (13)}, 2 {-1217282814 (13)},
;; 1 {-100016681 (13)}, 0 {1353249231 (13)}}}
```

The preceding example shows the result of performing LSH on the signature of user 13 with *k=27* and *r=3*. The buckets for 9 bands are returned. Next, we add further items to the locality-sensitive hash:

```
(defn ex-7-25 []
  (let [ratings (load-ratings "ua.base")
        user-ratings (group-by :user ratings)
        minhash (minhasher 27)
        user-a  (minhash (rated-items user-ratings 13))
        user-b  (minhash (rated-items user-ratings 655))]
    (-> (locality-sensitive-hash 3)
        (lsh-assoc {:id 13  :signature user-a})
        (lsh-assoc {:id 655 :signature user-b}))))

;; {:r 3, :bands {8 {220825369 (655 13)}, 7 {1126350710 (655),
;; -2054093854 (13)}, 6 {872296818 (655), 1177598806 (13)},
;; 5 {-1272446116 (655), -1809511158 (13)}, 4 {-154360221 (655),
;; -143738650 (13)}, 3 {123070264 (655), -704443054 (13)},
;; 2 {-1911274538 (655), -1217282814 (13)}, 1 {-115792260 (655),
;; -100016681 (13)}, 0 {-780811496 (655), 1353249231 (13)}}}
```

In the previous example, we can see that both the user IDs 655 and 13 are placed in the same bucket for band 8, although they're in different buckets for all the other bands.

The probability that the signatures agree for one particular band is s^r, where s is the true similarity of the sets and r is the length of each band. It follows that the probability that the signatures do not agree in at least one particular band is $1-s^r$ and so, the probability that signatures don't agree across all bands is $\left(1-s^r\right)^b$. Therefore, we can say the probability that two items become a candidates pair is $1-\left(1-s^r\right)^b$.

Regardless of the specific values of b and r, this equation describes an S-curve. The threshold (the value of the similarity at which the probability of becoming a candidate is 0.5) is a function of b and r. Around the threshold, the S-curve rises steeply. Thus, pairs with similarity above the threshold are very likely to become candidates, while those below are correspondingly unlikely to become candidates.

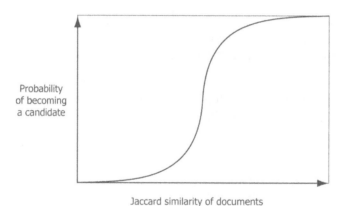

Probability
of becoming
a candidate

Jaccard similarity of documents

To search for candidate pairs, we now only need to perform the same process on a target signature and see which other items hash to the same buckets in the same bands:

```
(defn lsh-candidates [{:keys [bands r]} signature]
  (->> (buckets-for r signature)
       (mapcat (fn [[band bucket]]
                 (get-in bands [band bucket])))
       (distinct)))
```

The preceding code returns the distinct list of items that share at least one bucket in at least one band with the target signature:

```
(defn ex-7-26 []
  (let [ratings (load-ratings "ua.base")
        user-ratings (group-by :user ratings)
        minhash    (minhasher 27)
        user-b     (minhash (rated-items user-ratings 655))
```

```
        user-c      (minhash (rated-items user-ratings 405))
        user-a      (minhash (rated-items user-ratings 13))]
    (-> (locality-sensitive-hash 3)
        (lsh-assoc {:id 655 :signature user-b})
        (lsh-assoc {:id 405 :signature user-c})
        (lsh-candidates user-a))))
```

```
;; (655)
```

In the previous example, we associate the signature for users 655 and 405 into the locality-sensitive hash. We then ask for the candidates for user ID 13. The result is a sequence containing the single ID 655. Thus, 655 and 13 are candidate pairs and should be checked for similarity. User 405 has been judged by the algorithm as not being sufficiently similar, and we therefore will not check them for similarity.

 For more information on locality-sensitive hashing, MinHash, and other useful algorithms to deal with huge volumes of data, refer to the excellent *Mining of Massive Datasets* online book for free at http://www.mmds.org/.

Locality-sensitive hashing is a way of significantly reducing the space of pairwise comparisons that we need to make while comparing sets for similarity. Thus, with appropriate values set for *b* and *r*, locality-sensitive hashing allows us to precompute the user neighborhood. The task of finding similar users, given a target user, is as simple as finding the other users who share the same bucket across any of the bands; a task whose time complexity is related to the number of bands rather than the number of users.

Dimensionality reduction

What algorithms such as MinHash and LSH aim to do is reduce the quantity of data that must be stored without compromising on the essence of the original. They're a form of compression and they define helpful representations that preserve our ability to do useful work. In particular, MinHash and LSH are designed to work with data that can be represented as a set.

In fact, there is a whole class of dimensionality-reducing algorithms that will work with data that is not so easily represented as a set. We saw, in the previous chapter with k-means clustering, how certain data could be most usefully represented as a weighted vector. Common approaches to reduce the dimensions of data represented as vectors are principle component analysis and singular-value decomposition.

To demonstrate these, we'll return to Incanter and make use of one of its included datasets: the Iris dataset:

```
(defn ex-7-27 []
  (i/view (d/get-dataset :iris)))
```

The previous code should return the following table:

:Sepal.Length	:Sepal.Width	:Petal.Length	:Petal Width	:Species
5.1	3.5	1.4	0.2	setosa
4.9	3.0	1.4	0.2	setosa
4.7	3.2	1.3	0.2	setosa
4.6	3.1	1.5	0.2	setosa
5.0	3.6	1.4	0.2	setosa
5.4	3.9	1.7	0.4	setosa
4.6	3.4	1.4	0.3	setosa

The first four columns of the Iris dataset contain measurements of the sepal length, sepal width, petal length, and petal width of Iris plants. The dataset is ordered by the species of plants. Rows 0 to 49 represent Iris setosa, rows 50 to 99 represent Iris virsicolor, and rows above 100 contain Iris virginica. The exact species aren't important; we'll only be interested in the differences between them.

Plotting the Iris dataset

Let's visualize some of the attributes of the Iris dataset on a scatter plot. We'll make use of the following helper function to plot each of the species as a separate color:

```
(defn plot-iris-columns [a b]
  (let [data (->> (d/get-dataset :iris)
                  (i/$ [a b])
                  (i/to-matrix))]
    (-> (c/scatter-plot (i/$ (range 50) 0 data)
                        (i/$ (range 50) 1 data)
                        :x-label (name a)
                        :y-label (name b))
        (c/add-points (i/$ (range 50 100) 0 data)
                      (i/$ (range 50 100) 1 data))
        (c/add-points (i/$ [:not (range 100)] 0 data)
                      (i/$ [:not (range 100)] 1 data))
        (i/view))))
```

Having defined this function, let's see how the sepal widths and lengths compare for each of the three species:

```
(defn ex-7-28 []
  (plot-iris-columns :Sepal.Width
                     :Sepal.Length))
```

The previous example should generate the following chart:

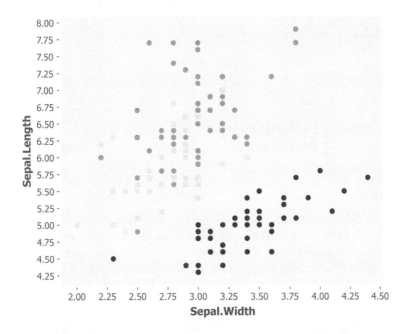

We can see how one of the species is quite different from the other two while comparing these two attributes, but two of the species are barely distinguishable: the widths and heights for several of the points are evenly overlaid.

Let's instead plot the petal width and height to see how these compare:

```
(defn ex-7-29 []
  (plot-iris-columns :Petal.Width
                     :Petal.Length))
```

This should generate the following chart:

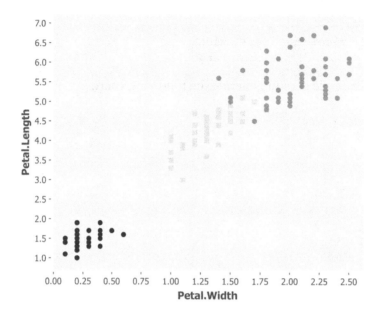

This does a much better job of distinguishing between the different species. This is partly because the variance of the petal width and length is greater — the length, for example, stretches a full 6 units on the *y* axis. A useful side effect of this greater spread is that it allows us to draw a much clearer distinction between the species of Iris.

Principle component analysis

In principle component analysis, often abbreviated to PCA, we're looking to find a rotation of data that maximizes the variance. In the previous scatter plot, we identified a way of looking at the data that provided a high degree of variance on the *y* axis, but the variance of the *x* axis was not as great.

We have four dimensions available in the Iris dataset, each representing the value of the length and width of a petal or a sepal. Principle component analysis allows us to determine whether there is a another basis, which is some linear combination of all the available dimensions, that best re-expresses our data to maximize the variance.

We can apply principle component analysis with the Incanter.stats' `principle-components` function. In the following code, we pass it a matrix of data and plot the first two returned rotations:

```
(defn ex-7-30 []
  (let [data (->> (d/get-dataset :iris)
                  (i/$ (range 4))
                  (i/to-matrix))
        components (s/principal-components data)
        pc1 (i/$ 0 (:rotation components))
        pc2 (i/$ 1 (:rotation components))
        xs (i/mmult data pc1)
        ys (i/mmult data pc2)]
    (-> (c/scatter-plot (i/$ (range 50) 0 xs)
                        (i/$ (range 50) 0 ys)
                        :x-label "Principle Component 1"
                        :y-label "Principle Component 2")
        (c/add-points (i/$ (range 50 100) 0 xs)
                      (i/$ (range 50 100) 0 ys))
        (c/add-points (i/$ [:not (range 100)] 0 xs)
                      (i/$ [:not (range 100)] 0 ys))
        (i/view))))
```

The preceding example produces the following chart:

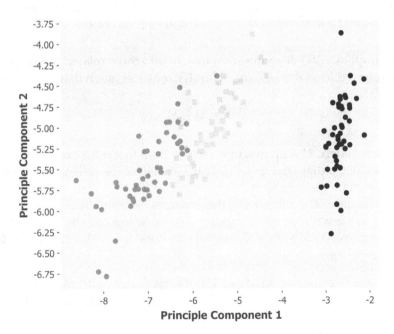

Notice how the axes can no longer be identified as being sepals or petals—the components have been derived as a linear combination of the values across all the dimensions and define a new basis to view the data that maximizes the variance within each component. In fact, the `principle-component` function returns `:std-dev` along with `:rotation` for each dimension.

 For interactive examples demonstrating principle component analysis, see `http://setosa.io/ev/principal-component-analysis/`.

As a result of taking the principle components of the data, the variance across the *x* and the *y* axis is greater than even the previous scatter plot showing petal width and length. The points corresponding to the different species of iris are therefore spread out as wide as they can be, so the relative difference of the species is clearly observable.

Singular value decomposition

A technique that's closely related to PCA is **Singular Value Decomposition (SVD)**. SVD is, in fact, a more general technique than PCA which also seeks to change the basis of a matrix.

 An excellent mathematical description of PCA and its relationship to SVD is available at `http://arxiv.org/pdf/1404.1100.pdf`.

As its name implies, SVD decomposes a matrix into three related matrices, commonly referred to as the U, Σ (or S), and V matrices, such that:

$$X = U \Sigma V^{T}$$

If X is an m x n matrix, U is an m x m matrix, Σ is an m x n matrix, and V is an n x n matrix. Σ is, in fact, a diagonal matrix, meaning that all the cells with the exception of those on the main diagonal (top left to bottom right) are zero. Although clearly, it need not be square. The columns of the matrices returned by SVD are ordered by their singular value with the most important dimensions coming first. SVD thus allows us to represent the matrix X more approximately by discarding the least important dimensions.

For example, the decomposition of our 150 x 4 Iris matrix will result in a U of 150 x 150, Σ of 150 x 4 and V of 4 x 4. Multiplying these matrices together will yield our original Iris matrix.

However, we could choose instead to take only the top two singular values and adjust our matrices such that U is 150 x 2, Σ is 2 x 2, and V is 2 x 4. Let's construct a function that takes a matrix and projects it into a specified number of dimensions by taking this number of columns from each of the U, Σ, and V matrices:

```
(defn project-into [matrix d]
  (let [svd (i/decomp-svd matrix)]
    {:U (i/$ (range d) (:U svd))
     :S (i/diag (take d (:S svd)))
     :V (i/trans
          (i/$ (range d) (:V svd)))}))
```

Here, d is the number of dimensions that we want to retain. Let's demonstrate this with a simple example by taking a multivariate normal distribution generated by Incanter using s/sample-mvn and reducing it to just one dimension:

```
(defn ex-7-31 []
  (let [matrix (s/sample-mvn 100
                             :sigma (i/matrix [[1 0.8]
                                               [0.8 1]]))]
    (println "Original" matrix)
    (project-into matrix 1)))

;; Original  A 100x2 matrix
;; :U  A 100x1 matrix
;; :S  A 1x1 matrix
;; :V  A 1x2 matrix
```

The output of the previous example contains the most important aspects of the data reduced to just one dimension. To recreate an approximation of the original dataset in two dimensions, we can simply multiply the three matrices together. In the following code, we project the one-dimensional approximation of the distribution back into two dimensions:

```
(defn ex-7-32 []
  (let [matrix (s/sample-mvn 100
                             :sigma (i/matrix [[1 0.8]
                                               [0.8 1]]))
        svd (project-into matrix 1)
        projection (i/mmult (:U svd)
                            (:S svd)
                            (:V svd))]
    (-> (c/scatter-plot (i/$ 0 matrix) (i/$ 1 matrix)
                        :x-label "x"
                        :y-label "y"
```

```
                    :series-label "Original"
                    :legend true)
    (c/add-points (i/$ 0 projection) (i/$ 1 projection)
                    :series-label "Projection")
    (i/view))))
```

This produces the following chart:

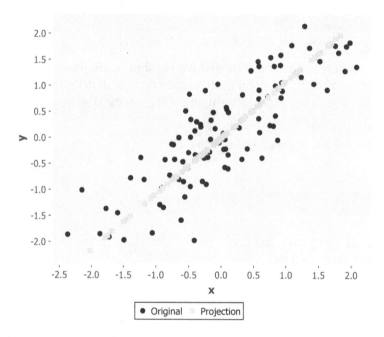

Notice how SVD has preserved the primary feature of the multivariate distribution, the strong diagonal, but has collapsed the variance of the off-diagonal points. In this way, SVD preserves the most important structure in the data while discarding less important information. Hopefully, the earlier example makes it even clearer than the PCA example that the preserved features need not be explicit in the original data. In the example, the strong diagonal is a *latent* feature of the data.

Latent features are those which are not directly observable, but which can be inferred from other features. Sometimes, latent features refer to aspects that could be measured directly, such as the correlation in the previous example or — in the context of recommendation — they can be considered to represent underlying preferences or attitudes.

Having observed the principle of SVD at work on the earlier synthetic data, let's see how it performs on the Iris dataset:

```
(defn ex-7-33 []
  (let [svd (->> (d/get-dataset :iris)
                 (i/$ (range 4))
                 (i/to-matrix)
                 (i/decomp-svd))
        dims 2
        u (i/$      (range dims) (:U svd))
        s (i/diag  (take dims    (:S svd)))
        v (i/trans (i/$ (range dims) (:V svd)))
        projection (i/mmult u s v)]
    (-> (c/scatter-plot (i/$ (range 50) 0 projection)
                        (i/$ (range 50) 1 projection)
                        :x-label "Dimension 1"
                        :y-label "Dimension 2")
        (c/add-points (i/$ (range 50 100) 0 projection)
                      (i/$ (range 50 100) 1 projection))
        (c/add-points (i/$ [:not (range 100)] 0 projection)
                      (i/$ [:not (range 100)] 1 projection))
        (i/view))))
```

This code generates the following chart:

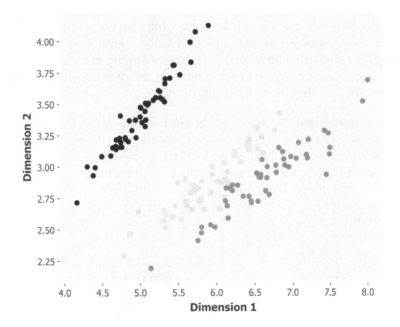

After comparing the Iris charts for PCA and SVD, it should be clear that the two approaches are closely related. This scatter plot looks a lot like an inverted version of the PCA plot that we saw previously.

Let's return to the problem of movie recommendation now, and see how dimensionality reduction could assist. In the next section, we'll make use of the Apache Spark distributed computing framework and an associated machine learning library, MLlib, to perform movie recommendations on dimensionally-reduced data.

Large-scale machine learning with Apache Spark and MLlib

The Spark project (`https://spark.apache.org/`) is a cluster computing framework that emphasizes low-latency job execution. It's a relatively recent project, growing out of UC Berkley's AMP Lab in 2009.

Although Spark is able to coexist with Hadoop (by connecting to the files stored on **Hadoop Distributed File System** (**HDFS**), for example), it targets much faster job execution times by keeping much of the computation in memory. In contrast with Hadoop's two-stage MapReduce paradigm, which stores files on the disk in between each iteration, Spark's in-memory model can perform tens or hundreds of times faster for some applications, particularly those performing multiple iterations over the data.

In *Chapter 5*, *Big Data*, we discovered the value of iterative algorithms to the implementation of optimization techniques on large quantities of data. This makes Spark an excellent choice for large-scale machine learning. In fact, the MLlib library (`https://spark.apache.org/mllib/`) is built on top of Spark and implements a variety of machine learning algorithms out of the box.

We won't provide an in-depth account of Spark here, but will explain just enough on the key concepts required to run a Spark job using the Clojure library, Sparkling (`https://github.com/gorillalabs/sparkling`). Sparkling wraps much of Spark's functionality behind a friendly Clojure interface. In particular, the use of the thread-last macro `->>` to chain Spark operations together can make Spark jobs written in Sparkling appear a lot like the code we would write to process data using Clojure's own sequence abstractions.

 Be sure also to check out Flambo, which makes use of the thread-first macro to chain tasks: `https://github.com/yieldbot/flambo`.

We're going to be producing recommendations based on the MovieLens ratings, so the first step will be to load this data with Sparkling.

Loading data with Sparkling

Spark can load data from any storage source supported by Hadoop, including the local file system and HDFS, as well as other data sources such as Cassandra, HBase, and Amazon S3. Let's start with the basics by writing a job to simply count the number of ratings.

The MovieLens ratings are stored as a text file, which can be loaded in Sparkling using the text-file function in the sparkling.core namespace (referred to as spark in the code). To tell Spark where the file is located, we pass a URI that can point to a remote source such as hdfs://..., s3n://.... Since we're running Spark in local mode, it could simply be a local file path. Once we have the text file, we'll call spark/count to get the number of lines:

```
(defn count-ratings [sc]
  (-> (spark/text-file sc "data/ml-100k/ua.base")
      (spark/count)))

(defn ex-7-34 []
  (spark/with-context sc (-> (conf/spark-conf)
                             (conf/master "local")
                             (conf/app-name "ch7"))
    (count-ratings sc)))

;; 90570
```

If you run the previous example, you may see many logging statements from Spark printed to the console. One of the final lines will be the count that has been calculated.

Notice that we have to pass a Spark context as the first argument to the text-file function. The Spark context tells Spark how to access your cluster. The most basic configuration specifies the location of the Spark master and the application name Spark should use for this job. For running locally, the Spark master is "local", which is useful for REPL-based interactive development.

Mapping data

Sparkling provides analogues to many of the Clojure core sequence functions you would expect such as map, reduce, and filter. At the beginning of this chapter, we stored our ratings as a map with the :item, :user, and :rating keys. While we could parse our data into a map again, let's parse each rating into a Rating object instead. This will allow us to more easily interact with MLlib later in the chapter.

The Rating class is defined in the org.apache.spark.mllib.recommendation package. The constructor takes three numeric arguments: representations of the user, the item, and the user's rating for the item. As well as creating a Rating object, we're also calculating the time modulo 10, returning a number between 0 and 9 and creating tuple of both values:

```
(defn parse-rating [line]
  (let [[user item rating time] (->> (str/split line #"\t")
                                     (map parse-long))]
    (spark/tuple (mod time 10)
                 (Rating. user item rating)))))

(defn parse-ratings [sc]
  (->> (spark/text-file sc "data/ml-100k/ua.base")
       (spark/map-to-pair parse-rating)))

(defn ex-7-35 []
  (spark/with-context sc (-> (conf/spark-conf)
                             (conf/master "local")
                             (conf/app-name "ch7"))
    (->> (parse-ratings sc)
         (spark/collect)
         (first))))

;; #sparkling/tuple [8 #<Rating Rating(1,1,5.0)>]
```

The returned value is a tuple with an integer key (defined as the time modulo 10) and a rating as the value. Having a key which partitions the data into ten groups will be useful when we come to split the data into test and training sets.

Distributed datasets and tuples

Tuples are used extensively by Spark to represent pairs of keys and values. In the preceding example the key was an integer, but this is not a requirement—keys and values can be any type serializable by Spark.

Datasets in Spark are represented as **Resilient Distributed Datasets (RDDs)**. In fact, RDDs are the core abstraction that Spark provides—a fault-tolerant collection of records partitioned across all the nodes in your cluster that can be operated in parallel. There are two fundamental types of RDDs: those that represent sequences of arbitrary objects (such as the kind returned by `text-file`—a sequence of lines), and those which represent sequences of key/value pairs.

We can convert between plain RDDs and pair RDDs simply, and this is accomplished in the previous example with the `map-to-pair` function. The tuple returned by our `parse-rating` function specifies the key and the value that should be used for each pair in the sequence. As with Hadoop, there's no requirement that the key be unique within the dataset. In fact, as we'll see, keys are often a useful means of grouping similar records together.

Filtering data

Let's now filter our data based on the value of the key and create a subset of the overall data that we can use for training. Like the core Clojure function of the same name, Sparkling provides a `filter` function that will keep only those rows for which a predicate returns logical true.

Given our pair RDD of ratings, we can filter only those ratings that have a key value less than 8. Since the keys roughly and uniformly distributed integers 0-9, this will retain approximately 80 percent of the dataset:

```
(defn training-ratings [ratings]
  (->> ratings
       (spark/filter (fn [tuple]
                       (< (s-de/key tuple) 8)))
       (spark/values)))
```

Our ratings are stored in a pair RDD, so the result of filter is also a pair RDD. We're calling `values` on the result so that we're left with a plain RDD containing only the `Rating` objects. This will be the RDD that we pass to our machine learning algorithm. We perform exactly the same process, but for the keys greater than or equal to 8, to obtain the test data we'll be using.

Persistence and caching

Spark's actions are lazy and won't be calculated until they're needed. Similarly, once data has been calculated, it won't be explicitly cached. Sometimes, we'd like to keep data around though. In particular, if we're running an iterative algorithm, we don't want the dataset to be recalculated from source each time we perform an iteration. In cases where the results of a transformed dataset should be saved for subsequent use within a job, Spark provides the ability to persist RDDs. Like the RDDs themselves, the persistence is fault-tolerant, meaning that if any partition is lost, it will be recomputed using the transformations that originally created it.

We can persist an RDD using the spark/persist function, which expects us to pass the RDD and also configure the storage level most appropriate for our application. In most cases, this will be in-memory storage. But in cases where recomputing the data would be computationally expensive, we can spill to disk or even replicate the cache across disks for fast fault recovery. In-memory is most common, so Sparkling provides the spark/cache function shorthand that will set this storage level on an RDD:

```
(defn ex-7-36 []
  (spark/with-context sc (-> (conf/spark-conf)
                             (conf/master "local")
                             (conf/app-name "ch7"))
    (let [ratings (spark/cache (parse-ratings sc))
          train (training-ratings ratings)
          test  (test-ratings ratings)]
      (println "Training:" (spark/count train))
      (println "Test:"     (spark/count test)))))

;; Training: 72806
;; Test: 8778
```

In the preceding example, we cache the result of the call to parse-ratings. This means that the loading and parsing of ratings is performed a single time, and the training and test ratings functions both use the cached data to filter and perform their counts. The call to cache optimizes the performance of jobs and allows spark to avoid recalculating data more than necessary.

Machine learning on Spark with MLlib

We've covered enough of the basics of Spark now to use our RDDs for machine learning. While Spark handles the infrastructure, the actual work of performing machine learning is handled by an apache Spark subproject called MLlib.

An overview of all the capabilities of the MLlib library are at
`https://spark.apache.org/docs/latest/mllib-guide.html`.

MLlib provides a wealth of machine learning algorithms for use on Spark, including those for regression, classification, and clustering covered elsewhere in this book. In this chapter, we'll be using the algorithm MLlib provides for performing collaborative filtering: alternating least squares.

Movie recommendations with alternating least squares

In *Chapter 5, Big Data*, we discovered how to use gradient descent to identify the parameters that minimize a cost function for a large quantity of data. In this chapter, we've seen how SVD can be used to calculate latent factors within a matrix of data through decomposition.

The **alternating least squares (ALS)** algorithm can be thought of as a combination of both of these approaches. It is an iterative algorithm that uses least-squares estimates to decompose the user-movies matrix of rankings into two matrices of latent factors: the user factors and the movie factors.

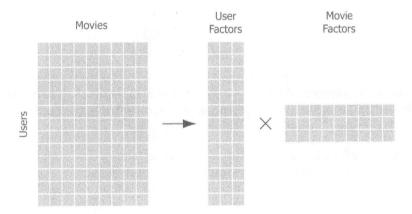

Alternating least squares is therefore based on the assumption that the users' ratings are based on some latent property of the movie that can't be measured directly, but can be inferred from the ratings matrix. The earlier diagram shows how the sparse matrix of user-movie ratings can be decomposed into two matrices containing the user factors and the movie factors. The diagram associates just three factors with each user and movie, but let's make it even more simplistic by just using two factors.

We could hypothesize that all the movies exist in a two-dimensional space identified by their level of action, romance, and how realistic (or not) they may be. We visualize such a space as follows:

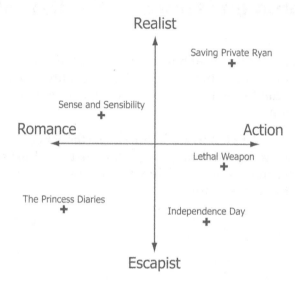

We could likewise imagine all the users represented in an equivalent two-dimensional space, where their tastes were simply expressed as their relative preference for **Romance/Action** and **Realist/Escapist**.

Once we've reduced all the movies and users to their factor representation, the problem of prediction is reduced to a simple matrix multiplication—our predicted rating for a user, given a movie, is simply the product of their factors. The challenge for ALS then is to calculate the two factor matrices.

ALS with Spark and MLlib

At the time of writing, no Clojure wrapper exists for the MLlib library, so we'll be using Clojure's interop capabilities to access it directly. MLlib's implementation of alternating least squares is provided by the ALS class in the `org.apache.spark.mllib.recommendation` package. Training ALS is almost as simple as calling the `train` static method on the class with our RDD and provided arguments:

```
(defn alternating-least-squares [data {:keys [rank num-iter
                                              lambda]}]
  (ALS/train (to-mllib-rdd data) rank num-iter lambda 10))
```

The slight complexity is that the RDD of training data returned by our preceding Sparkling job is expressed as a `JavaRDD` type. MLlib, since it has no Java API, expects to receive standard Spark `RDD` types. Converting between the two is a straightforward enough process, albeit somewhat tedious. The following functions convert back and forth between RDD types; into `RDD`s ready for consumption by MLlib and then back into `JavaRDD`s for use in Sparkling:

```
(defn to-mlib-rdd [rdd]
  (.rdd rdd))

(defn from-mlib-rdd [rdd]
  (JavaRDD/fromRDD rdd scala/OBJECT-CLASS-TAG))
```

The second argument in `from-mllib-rdd` is a value defined in the `sparkling.scalaInterop` namespace. This is required to interact with the JVM bytecode generated by Scala's function definition.

 For more on Clojure/Scala interop consult the excellent from the scala library by Tobias Kortkamp at `http://t6.github.io/from-scala/`.

With the previous boilerplate out of the way, we can finally perform ALS on the training ratings. We do this in the following example:

```
(defn ex-7-37 []
  (spark/with-context sc (-> (conf/spark-conf)
                             (conf/master "local")
                             (conf/app-name "ch7"))
    (-> (parse-ratings sc)
        (training-ratings)
        (alternating-least-squares {:rank 10
                                    :num-iter 10
                                    :lambda 1.0}))))
```

The function takes several arguments—rank, num-iter, and lambda, and it returns a MLlib MatrixFactorisationModel function. The rank is the number of features to use for the factor matrices.

Making predictions with ALS

Once we've calculated MatrixFactorisationModel, we can use it to make predictions with the recommendProducts method. This expects to receive the ID of the user to recommend to and the number of recommendations to return:

```
(defn ex-7-38 []
  (spark/with-context sc (-> (conf/spark-conf)
                             (conf/master "local")
                             (conf/app-name "ch7"))
    (let [options {:rank 10
                   :num-iter 10
                   :lambda 1.0}
          model (-> (parse-ratings sc)
                    (training-ratings )
                    (alternating-least-squares options))]
      (into [] (.recommendProducts model 1 3)))))

;; [#<Rating Rating(1,1463,3.869355232995907)>
;; #<Rating Rating(1,1536,3.7939806028920993)>
;; #<Rating Rating(1,1500,3.7130689437266646)>]
```

You can see that the output of the model, like the input, are the Rating objects. They contain the user ID, the item ID, and a predicted rating calculated as the product of the factor matrices. Let's make use of the function that we defined at the beginning of the chapter to give these ratings names:

```
(defn ex-7-39 []
  (spark/with-context sc (-> (conf/spark-conf)
                             (conf/master "local")
                             (conf/app-name "ch7"))
    (let [items    (load-items "u.item")
          id->name (fn [id] (get items id))
          options {:rank 10
                   :num-iter 10
                   :lambda 1.0}
          model (-> (parse-ratings sc)
```

```
                    (training-ratings )
                    (alternating-least-squares options))]
       (->> (.recommendProducts model 1 3)
            (map (comp id->name #(.product %)))))))))

;; ("Boys, Les (1997)" "Aiqing wansui (1994)"
;; "Santa with Muscles (1996)")
```

It's not particularly clear that these are good recommendations though. For this, we'll need to evaluate the performance of our ALS model.

Evaluating ALS

Unlike Mahout, Spark doesn't include a built-in evaluator for the model, so we're going to have to write our own. One of the simplest evaluators, and one we've used already in this chapter, is the root mean square error (RMSE) evaluator.

The first step for our evaluation is to use the model to predict ratings for all of our training set. Spark's implementation of ALS includes a predict function that we can use, which will accept an RDD containing all of the user IDs and item IDs to return predictions for:

```
(defn user-product [rating]
  (spark/tuple (.user rating)
               (.product rating)))

(defn user-product-rating [rating]
  (spark/tuple (user-product rating)
               (.rating rating)))

(defn predict [model data]
  (->> (spark/map-to-pair user-product data)
       (to-mlib-rdd data)
       (.predict model)
       (from-mlib-rdd)
       (spark/map-to-pair user-product-rating)))
```

The .recommendProducts method we called previously uses the model to return product recommendations for a specific user. By contrast, the .predict method will predict the rating for many users and items at once.

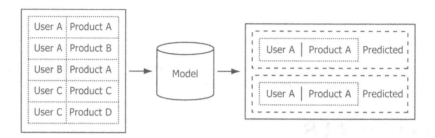

The result of our call to the .predict function is a pair RDD, where the key is itself a tuple of user and product. The value of the pair RDD is the predicted rating.

Calculating the sum of squared errors

To calculate the difference between the predicted rating and the actual rating given to the product by the user, we'll need to join the predictions and the actuals together based on a matching user/product tuple. As the keys will be the same in both the predictions and actuals RDDs, we can simply pass them both to Sparkling's join function:

```
(defn squared-error [y-hat y]
  (Math/pow (- y-hat y) 2))

(defn sum-squared-errors [predictions actuals]
  (->> (spark/join predictions actuals)
       (spark/values)
       (spark/map (s-de/val-val-fn squared-error))
       (spark/reduce +)))
```

We can visualize the whole `sum-squared-errors` function as the following flow, comparing the predicted and actual ratings:

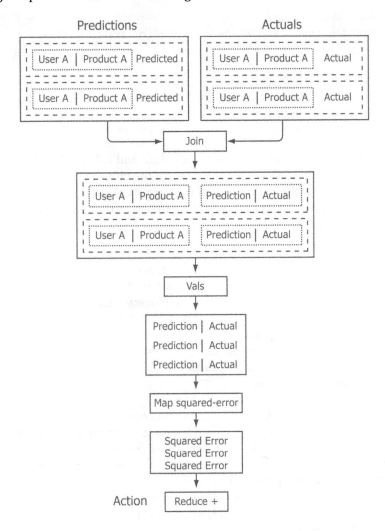

Once we've calculated the `sum-squared-errors`, calculating the root mean square is simply a matter of dividing it by the count and taking the square root:

```
(defn rmse [model data]
  (let [predictions  (spark/cache (predict model data))
        actuals (->> (spark/map-to-pair user-product-rating
                                        data)
                  (spark/cache))]
    (-> (sum-squared-errors predictions actuals)
        (/ (spark/count data))
        (Math/sqrt))))
```

The `rmse` function will take a model and some data and calculate RMSE of the prediction against the actual rating. Earlier in the chapter, we plotted the different values of RMSE as the size of the neighborhood changed with a user-based recommender. Let's employ the same technique now, but alter the rank of the factor matrix:

```
(defn ex-7-40 []
  (spark/with-context sc (-> (conf/spark-conf)
                             (conf/master "local")
                             (conf/app-name "ch7"))
    (let [options {:num-iter 10 :lambda 0.1}
          training (-> (parse-ratings sc)
                       (training-ratings)
                       (spark/cache))
          ranks    (range 2 50 2)
          errors   (for [rank ranks]
                     (doto (-> (als training
                                    (assoc options :rank rank))
                               (rmse training))
                       (println "RMSE for rank" rank)))]
      (-> (c/scatter-plot ranks errors
                          :x-label "Rank"
                          :y-label "RMSE")
          (i/view)))))
```

The earlier code generates the following plot:

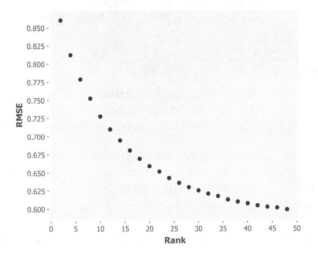

Observe how, as we increase the rank of the factor matrix, the ratings returned by our model become closer and closer to the ratings that the model was trained on. As the dimensions of the factor matrix grow, it can capture more of the variation in individual users' ratings.

What we'd really like to do though is to see how well the recommender performs against the test set—the data it hasn't already seen. The final example in this chapter, ex-7-41, runs the preceding analysis again, but tests the RMSE of the model against the test set rather than the training set. The example generates the following plot:

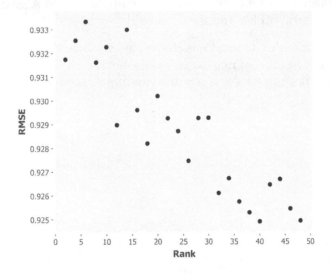

As we would hope, the RMSE of the predictions fall as the rank of the factor matrix is increased. A larger factor matrix is able to capture more of the latent features that lie within the ratings, and more accurately predict the rating a user will give a movie.

Summary

We've covered a lot of ground in this chapter. Although the subject was principally recommender systems, we've also discussed dimensionality reduction and introduced the Spark distributed computation framework as well.

We started by discussing the difference between content- and collaborative filtering-based approaches to the problem of recommendation. Within the context of collaborative filtering, we discussed item-item recommenders and built a Slope One recommender. We also discussed user-user recommenders and used Mahout's implementations of a variety of similarity measures and evaluators to implement and test several user-based recommenders too. The challenge of evaluation provided an opportunity to introduce the statistics of information retrieval.

We spent a lot of time in this chapter covering several different types of dimensionality reduction. For example, we learned about the probabilistic methods offered by Bloom filters and MinHash, and the analytic methods offered by principle component analysis and singular value decomposition. While not specific to recommender systems, we saw how such techniques could be used to help implement more efficient similarity comparisons.

Finally, we introduced the distributed computation framework Spark and learned how the alternating least squares algorithm uses dimensionality reduction to discover latent factors in a matrix of ratings. We implemented ALS and a RMSE evaluator using Spark, MLlib, and the Clojure library Sparkling.

Many of the techniques we learned this chapter are very general, and the next chapter will be no different. We'll continue to explore the Spark and Sparkling libraries as we learn about network analysis: the study of connections and relationships.

8
Network Analysis

"The enemy of my enemy is my friend."

- Ancient proverb

This chapter concerns itself with graphs in the mathematical rather than the visual sense. A graph is simply a set of vertices connected by the edges and the simplicity of this abstraction means that graphs are everywhere. They are an effective model for structures as diverse as the hyperlink structure of the web, the physical structure of the internet, and all sorts of networks: roads, telecommunications, and social networks.

Thus, network analysis is hardly new, but it has become particularly popular with the rise of social network analysis. Among the largest sites on the web are social networks, and Google, Facebook, Twitter, and LinkedIn all make use of large-scale graph processing to mine their users' data. The huge importance of targeted advertising for the monetization of websites means that there is a large financial reward for companies that effectively infer internet users' interests.

In this chapter, we'll use publicly available Twitter data to demonstrate the principles of network analysis. We'll apply pattern matching techniques such as triangle counting to look for a structure within the graph and apply whole-graph processing algorithms such as label propagation and PageRank to tease out the network structure of the graph. Ultimately, we'll use these techniques to identify the interests of a set of Twitter communities from their most influential members. We'll do all of this using Spark and a library called GraphX which uses the Spark distributed computation model to process very large graphs.

But before we scale up, we'll begin our exploration of graphs by considering a different sort of problem: that of graph traversal. For this, we'll make use of the Clojure library Loom.

Download the data

This chapter makes use of the data of follower data from the Twitter social network. The data is provided as a part of the Stanford Large Network Dataset Collection. You can download the Twitter data from `https://snap.stanford.edu/data/egonets-Twitter.html`.

We'll be making use of both the `twitter.tar.gz` file and the `twitter_combined.txt.gz` files. Both of these files should be downloaded and decompressed inside the sample code's data directory.

 The sample code for this chapter is available at `https://github.com/clojuredatascience/ch8-network-analysis`.

As usual, a script has been provided that will do this for you. You can run it by executing the following command line from within the project directory:

`script/download-data.sh`

If you'd like to run this chapter's examples, make sure you download the data before continuing.

Inspecting the data

Let's look at one of the files in the Twitter directory, specifically the `twitter/98801140.edges` file. If you open it in a text editor, you'll see that each line of the file consists of a pair of integers separated by a space. The data is in what's known as an edge list format. It's one of the two primary ways of storing graphs (the other being the adjacency list format, which we'll come to later). The following code uses Clojure's `line-seq` function to read the file one line at a time and convert it into a tuple:

```
(defn to-long [l]
  (Long/parseLong l))

(defn line->edge [line]
  (->> (str/split line #" ")
       (mapv to-long)))

(defn load-edges [file]
  (->> (io/resource file)
       (io/reader)
```

```
      (line-seq)
      (map line->edge)))

  (defn ex-8-1 []
    (load-edges "twitter/98801140.edges"))
```

If you execute (ex-8-1) in the REPL or run the following on the command line, you should see the following sequence:

```
lein run -e 8.1
;;([100873813 3829151] [35432131 3829151] [100742942 35432131]
;;  [35432131 27475761] [27475761 35432131])
```

This simple sequence of pairs of numbers, each representing an edge, is already enough to represent the essence of the graph. It's not intuitive to see how the edges relate to each other, so let's visualize it.

Visualizing graphs with Loom

For the first half of this chapter, we'll be using Loom (https://github.com/aysylu/loom) to process our graphs. Loom defines an API to create and manipulate graphs. It also contains many built-in graph traversal algorithms. We'll come to these shortly.

Firstly, we'll want to visualize our graph. For this, Loom relies on a system-level library called GraphViz. If you like to be able to replicate many of the images in this chapter, you'll need to install GraphViz now. If you're not sure that you have it installed, try running the following on the command line:

```
dot -V
```

 GraphViz is available from http://graphviz.org/ and there are installers for Linux, MacOS, and Windows. GraphViz isn't a requirement to run all the examples in this chapter, just the ones that visualize the graphs.

Loom is able to create a graph from a sequence of edges like the ones we have when we apply the loom/graph function to the sequence. We'll require loom.graph as loom and loom.io as lio in the following examples. If you have GraphViz installed, run the following example:

```
  (defn ex-8-2 []
    (->> (load-edges "twitter/98801140.edges")
         (apply loom/graph)
         (lio/view)))
```

You should see a result like the following schematic representation:

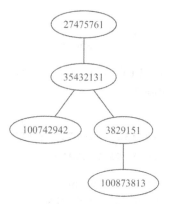

Depending on your version of GraphViz, you may not get exactly the same layout as the previous version, but it doesn't matter. The relative positions of the nodes and the edges in the image aren't important. The only important fact about the graph is which nodes are connected to which other nodes.

As a Clojure programmer, you're familiar with tree structures as the nested structure of S-expressions and you've probably noticed that this graph looks a lot like a tree. In fact, a tree is just a special kind of graph: one that contains no loops. We refer to such graphs as **acyclic**.

In this graph there are only four edges, whereas there were five in the edge list we saw in the first example. This is because edges can be directed. They go from a node to another node. We can load directed graphs with Loom using the `loom/digraph` function:

```
(defn ex-8-3 []
  (->> (load-edges "twitter/98801140.edges")
       (apply loom/digraph)
       (lio/view)))
```

This code generates the following image:

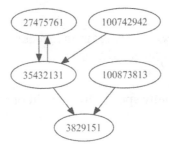

Notice how the act of adding directions to our edges has fundamentally altered the way we read the graph. In particular, the graph is clearly no longer a tree. Directed graphs are extremely important in cases where we want to represent an action that's performed on something by something else.

For example, in Twitter's social graph, an account may follow one account, but the act may not be reciprocal. Using Twitter's terminology, we can refer to either the followers or the friends of an account. A follow represents an outgoing edge, whereas a friend is an incoming edge. In the previous graph, for example, account **382951** has two followers: accounts **35432131** and **100873813**.

There are now two edges between nodes **27475761** and **35432131**. This means that it's possible to get from one node back to the other. We call this a cycle. The technical term for a graph such as the earlier one is a directed, **cyclic** graph.

 A cycle in a graph means that it's possible to get back to a node by moving only in the direction of edges. If a graph contains no such loops, then the graph is said to be acyclic. A **Directed Acyclic Graph (DAG)**, is a model for a huge variety of hierarchical or ordered phenomena such as dependency graphs, family trees, and file system hierarchies.

We've seen that graphs can be directed or undirected. The third main type of graph is the **weighted** graph. A weight may be usefully associated with an edge to represent the strength of a connection between two nodes. For example, if the graph represents a social network, the weight between two accounts might be the strength of their connection (for example, their frequency of communication).

We can load a weighted graph in `loom` with either the `loom/weighted-graph` or `loom/weighted-digraph` functions:

```
(defn ex-8-4 []
  (->> (load-edges "twitter/98801140.edges")
       (apply loom/weighted-digraph)
       (lio/view)))
```

Our input graph doesn't actually specify the weight of the edges. Loom's default weight for all the edges is **1**.

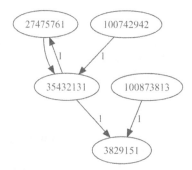

Another aspect in which graphs can differ is whether its vertices and edges are typed, representing different entities or connections between them. For example, the Facebook graph contains many types of entities: notably "pages" and "people". People can "like" the pages, but they can't "like" other people. In heterogeneous graphs where nodes of type "A" are always connected to type "B" and vice versa (but never to each other), the graph is said to be **bipartite**. Bipartite graphs can be represented as two disjoint sets, where nodes in one set only ever link to the nodes in the other set.

Graph traversal with Loom

Traversal algorithms concern themselves with the ways of exploring the graph in a systematic way. Given the huge variety of phenomena that can be modeled with graphs, such algorithms could have a huge variety of uses.

The algorithms we'll consider in the next few sections concern some of the most common tasks such as:

- Determining whether a path exists that traces each edge exactly once
- Determining the shortest path between two vertices
- Determining the shortest tree that connects all the vertices

If the graph in question represented the road network covered by a delivery driver's round, the vertices could represent intersections. Finding a path that traces each edge exactly once would be the way a delivery driver would travel all the roads without doubling back or passing the same addresses twice. The shortest path between the two vertices would be the most efficient way to navigate from one address to the next delivery. Finally, the shortest tree connecting all the vertices would be the most effective way to connect all of the vertices: perhaps, to lay a roadside power line for the lights at each intersection.

The seven bridges of Königsberg

The city of Königsberg in Prussia (now Kaliningrad, Russia) was set on both sides of the Pregel River, and included two large islands that were connected to each other and the mainland by seven bridges. The Seven bridges of Königsberg is a historically notable problem in mathematics that laid the foundation for graph theory and prefigured the idea of topology. The name Pregel will appear again later in this chapter.

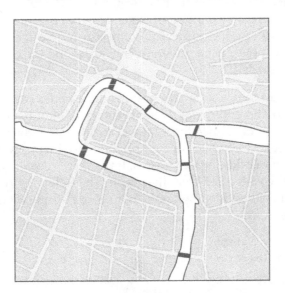

The problem was to find a walk through the city that would cross each bridge once and only once. The islands could not be reached by any route other than the bridges and the bridges had to be crossed completely every time; one could not walk halfway onto the bridge and then turn around and later cross the other half from the other side (though the walk need not start and end at the same spot).

Euler realized that the problem has no solution: that there could be no non-retracing route via the bridges, and the difficulty led to the development of a technique that established this assertion with mathematical rigor. The only structure of the problem that mattered were the connections between the bridges and landmasses. The essence of the problem could be preserved by representing the bridges as edges in a graph.

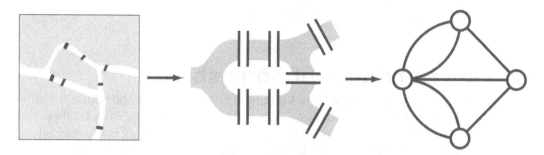

Euler observed that (except at the endpoints of the walk) one enters a vertex by one edge and leaves the vertex by a different edge. If every edge has been traversed exactly once, it follows that the number of connecting edges for each node must be even (half of them will have been traversed "inwards" and the other half will have been traversed "outwards").

Therefore, for an Euler tour to exist in a graph, all the nodes (with the possible exception of the start and end node) must have an even number of connecting edges. We refer to the number of connecting edges as the degree of the node. Determining whether or not an Euler tour exists in a graph therefore is simply a matter of counting the number of odd-degree vertices. If there are zero or two vertices, then an Euler tour can be constructed from the graph. The following function makes use of two utility functions provided by Loom, out-degree and nodes, to check for the presence of an Euler tour:

```
(defneuler-tour? [graph]
  (let [degree (partial loom/out-degree graph)]
    (->> (loom/nodes graph)
         (filter (comp odd? degree))
         (count)
         (contains? #{0 2})))))
```

In this code, we used Loom's out-degree function to calculate the degree of each node in the graph. We filter just the odd degree vertices and verify that the count is either 0 or 2. If it is, an Euler tour exists.

Breadth-first and depth-first search

The previous example is historically notable, but a more common desire in graph traversal is to find a node within the graph starting from some other node. There are several ways of addressing this challenge. For unweighted graphs such as our Twitter follow graph, the most common are breadth first and depth first search.

Breadth first search starts with a particular vertex and then searches each of its neighbors for the target vertex. If the vertex isn't found, it searches each of the neighbor's neighbors in turn, until either the vertex is found or the entire graph has been traversed.

The following diagram shows the order in which the vertices are traversed, beginning at the top and working down in tiers, from left to right:

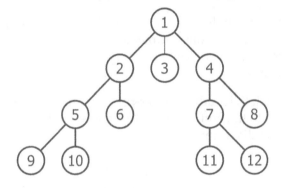

Loom contains a variety of traversal algorithms in the `loom.alg` namespace. Let's perform breadth first search on the same Twitter followers graph we have been studying, which is repeated for convenience:

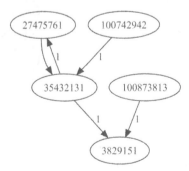

Breadth-first traversal is provided as the bf-traverse function. This will return a sequence of vertices in the order that they were visited which will allow us to see how breadth-first search traverses the graph:

```
(defn ex-8-5 []
  (let [graph (->> (load-edges "twitter/98801140.edges")
                   (apply loom/digraph))]
    (alg/bf-traverse graph 100742942)))

;; (100742942 35432131 27475761 3829151)
```

We're using the bf-traverse function to perform a traversal of the graph, beginning at node 100742942. Notice how the response does not contain the node 100873813. There's no way of traversing the graph to this vertex, following only the direction of the edges. The only way to get to vertex 100742942 would be to start there.

Also, note that 35432131 is only listed once, even though it's connected to both 27475761 and 3829151. Loom's implementation of breadth first search maintains a set of the visited vertices in memory. Once a vertex is visited, it need not be visited again.

An alternative approach to breadth-first search is depth-first search. This algorithm proceeds immediately to the bottom of the tree and visits the nodes in the order shown in the following diagram:

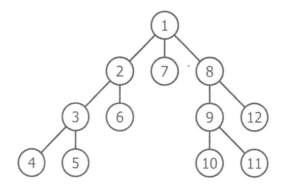

Loom includes a depth-first search as pre-traverse:

```
(defn ex-8-6 []
  (let [graph (->> (load-edges "twitter/98801140.edges")
                   (apply loom/digraph))]
    (alg/pre-traverse graph 100742942)))

;; (100742942 35432131 3829151 27475761)
```

The advantage of depth-first search is that it has a much lower memory requirement than breadth-first search, because it's not necessary to store all of the nodes at each tier. This may make it less memory-intensive for large graphs.

However, depending on the circumstances, either a depth-first or breadth-first search may be more convenient. For example, if we were traversing a family tree, looking for a living relative, we could assume that person would be near the bottom of the tree, so a depth-first search may reach the target more quickly. If we were looking for an ancient ancestor, then a depth first search might waste its time checking a large number of more recent relatives and take much longer to reach the target.

Finding the shortest path

The algorithms presented earlier traversed the graph vertex by vertex and returned a lazy sequence of all the nodes in the graph. They were convenient for illustrating the two primary ways of navigating the graph structures. However, a more common task would be to find the shortest path from one vertex to another. This means that we'll be interested only in the sequence of nodes that lie between them.

If we have an unweighted graph, such as the previous graphs, we'll usually count the distance as the number of "hops": a hop being the step between two neighboring nodes. The shortest path will have the fewest number of hops. Breadth-first search is, in general, a more efficient algorithm to use in this case.

Loom implements the breadth-first shortest path as the `bf-path` function. To demonstrate it, let's load a more complex Twitter graph:

```
(defn ex-8-7 []
  (->> (load-edges "twitter/396721965.edges")
       (apply loom/digraph)
       (lio/view)))
```

This code generates the following graph:

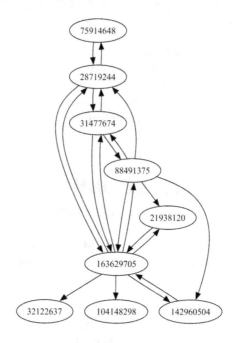

Let's see if we can identify the shortest path between the top and bottom nodes: **75914648** and **32122637**. There are many paths that the algorithm could return, but we want to identify the path that goes through points **28719244** and **163629705**. This is the one with the fewest hops.

```
(defn ex-8-8 []
  (let [graph (->> (load-edges "twitter/396721965.edges")
                   (apply loom/digraph))]
    (alg/bf-path graph 75914648 32122637)))

;;(75914648 28719244 163629705 32122637)
```

Indeed it does.

Loom also implements a bidirectional breadth-first shortest path algorithm as bf-path-bi. This searches in parallel from both the source and the destination and may find the shortest path much faster on certain types of graphs.

What if the graph is weighted? In this case, the fewest hops might not correspond to the shortest path between two nodes, because this path might be associated with a large weight. In this case, Dijkstra's algorithm is a method to find the shortest cost path between two nodes. The path may take a larger number of hops, but the sum of the edge weights traversed would be the lowest:

```
(defn ex-8-9 []
  (let [graph (->> (load-edges "twitter/396721965.edges")
                   (apply loom/weighted-digraph))]
    (-> (loom/add-edges graph [28719244 163629705 100])
        (alg/dijkstra-path 75914648 32122637)))))

;;(75914648 28719244 31477674 163629705 32122637)
```

In this code, we loaded the graph as a weighted digraph and updated the edge between node `28719244` and `163629705` to have a weight of `100`. All the other edges have a default weight of `1`. This has the effect of assigning a very high cost to the most direct path, and so an alternative path is found.

Dijkstra's algorithm is particularly valuable for route finding. For example, if the graph models the road network, the best route may be the one that takes major roads, rather than the one which takes the fewest number of steps. Or, depending on the time of day and the amount of traffic on the roads, the cost associated with particular routes may change. In this case, Dijkstra's algorithm would be able to determine the best route at any time of the day.

An algorithm called **A*** (pronounced A-star) optimizes Dijkstra's algorithm by allowing a heuristic function. It's implemented as `alg/astar-path` in Loom. The heuristic function returns an expected cost to the destination. Any function can be used as a heuristic as long as it does not over-estimate the true cost. The use of this heuristic allows the A* algorithm to avoid making an exhaustive search of the graph and thus, it can be much quicker. For more information on A* algorithm, refer to `https://en.wikipedia.org/wiki/A*_search_algorithm`.

Let's continue to consider weighted graphs and ask how we could construct a tree that connects all the nodes with the shortest cost. Such a tree is referred to as the minimum spanning tree.

Minimum spanning trees

With the help of the previous algorithms, we considered how to traverse the graph between two points. However, what if we want to discover a route that connects all the nodes in the graph? In this case, we could use a minimum spanning tree. We can think of a minimum spanning tree as a hybrid of the full-graph traversal algorithms we have considered and the shortest path algorithm we saw recently.

Minimum spanning trees are particularly useful for weighted graphs. If the weight represents the cost of connecting two vertices, the minimum spanning tree finds the minimum cost of connecting the whole graph. They occur in problems such as network design. If the nodes represent offices, for example, and the edge weights represent the cost of phone lines between offices, the minimum spanning tree will provide the set of phone lines that connect all the offices with the lowest total cost.

Loom's implementation of minimum spanning trees makes use of Prim's algorithm and is available as the `prim-mst` function:

```
(defn ex-8-10 []
  (let [graph (->> (load-edges "twitter/396721965.edges")
                   (apply loom/weighted-graph))]
    (-> (alg/prim-mst graph)
        (lio/view))))
```

This will return the following graph:

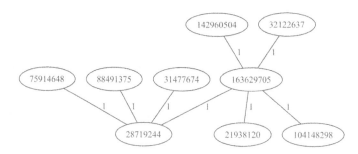

If, once again, we update the edge between vertices **28719244** and **163629705** to be 100, we will be able to observe the difference it makes to the minimum spanning tree:

```
(defn ex-8-11 []
  (let [graph (->> (load-edges "twitter/396721965.edges")
                   (apply loom/weighted-graph))]
    (-> (loom/add-edges graph [28719244 163629705 100])
        (alg/prim-mst)
        (lio/view))))
```

This code returns the following chart:

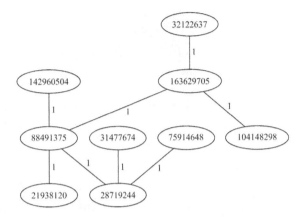

The tree has been reconfigured to bypass the edge with the highest cost.

Subgraphs and connected components

A minimum spanning tree can only be specified for *connected* graphs, where all the nodes are connected to all the others by at least one path. Where the graphs are not connected, we're clearly unable to construct a minimum spanning tree (although we could construct a minimum spanning forest instead).

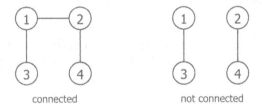

If a graph contains a set of subgraphs that are internally connected but are not connected to each other, then the subgraphs are referred to as connected components. We can observe the connected components if we load a still more complicated network:

```
(defn ex-8-12 []
  (->> (load-edges "twitter/15053535.edges")
       (apply loom/graph)
       (lio/view)))
```

This example generates the following image:

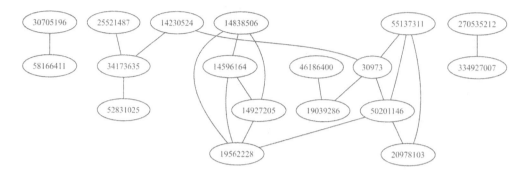

Thanks to the layout of the graph, we can easily see that there are three connected components and Loom will calculate these for us with the `connected-components` function. We'll see later in this chapter how we can implement an algorithm to calculate this for ourselves:

```
(defn ex-8-13 []
  (->> (load-edges "twitter/15053535.edges")
       (apply loom/graph)
       (alg/connected-components)))

;;[[30705196 58166411] [25521487 34173635 14230524 52831025 30973
;; 55137311 50201146 19039286 20978103 19562228 46186400
;;14838506 14596164 14927205] [270535212 334927007]]
```

A directed graph is strongly connected if there is a path from every node to every other node. A directed graph is weakly connected if, only treating all the edges as being undirected, there is a path from every node to every other node.

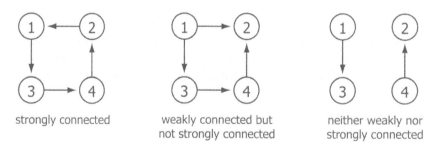

Let's load the same graph as a directed graph to see if there are any strongly connected components:

```
(defn ex-8-14 []
  (->> (load-edges "twitter/15053535.edges")
       (apply loom/digraph)
       (lio/view)))
```

This example generates the following image:

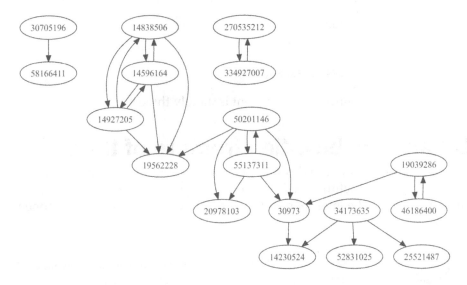

There are three weakly connected components as before. It's quite difficult to visually determine how many strongly connected components there are by just looking at the graph. Kosaraju's algorithm will calculate the number of strongly connected components in a graph. It's implemented by Loom as the `alg/scc` function:

```
(defn ex-8-15 []
  (->> (load-edges "twitter/15053535.edges")
       (apply loom/digraph)
       (alg/scc)
       (count)))
```

```
;; 13
```

Kosaraju's algorithm makes use of the interesting property that the transpose graph—one with all the edges reversed—has exactly the same number of connected components as the input graph. The response contains all the strongly connected components (even the degenerate cases containing only one node) as sequence vectors. If we sort by length in descending order the first component will be the largest:

```
(defn ex-8-16 []
  (->> (load-edges "twitter/15053535.edges")
       (apply loom/digraph)
       (alg/scc)
       (sort-by count >)
       (first)))

;; [14927205 14596164 14838506]
```

The largest strongly connected component is merely three nodes.

SCC and the bow-tie structure of the web

Weakly and strongly connected components can provide an informative way of understanding the structure of a directed graph. For example, research performed on the link structure of the internet has shown that strongly connected components can grow very large indeed.

 The paper from which the following numbers are quoted is available online at http://www9.org/w9cdrom/160/160.html.

Although the following numbers are from a study undertaken in 1999 and so they are therefore very out of date, we can see that at the center of the web was one large strongly connected component consisting of 56 million pages. This meant that from any page within the strongly connected component, you could reach any other within the strongly connected component only by following the outbound hyperlinks.

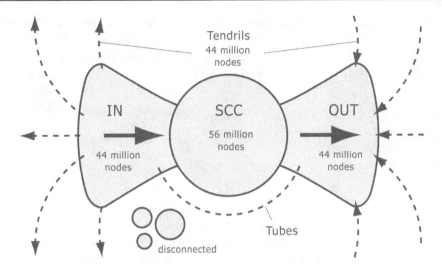

44 million pages linked into the SCC, but were not linked from it, and 44 million pages were linked from the SCC, but did not link back. Only very few links bypassed the SCC entirely (the "tubes" in the preceding illustration).

Whole-graph analysis

Let's turn our attention away from the smaller graphs we've been working with towards the larger graph of followers provided by the `twitter_combined.txt` file. This contains over 2.4 million edges and will provide a more interesting sample to work with.

One of the simplest metrics to determine about a whole graph is its density. For directed graphs, this is defined as the number of edges $|E|$, over the number of vertices $|V|$ multiplied by one less than itself.

$$D = \frac{|E|}{|V|(|V|-1)}$$

For a connected graph (one where every vertex is connected to every other vertex by an edge), the density would be 1. By contrast, a disconnected graph (one with no edges) would have a density of 0. Loom implements graph density as the `alg/density` function. Let's calculate the density of the larger Twitter graph:

```
(defn ex-8-17 []
  (->> (load-edges "twitter_combined.txt")
       (apply loom/digraph)
       (alg/density)
       (double)))
```

```
;; 2.675E-4
```

This seems very sparse, but bear in mind that a value of 1 would correspond to every account following every other account, which is clearly not the case on social networks. Some accounts may have many connections, while others may have none at all.

Let's see how the edges are distributed among nodes. We can re-use Loom's `out-degree` function to count the number of outgoing edges from each node and plot a histogram of the distribution using the following code:

```
(defn ex-8-18 []
  (let [graph (->> (load-edges "twitter_combined.txt")
                   (apply loom/digraph))
        out-degrees (map #(loom/out-degree graph %)
                         (loom/nodes graph))]
    (-> (c/histogram out-degrees :nbins 50
                     :x-label "Twitter Out Degrees")
        (i/view))))
```

This generates the following histogram:

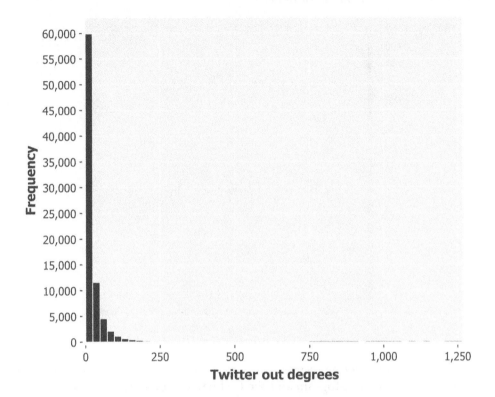

The distribution of out-degrees looks a lot like the exponential distribution we first encountered in *Chapter 2, Inference*. Notice how most people have very few out-degrees, but a handful have over a thousand.

Let's also plot the histogram of in-degrees. On Twitter, the in-degree corresponds to the number of followers an account has.

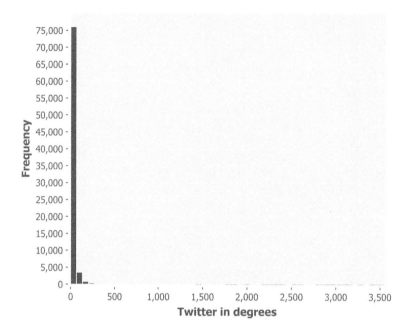

The distribution of in-degrees is even more extreme: the tail extends further to the right than the previous histogram and the first bar is even taller than before. This corresponds to most accounts having very few followers but a handful having several thousand.

Contrast the previous histograms to the degree distribution we get when we generate a random graph of edges and nodes. Next, we use Loom's gen-rand function to generate a random graph with 10,000 nodes and 1,000,000 edges:

```
(defn ex-8-20 []
  (let [graph (generate/gen-rand (loom/graph) 10000 1000000)
        out-degrees (map #(loom/out-degree graph %)
                         (loom/nodes graph))]
    (-> (c/histogram out-degrees :nbins 50
                     :x-label "Random out degrees")
        (i/view))))
```

This generates the following histogram:

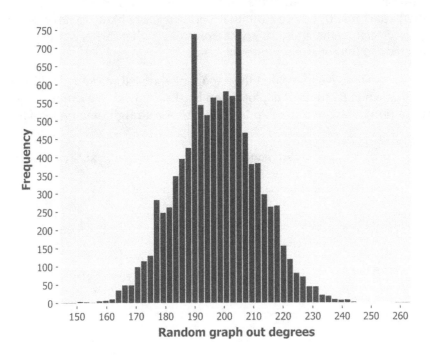

The random graph shows that the mean number of out-degrees for a graph of ten thousand vertices connected by a million edges is around 200. The distribution of the degrees is approximately normal. It's very apparent that the Twitter graph hasn't been generated by a random process.

Scale-free networks

The Twitter degree histograms are a characteristic of power-law degree distributions. Unlike the normally distributed, randomly generated graph, the Twitter histograms show that a few vertices are connected to a large majority of the edges.

The term "scale-free network" was coined by researchers at the University of Notre Dame in 1999 to describe the structure they observed on the World Wide Web.

In the graphs that model human interactions, we'll often observe a power law of connectedness. This is also called the **Zipf** scale and it indicates the so-called "law of preferential attachment", where a popular vertex is more likely to develop additional connections. Social media sites are prime examples of this sort of a process, where new users tend to follow already popular users.

In *Chapter 2, Inference,* we identified the exponential distribution by looking for a straight line when the data was plotted on log-linear axes. We can most easily determine a power-law relationship by looking for a straight line on log-log axes:

```
(defn ex-8-21 []
  (let [graph (->> (load-edges "twitter_combined.txt")
                   (apply loom/digraph))
        out-degrees (map #(loom/out-degree graph %)
                         (loom/nodes graph))
        points (frequencies out-degrees)]
    (-> (c/scatter-plot (keys points) (vals points))
        (c/set-axis :x (c/log-axis :label "log(out-degree)"))
        (c/set-axis :y (c/log-axis :label "log(frequency)"))
        (i/view))))
```

This code returns the following plot:

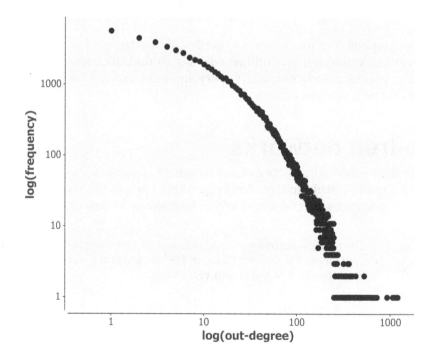

Although not perfectly linear, the earlier chart is enough to show that a power law distribution is at work in the Twitter graph. If we visualize the connections between the nodes and edges in the graph, scale-free networks will be recognizable because of their characteristic "clustered" shape. Popular vertices tend to have a halo of other vertices around them.

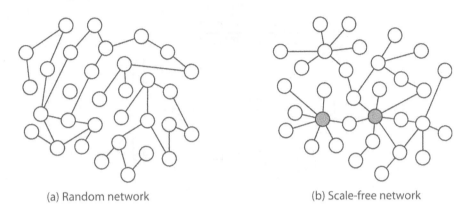

(a) Random network   (b) Scale-free network

Scaling up to the full Twitter combined dataset has caused the previous examples to run much more slowly, even though this graph is tiny in comparison to many social networks. The rest of this chapter will be devoted to a graph library that runs on top of the Spark framework called **GraphX**. GraphX expresses many of the algorithms we've covered already this chapter, but can take advantage of the Spark distributed computation model to process much larger graphs.

Distributed graph computation with GraphX

GraphX (`https://spark.apache.org/graphx/`) is a distributed graph processing library that is designed to work with Spark. Like the MLlib library we used in the previous chapter, GraphX provides a set of abstractions that are built on top of Spark's RDDs. By representing the vertices and edges of a graph as RDDs, GraphX is able to process very large graphs in a scalable way.

We've seen in previous chapters how to process a large dataset using MapReduce and Hadoop. Hadoop is an example of a data-parallel system: the dataset is divided into groups that are processed in parallel. Spark is also a data-parallel system: RDDs are distributed across the cluster and processed in parallel.

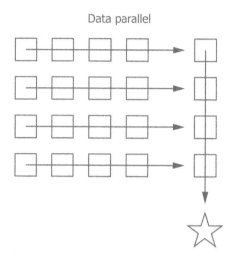

Data-parallel systems are appropriate ways of scaling data processing when your data closely resembles a table. Graphs, which may have complex internal structure, are not most efficiently represented as tables. Although graphs can be represented as edge lists, as we've seen, processing a graph stored in this way may involve complex joins and excessive data movement around the cluster because of how interconnected the data is.

The growing scale and significance of graph data has driven the development of numerous new graph-parallel systems. By restricting the types of computation that can be expressed and introducing techniques to partition and distribute graphs, these systems can efficiently execute sophisticated graph algorithms orders of a magnitude faster than general data-parallel systems.

 Several libraries bring graph-parallel computation to Hadoop, including Hama, (https://hama.apache.org/) and Giraph (http://giraph.apache.org/).

The GraphX library brings graph-parallel computation to Spark. One of the advantages of using Spark as the engine for graph processing is that its in-memory computation model is well-suited to the iterative nature of many graph algorithms.

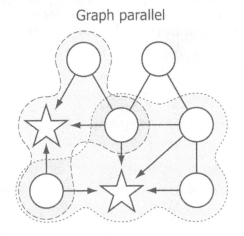

This diagram illustrates the challenge of processing graphs in parallel where the nodes may be interconnected. By processing the data within the graph topology, GraphX avoids excessive data movement and duplication. GraphX extends Spark's RDD abstraction by introducing the Resilient Distributed Graph, or RDG, and a set of functions to query and transform the graph in a structurally-aware way.

Creating RDGs with Glittering

Spark and GraphX are libraries that are predominantly written in Scala. In this chapter, we'll be using the Clojure library Glittering (`https://github.com/henrygarner/glittering`) to interact with GraphX. In much the same way that Sparkling provides a thin Clojure wrapper around Spark, Glittering provides a thin Clojure wrapper around GraphX.

Our first task will be to create a graph. Graphs can be instantiated in two ways: either by supplying two RDD representations (one containing the edges and the other the vertices), or simply by supplying an RDD of edges. If only the edges are supplied, then we will supply a default value for each node. We'll see how to do this next.

Since GraphX leverages Spark, every job requires an associated Spark context. In the previous chapter, we used Sparkling's `sparkling.conf/conf` default configuration. However, in this chapter, we'll use the default configuration provided by Glittering. Glittering extends Sparkling's defaults with the configuration necessary to serialize and deserialize GraphX types. In the following code, we'll include `glittering.core` as `g` and create a small graph of only three edges using Glittering's graph constructor:

```
(defn ex-8-22 []
  (spark/with-context sc (-> (g/conf)
                             (conf/master "local")
                             (conf/app-name "ch8"))
    (let [vertices [[1 "A"] [2 "B"] [3 "C"]]
          edges [(g/edge 1 2 0.5)
                 (g/edge 2 1 0.5)
                 (g/edge 3 1 1.0)]]
      (g/graph (spark/parallelize sc vertices)
               (spark/parallelize sc edges)))))

;; #<GraphImpl org.apache.spark.graphx.impl.GraphImpl@adb2324>
```

The result is a GraphX graph object. Note that edges are provided as an RDD of g/edges: the `g/edge` function will create an edge type given a source ID, destination ID, and an optional edge attribute. Edge attributes can be any object that Spark can serialize. Note that vertices can have attributes too ("A", "B", and "C" in the previous example).

An alternative way of constructing a graph is to use the `g/graph-from-edges` constructor. This will return a graph based solely on the RDD of edges. The Twitter data is supplied in the edge list format, so this is the function we'll use to load it. In the next code, we'll load the full `twitter_combined.txt` as a text file and create an edge list from it by mapping over the lines of the file. From each line, we'll create an edge of weight 1.0:

```
(defn line->edge [line]
  (let [[from to] (map to-long (str/split line #" "))]
    (g/edge from to 1.0)))

(defn load-edgelist [sc path]
  (let [edges (->> (spark/text-file sc path)
                   (spark/map line->edge))]
    (g/graph-from-edges edges 1.0)))

(defn ex-8-23 []
  (spark/with-context sc (-> (g/conf)
```

```
                    (conf/master "local")
                    (conf/app-name "ch8"))
    (load-edgelist sc "data/twitter_combined.txt"))))
```

```
;;#<GraphImpl org.apache.spark.graphx.impl.GraphImpl@c63044d>
```

The second argument to the `graph-from-edges` function is a default value to use as each vertex's attribute: the vertex attributes can't be provided in an edge list.

Measuring graph density with triangle counting

GraphX comes with a small selection of built-in graph algorithms, which Glittering makes available in the `glittering.algorithms` namespace. Before covering Glittering's API in more detail, let's run one of these on the Twitter follows graph. We'll show how to use Glittering to create a simple graph processing job, and then show how to use more of Glittering's API to implement the algorithm ourselves using GraphX's graph-parallel primitives.

Triangle counting is an algorithm to measure the density of the graph in the vicinity of each node. It's similar in principle to counting degrees, but also accounts for how well our neighbors are connected to each other. We can picture the process using this very simple graph:

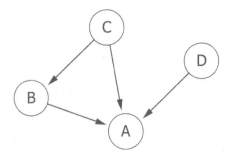

In this example, we can see that vertices A, B, and C all participate in one triangle, and vertex D participates in none. Both B and C follow A, but C also follows B. In the context of social network analysis, triangle counting is a measure of how many friends of friends also know each other. In tight-knit communities, we would expect the number of triangles to be high.

Triangle counting is already implemented by GraphX and is accessible as the `triangle-count` function in the `glittering.algorithms` namespace. Before we use this particular algorithm, GraphX requires us to do two things:

1. Point the edges in the "canonical" direction.
2. Ensure the graph is partitioned.

Both of these steps are the artifacts of the way triangle counting is implemented in GraphX. GraphX allows there to be multiple edges between two vertices, but triangle counting seeks only to count the distinct edges. The previous two steps ensure that GraphX is able to efficiently calculate the distinct edges before performing the algorithm.

The canonical direction of an edge always points from a smaller node ID to a larger node ID. We can achieve this by ensuring all the edges are created in this direction when we first construct our edge RDD:

```
(defn line->canonical-edge [line]
  (let [[from to] (sort (map to-long (str/split line #" ")))]
    (glitter/edge from to 1.0)))

(defn load-canonical-edgelist [sc path]
  (let [edges (->> (spark/text-file sc path)
                   (spark/map line->canonical-edge))]
    (glitter/graph-from-edges edges 1.0)))
```

By sorting the `from` and `to` IDs before we create the edge, we ensure that the `from` ID is always lower than the `to` ID. This is the first step towards making duplicate edge removal more efficient. The second is to choose a partitioning strategy for the graph. The next section describes our options.

GraphX partitioning strategies

GraphX is built for distributed computation and so it must partition graphs across multiple machines. In general, there are two approaches that you could take while partitioning graphs: the 'edge cut' and 'vertex cut' approach. Each makes a different trade-off.

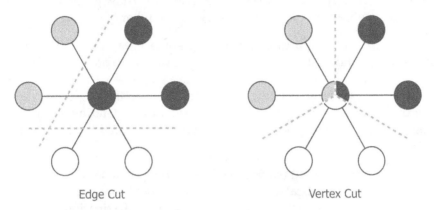

Edge Cut   Vertex Cut

The edge cut strategy may seem the most "natural" way to partition a graph. By splitting the graph along the edges, it ensures that each vertex is assigned to exactly one partition indicated by the shade of gray. This presents an issue for the representation of edges that span partitions though. Any computation along the edge will necessarily need to be sent from one partition to another, and minimizing network communication is key to the implementation of efficient graph algorithms.

GraphX implements the "vertex cut" approach, which ensures that the edges are assigned to partitions and that the vertices may be shared across partitions. This appears to simply move the network communication to a different part of the graph—from the edges to the vertices—but GraphX provides a number of strategies that allow us to ensure that vertices are partitioned in the most appropriate way for the algorithm we wish to apply.

Glittering provides the `partition-by` function, which accepts a keyword representing the strategy to partition the graph. Accepted values are `:edge-partition-1d`, `:edge-partition-2d`, `:canonical-random-vertex-cut`, and `:random-vertex-cut`.

Your choice about which partitioning strategy to use is based on the structure of the graph and the algorithm you will apply. The :edge-partition-1d strategy ensures that all the edges with the same source are partitioned together. This means that operations that aggregate edges by the source (for example, counting outgoing edges) have all the data they require on an individual machine. Although this minimizes network traffic, it also means that with power-law graphs a few partitions may receive a significant proportion of the overall number of edges.

The :random-vertex-cut partitioning strategy splits a graph into edges based on both the source and destination vertices. This can help to create more balanced partitions at the cost of run-time performance, as a single source or destination node may be spread across many machines in the cluster. Even the edges that connect the same pair of nodes may be spread across two machines depending on the direction of the edge. To group edges regardless of direction, we can use :canonical-random-vertex-cut.

Finally, :edge-partition-2d partitions edges by both their source and destination vertex using a more sophisticated partitioning strategy. As with the :canonical-random-vertex-cut, nodes sharing both a source and a destination will be partitioned together. In addition, the strategy places an upper limit on the number of partitions that each node will be spread across. Where an algorithm aggregates information about edges sharing both a source and a destination node, and also by source or destination independently, this may be the most efficient strategy to use.

Running the built-in triangle counting algorithm

We've already seen how to load our edges in the canonical direction. The next step is to choose a partitioning strategy, and we'll go for :random-vertex-cut. The following example shows the full sequence of loading and partitioning the graph, performing triangle counting and visualizing the results using Incanter:

```
(defn ex-8-24 []
  (spark/with-context sc (-> (g/conf)
                             (conf/master "local")
                             (conf/app-name "ch8"))
    (let [triangles (->> (load-canonical-edgelist
                          sc "data/twitter_combined.txt")
                         (g/partition-by :random-vertex-cut)
                         (ga/triangle-count)
                         (g/vertices)
                         (to-java-pair-rdd)
                         (spark/values)
```

```
                    (spark/collect)
                    (into [])))
        data (frequencies triangles)]
    (-> (c/scatter-plot (keys data) (vals data))
        (c/set-axis :x (c/log-axis :label "# Triangles"))
        (c/set-axis :y (c/log-axis :label "# Vertices"))
        (i/view)))))
```

The output of `triangle-count` is a new graph where the attribute of each vertex is a count of the number of triangles that the vertex participates in. The ID of the vertex is unchanged. We're only interested in the triangle counts themselves—the vertex attributes of the returned graph—so we extract `values` from the vertices. The `spark/collect` function gathers all the values into a single Clojure sequence, so it's not something we'd want to do on a very large graph.

Having gathered the count of triangles, we calculate the frequency of each count and visualize the result on a log-log scatter plot using Incanter. The output is shown next:

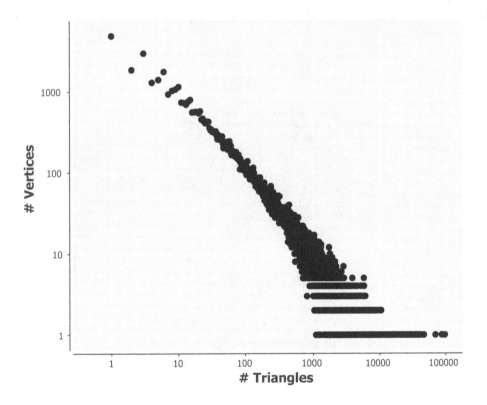

Once again, we see the effect of a power law distribution. A few nodes connect a very large number of triangles.

Running a built-in algorithm has allowed us to see how to create and manipulate a graph, but the real power of GraphX is the way it allows us to express this sort of computation efficiently for ourselves. In the next section, we'll see how to accomplish triangle counting using lower-level functions.

Implement triangle counting with Glittering

There are many ways to count the number of triangles in a graph, but GraphX implements the algorithm in the following way:

1. Compute the set of neighbors for each vertex.
2. For each edge, compute the intersection of the vertices at either end.
3. Send the count of the intersection to both vertices.
4. Compute the sum of the counts for each vertex.
5. Divide by two, since each triangle is counted twice.

The following diagram shows the steps on our simple graph consisting of only one triangle:

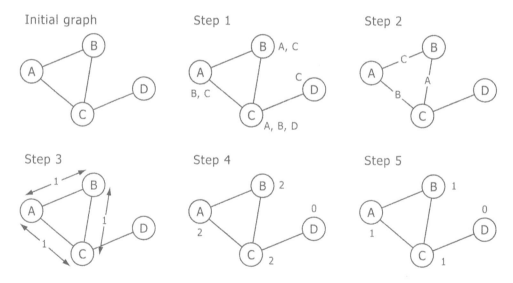

The algorithm ignores the direction of the edges and, as mentioned previously, expects the edges between any two nodes to be distinct. We'll therefore continue to work on the partitioned graph with the canonical edges we defined in the previous section.

The full code to perform triangle counting isn't very long, so it's presented in full next. It's representative of most of the algorithms we'll cover for the rest of the chapter so, once we've presented the code, we'll walk through each of the steps one at a time:

```
(defn triangle-m [{:keys [src-id src-attr dst-id dst-attr]}]
  (let [c (count (set/intersection src-attr dst-attr))]
    {:src c :dst c}))


(defn triangle-count [graph]
  (let [graph (->> (g/partition-by :random-vertex-cut graph)
                   (g/group-edges (fn [a b] a)))
        adjacent (->> (g/collect-neighbor-ids :either graph)
                      (to-java-pair-rdd)
                      (spark/map-values set))
        graph (g/outer-join-vertices
                (fn [vid attr adj] adj) adjacent graph)
        counters (g/aggregate-messages triangle-m + graph)]
    (->> (g/outer-join-vertices (fn  [vid vattr counter]
                                  (/ counter 2))
                                counters graph)
         (g/vertices))))
```

For the algorithm to work, the input graph needs to have distinct edges. Once the canonical graph has been partitioned, we make sure the edges are distinct by calling `(g/group-edges (fn [a b] a) graph)` on the graph. The `group-edges` function is similar to `reduce` and it reduces over the collection of edges that share the same start and end node. We're simply choosing to keep the first edge. The attributes of the edge don't factor into triangle counting, only the fact that there is one.

Step one – collecting neighbor IDs

At step one, we want to collect the neighbor IDs for each vertex. Glittering makes this operation available as the `g/collect-neighbor-ids` function. We can choose to collect only the incoming or outgoing edges with `:in` or `:out`, respectively, or the edges in either direction with `:either`.

The `g/collect-neighbor-ids` function returns a pair RDD with the key being the vertex ID in question and the value being the sequence of neighbor IDs. Like MLlib in the previous chapter, the RDD is not the `JavaRDD` class that Sparkling expects, and so we must convert it accordingly. Once we've done so, converting the sequence of neighbor IDs into a set is as simple as calling `set` on each of the values in the pair RDD. The result of step one is a PairRDD containing the of node ID and set of neighbor IDs, so we've flattened the graph to a series of sets stored as the value of `adjacent`.

This graph representation, as a sequence of sets of connected vertices, is commonly known as an adjacency list. Along with the edge list, it's one of the two primary means of representing graphs.

Step two requires us to assign values to the graph edges though, so we'll want to preserve the graph structure. We use the `g/outer-join-vertices` function to combine `adjacent` and the original graph. Given a graph and a pair RDD indexed by vertex ID, `outer-join-vertices` allows us to supply a function whose return value will be assigned as the attribute of each vertex in the graph. The function receives three arguments: the vertex ID, the current vertex attribute, and the value associated with the vertex ID in the pair RDD being outer joined to the graph. In the earlier code, we return the set of adjacent vertices as the new vertex attribute.

Steps two, three, and four – aggregate messages

The next several steps are handled by one function, `g/aggregate-messages`, the workhorse function of GraphX's graph-parallel implementation. It requires two arguments: a message sending function and a message combining function. In the way they work together, these two functions are like map and reduce adapted for the vertex-centric view of graph-parallel computation.

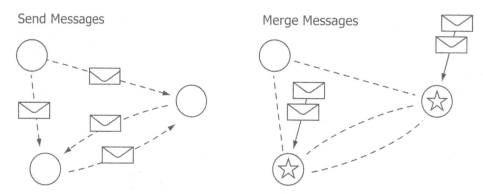

The send message function is responsible for sending messages along edges. The function is called once for each edge, but it can send multiple messages to either the source or destination vertex. The input to the function is a triplet (an edge with two connected vertices) and it responds with a sequence of messages. A message is a key/value pair where the key is one of `:src` or `:dst` and the value is the message to be sent. In the previous example, this is implemented as a map with the `:src` and `:dst` keys.

The merge message function is responsible for combining all the messages for a particular vertex. In the earlier code, each message is a number and therefore the merge function has a sequence of numbers to merge. We can achieve this simply by passing + as the merge function.

Step five – dividing the counts

The final step of triangle counting is to divide the counts we have calculated for each vertex ID by two, since each triangle is counted twice. In the earlier code, we do this while simultaneously updating the vertex attributes with the triangle count using outer-join-vertices.

Running the custom triangle counting algorithm

With all of the earlier steps in place, we can run our custom triangle counting algorithm using Glittering. Let's first run it on one of our Twitter follow graphs from the beginning of the chapter to see the result we get:

```
(defn ex-8-25 []
  (spark/with-context sc (-> (g/conf)
                             (conf/master "local")
                             (conf/app-name "triangle-count"))
    (->> (load-canonical-edgelist
          sc "data/twitter/396721965.edges")
         (triangle-count)
         (spark/collect)
         (into []))))

;; #sparkling/tuple [21938120 1] #sparkling/tuple [31477674 3]
;; #sparkling/tuple [32122637 0] ...]
```

The result is a series of tuples with the vertex ID as the key and number of connected triangles as the value.

If we want to see how many triangles were there in the entire Twitter dataset, we could extract the values from the resulting graph (the values), add them up, and then divide them by three. Let's do this now:

```
(defn ex-8-26 []
  (spark/with-context sc (-> (g/conf)
                             (conf/master "local")
                             (conf/app-name "triangle-count"))
```

```
(let [triangles (->> (load-canonical-edgelist
                       sc "data/twitter_combined.txt")
                      (triangle-count)
                      (to-java-pair-rdd)
                      (spark/values)
                      (spark/reduce +))]
  (/ triangles 3))))
```

The algorithm shouldn't take too long to run. Our custom triangle counting code will be performant enough to run on the entire combined Twitter dataset.

If `aggregate-messages` is like a single step of MapReduce programming, we'll often end up performing it iteratively. Many graph algorithms will want to run to convergence. In fact, GraphX provides an alternative function that we will be able to use in this case called the **Pregel API**. We'll discuss it in detail in the next section.

The Pregel API

The Pregel API is GraphX's main abstraction to express custom, iterative, graph-parallel computation. It's named after Google's internal system for running large-scale graph processing, about which they published a paper in 2010. You may remember that it was also the river upon which the town of Königsberg was built.

Google's Pregel paper popularized the "think like a vertex" approach to graph parallel computation. Pregel's model fundamentally uses the message passing between the vertices in the graph organized into a series of steps called **supersteps**. At the beginning of each superstep, Pregel runs a user-specified function on each vertex, passing all the messages sent to it in the previous superstep. The vertex function has the opportunity to process each of these messages and send messages to other vertices in turn. Vertices can also "vote to halt" the computation and, when all the vertices have voted to halt, the computation will terminate.

The `pregel` function implemented by Glittering implements a very similar approach to graph processing. The primary difference is that the vertices don't vote to halt: the computation terminates either when there are no more messages being sent or when a specified number of iterations has been exceeded.

While the aggregate-messages function introduced in the previous section makes use of two symbiotic functions to express its intent, the `pregel` function makes use of three related functions, applied iteratively, to implement graph algorithms. The first two are the message function and the message combiner we encountered before, the third is the "vertex program": a function that processes the incoming messages for each vertex. The return value of this function is assigned as the vertex attribute for the next superstep.

Let's see how the `pregel` function works in practice by implementing an algorithm we've already covered in this chapter: connected components.

Connected components with the Pregel API

Connected components can be expressed as an iterative algorithm in the following way:

1. Initialize all vertex attributes to the vertex ID.

2. For each edge, determine whether the source or destination vertex attribute is the lowest.

3. Down each edge, send the lower of the two attributes to the opposite vertex.

4. For each vertex, update attribute to be the lowest of the incoming messages.

5. Repeat until the node attributes no longer change.

As before, we can visualize the process on a simple graph of four nodes.

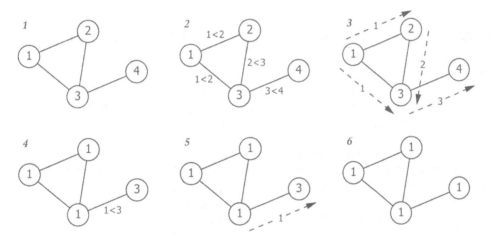

We can see how in six steps the graph has converged to a state where all the nodes have the lowest connected vertex ID as their attribute. Since the messages only travel along the edges, any nodes that don't share any edges will converge to different values. All the vertices that share the same attribute once the algorithm has converged will therefore be a part of the same connected component. Let's see the finished code first and we'll walk through the code in steps immediately afterwards:

```
(defn connected-component-m [{:keys [src-attr dst-attr]}]
  (cond
    (< src-attr dst-attr) {:dst src-attr}
```

```
        (> src-attr dst-attr) {:src dst-attr}))

  (defn connected-components [graph]
    (->> (glitter/map-vertices (fn [id attr] id) graph)
         (p/pregel {:vertex-fn (fn [id attr msg]
                                 (min attr msg))
                    :message-fn connected-component-m
                    :combiner min}))))
```

Using the g/pregel function is all that's required to implement an iterative connected components algorithm.

Step one – map vertices

Initializing all the vertex attributes to the vertex ID is handled outside of the pregel function by the g/map-vertices function. We pass it a function of two arguments, the vertex ID and vertex attribute, and it returns the vertex ID to be assigned as the vertex attribute.

Steps two and three – the message function

Glittering's pregel function expects to receive a map specifying at least three functions: a message function, a combiner function, and a vertex function. We'll discuss the last of these in more detail shortly. However, the first of these is responsible for steps two and three: for each edge, determining which connected node has the lower attribute and sending this value to the opposing node.

We introduced the message function along with the custom triangle counting function earlier in the chapter. This function receives the edge as a map and returns a map in return describing the messages to be sent. This time, only one message is sent: the src-attr attribute to the destination node if the source attribute is lower or the dst-attr attribute to the source node if the destination attribute is lower.

The combiner function aggregates all the incoming messages for a vertex. The combiner function for the connected components is simply the min function: we're only interested in the minimum value sent to each vertex.

Step four – update the attributes

In step four, each vertex updates its attribute to equal the lowest of its current attribute and the value of all the received messages. If any of its incoming messages is lower than its current attribute, it will update its attribute to equal the lowest. This step is handled by the vertex program, the third of Pregel's three symbiotic functions.

The vertex function for connected components is also trivial: for each vertex, we want to return the lower of the current vertex attribute and the lowest incoming message (as determined by the combiner function in the previous step). The return value will be used as the vertex attribute for the next superstep.

Step five – iterate to convergence

Step five is something we get "for free" with the `pregel` function. We didn't specify the maximum number of iterations, so the three functions just described will be run repeatedly until there are no more messages to be sent. For this reason (and for reasons of efficiency), it's important that our message function only sends messages when it needs to. This is why our `cond` value in the earlier message function ensures we don't send a message if the source and destination attributes are already equal.

Running connected components

Having implemented the previous connected components function, we use it in the following example:

```
(defn ex-8-27 []
  (spark/with-context sc (-> (g/conf)
                             (conf/master "local")
                             (conf/app-name "cljds.ch8"))
    (->> (load-edgelist sc "data/twitter/396721965.edges")
         (connected-components)
         (g/vertices)
         (spark/collect)
         (into []))))

;; [#sparkling/tuple [163629705 21938120] #sparkling/tuple
;; [88491375 21938120] #sparkling/tuple [142960504 21938120] ...
```

By converting the graph back into an RDD, we can perform analysis in a data-parallel way. For example, we could determine the size of all of the connected components by counting the number of nodes that share the same attribute.

Calculating the size of the largest connected component

In the next example, we'll use the same connected components function, but count the size of each connected component. We'll achieve this with Sparkling's count-by-value function:

```
(defn ex-8-28 []
  (spark/with-context sc (-> (g/conf)
                             (conf/master "local")
                             (conf/app-name "ch8"))
    (->> (load-canonical-edgelist
          sc "data/twitter_combined.txt")
         (connected-components)
         (g/vertices)
         (to-java-pair-rdd)
         (spark/values)
         (spark/count-by-value)
         (into []))))

;; [[12 81306]]
```

Code such as the previous example is one of the great benefits of using GraphX and Glittering. We can take flat data represented as an edge list, convert it into a graph structure to perform an iterative graph algorithm, and then convert the results back into a flat structure to calculate aggregates: all in a single pipeline.

The example's response indicates that all of our vertices — 81,306 of them — are in one large connected component. This shows that everyone in the graph is connected to everyone else, either as a friend or a follower.

While it's useful to know that there are no isolated groups of users, it would be more interesting to understand how the users are organized within the connected component. If certain groups of users tend to be more densely connected to each other, then we could think of these users as forming a community.

Detecting communities with label propagation

A community can be defined informally as a group of vertices that are more strongly connected to each other than they are to the vertices outside the community.

> If every vertex is connected to every other vertex within the community, then we would call the community a clique.

Communities therefore correspond to increased density in the graph. We could think of communities within the Twitter network as groups of followers who tend to also follow each other's followers. Smaller communities might correspond to friendship groups, while larger communities are more likely to correspond to shared interest groups.

Community detection is a general technique and there are many algorithms that are capable of identifying communities. Depending on the algorithm, communities may overlap so that a user could be associated with more than one community. The algorithm we'll be looking at next is called **label propagation** and it assigns each user to a maximum of one community.

Label propagation can be implemented iteratively with the following steps:

1. Initialize all the vertex attributes to equal the vertex ID.
2. For each edge, send the source and destination attributes to the opposing node.
3. For each vertex, calculate the frequency of each incoming attribute.
4. For each vertex, update the attribute to be the most frequent of the incoming attributes.
5. Repeat until convergence or until maximum iteration count is reached.

The steps of the algorithm are shown next on a graph with two communities. Each community is also a clique, but this is not a requirement for label propagation to work in general.

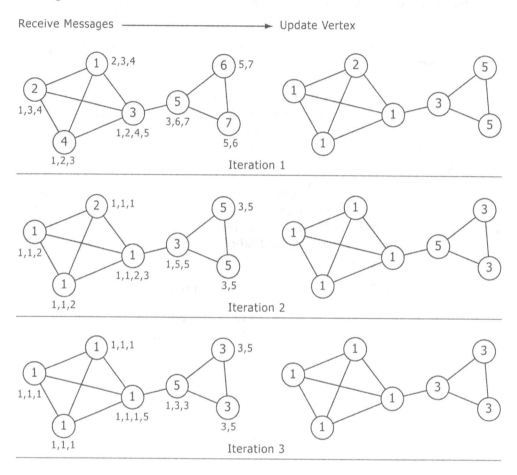

The code for label propagation using the `pregel` function is as follows:

```
(defn label-propagation-v [id attr msg]
  (key (apply max-key val msg)))

(defn label-propagation-m [{:keys [src-attr dst-attr]}]
  {:src {dst-attr 1}
   :dst {src-attr 1}})

(defn label-propagation [graph]
  (->> (glitter/map-vertices (fn [vid attr] vid) graph)
```

```
(p/pregel {:message-fn label-propagation-m
           :combiner (partial merge-with +)
           :vertex-fn label-propagation-v
           :max-iterations 10}))))
```

As before, let's walk through the code step by step.

Step one – map vertices

Step one for label propagation is identical to step one for the connected components algorithm we defined earlier. We use the `g/map-vertices` function to update each vertex attribute to equal the vertex ID.

Step two – send the vertex attribute

In step two, we send the opposing vertex attribute along each edge. Step three will require us to count the most frequent of the incoming attributes, so each message is a map of attribute to the value "1".

Step three – aggregate value

The combiner function receives all the messages for a vertex and produces an aggregate value. Since the messages are maps of attribute value to the number "1", we can use Clojure's `merge-with` function to combine the messages together with +. The result will be a map of attribute to frequency.

Step four – vertex function

Step four is handled by the vertex function. Given the frequency counts of all the incoming attributes, we want to pick the most frequent one. The `(apply max-key val msg)` expression returns the key/value pair from the map associated with the greatest value (the highest frequency). We pass this value to `key` to return the attribute associated with this value.

Step five – set the maximum iterations count

As with the connected components algorithm, iteration is the default behavior of the `pregel` function while there are messages to be sent. Unlike the connected components algorithm, we don't have a conditional clause in the earlier `message` function. In order to avoid an infinite loop, we pass `:max-iterations` of 10 in the map of options to `pregel`.

Running label propagation

The following example makes use of the previous code to perform label propagation on the full Twitter dataset. We calculate the size of each community with Sparkling's `count-by-value` function and calculate the frequencies of the counts. The resulting histogram is then visualized on a log-log scatterplot using Incanter to show the distribution of community sizes:

```
(defn ex-8-29 []
  (spark/with-context sc (-> (g/conf)
                             (conf/master "local")
                             (conf/app-name "ch8"))
    (let [xs (->> (load-canonical-edgelist
                    sc "data/twitter_combined.txt")
                  (label-propagation)
                  (g/vertices)
                  (to-java-pair-rdd)
                  (spark/values)
                  (spark/count-by-value)
                  (vals)
                  (frequencies))]
      (-> (c/scatter-plot (keys xs) (vals xs))
          (c/set-axis :x (c/log-axis :label "Community Size"))
          (c/set-axis :y (c/log-axis :label "# Communities"))
          (i/view)))))
```

This code generates the following chart:

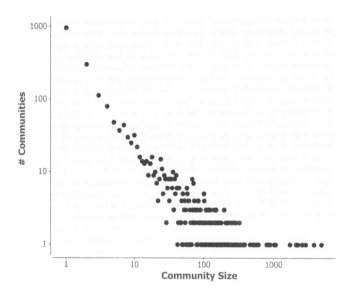

As we may have come to expect, the distribution of community sizes is also a power law: small communities are much more common than larger communities. The largest communities have around 10,000 members, while the smallest consist of just one member. We're beginning to tease apart the structure of the Twitter graph: we have a sense of how users are distributed into groups and we can hypothesize that the larger communities are likely to represent groups united by a shared interest.

In the final pages of this chapter, let's see whether we can establish what unites the largest of these communities. There are numerous ways we could go about this. If we had access to the tweets themselves, we could perform text analysis of the kind we performed in *Chapter 6, Clustering* to see whether there were particular words—or particular languages—more frequently used among these groups.

This chapter is about network analysis though, so let's just use the structure of the graph to identify the most influential accounts in each community. The list of the top ten most influential accounts might give us some indication of what resonates with their followers.

Measuring community influence using PageRank

One simplistic way of measuring influence within a community is to calculate how many incoming edges a particular vertex has. On Twitter, this would correspond to an account with a large number of followers. Such accounts represent the most "popular" within the network.

Counting incoming edges is a simplistic way to measure influence because it treats all the incoming edges as being equal. In social graphs, this is often not the case, as certain followers will themselves be popular accounts and therefore their follow carries more importance than a follower who has no followers themselves.

 PageRank was developed at Stanford University in 1996 by Larry Page and Sergey Brin as part of the research project that ultimately became Google. PageRank works by counting both the number and quality of links to a page to determine a rough estimate of how important the website is.

The importance of an account is therefore based on two things: the number of followers and the importance of each of those followers. The importance of each follower is calculated in the same way. PageRank therefore has a recursive definition: it appears that we must calculate the importance of the followers before we can calculate the importance of the account, and so on.

The flow formulation

Fortunately, it's possible to calculate PageRank iteratively. First, we initialize all the vertices to have the same weight. This could be a weight of one; in which case, the sum of all the weights equals the number of vertices N. Or, it could be a weight of $\frac{1}{N}$; in which case, the sum of all the weights will equal one. Although it doesn't change the fundamental algorithm, the latter is often preferred, as it means the results of PageRank can be interpreted as probabilities. We'll be implementing the former.

This initial weight is the PageRank r of each account at the start of the algorithm. At iteration one, each account sends an equal proportion of its own rank to all the pages it follows. After this step, the rank of account j and r_j is defined as the sum of all the incoming ranks. We can express this with the following equation:

$$r_j = \sum_{i \to j} \frac{r_i}{n_i}$$

Here, r_i is the rank of a follower and ni is the count of accounts they follow. Account j receives a proportion of the rank, $\frac{r_i}{n_i}$, from all of their followers.

If this were all there was to PageRank, then the accounts with no followers would already have zero rank and, at every iteration, the most popular pages would just get more and more popular. PageRank therefore also includes a damping factor. This factor ensures that even the least popular accounts retain some weight and that the algorithm can converge to stable values. This can be expressed by modifying the previous equation:

$$r_j = \frac{1-d}{N} - d \sum_{i \to j} \frac{r_i}{n_i}$$

Here, d is the damping factor. A common damping factor to use is 85 percent.

The effect of the damping factor for a group of eleven accounts is visualized in the following diagram:

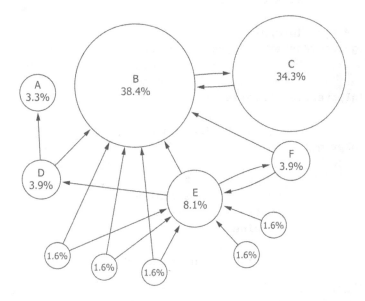

Without the damping factor, all the weight would eventually accrue on accounts **A**, **B**, and **C**. With the damping factor, even the small accounts with no follows continue to receive a small percentage of the overall weight. Even though account **E** has more followers, account **C** has a higher rank, because it is followed by high-ranking account.

Implementing PageRank with Glittering

We implement PageRank with the `pregel` function in the following example code. The structure of the code should be familiar to you by now, although we will be making use of several new Glittering functions:

```
(def damping-factor 0.85)

(defn page-rank-v [id prev msgsum]
  (let [[rank delta] prev
        new-rank (+ rank (* damping-factor msgsum))]
    [new-rank (- new-rank rank)]))

(defn page-rank-m [{:keys [src-attr attr]}]
```

```
    (let [delta (second src-attr)]
      (when (> delta 0.1)
        {:dst (* delta attr)}))))

(defn page-rank [graph]
  (->> (glitter/outer-join-vertices (fn [id attr deg] (or deg 0))
                                    (glitter/out-degrees graph)
                                    graph)
       (glitter/map-triplets (fn [edge]
                               (/ 1.0 (glitter/src-attr edge))))
       (glitter/map-vertices (fn [id attr] (vector 0 0)))
       (p/pregel {:initial-message (/ (- 1 damping-factor)
                                      damping-factor)
                  :direction :out
                  :vertex-fn page-rank-v
                  :message-fn page-rank-m
                  :combiner +
                  :max-iterations 20})
       (glitter/map-vertices (fn [id attr] (first attr)))))
```

We begin in the usual way, using `outer-join-vertices` to join `out-degrees` of every node to itself. After this step, every node's attribute is equal to its number of outgoing links. Then, we use `map-triplets` to set all the `edge` attributes to be the inverse of their source vertex's attribute. The net effect is that each vertex's rank is split equally among all of its outgoing edges.

After this initialization step, we use `map-edges` to set the attribute of each node to the default value: a vector of two zeros. The vector contains the current page rank and the difference between this iteration's rank and the previous iteration's rank. Based on the size of the difference, our `message` function is able to decide whether or not to keep iterating.

Sort by highest influence

Before we run PageRank on the communities identified by label propagation, we'll implement a utility function to list just the top 10 accounts in descending order of their ranks. The `top-n-by-pagerank` function will allow us to only show the accounts with the largest rank:

```
(defn top-n-by-pagerank [n graph]
  (->> (page-rank graph)
       (g/vertices)
       (to-java-pair-rdd)
       (spark/map-to-pair
        (s-de/key-value-fn
```

```
      (fn [k v]
        (spark/tuple v k))))
    (spark/sort-by-key false)
    (spark/take n)
    (into []))))
```

Once again, the fact that we can easily convert between graph and table representations of our data to enable this sort of data manipulation is one of the major benefits of using Glittering and Sparkling together for the graph analysis.

Finally, it will also be useful to have a function that returns the most frequently occurring node attributes appearing in the first line:

```
(defn most-frequent-attributes [graph]
  (->> (g/vertices graph)
       (to-java-pair-rdd)
       (spark/values)
       (spark/count-by-value)
       (sort-by second >)
       (map first)))
```

Given the output of label propagation, this function will return the community IDs as a sequence in the order of descending sizes.

Running PageRank to determine community influencers

At last, we can bring together all the earlier code to identify the most resonant interests of the communities identified by label propagation. Unlike the other algorithms we've implemented with Glittering so far, we're sending our messages in the direction of follow rather than in the canonical direction. Therefore in the next example, we'll load the graph with `load-edgelist`, which preserves the follow direction:

```
(defn ex-8-30 []
  (spark/with-context sc (-> (g/conf)
                             (conf/master "local")
                             (conf/app-name "ch8"))
    (let [communities (->> (load-edgelist
                             sc "data/twitter_combined.txt")
                           (label-propagation))
          by-popularity (most-frequent-attributes 2 communities)]
      (doseq [community (take 10 by-popularity)]
        (println
          (pagerank-for-community community communities)))))))
```

This code will take a little while to run, but will eventually return a sequence of the most important nodes in each of the ten most popular community graphs as shown in the following example:

```
;;[#sparkling/tuple [132.8254006818738 115485051]
;;#sparkling/tuple [62.13049747055527 62581962]
;;#sparkling/tuple [49.80716333905785 65357070]
;;#sparkling/tuple [46.248688749879875 90420314] ...]
```

The first element of each tuple is the PageRank we've calculated for the vertex and the second element of each tuple is the node ID. The Twitter vertex IDs correspond to Twitter's own IDs. The accounts haven't been anonymized, so we can look up the Twitter accounts they correspond to.

At the time of writing, we can look up a Twitter account by ID using Twitter's Intent API available at https://twitter.com/intent/user?user_id={$USER_ID}. Substituting {$USER_ID} for Twitter's numeric ID will return the basic profile information.

The accounts with the highest PageRank in community one are American comic and talk show host Conan O'Brien with Barack Obama, Felicia Day, and Neil Patrick Harris. We could broadly categorize these people as American celebrities. It's not entirely surprising that on Twitter, the largest community is gathered around some of the largest accounts with the broadest general appeal.

Moving down the list, the second-largest community features among its top influencers the band Paramore, its members Hayley and Taylor, as well as Lady Gaga. This community clearly has a very specific set of musical interests.

Communities three and four both appear to have a strong gaming bias featuring X-Box, PlayStation, Steam, and Marcus Persson (the creator of Minecraft) as their top influencers.

Bear in mind that we've already established that the whole graph is a part of one connected component, so we're not looking at disjoint sets of users. Using a combination of label propagation and PageRank, we are able to determine the groups of Twitter users with related interests.

Summary

In this chapter, we've learned about graphs: a useful abstraction to model a huge variety of phenomena. We started the chapter using the Clojure library Loom to visualize and traverse small graphs of Twitter followers. We learned about two different methods of graph traversal, depth-first and breadth-first search, and the effect of changing edge weights on the paths discovered by Dijkstra's algorithm and Prim's algorithm. We also looked at the density of the whole graph and plotted the degree distributions to observe the difference between random and scale-free graphs.

We introduced GraphX and the Clojure library Glittering as a means of processing large graphs in a scalable way using Spark. In addition to providing several built-in graph algorithms, Glittering also exposes GraphX's Pregel API: a set of three symbiotic functions to express graph algorithms in a vertex-centric way. We showed that this alternative model of computation could be used to express triangle counting, connected components, label propagation, and finally PageRank algorithms, and chained our label propagation and PageRank steps together to determine the top influencers for a set of Twitter communities.

This was our last chapter using parallel computing techniques. In the next chapter, we'll focus on local data processing, but we'll continue the thread of recursive analysis. We'll cover methods to deal with time series data—ordered sequences of observations in time—and demonstrate how recursive functions can be used to produce forecasts.

9
Time Series

"Again time elapsed."

- Carolyn Keene, The Secret of the Old Clock

In several of the previous chapters, we saw how we can apply iterative algorithms to identify solutions to complex equations. We first encountered this with gradient descent—both batch and stochastic—but most recently we saw it in community detection in graphs using the graph-parallel model of computation.

This chapter is about time series data. A time series is any data series that consists of regular observations of a quantity arranged according to the time of their measurement. For many of the techniques in this chapter to work, we require that the intervals between successive observations are all equal. The period between measurements could be monthly in the case of sales figures, daily in the case of rainfall or stock market fluctuations, or by minute in the case of hits to a high-traffic website.

For us to be able to predict the future values of a time series, we require that the future values are, to some extent, based on the values that have come before. This chapter is therefore also about recursion: how we can build up a sequence where each new value is a function of the previous values. By modeling a real time series as a process where new values are generated in this way, we hope to be able to simulate the sequence forwards in time and produce a forecast.

Before we get to recursion though, we'll learn how we can adapt a technique we've already encountered—linear regression—to fit curves to time series data.

About the data

This chapter will make use of two datasets that come pre-installed with Incanter: the **Longley dataset**, which contains data on seven economic variables measured in the United States between the years 1947 to 1962, and the **Airline dataset**, which contains the monthly total airline passengers from January 1949 to December 1960.

 You can download the source code for this chapter from https://github.com/clojuredatascience/ch9-time-series.

The Airline dataset is where we will spend most of our time in this chapter, but first let's look at the Longley dataset. It contains columns including the gross domestic product (GDP), the number of employed and unemployed people, the population, and the size of the armed forces. It's a classic dataset for analyzing multicollinearity since many of the predictors are themselves correlated. This won't affect the analysis we're performing since we'll only be using one of the predictors at a time.

Loading the Longley data

Since Incanter includes the Longley dataset as part of its sample datasets library, loading the data in is a simple matter of calling `incanter.datasets/get-dataset` with `:longley` as the only argument. Once loaded, we'll view the dataset with `incanter.core/view`:

```
(defn ex-9-1 []
  (-> (d/get-dataset :longley)
      (i/view)))
```

The data should look something like this:

:y	:x1	:x2	:x3	:x4	:x5	:x6
60323	83.0	234289	2356	1590	107608	1947
61122	88.5	259426	2325	1456	108632	1948
60171	88.2	258054	3682	1616	109773	1949
61187	89.5	284599	3351	1650	110929	1950
63221	96.2	328975	2099	3099	112075	1951
63639	98.1	346999	1932	3594	113270	1952
64989	99.0	365385	1870	3547	115094	1953
63761	100.0	363112	3578	3350	116219	1954
66019	101.2	397469	2904	3048	117388	1955
67857	104.6	419180	2822	2857	118734	1956
68169	108.4	442769	2936	2798	120445	1957
66513	110.8	444546	4681	2637	121950	1958
68655	112.6	482704	3813	2552	123366	1959
69564	114.2	502601	3931	2514	125368	1960
69331	115.7	518173	4806	2572	127852	1961
70551	116.9	554894	4007	2827	130081	1962

The data was originally published by the National Institute for Standards and Technology as a statistical reference dataset and the column descriptions are listed on their website at http://www.itl.nist.gov/div898/strd/lls/data/LINKS/i-Longley.shtml. We'll be considering the final three columns **x4**: the size of the armed forces, **x5**: the "non-institutional" population aged 14 and over, and **x6**: the year.

First, let's see how population changes with respect to time:

```
(defn ex-9-2 []
  (let [data (d/get-dataset :longley)]
    (-> (c/scatter-plot (i/$ :x6 data)
                        (i/$ :x5 data)
                        :x-label "Year"
                        :y-label "Population")
        (i/view))))
```

The preceding code generates the following chart:

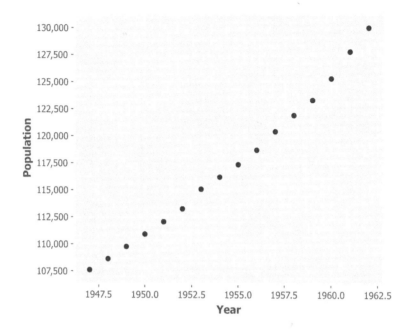

The plot of population against year shows a very clear not-quite-linear relationship. The slight curve suggests that the population growth rate is increasing as the population increases.

> Recall Gibrat's law from *Chapter 3, Correlation*, the growth rate of firms is proportional to their size. It's common to see growth curves similar to the preceding one when analyzing populations where Gibrat's law applies: the rate of growth will tend to increase over time.

We have seen how to fit a straight line through data with Incanter's linear model. Perhaps surprisingly, it's also possible to fit curves with the `linear-model` function.

Fitting curves with a linear model

First, let's remind ourselves how we would fit a straight line using Incanter's
`linear-model` function. We want to extract the x5 and x6 columns from the
dataset and apply them (in that order: x6, the year, is our predictor variable)
to the `incanter.stats/linear-model` function.

```
(defn ex-9-3 []
  (let [data  (d/get-dataset :longley)
        model (s/linear-model (i/$ :x5 data)
                              (i/$ :x6 data))]
    (println "R-square" (:r-square model))
    (-> (c/scatter-plot (i/$ :x6 data)
                        (i/$ :x5 data)
                        :x-label "Year"
                        :y-label "Population")
        (c/add-lines (i/$ :x6 data)
                     (:fitted model))
        (i/view))))

;; R-square 0.9879
```

The preceding code generates the following chart:

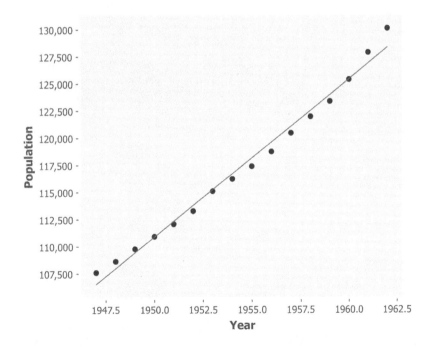

While the straight line is a close fit to the data—generating an R^2 of over 0.98—it doesn't capture the curve of the line. In particular, we can see that points diverge from the line at either end and in the middle of the chart. Our straightforward model has high bias and is systematically under- and over-predicting the population depending on the year. A plot of the residuals would clearly show that the errors are not normally distributed with equal variance.

The `linear-model` function is so-called because it generates models that have a linear relationship with their parameters. However, and perhaps surprisingly, it's capable of generating non-linear predictions, provided we supply it with non-linear features. For example, we could add the year squared as a parameter, in addition to the year. In the following code, we do this using Incanter's `bind-columns` function to create a matrix of both of these features:

```
(defn ex-9-4 []
  (let [data  (d/get-dataset :longley)
        x     (i/$ :x6 data)
        xs    (i/bind-columns x (i/sq x))
        model (s/linear-model (i/$ :x5 data) xs)]
    (println "R-square" (:r-square model))
    (-> (c/scatter-plot (i/$ :x6 data)
                        (i/$ :x5 data)
                        :x-label "Year"
                        :y-label "Population")
        (c/add-lines (i/$ :x6 data)
                    (:fitted model))
        (i/view))))

;; 0.9983
```

Our R^2 has increased and we get the following chart:

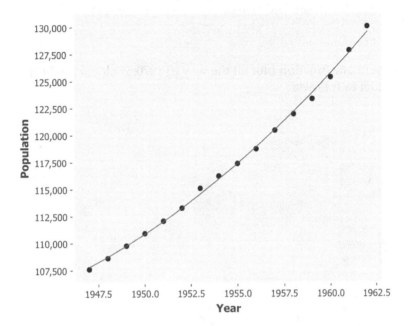

This appears to be a much better fit for the data. We can use our model for forecasting by creating a `forecast` function that takes the coefficients of the model and returns a function of x, the year, that multiplies them them by the features we've defined:

```
(defn forecast [coefs]
  (fn [x]
    (first
      (i/mmult (i/trans coefs)
               (i/matrix [1.0 x (i/sq x)])))))
```

The coefficients includes a parameter for the bias term, so we're multiplying the coefficients by *1.0, x,* and x^2.

```
(defn ex-9-5 []
  (let [data  (d/get-dataset :longley)
        x     (i/$ :x6 data)
        xs    (i/bind-columns x (i/sq x))
        model (s/linear-model (i/$ :x5 data) xs)]
    (-> (c/scatter-plot (i/$ :x6 data)
                        (i/$ :x5 data)
```

```
              :x-label "Year"
              :y-label "Population")
  (c/add-function (forecast (:coefs model))
              1947 1970)
  (i/view))))
```

Next, we extend our function plot all the way to 1970 to more clearly see the curve of the fitted model as follows:

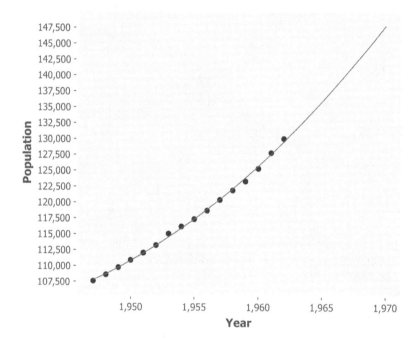

Of course, we are extrapolating beyond the bounds of our data. As discussed back in *Chapter 3, Correlation*, it is generally unwise to extrapolate very far. To illustrate why more clearly, let's turn our attention to another column in the Longley dataset, the size of the armed forces: x6.

We can plot this in the same way as before:

```
(defn ex-9-6 []
  (let [data (d/get-dataset :longley)]
    (-> (c/scatter-plot (i/$ :x6 data)
                    (i/$ :x4 data)
                    :x-label "Year"
                    :y-label "Size of Armed Forces")
        (i/view))))
```

This generates the following chart:

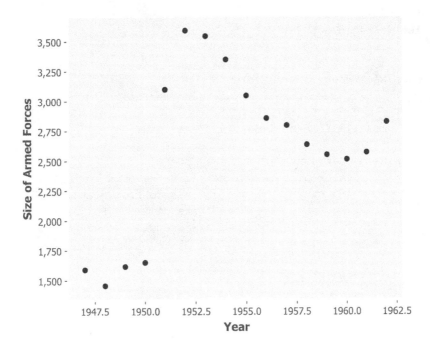

This is clearly a much more complicated series. We can see a sharp increase in the size of the armed forces between 1950 and 1952 followed by a gentle decline. On June 27th 1950, President Truman ordered air and naval forces to assist South Korea in what would become known as the Korean War.

To fit a curve to these data, we'll need to generate higher order polynomials. First, let's construct a `polynomial-forecast` function that will create the higher-order features for us automatically, based on a single x and the highest-degree polynomial to create:

```
(defn polynomial-forecast [coefs degree]
  (fn [x]
    (first
      (i/mmult (i/trans coefs)
               (for [i (range (inc degree))]
                 (i/pow x i))))))
```

For example, we could train a model all the way up to x^{11} using the following code:

```
(defn ex-9-7 []
  (let [data (d/get-dataset :longley)
        degree 11
        x   (s/sweep (i/$ :x6 data))
        xs (reduce i/bind-columns
                   (for [i (range (inc degree))]
                     (i/pow x i)))
        model (s/linear-model (i/$ :x4 data) xs
                              :intercept false)]
    (println "R-square" (:r-square model))
    (-> (c/scatter-plot  (i/$ 1 xs) (i/$ :x4 data)
                         :x-label "Distance from Mean (Years)"
                         :y-label "Size of Armed Forces")
        (c/add-function (polynomial-forecast (:coefs model)
                                             degree)
                        -7.5 7.5)
        (i/view))))
```

```
;; R-square 0.9755
```

The preceding code generates the following chart:

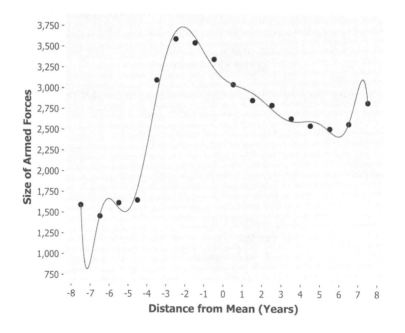

The curve fits the data quite well, with an R^2 of over 0.97. However, it should come as no surprise to you now to discover that we are overfitting the data. The model we have built is unlikely to have very much forecasting power. In fact, if we extend the range of the chart to the right, as we do with ex-9-8 to show predictions into the future, we obtain the following:

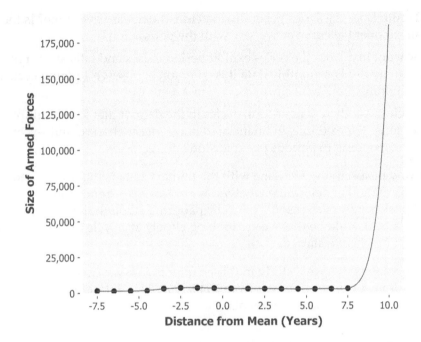

Just two-and-a-half years after the last measured data point, our model is predicting that the military will grow more than 500 percent to over 175,000 people.

Time series decomposition

One of the problems that we have modeling the military time series is that there is simply not enough data to be able to produce a general model of the process that produced the series. A common way to model a time series is to decompose the series into a number of separate components:

- **Trend**: Does the series generally increase or decrease over time? Is the trend an exponential curve as we saw with the population?

- **Seasonality**: Does the series exhibit periodic rises and falls at a set number of intervals? For monthly data it is common to observe a period cycle of 12 months.

- **Cycles**: Are there longer-term cycles in the dataset that span multiple seasons? For example, in financial data we might observe multi-year cycles corresponding to periods of expansion and recession.

Another way of specifying the issue with the military data is that there is not enough information to determine whether or not there is a trend, and whether the observed peak is part of a seasonal or cyclic pattern. Although the data appears to trend upwards, it could be that we are looking closely at a cycle that will eventually decline back to where it started.

One of the datasets that we'll study in this chapter is a classic time series looking at monthly airline passenger numbers from 1949-1960. This dataset is larger and clearly exhibits trend and seasonal components.

Inspecting the airline data

Like the Longley dataset, the Airline dataset is part of Incanter's datasets library. We load the incanter.datasets library as d and incanter.code as i.

```
(defn ex-9-9 []
  (-> (d/get-dataset :airline-passengers)
      (i/view)))
```

The first few rows should look like this:

:year	:passengers	:month
1949	112	Jan
1950	115	Jan
1951	145	Jan
1952	171	Jan
1953	196	Jan
1954	204	Jan
1955	242	Jan
1956	284	Jan
1957	315	Jan
1958	340	Jan
1959	360	Jan

When analyzing time series, it's important that the data is ordered sequentially in time. This data is ordered by year and alphabetically by month. All the January data is followed by all the February data, and so on. To proceed further, we'll need to convert the year and month columns into a single column we can sort by. For this, we'll use the `clj-time` library (`https://github.com/clj-time/clj-time`) once again.

Visualizing the airline data

When parsing times previously in *Chapter 3, Correlation,* we were able to take advantage of the fact that the string representation of the time was a default format that clj-time understood. Clj-time is not able to automatically infer all time representations of course. Particularly problematic is the difference between the *mm/dd/yyyy* American format and the *dd/mm/yyyy* favored by most of the rest of the world. The `clj-time.format` namespace provides a `parse` function that allows us to pass a format string instructing the library how it should interpret the string. We're including the `format` namespace as `tf` in the following code and specifying that our time will be expressed in the format `"MMM YYYY"`.

 A list of formatter strings used by clj-time is available at `http://www.joda.org/joda-time/key_format.html`.

In other words, three characters of "month" followed by four characters of "year".

```
(def time-format
  (tf/formatter "MMM YYYY"))

(defn to-time [month year]
  (tf/parse time-format (str month " " year)))
```

With the earlier functions in place we can parse our year and month columns into a single time, order them sequentially, and extract the passenger numbers:

```
(defn airline-passengers []
  (->> (d/get-dataset :airline-passengers)
       (i/add-derived-column :time [:month :year] to-time)
       (i/$order :time :asc)
       (i/$ :passengers)))
```

The result is a sequence of numbers representing the passenger count in order of ascending time. Let's visualize this as a line chart now:

```
(defn timeseries-plot [series]
  (-> (c/xy-plot (range (count series)) series
                 :x-label "Time"
                 :y-label "Value")
      (i/view)))

(defn ex-9-10 []
  (-> (airline-passengers)
      (timeseries-plot)))
```

The preceding code generates the following chart:

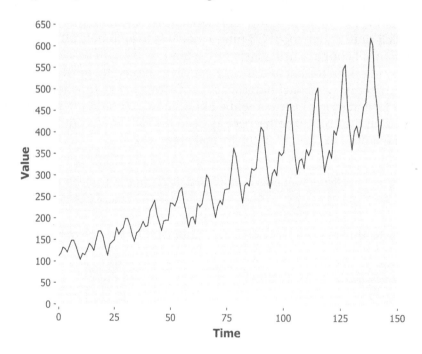

You can see how the data has a pronounced seasonal pattern (repeating every 12 months), an upward trend, and a gentle growth curve.

The variance to the right of the chart is greater than the variance to the left, so we say that the data is exhibiting some **heteroscedasticity**. We'll want to remove the increase in variance and also the upward trend from the dataset. This will yield a time series which is **stationary**.

Stationarity

A stationary time series is one whose statistical properties are constant in time. Most statistical forecasting methodologies assume the series has been transformed to be stationary. A prediction is made much easier with a stationary time series: we assume the statistical properties of the series will be the same in the future as they have been in the past. To remove both the increasing variance and the growth curve from the airline data, we can simply take the logarithm of the passenger numbers:

```
(defn ex-9-11 []
  (-> (airline-passengers)
      (i/log)
      (timeseries-plot)))
```

This generates the following chart:

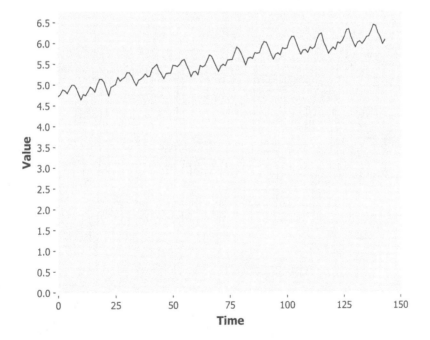

The effect of taking the logarithm is twofold. Firstly, the heteroscedasticity evident in the initial chart has been removed. Secondly, the exponential growth curve has been reduced to a straight line.

This has made the data much easier to work with but we still have a trend, also known as **drift**, in the series. To get a truly stationary time series, we'll want to stabilize the mean as well. There are several ways to do this.

De-trending and differencing

The first method is de-trending the series. After taking the logarithm, the airline dataset contains a very strong linear trend. We could fit a linear model to this data and then plot the residuals:

```
(defn ex-9-12 []
  (let [data (i/log (airline-passengers))
        xs   (range (count data))
        model (s/linear-model data xs)]
    (-> (c/xy-plot xs (:residuals model)
                   :x-label "Time"
                   :y-label "Residual")
        (i/view))))
```

This generates the following chart:

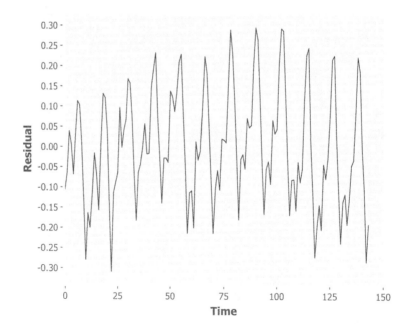

The residual plot shows a series whose mean is much more stable than the original series and the upward trend has been entirely removed. Unfortunately, though, the residuals don't appear to be quite normally distributed around the new mean. In particular there appears to be a "hump" in the middle of the chart. This suggests that our linear model is not performing ideally on the airline data. We could fit a curve to the data like we did at the beginning of the chapter, but let's instead look at another method of making time series stationary.

The second method is differencing. If we subtract the value of the directly preceding point from each point in the time series, we'll obtain a new time series (one data point shorter) that contains only the differences between successive points.

```
(defn difference [series]
  (map - (drop 1 series) series))

(defn ex-9-13 []
  (-> (airline-passengers)
      (i/log)
      (difference)
      (timeseries-plot)))
```

We can see the effect in the following chart:

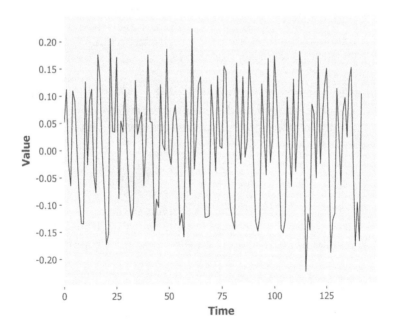

Notice how the upward trend has been replaced with a series of fluctuations around a constant mean value. The mean is slightly above zero, corresponding to an increased propensity for differences to be positive and leading to the upward trend we observe.

Both techniques aim to result in a series whose mean is constant. In some cases, it may be necessary to difference the series more than once, or to apply differencing after de-trending to obtain a series which a truly a stable mean. Some drift is still evident in the series after de-trending, for example, so we'll use the differenced data for the rest of this chapter.

Before moving on to discuss how to model such time series for forecasting, let's take a detour to think about what a time series is, and how we might model a time series as a recursive process.

Discrete time models

Discrete time models, such as the ones we have been looking at so far, separate time into slices at regular intervals. For us to be able to predict future values of time slices, we assume that they are dependent on past slices.

 Time series can also be analyzed with respect to frequency rather than time. We won't discuss frequency domain analysis in this chapter but the book's wiki at http://wiki.clojuredatascience.com contains links to further resources.

In the following, let y_t denote the value of an observation at time t. The simplest time series possible would be one where the value of each time slice is the same as the one directly preceding it. The predictor for such a series would be:

$$\hat{y}_{t+1|t} = y_t$$

This is to say that the prediction at time $t + 1$ given t is equal to the observed value at time t. Notice that this definition is recursive: the value at time t depends on the value at $t - 1$. The value at $t - 1$ depends on the value at $t - 2$, and so on.

We could model this "constant" time series as a lazy sequence in Clojure, where each value in the sequence is a constant value:

```
(defn constant-series [y]
  (cons y (lazy-seq (constant-series y))))

(defn ex-9-14 []
  (take 5 (constant-series 42)))

;; (42 42 42 42 42)
```

Notice how the definition of `constant-series` contains a reference to itself. This is a recursive function definition that creates an infinite lazy sequence from which we can consume values.

The next time slice, at time $t + 1$, the actual value is observed to be y_{t+1}. If this value and our predicted value $\hat{y}_{t+1|t}$ differ, then we can compute this difference as the error of our prediction:

$$\varepsilon_{t+1} = y_{t+1} - \hat{y}_{t+1|t}$$

By combining the two previous equations we obtain the stochastic model for a time series.

$$y_t = y_{t-1} + \varepsilon_t$$

In other words, the value at the current time slice is the value at the previous time slice, plus some error.

Random walks

One of the simplest stochastic processes is the random walk. Let's extend our `constant-series` into a `random-walk` process. We'll want our errors to be normally distributed with a zero mean and constant variance. Let's simulate random noise with a call to Incanter's `stats/sample-normal` function.

```
(defn random-walk [y]
  (let [e (s/sample-normal 1)
        y (+ y e)]
    (cons y (lazy-seq (random-walk y)))))

(defn ex-9-15 []
  (->> (random-walk 0)
       (take 50)
       (timeseries-plot)))
```

You'll get a different result, of course, but it should look similar to the following chart:

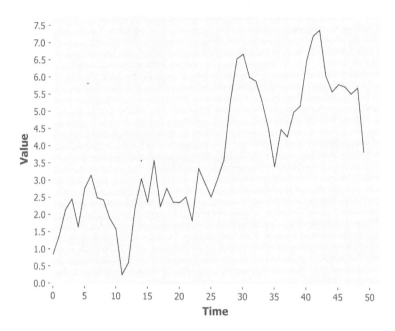

The random walk model is very often seen in finance and econometrics.

The term *random walk* was first introduced by Karl Pearson in 1905. Many processes — from fluctuating stock prices to the path traced by a molecule as it travels in a gas — can be modeled as simple random walks. In 1973, the Princeton economist Burton Gordon Malkiel argued in his book *A Random Walk Down Wall Street* that stock prices evolve according to a random walk as well.

The random walk is not entirely unpredictable. Although the difference between each point and the next is governed by a random process, the variance of that difference is constant. This means that we can estimate confidence intervals for the magnitude of each step. However, since the mean is zero we cannot say with any confidence whether the difference will be positive or negative relative to the current value.

Autoregressive models

We've seen already in this chapter how to use a linear model to make a prediction based on a linear combination of predictors. In an autoregressive model we forecast the variable of interest by using a linear combination of the past values of the variable.

The autoregressive model regresses the predictor against itself. In order to see how this works in practice, let's look at the following code:

```
(defn ar [ys coefs sigma]
  (let [e (s/sample-normal 1 :sd sigma)
        y (apply + e (map * ys coefs))]
    (cons y (lazy-seq
              (ar (cons y ys) coefs sigma)))))
```

This shares much in common with the random walk recursive definition that we encountered a few pages previously. This time, however, we're generating each new y as a product of previous ys and the coefs.

We can generate an autoregressive series with a call to our new ar function, passing the previous ys and the coefficients of the autoregressive model:

```
(defn ex-9-16 []
  (->> (ar [1] [2] 0)
       (take 10)
       (timeseries-plot)))
```

This generates the following chart:

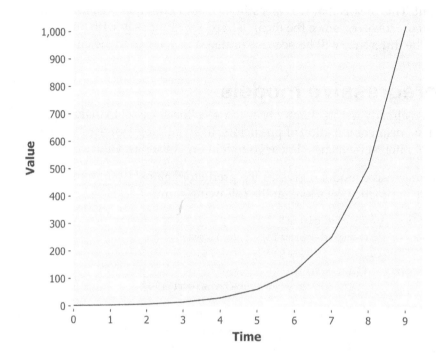

By taking an initial value of 1.0 and a coefficient of 2.0, with zero noise, we're creating an exponential growth curve. Each time step in the series is a power of two.

The autoregressive series is said to be *autocorrelated*. In other words, each point is linearly correlated to its preceding points. In the earlier case, this is simply twice the preceding value. The quantity of coefficients is said to be the order of the autocorrelation model and is often denoted by the letter p. The preceding example is therefore an autoregressive process with $p=1$, or an *AR(1)* process.

More intricate autoregressive series can be generated by increasing p.

```
(defn ex-9-17 []
  (let [init (s/sample-normal 5)]
    (->> (ar init [0 0 0 0 1] 0)
         (take 30)
         (timeseries-plot))))
```

For example, the previous code generates an autoregressive time series of order 5, or an *AR(5)* series. The effect is visible in the series as a regular cycle with a period of 5 points.

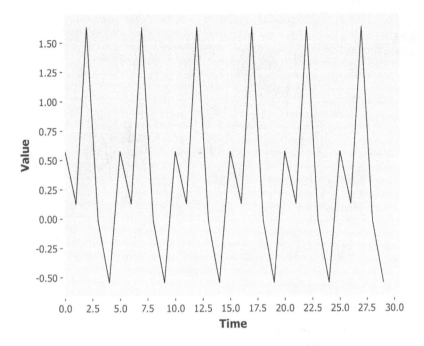

We can combine the autoregressive model together with some noise to introduce a component of the random walk we saw previously. Let's increase sigma to 0.2:

```
(defn ex-9-18 []
  (let [init (s/sample-normal 5)]
    (->> (ar init [0 0 0 0 1] 0.2)
         (take 30)
         (timeseries-plot))))
```

This generates the following chart:

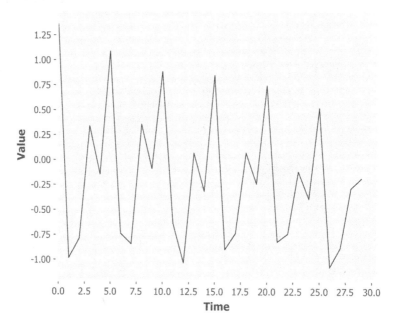

Notice how the characteristic "seasonal" cycle every five points is preserved, but has been combined with an element of noise too. Although this is simulated data, this simple model is beginning to approach the sort of series that regularly appears in time series analysis.

The general equation for an AR model of one lag is given by:

$$y_t = c + \varepsilon_t + \varphi_1 y_{t-1}$$

where c is some constant, ε_t is the error, y_{t-1} is the value of the series at the previous time step, and φ_1 is the coefficient denoted by the Greek symbol *phi*. More generally, the equation for an autoregressive model up to p lags is given by:

$$y_t = c + \varepsilon_t + \varphi_1 y_{t-1} + \ldots + \varphi_p y_{t-p}$$

Since our series are stationary, we have omitted the constant term c in the code.

Determining autocorrelation in AR models

Just as linear regression can establish a (linear) correlation between multiple independent variables, autoregression can establish a correlation between a variable and itself at different points in time.

Just as in linear regression we sought to establish correlation between the predictors and the response variable, so in time series analysis we seek to establish an autocorrelation with the time series and itself at a certain number of lags. Knowing the number of lags for which autocorrelation exists allows us to calculate the order of the autoregressive model.

It follows that we want to study the autocorrelation of the series at different lags. For example, a lag of zero will mean that we compare each point with itself (an autocorrelation of 1.0). A lag of 1 will mean that we compare each point with the directly preceding point. The **autocorrelation function (ACF)** is a linear dependence between a dataset and itself with a given lag. The ACF is therefore parameterized by the lag, k.

$$\rho_{y|k} = \text{corr}\left(y_t, y_{t-k}\right)$$

Incanter contains an `auto-correlation` function that will return the autocorrelation for a given sequence and lag. However, we're defining our own `autocorrelation` function that will return the `autocorrelation` for a sequence of lags:

```
(defn autocorrelation* [series variance n k]
  (let [lag-product (->> (drop k series)
                         (map * series)
                         (i/sum))]
    (cons (/ lag-product variance n)
          (lazy-seq
            (autocorrelation* series variance n (inc k))))))

(defn autocorrelation [series]
  (autocorrelation* (s/sweep series)
                    (s/variance series)
                    (dec (count series)) 0))
```

Before calculating the autocorrelation, we use `sweep` function of `incanter.stats` to remove the mean from the series. This means that we can simply multiply the values of the series together with the values at lag k to determine whether they have a tendency to vary together. If they do, their products will be positive; if not, their products will be negative.

This function returns an infinite lazy sequence of autocorrelation values corresponding to the autocorrelation of lags *0...k*. Let's define a function for plotting these values as a bar chart. As with the `timeseries-plot`, this function will accept an ordered sequence of values:

```
(defn bar-plot [ys]
  (let [xs (range (count ys))]
    (-> (c/bar-chart xs ys
                     :x-label "Lag"
                     :y-label "Value")
        (i/view))))
```

```
(defn ex-9-19 []
  (let [init (s/sample-normal 5)
        coefs [0 0 0 0 1]]
    (->> (ar init coefs 0.2)
         (take 100)
         (autocorrelation)
         (take 15)
         (bar-plot))))
```

This generates the following chart:

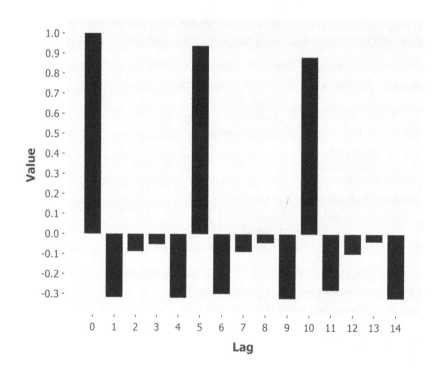

The peaks every 5 lags are consistent with our *AR(5)* series generator. They diminish over time as noise interferes with the signal and decreases the measured autocorrelation.

Moving-average models

An assumption of AR models is that noise is random with constant mean and variance. Our recursive AR function sampled values from the normal distribution to generate noise that satisfied these assumptions. In an AR process, therefore, the noise terms are *uncorrelated* with each other.

In some processes, though, the noise terms themselves are not uncorrelated. For an example of this consider a time series that reports the daily number of barbeques sold. We might observe peaks every 7 days corresponding to customers' increased likelihood of buying barbeques at the weekend. Occasionally, we might observe a period of several weeks where the total sales are down, and other periods of several weeks where the sales are correspondingly up. We might reason that this is due to the weather, with poor sales corresponding to a period of cold or rainy weather and good sales corresponding to a period of favorable weather. Whatever the cause, it will appear in our data as a pronounced shift in the mean value of the series. Series that exhibit this behavior are called **moving-average (MA)**, models.

A first-order moving-average model, denoted by *MA(1)*, is:

$$y_t = \mu + \varepsilon_t + \theta_1 \varepsilon_{t-1}$$

where μ is the mean of the series, ε_t are the noise values, and θ_1 is the parameter to the model. More generally for q terms the MA model is given by:

$$y_t = \mu + \varepsilon_t + \theta_1 \varepsilon_{t-1} + \ldots + \theta_q \varepsilon_{t-q}$$

Thus, an MA model is conceptually a linear regression of the current value of the series against current and previous (unobserved) white noise error terms or random shocks. The error terms at each point are assumed to be mutually independent and come from the same (usually normal) distribution with zero mean and constant variance.

In MA models, we make the assumption that the noise values themselves are autocorrelated. We can model it like this:

```
(defn ma [es coefs sigma]
  (let [e (s/sample-normal 1 :sd sigma)
        y (apply + e (map * es coefs))]
    (cons y (lazy-seq
              (ma (cons e es) coefs sigma)))))
```

Here, `es` are the previous errors, `coefs` are the parameters to the MA model, and `sigma` is the standard deviation of the errors.

Notice how the function differs from the `ar` function previously defined. Instead of retaining a sequence of the previous *ys*, we retain a sequence of the previous *es*. Let's see what sort of series an MA model generates:

```
(defn ex-9-20 []
  (let [init (s/sample-normal 5)
        coefs [0 0 0 0 1]]
    (->> (ma init coefs 0.5)
         (take 100)
         (timeseries-plot))))
```

This generates a graph similar to the following:

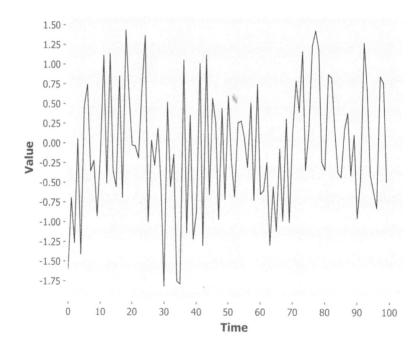

You can see that the chart for an MA lacks the obvious repetition of the AR model. Viewed over a longer series of points, though, you can see how it reintroduces *drift* into the model as the reverberations of one random shock are perpetuated in a new temporary mean.

Determining autocorrelation in MA models

You may wonder if an autocorrelation plot would help identify an MA process. Let's plot that now. An MA model can be harder to spot, so we'll generate more points before plotting the autocorrelation.

```
(defn ex-9-21 []
  (let [init (s/sample-normal 5)
        coefs [0 0 0 0 1]]
    (->> (ma init coefs 0.2)
         (take 5000)
         (autocorrelation)
         (take 15)
         (bar-plot))))
```

This generates the following chart:

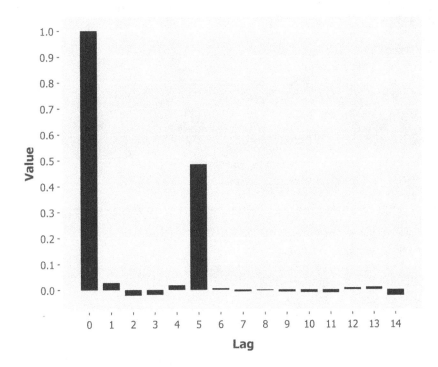

You can see on the preceding chart how it clearly shows the order of the MA process with a pronounced peak at lag 5. Notice though that, unlike the autoregressive process, there is no recurring peak every 5 lags. It's a feature of the MA process that, since the process introduces drift into the mean, autocorrelation for the other lags is greatly diminished.

Combining the AR and MA models

The AR and MA models that we've been considering so far this chapter are two different but closely related ways of generating autocorrelated time series. They are not mutually exclusive, though, and when trying to model real time series you'll often encounter situations where the series appears to be a mixture of both.

$$y_t = c + \varepsilon_t + \sum_{i=1}^{p} \varphi_i y_{t-i} + \sum_{i=1}^{q} \theta_i \varepsilon_{t-i}$$

We can combine both AR and MA processes into a single ARMA model, with two sets of coefficients: those of the autoregressive model and those of the moving-average model. The number of coefficients for each model need not be identical, and by convention the order of the AR model is identified by p and the order of the MA model identified by q.

```
(defn arma [ys es ps qs sigma]
  (let [e  (s/sample-normal 1 :sd sigma)
        ar (apply + (map * ys ps))
        ma (apply + (map * es qs))
        y  (+ ar ma e)]
    (cons y (lazy-seq
              (arma (cons y ys)
                    (cons e es)
                    ps qs sigma)))))
```

Let's plot a longer series of points to see what sort of structure emerges:

```
(defn ex-9-22 []
  (let [ys (s/sample-normal 10 :sd 1.0)
        es (s/sample-normal 10 :sd 0.2)
        ps [0 0 0 0.3 0.5]
        qs [0.2 0.8]]
    (->> (arma ys es ps qs 0.2)
         (take 500)
         (timeseries-plot))))
```

Notice how we're specifying a different number of parameters for the AR and MA portions of the model: 5 parameters for the AR and 2 parameters for the MA model. This is referred to as an *ARMA(5,2)* model.

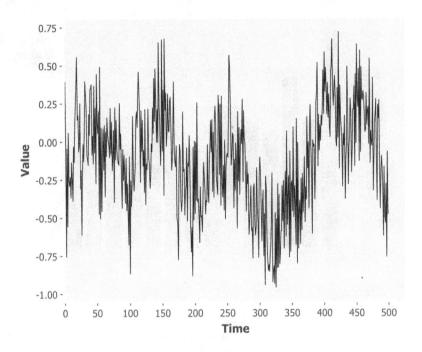

The plot of the earlier ARMA model over a longer series of points allows the effect of the MA terms to become visible. At this scale we can't see the effect of the AR component, so let's run the series though an autocorrelation plot as before:

```
(defn ex-9-23 []
  (let [ys (s/sample-normal 10 :sd 1.0)
        es (s/sample-normal 10 :sd 0.2)
        ps [0 0 0 0.3 0.5]
        qs [0.2 0.8]]
    (->> (arma ys es ps qs 0.2)
         (take 500)
         (autocorrelation)
         (take 15)
         (bar-plot))))
```

You should see a chart similar to the following:

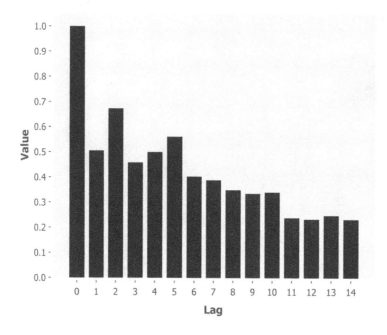

Far from making the order of the series clearer, with more data and both AR and MA components in the series the ACF plot is not very useful and quite unlike the strikingly clear autocorrelation plots that we have been looking at so far. The autocorrelation decays slowly to zero making it impossible to determine the order of the AR and MA processes, even though we've provided it with a large quantity of data.

The reason for this is that the MA portion of the model is overwhelming the AR portion of the model. We can't determine a cyclic pattern in the data because it is hidden behind a moving average that makes all points that are close to each other appear correlated. The best approach to fixing this is to plot the partial autocorrelation.

Calculating partial autocorrelation

The **partial autocorrelation function (PACF)** aims to address the issue of spotting cyclic components in a hybrid ARMA model. It's defined as the correlation coefficient between y_t and y_{t+k} given all the in-between observations. In other words, it's the autocorrelation at lag k that isn't already accounted for by lags 1 through k-1.

The first order, lag 1 partial autocorrelation is defined to equal the first order autocorrelation. The second order, lag 2 partial autocorrelation is equal to:

$$R(t,t-2) = \frac{\text{cov}(y_t, y_{t-2} \mid y_{t-1})}{\sqrt{\text{var}(y_t \mid y_{t-1}) \, \text{var}(y_{t-2} \mid y_{t-1})}}$$

This is the correlation between values two time periods apart, y_t and y_{t-2}, conditional on knowledge of y_{t-1}. In a stationary time series, the two variances in the denominator will be equal.

The third order, lag 3 partial autocorrelation is equal to:

$$R(t,t-3) = \frac{\text{cov}(y_t, y_{t-3} \mid y_{t-1}, y_{t-2})}{\sqrt{\text{var}(y_t \mid y_{t-1}, y_{t-2}) \, \text{var}(y_{t-3} \mid y_{t-1}, y_{t-2})}}$$

And so on, for any lag.

Autocovariance

The equations for partial autocorrelation require us to calculate the covariance of our data with itself at some lag. This is called the **autocovariance**. We have seen in previous chapters how to measure the covariance between two series of data, the tendency of two or more attributes to vary together. This function is very similar to the autocorrelation function we defined earlier in the chapter, and calculates the autocovariance for a range of lags beginning at zero:

```
(defn autocovariance* [series n k]
  (let [lag-product (->> (drop k series)
                         (map * series)
                         (i/sum))]
    (cons (/ lag-product n)
          (lazy-seq
           (autocovariance* series n (inc k))))))

(defn autocovariance [series]
  (autocovariance* (s/sweep series) (count series) 0))
```

As before, the return value will be a lazy sequence of lags, so we'll be sure to take only the values we need.

PACF with Durbin-Levinson recursion

Because of the need to account for previously explained variation, calculating
partial autocorrelation is a lot more involved than calculating autocorrelation.
The Durbin-Levinson algorithm provides a way to calculate it recursively.

 Durbin-Levinson recursion, or simply Levinson Recursion, is a
method for calculating the solution to equations involving matrices
with constant values on the diagonals (called **Toeplitz matrices**).
More information is available at `https://en.wikipedia.org/`
`wiki/Levinson_recursion`.

An implementation of Levinson recursion is shown as follows. The math is beyond
the scope of this book, but the general shape of the recursive function should be
familiar to you now. At each iteration, we calculate the partial autocorrelation with a
function of the previous partial autocorrelations and the autocovariance.

```
(defn pac* [pacs sigma prev next]
  (let [acv (first next)
        sum (i/sum (i/mult pacs (reverse prev)))
        pac (/ (- acv sum) sigma)]
    (cons pac
          (lazy-seq
            (pac* (->> (i/mult pacs pac)
                       (reverse)
                       (i/minus pacs)
                       (cons pac))
                  (* (- 1 (i/pow pac 2)) sigma)
                  (cons acv prev)
                  (rest next))))))

(defn partial-autocorrelation [series]
  (let [acvs (autocovariance series)
        acv1 (first  acvs)
        acv2 (second acvs)
        pac  (/ acv2 acv1)]
    (concat [1.0 pac]
            (pac* (vector pac)
                  (- acv1 (* pac acv2))
                  (vector acv2)
                  (drop 2 acvs)))))
```

As before, this function will create an infinite lazy sequence of partial
autocorrelations, so we have to take only the numbers that we actually want from it.

Plotting partial autocorrelation

Now that we've implemented a function to calculate the partial autocorrelations of a time series, let's plot them. We'll use the same ARMA coefficients as before so we can compare the difference.

```
(defn ex-9-24 []
  (let [ys (s/sample-normal 10 :sd 1.0)
        es (s/sample-normal 10 :sd 0.2)
        ps    [0 0 0 0.3 0.5]
        qs    [0.2 0.8]]
    (->> (arma ys es ps qs 0.2)
         (take 500)
         (partial-autocorrelation)
         (take 15)
         (bar-plot)))))
```

This should generate a bar chart similar to the following:

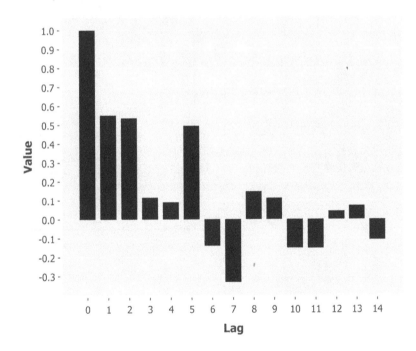

Fortunately, this is rather different from the ACF plot that we created previously. There is a high partial autocorrelation at lags 1 and 2. This suggests that an *MA(2)* process is at work. Then, there is low partial autocorrelation until lag 5. This suggests that there is a an *AR(5)* model at work too.

Determining ARMA model order with ACF and PACF

The differences between ACF and PACF plots are useful to help with selecting the most appropriate model for the time series. The following table describes the appearance of ACF and PACF plots for idealized AR and MA series.

Model	ACF	PACF
AR(p)	Decays gradually	Cuts off after p lags
MA(q)	Cuts off after q lags	Decays gradually
ARMA(p,q)	Decays gradually	Decays gradually

We are often not confronted with data that confirms to these ideals though. Given a real time series, particularly one without a significant number of points, it's not always obvious which would be the most appropriate model. The best course of action is often to pick the simplest model (the one with the lowest order) capable of describing your data.

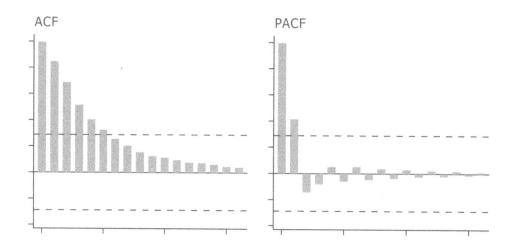

The preceding illustration shows sample ACF and PACF plots for an idealized *AR(1)* series. Next are sample ACF and PACF plots for an idealized *MA(1)* series.

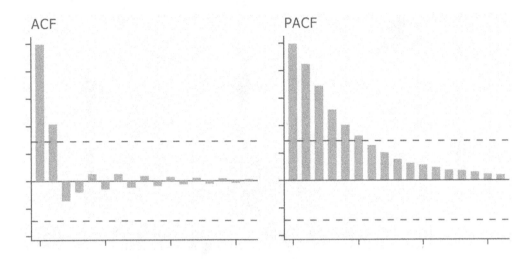

The dotted lines on the graphics indicate the threshold of significance. In general, we are not able to produce a model that perfectly captures all the autocorrelations in the time series and the significance threshold helps us prioritize the most important. A simple formula for determining significance threshold with an *a* of 5 percent is:

$$\pm \frac{2}{\sqrt{n}}$$

Here, *n* is the number of points in the time series. If all points in the ACF and PACF are close to zero, the data are basically random.

ACF and PACF of airline data

Let's return to the airline data that we started considering earlier and plot the ACF of the data for the first 25 lags.

```
(defn ex-9-25 []
  (->> (airline-passengers)
       (difference)
       (autocorrelation)
       (take 25)
       (bar-plot)))
```

This code generates the following chart:

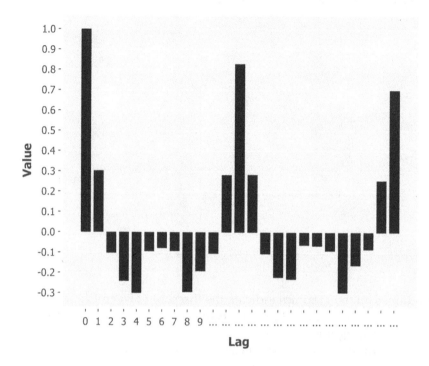

You can see that there are regular peaks and troughs in the data. The first peak is at lag 12; the second is at lag 24. Since the data is monthly, these peaks correspond to an annual, seasonal, cycle. Since we have 144 points in our time series, the threshold for significance is about $\frac{2}{\sqrt{144}}$ or 0.17.

Next, let's look at the partial autocorrelation plot for the airline data:

```
(defn ex-9-26 []
  (->> (airline-passengers)
       (difference)
       (partial-autocorrelation)
       (take 25)
       (bar-plot)))
```

This code generates the following chart:

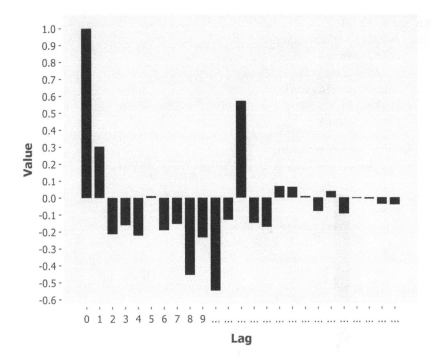

The partial autocorrelation plot also has a peak at lag 12. Unlike the autocorrelation plot it doesn't have a peak at lag 24 because the periodic autocorrelation has already been accounted for at lag 12.

Although this appears to suggest an AR(12) model will be appropriate, that will create a large number of coefficients to learn, especially on a relatively small amount of data. Since the periodic cycle is seasonal, we ought to remove it with a second phase of differencing.

Removing seasonality with differencing

We have already differenced the data once, meaning that our model is referred to as an **autoregressive integrated moving-average (ARIMA)** model. The level of differencing is given the parameter d, and the full model order can therefore be specified as $ARIMA(p,d,q)$.

We can difference the data a second time to remove the strong seasonality in the data. Let's do this next:

```
(defn ex-9-27 []
  (->> (airline-passengers)
       (difference)
       (difference 12)
       (autocorrelation)
       (take 15)
       (bar-plot)))
```

First, we plot the autocorrelation:

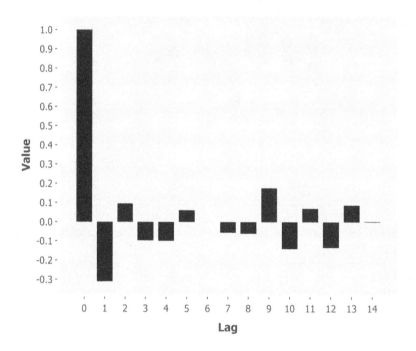

Next, the partial autocorrelation:

```
(defn ex-9-28 []
  (->> (airline-passengers)
       (difference)
       (difference 12)
       (partial-autocorrelation)
       (take 15)
       (bar-plot)))
```

This generates the following chart:

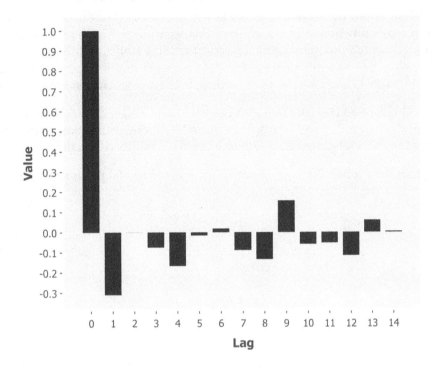

The strong seasonal cycle accounted for most of the significance in the charts. We're left with negative autocorrelation at lag 1 on both charts, and a barely significant autocorrelation at lag 9 on the ACF. A general rule of thumb is that positive autocorrelation is best treated by adding an *AR* term to the model, while negative autocorrelation is usually best treated by adding an *MA* term to the model.

It appears based on the preceding charts that a justified model is an *MA(1)* model. This would probably be a good enough model for this case, but let's use this as an opportunity to demonstrate how to fit a large number of parameters to a model by trying to capture the *AR(9)* autocorrelation as well.

We'll consider an alternative to the cost function, the likelihood, which measures how closely the given model fits the data. The better the model fits, the greater the likelihood. Thus, we will want to maximize the likelihood, a goal also known as **maximum likelihood estimation**.

Maximum likelihood estimation

On several occasions throughout this book, we've expressed optimization problems in terms of a cost function to be minimized. For example, in *Chapter 4, Classification,* we used Incanter to minimize the logistic cost function whilst building a logistic regression classifier, and in *Chapter 5, Big Data,* we used gradient descent to minimize a least-squares cost function when performing batch and stochastic gradient descent.

Optimization can also be expressed as a benefit to maximize, and it's sometimes more natural to think in these terms. Maximum likelihood estimation aims to find the best parameters for a model by maximizing the likelihood function.

Let's say that the probability of an observation x given model parameters β is written as:

$$P(x \mid \beta)$$

Then, the likelihood can be expressed as:

$$L(\beta \mid x)$$

The likelihood is a measure of the *probability of the parameters*, given the data. The aim of maximum likelihood estimation is to find the parameter values that make the observed data most likely.

Calculating the likelihood

Before calculating the likelihood for a time series, we'll illustrate the process by way of a simple example. Say we toss a coin 100 times and observe 56 heads, h, and 44 tails, t. Rather than assume that we have a fair coin with $P(h)=0.5$ (and therefore that the slightly unequal totals are the result of chance variation), instead we could ask whether the observed values differ significantly from 0.5. We can do this by asking what value of $P(h)$ makes the observed data most likely.

```
(defn ex-9-29 []
  (let [data 56
        f (fn [p]
            (s/pdf-binomial data :size 100 :prob p))]
    (-> (c/function-plot f 0.3 0.8
                         :x-label "P"
                         :y-label "Likelihood")
        (i/view))))
```

In the preceding code, we're using binomial distribution to model the sequence of coin tosses (recall from *Chapter 4, Classification*, that binomial distribution is used to model the number of times a binary outcome is expected to occur). The key point is that the data is fixed, and we're plotting the varying probabilities of observing that data given different parameters to the binomial distribution. The following plot shows the likelihood surface:

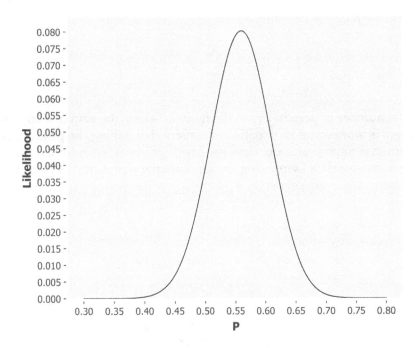

As we might have expected, the most likely parameter to the binomial distribution is *p=0.56*. This contrived example could have more easily been calculated by hand, but the principle of maximum likelihood estimation is able to cope with much more complicated models.

In fact, our ARMA model is one such complicated model. The math for calculating the likelihood of time series parameters is beyond the scope of this book. We'll be making use of the Clojure library Succession (https://github.com/henrygarner/succession) to calculate the likelihood for our time series.

It is often the case that we work with the log-likelihood rather than the likelihood. This is simply for mathematical convenience, since the log-likelihood:

$$LL(\beta \mid x) = \log \prod_{i=1}^{k} f(x_i \mid \beta_i)$$

can be re-written as:

$$LL(\beta \mid x) = \sum_{i=1}^{k} \log f(x_i \mid \beta_i)$$

Here, k is the number of parameters to the model. Taking the sum of a large number of parameters is more computationally convenient than taking the product, so the second formula is often preferred. Let's get a feel for how the likelihood function behaves on some test data by plotting the log-likelihood of different parameters against a simple *AR(2)* time series.

```
(defn ex-9-30 []
  (let [init  (s/sample-normal 2)
        coefs [0 0.5]
        data  (take 100 (ar init coefs 0.2))
        f     (fn [coef]
                (log-likelihood [0 coef] 2 0 data))]
    (-> (c/function-plot f -1 1
                         :x-label "Coefficient"
                         :y-label "Log-Likelihood")
        (i/view))))
```

The preceding code generates the following chart:

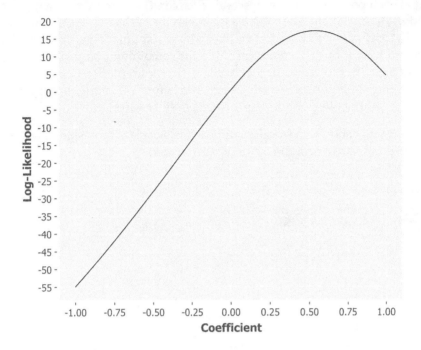

The peak of the curve corresponds to the best estimate for the parameters, given the data. Notice how the peak in the preceding plot is a little higher than 0.5: the noise we added to the model has meant that the best estimate is not exactly 0.5.

Estimating the maximum likelihood

The number of parameters to our ARMA model is large, and so to determine the maximum likelihood we're going to use an optimization method that performs well in high-dimensional spaces. The method is called the **Nelder-Mead**, or **simplex**, method. In a space of n dimensions, a simplex is a *polytope* of $n+1$ vertices.

 A polytope is a geometric object with flat sides that can exist in an arbitrary number of dimensions. A two-dimensional polygon is 2-polytope, and a three dimensional polyhedron is a 3-polytope.

The advantage of simplex optimization is that it doesn't need to calculate the gradient at each point in order to descend (or ascend) to a more optimal position. The Nelder-Mead method extrapolates the behavior of the objective function measured at each test point on the simplex. The worst point is replaced with a point created by reflecting through the centroid of the remaining points. If the new point is better than the current best point then we stretch the simplex out exponentially along this line. If the new point isn't much better than before we could be stepping across a valley, so we contract the simplex towards a possibly better point.

The following plot shows an example of how the simplex, represented as a triangle, reflects and contracts to find the optimal parameters.

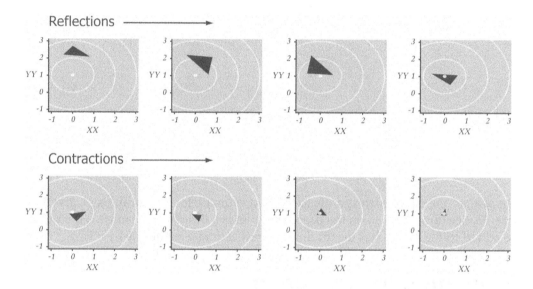

The simplex is always represented as a shape whose number of vertices is one greater than the number of dimensions. The simplex for two-dimensional optimization, as in the preceding plot, is represented by a triangle. For an arbitrary *n*-dimensional space, the simplex will be represented as a polygon of *n+1* vertices.

 The simplex method is also called the **amoeba method** due to the way it appears to crawl towards a more optimal position.

The simplex method of optimization isn't implemented in Incanter, but it's available in the Apache Commons Math library (http://commons.apache.org/proper/commons-math/). To use it, we'll need to wrap our objective function, the log-likelihood, in a representation that the library understands.

Nelder-Mead optimization with Apache Commons Math

Apache Commons Math is a large and sophisticated library. We can't cover more than the barest essentials here. The next example is provided simply to illustrate how to integrate Clojure code with the Java interfaces provided by the library.

 An overview of Apache Commons Math's extensive optimization capabilities is available at `http://commons.apache.org/ proper/commons-math/userguide/optimization.html`.

The Apache Commons Math library expects that we'll provide an `ObjectiveFunction` to be optimized. Next, we create one by reifying a `MultivariateFunction`, since our objective function needs to be supplied with multiple parameters. Our response will be a single value: the log-likelihood.

```
(defn objective-function [f]
  (ObjectiveFunction. (reify MultivariateFunction
                        (value [_ v]
                          (f (vec v))))))
```

The preceding code will return an `ObjectiveFunction` representation of an arbitrary function `f`. A `MultivariateFunction` expects to receive a parameter vector `v`, which we pass straight through to our `f`.

With this in place, we use some Java interop to call `optimize` on a `SimplexOptimizer` with some sensible default values. Our `InitialGuess` at the parameters is simply an array of zeros. The `NelderMeadSimplex` must be initialized with a default step size for each dimension, which can be any value except zero. We're picking a value of 0.2 for each parameter.

```
(defn arma-model [p q ys]
  (let [m (+ p q)
        f (fn [params]
            (sc/log-likelihood params p q ys))
        optimal (.optimize (SimplexOptimizer. 1e-10 1e-10)
                           (into-array
                            OptimizationData
                            [(MaxEval. 100000)
                             (objective-function f)
                             GoalType/MAXIMIZE
                             (->> (repeat 0.0)
                                  (take m)
                                  (double-array)
                                  (InitialGuess.))
```

```
                               (->> (repeat 0.1)
                                    (take m)
                                    (double-array)
                                    (NelderMeadSimplex.))])))
            point (-> optimal .getPoint vec)
            value (-> optimal .getValue)]
        {:ar (take p point)
         :ma (drop p point)
         :ll value}))

(defn ex-9-31 []
  (->> (airline-passengers)
       (i/log)
       (difference)
       (difference 12)
       (arma-model 9 1)))
```

Our model is a large one with many parameters and so the optimization will take a while to converge. If you run the preceding example you should eventually see returned parameters similar to those shown next:

```
;; {:ar (-0.23769808471685377 -0.012617164166298971 ...),
;;  :ma (-0.14754455658280236),
;;  :ll 232.97813750669314}
```

These are the maximum likelihood estimates for our model. Also included in the response is the log-likelihood for the model with the maximum-likelihood parameters.

Identifying better models with Akaike Information Criterion

When evaluating multiple models, it might appear that the best model is the one with the greatest maximum likelihood estimate. After all, the estimate has determined that the model is the best candidate for generating the observed data. However, the maximum likelihood estimate takes no account of the complexity of the model and, in general, simpler models are to be preferred. Think back to the beginning of the chapter and our high-order polynomial model that had a high R^2 but provided no predictive power.

The **Akaike Information Criterion (AIC)** is a method for comparing models that rewarded goodness of fit, as assessed by the likelihood function, but includes a penalty that is a function of the number of parameters. This penalty discourages overfitting, since increasing the number of parameters to the model almost always improves the goodness of fit.

The AIC can be calculated from the following formula:

$$AIC = 2k - 2\log L$$

Here, k is the number of parameters to the model and L is the likelihood function. We can calculate the AIC in the following way in Clojure with the parameter counts p and q.

```
(defn aic [coefs p q ys]
  (- (* 2 (+ p q 1))
     (* 2 (log-likelihood coefs p q ys))))
```

If we were to produce multiple models and pick the best one, we would want to pick the one with the lowest AIC.

Time series forecasting

With the parameter estimates having been defined, we're finally in a position to use our model for forecasting. We've actually already written most of the code we need to do this: we have an `arma` function that's capable of generating an autoregressive moving-average series based on some seed data and the model parameters p and q. The seed data will be our measured values of y from the airline data, and the values of p and q will be the parameters that we calculated using the Nelder-Mead method.

Let's plug those numbers into our ARMA model and generate a sequence of predictions for y:

```
(defn ex-9-32 []
  (let [data (i/log (airline-passengers))
        diff-1  (difference 1 data)
        diff-12 (difference 12 diff-1)
        forecast (->> (arma (take 9 (reverse diff-12))
                         []
                         (:ar params)
                         (:ma params) 0)
                      (take 100)
                      (undifference 12 diff-1)
                      (undifference 1 data))]
    (->> (concat data forecast)
         (i/exp)
         (timeseries-plot))))
```

The preceding code generates the following chart:

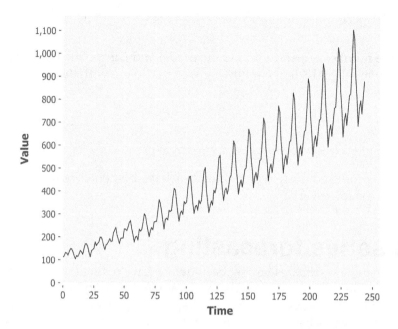

The line up to time slice 144 is the original series. The line subsequent to this point is our forecast series. The forecast looks a lot like we might have hoped: the exponentially increasing trend continues, as do the regular seasonal pattern of peaks and troughs.

In fact, the forecast is almost too regular. Unlike the series at points 1 to 144, our forecast contains no noise. Let's add some noise to make our forecast more realistic. To determine how much noise is justified, we could look to see what the error was in our past forecasting. To avoid our errors compounding, we should make predictions one time step ahead, and observe the difference between the prediction and the actual value.

Let's run our ARMA function with a sigma of 0.02:

```
(defn ex-9-33 []
  (let [data (i/log (airline-passengers))
        diff-1  (difference 1 data)
        diff-12 (difference 12 diff-1)
        forecast (->> (arma (take 9 (reverse diff-12))
                        []
                        (:ar params)
```

```
                (:ma params) 0.02)
                (take 10)
                (undifference 12 diff-1)
                (undifference 1 data))]
    (->> (concat data forecast)
        (i/exp)
        (timeseries-plot))))
```

The preceding code may generate a chart like the following:

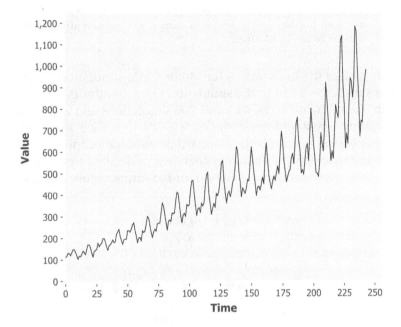

Now we get a sense of the volatility of the forecast. By running the simulation several times we can get a sense of the variety of different possible outcomes. What would be useful is if we could determine the confidence interval of our predictions: the upper and lower expectation of all future series, including noise.

Forecasting with Monte Carlo simulation

Although analytic methods do exist for calculating the expected future value of a time series, together with confidence intervals, we'll use this final section to arrive at these values through simulation instead. By studying the variation amongst many forecasts we can arrive at confidence intervals for our model predictions.

For example, if we run a very large number of simulations we can calculate the 95 percent confidence intervals on our future predictions based on the range within which values fall 95 percent of the time. This is the essence of the Monte Carlo simulation, which is a commonly used statistical tool for problems that are analytically intractable.

The Monte Carlo method was developed and used systematically during the Manhattan Project, the American World War II effort to develop nuclear weapons. John Von Neumann and Stanislaw Ulam suggested it as a means to investigate properties of neutron travel through radiation shielding and named the method after the Monte Carlo Casino in Monaco.

We've already laid all the foundations for Monte Carlo simulations of the time series forecasts. We simply need to run the simulation many hundreds of times and collect the results. In the following code, we run 1,000 simulations and gather the mean and standard deviation across all forecasts at each future time slice. By creating two new series (an upper bound that adds the standard deviation multiplied by 1.96 and a lower bound that subtracts the standard deviation multiplied by 1.96), we're able to visualize the 95 percent confidence interval for the future values of the series.

```
(defn ex-9-34 []
  (let [data (difference (i/log (airline-passengers)))
        init (take 12 (reverse data))
        forecasts (for [n (range 1000)]
                    (take 20
                          (arma init [0.0028 0.0028]
                                (:ar params1)
                                (:ma params1)
                                0.0449)))
        forecast-mean (map s/mean (i/trans forecasts))
        forecast-sd (-> (map s/sd (i/trans forecasts))
                        (i/div 2)
                        (i/mult 1.96))
        upper (->> (map + forecast-mean forecast-sd)
                   (concat data)
                   (undifference 0)
                   (i/exp))
        lower (->> (map - forecast-mean forecast-sd)
                   (concat data)
                   (undifference 0)
                   (i/exp))
        n (count upper)]
```

```
(-> (c/xy-plot    (range n) upper
                  :x-label "Time"
                  :y-label "Value"
                  :series-label "Upper Bound"
                  :legend true)
    (c/add-lines (range n) lower
                  :series-label "Lower Bound")
    (i/view))))
```

This generates the following chart:

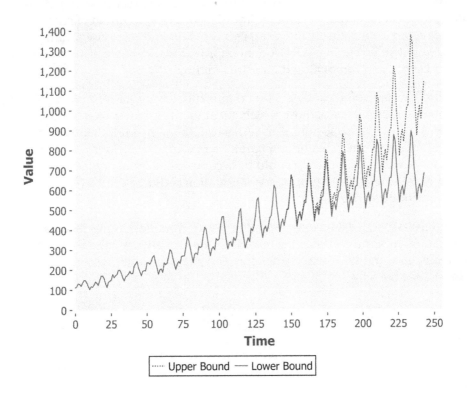

The upper and lower bounds provide the confidence intervals for our time series predictions into the future.

Summary

In this chapter, we've considered the task of analyzing discrete time series: sequential observations taken at fixed intervals in time. We've seen how the challenge of modeling such a series can be made easier by decomposing it into a set of components: a trend component, a seasonal component, and a cyclic component.

We've seen how ARMA models decompose a series further into autoregressive and moving-average components, each of which is in some way determined by past values of the series. This conception of a series is inherently recursive, and we've seen how Clojure's natural capabilities for defining recursive functions and lazy sequences lend themselves to the algorithmic generation of such series. By determining each value of the series as a function of the previous values, we implemented a recursive ARMA generator that was capable of simulating a measured series and forecasting it forwards in time.

We've also learned about expectation maximization: a way of reframing solutions to optimization problems as those which generate the greatest likelihood, given the data. And we've also seen how the Apache Commons Math library can be used to estimate the maximum likelihood parameters using the Nelder-Mead method. Finally, we saw how forecasting could be accomplished by playing the sequence forward in time, and how Monte Carlo simulation could be used to estimate the future error of the series.

In the final chapter, we'll turn our attention away from data analysis towards data visualization. In some respects, the most important challenge for data scientists is communication, and we'll see how Clojure can support us in presenting our data in the most effective way.

10
Visualization

"Numbers have an important story to tell. They rely on you to give them a clear and convincing voice."

- Stephen Few

Every chapter in this book has made use of visualization in some way, primarily using Incanter. Incanter is an effective tool to produce a wide variety of charts as we work, and these are often the ones we'll reach out for first while trying to understand a dataset. This initial phase is often called **exploratory data analysis** and, at this stage, we're interested in summarizing statistics such as the distribution of numerical data, the counts of the categorical data, and how the attributes in our data are correlated.

Having found a meaningful way to interpret data, we'll often want to communicate it to others. One of the most important tools for communication is visualization, and we may be required to convey subtle or complicated ideas to people without a strong analytical background. In this chapter, we'll use the library Quil—which grew out of software developed for visual artists—to produce attractive graphics that can help bring data to life. Visualization and communication design are large, rich fields that we will not cover in detail here. Instead, this chapter will offer two case studies showing how Clojure's data abstractions and Quil's drawing API can be used together for good effect.

We'll begin this chapter by coming full circle and returning to the data we used in *Chapter 1*, *Statistics*. We'll introduce Quil by demonstrating how to build a simple two-dimensional histogram from the Russian election data. Having covered the basics of drawing in Quil, we'll show how a few basic drawing instructions can combine to produce a compelling representation of the distribution of wealth in the United States.

Download the code and data

In this chapter, we'll return to the data we used in the very first chapter of this book: data from the 2011 Russian election. Back, in *Chapter 1, Statistics*, we used a scatter plot with transparency to visualize the relationship between voter turnout and the victor's percentage of the vote. In this chapter, we'll produce code to render the data as a two-dimensional histogram.

We'll also be making use of the data on the distribution of wealth in the United States. This data is so small that we won't have anything to download: we'll type the figures directly into the source code.

 The source code for this chapter is available at `https://github.com/clojuredatascience/ch10-visualization`.

The example code for this chapter contains a script to download the election data we used in *Chapter 1, Statistics*. Once you've downloaded the source code, you can execute the script by running the following command line from within the project root:

`script/download-data.sh`

If you downloaded the data for *Chapter 1, Statistics* previously, you can simply move the data files across into this chapter's data directory, if you prefer.

Exploratory data visualization

At the outset of any data science project, there is likely to be a period of iterative data exploration when you gain insight into the data. Throughout this book, Incanter has been our primary visualization tool. Although it includes a large number of charts there will be occasions when it won't contain the ideal chart for the data you seek to represent.

 Other Clojure libraries are stepping in to offer exploratory data visualization capabilities. For examples, see **clojurewerkz/envision** `https://github.com/clojurewerkz/envision` and Karsten Schmidt's **thi-ng/geom** at `https://github.com/thi-ng/geom/tree/master/geom-viz`.

For example, back in *Chapter 1, Statistics*, we used a scatter plot with alpha transparency to visualize the voter turnout proportion against the proportion of votes for the winner. This wasn't an ideal chart, because we were primarily interested in the density of points in a particular area. Alpha transparency helped reveal the structure of the data, but it wasn't an unambiguous representation. Some points were still too feint to be visible or so numerous that they appeared as one:

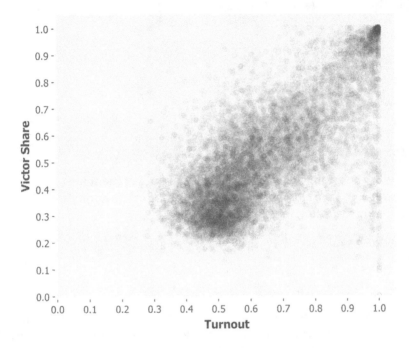

We could have solved these problems with a two-dimensional histogram. This type of plot uses color to communicate areas of high and low density over two dimensions. The chart is split into a grid with each cell of the grid signifying a range in both dimensions. The more the points fall into a cell of the grid, the greater is the density within the range.

Representing a two-dimensional histogram

A histogram is simply a representation of a continuous distribution into a series of bins. Histograms were introduced in *Chapter 1, Statistics* and, at the time, we wrote a binning function that would separate continuous data into discrete bins:

```
(defn bin [n-bins xs]
  (let [min-x    (apply min xs)
        range-x  (- (apply max xs) min-x)
        max-bin  (dec n-bins)
        bin-fn   (fn [x]
                   (-> (- x min-x)
                       (/ range-x)
                       (* n-bins)
                       (int)
                       (min max-bin)))]
    (map bin-fn xs)))
```

This code will take a range of continuous xs and bucket them into distinct groups based on the n-bins parameter. For example, binning the range between 0 and 19 into 5 bins yields the following sequence:

```
(defn ex-1-1 []
  (bin 5 (range 20)))

;;(0 0 0 0 1 1 1 1 2 2 2 2 3 3 3 3 4 4 4 4)
```

The bin function returns the bin index for each data point rather than the count, so we use Clojure's frequencies function to determine the count of the points falling into the bin:

```
(defn ex-1-2 []
  (frequencies (bin 5 (range 20))))

;;{0 4, 1 4, 2 4, 3 4, 4 4}
```

This is a reasonable representation of a one-dimensional histogram: as a map of the bins to be counted. To represent a two-dimensional histogram, we can simply perform the same calculation on both the *xs* and the *ys*. We map the vector function over the bin indices so that each point is converted into a representation of [x-bin y-bin]:

```
(defn histogram-2d [xsys n-bins]
  (-> (map vector
           (bin n-bins xs)
           (bin n-bins ys))
      (frequencies)))
```

This function returns a map keyed by a vector of two values. The frequencies function will now count all the points that share both an *x* and a *y* bin:

```
(defn ex-10-3 []
  (histogram-2d (range 20)
                (reverse (range 20)) 5))

;;{[0 4] 4, [1 3] 4, [2 2] 4, [3 1] 4, [4 0] 4}
```

We'll want to plot real data with our histogram, so let's load the Russian data from *Chapter 1, Statistics*. If you've downloaded the data into the sample code's data directory, you can run the following code:

```
(defn ex-10-4 []
  (let [data (load-data :ru-victors)]
    (histogram-2d (i/$ :turnout data)
                  (i/$ :victors-share data) 5)))

;; {[4 3] 6782, [2 2] 14680, [0 0] 3, [1 0] 61, [2 3] 2593,
;;  [3 3] 8171, [1 1] 2689, [3 4] 1188, [4 2] 3084, [3 0] 64,
;;  [4 1] 1131, [1 4] 13, [1 3] 105, [0 3] 6, [2 4] 193, [0 2] 10,
;;  [2 0] 496, [0 4] 1, [3 1] 3890, [2 1] 24302, [4 4] 10771,
;;  [1 2] 1170, [3 2] 13384, [0 1] 4, [4 0] 264}
```

We can see the huge range of values in the histogram bins: from just 1 in bin [0 4] to 24,302 in bin [2 1]. These counts will be the density values we plot on our histogram.

Using Quil for visualization

Quil (`https://github.com/quil/quil`) is a Clojure library that provides an enormous amount of flexibility to produce custom visualizations. It wraps Processing (`https://processing.org/`), a Java framework that's been actively developed for many years by visual artists and designers, which aims promote "software literacy in visual arts and visual literacy within technology".

Any visualization done with Quil involves creating a *sketch*. A sketch is processing's term for a running a program that consists of drawing instructions. Most API functions are available from the `quil.core` namespace. We'll include it in our code as q. Calling `q/sketch` without any arguments will cause an empty window to pop up (although it may be obscured by other windows).

Drawing to the sketch window

The default window size is 500px by 300px. We'd like our two-dimensional histogram to be square, so let's make the window 250px in both directions:

```
(q/sketch :size [250 250])
```

Since we have 5 bins for each of our two axes, it means that each bin will be represented by a square that is 50px wide and 50px high.

Quil provides the standard 2D shape primitives for drawing: points, lines, arcs, triangles, quadrilaterals, rectangles, and ellipses. To draw a rectangle, we call the `q/rect` function with the location specified as the x and y coordinates, as well as a width and height.

Let's draw a square at the origin, 50px across. There are a couple of ways to supply drawing instructions to Quil but, in this chapter, we'll pass what's known as a `setup` function. This is a function of no arguments that we pass to sketch. Our zero-argument function simply calls `rect` with a position [0, 0] and a width and height of 50:

```
(defn ex-10-5 []
  (let [setup #(q/rect 0 0 50 50)]
    (q/sketch :setup setup
              :size [250 250])))
```

The code generates the following image:

The rectangle may not be where you expected it to be, depending on your familiarity with computer graphics.

 Rectangles can also be drawn with rounded corners by passing a radius as the fifth argument. Different radii can be used for each corner by passing the values as arguments five to eight.

Before we proceed further, we need to understand Quil's coordinate system.

Quil's coordinate system

The coordinate system Quil uses is the same as processing and most other computer graphics programs. If you're unfamiliar with drawing, this may seem counter-intuitive that the origin is at the top left corner of the display. The y axis runs down the screen and the x axis runs to the right.

Clearly, this is not the direction of the *y* axis on most graphs, which means that the *y* coordinate will often need to be flipped while drawing.

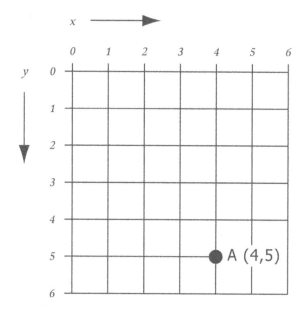

A common way to do this is to subtract the desired *y* value (as measured from the bottom of the sketch) from the height of the sketch. This transformation causes a *y* of zero to correspond to the bottom of the sketch. Greater values of *y* will correspond to the values higher up the sketch.

Plotting the grid

Let's put this into practice with a simple grid. The following function accepts a number of bins, n-bins, and a size parameter expressed as a vector of [width height]:

```
defn draw-grid [{:keys [n-bins size]}]
  (let [[width height] size
        x-scale (/ width n-bins)
        y-scale (/ height n-bins)
        setup (fn []
                (doseq [x (range n-bins)
                        y (range n-bins)
                        :let [x-pos (* x x-scale)
                              y-pos (- height
                                       (* (inc y) y-scale))]]
                  (q/rect x-pos y-pos x-scale y-scale)))]
    (q/sketch :setup setup :size size)))
```

From this, we can calculate `x-scale` and `y-scale`, a factor that enables us to convert bin index to pixel offset in each of the x and the y dimensions. These are used by our `setup` function that loops over both the x and the y bins, placing a rectangle for each bin.

 Notice how we're executing the loop inside `doseq`. Our drawing instructions are executed as a side effect. If we don't do this, Clojure's lazy evaluation would cause nothing to be drawn.

The previous code generates the following graphic:

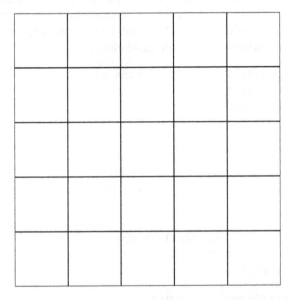

Having defined the earlier function, we've almost created a histogram. We just need to color each square in the grid with a color that represents an appropriate value for each bin in the histogram. To achieve this, we'll need two more functions: one to fetch the value from the data corresponding to the bin and the other to interpret these values as a color.

Specifying the fill color

Filling colors in Quil is achieved with the q/fill function. Any fill we specify will continue to be used until we specify a new fill.

 Many functions in Quil affect the current drawing context and are *stateful*. For example, when we specify a fill value, it will be used for all subsequent drawing instructions until the fill is altered. Other examples are fill, stroke, scale, and font.

The following code is an adapted version of our draw-grid function. The addition to draw-filled-grid is fill-fn: some way of coloring the rectangle at a point in the grid. The fill-fn function should be a function of two arguments, the x and y indices of the bin. It should return a representation that Quil can use as a fill:

```
(defn draw-filled-grid [{:keys [n-bins size fill-fn]}]
  (let [[width height] size
        x-scale (/ width n-bins)
        y-scale (/ height n-bins)
        setup (fn []
                (doseq [x (range n-bins)
                        y (range n-bins)
                        :let [x-pos (* x x-scale)
                              y-pos (- height
                                       (* (inc y) y-scale))]]
                  (q/fill (fill-fn x y))
                  (q/rect x-pos y-pos x-scale y-scale)))]
    (q/sketch :setup setup :size size)))
```

Quil's fill function accepts multiple arities:

- **One argument**: The RGB value (either as a number or the q/color representation)
- **Two arguments**: The RGB, as with one argument, plus an alpha transparency
- **Three arguments**: The red, green, and blue components of the color as numbers between 0 and 255 inclusive
- **Four arguments**: The red, green, blue, and alpha components as numbers

We'll see how to use the color representations shortly but, for now, we'll represent colors with a simple numeric representation: as a number between 0 and 255. When the same number is used for red, green, and blue (or when fill is called with one or two arguments), we get a gray color. 0 corresponds to black and 255 corresponds to white.

If we divide the frequency of the value in each bin in the histogram by the maximum value, we'll get a number between 0 and 1.0. Multiplying by 255 will yield a value that Quil will convert into a gray color for us. We do this in the following `fill-fn` implementation, passing it to the `draw-filled-grid` function that we defined earlier:

```
(defn ex-10-6 []
  (let [data (load-data :ru-victors)
        n-bins 5
        hist (histogram-2d (i/$ :turnout data)
                           (i/$ :victors-share data)
                           n-bins)
        max-val (apply max (vals hist))
        fill-fn (fn [x y]
                  (-> (get hist [x y] 0)
                      (/ max-val)
                      (* 255)))]
    (draw-filled-grid {:n-bins n-bins
                       :size [250 250]
                       :fill-fn fill-fn})))
```

The previous code generates the following graphic:

The chart is doing what we want, but it's a very crude representation of our data. Let's increase the number of bins to increase the resolution of our histogram:

```
(defn ex-10-7 []
  (let [data (load-data :ru-victors)
        n-bins 25
        hist (histogram-2d (i/$ :turnout data)
                           (i/$ :victors-share data)
                           n-bins)
        max-val (apply max (vals hist))
        fill-fn (fn [x y]
                  (-> (get hist [x y] 0)
                      (/ max-val)
                      (* 255)))]
    (draw-filled-grid {:n-bins n-bins
                       :size [250 250]
                       :fill-fn fill-fn})))
```

This code generates the following graphic:

With 25 rectangles along each of the x and the y axes, we have a finer-grained picture of the structure of the data. However, a side effect is that it's become hard to discern detail in the histogram, because of how dim most of the cells are. Part of the problem is that the top right corner has such a high value that even the central area (previously the brightest) is now not much more than a gray smudge.

There are two solutions to this problem:

- Mitigate the effect of the outlier by plotting the z-score instead of the actual value
- Diversify the range of visual queues by using a greater range of colors

We'll discover how to convert values into a full spectrum of colors in the next section, but first, let's convert the histogram value to a z-score. Plotting z-scores is a distribution-aware way of coloring the chart that will go a long way toward diminishing the effect of the extreme outlier in the top right corner. With a z-score, we'll be plotting the number of standard deviations away from the mean for each cell.

To accomplish this, we need to know two things: the mean and the standard deviation of the frequencies in the histogram:

```
(defn ex-10-8 []
  (let [data (load-data :ru-victors)
        n-bins 25
        hist (histogram-2d (i/$ :turnout data)
                           (i/$ :victors-share data)
                           n-bins)
        mean (s/mean (vals hist))
        sd   (s/sd   (vals hist))
        fill-fn (fn [x y]
                   (-> (get hist [x y] 0)
                       (- mean)
                       (/ sd)
                       (q/map-range -1 3 0 255)))]
    (draw-filled-grid {:n-bins n-bins
                       :size [250 250]
                       :fill-fn fill-fn})))
```

The preceding code subtracts the mean from each value in the histogram and divides it by the mean. This will yield a value with a mean of zero. 1 will represent one standard deviation from the mean, 2 will represent two standard deviations from the mean, and so on.

Quil exposes a useful `map-range` function that will take one range of values and map it onto another range of values. For example, we could take the desired range of standard deviations (-1 to 3 in the earlier example) and map them onto the range 0 and 255. This would correspond to four standard deviations of the distribution being represented as the full range of gray from black to white. Any data exceeding this range would simply be clipped.

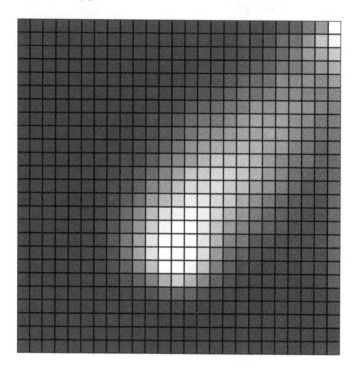

The result is a much more striking representation of the data in grayscale. The use of z-scores has brought more detail out in the main body of the histogram and we can perceive more of the variation in the tail.

However, the histogram is still not quite as clear as it could be, as distinguishing between the different shades of gray can be challenging. Where cells aren't adjacent to each other, it can be hard to determine whether they share the same value.

We can increase the range open to us by making use of color to represent each cell. This makes the histogram more like a heat map: "cooler" colors such as blue and green represent low values, while "hotter" colors such as orange and red represent the most dense regions of the heatmap.

Color and fill

To create a heat map version of our two-dimensional histogram, we'll have to take our *z*-score and find some way of mapping it to a color value. Rather than showing a discrete palette of colors, say 5, our heat map should have a smooth palette containing all the colors in the spectrum.

 For those reading the print book or in black and white, you can download color images from Packt Publishing's website https://www.packtpub.com/sites/default/files/downloads/Clojure_for_Data_Science_ColorImages.pdf.

This is exactly what the Quil function q/lerp-color does. Given two colors and a ratio between zero and one, lerp-color will return a new color that interpolates between them. An amount of zero will return the first color and one the second, while 0.5 will return a color halfway between the two:

```
(defn z-score->heat [z-score]
  (let [colors [(q/color 0 0 255)      ;; Blue
                (q/color 0 255 255)  ;; Turquoise
                (q/color 0 255 0)      ;; Green
                (q/color 255 255 0)  ;; Yellow
                (q/color 255 0 0)]   ;; Red
        offset  (-> (q/map-range z-score -1 3 0 3.999)
                    (max 0)
                    (min 3.999))]
    (q/lerp-color (nth colors offset)
                  (nth colors (inc offset))
                  (rem offset 1)))))
```

This code makes use of an array of colors in the order of the spectrum. We use q/map-range to determine which two colors we will interpolate between and call q/lerp-color with the floating-point portion of the range.

We've already implemented a draw-filled-grid function that accepts fill-fn to determine which color should be used to fill the grid. Let's pass our z-score->heat function to it now:

```
(defn ex-10-9 []
  (let [data (load-data :ru-victors)
        n-bins 25
        hist (histogram-2d (i/$ :turnout data)
                           (i/$ :victors-share data)
                           n-bins)
```

```
mean (s/mean (vals hist))
sd   (s/sd   (vals hist))
fill-fn (fn [x y]
            (-> (get hist [x y] 0)
                (- mean)
                (/ sd)
                (z-score->heat)))]
    (draw-filled-grid {:n-bins n-bins
                       :size [250 250]
                       :fill-fn fill-fn})))
```

This code generates the following graphic:

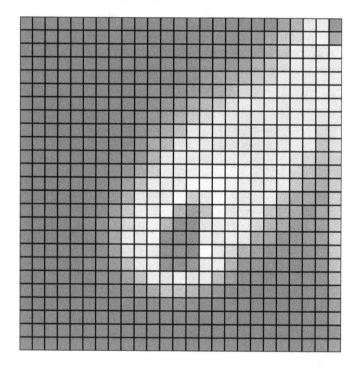

The heat map has exposed even more of the internal structure of the data. In particular, while the strong diagonal shape of the data is still evident, we can now see more of the variation within it. Details that were previously hard to determine (either because the region was too dense or too sparse) have become more apparent.

Outputting an image file

Now that we're happy with the histogram, we want to output a high-quality version. By adding a call to q/save within the setup function, passing a filename, Quil will output to a file as well as the screen. The format of the image created will depend on the filename suffix: .tif for TIFF files, .jpg for JPEG files, .png for PNG files, and .tga for TARGA files:

```
(defn draw-filled-grid [{:keys [n-bins size fill-fn]}]
  (let [[width height] size
        x-scale (/ width n-bins)
        y-scale (/ height n-bins)
        setup (fn []
                (doseq [x (range n-bins)
                        y (range n-bins)
                        :let [x-pos (* x x-scale)
                              y-pos (- height
                                       (* (inc y) y-scale))]]
                  (q/fill (fill-fn x y))
                  (q/rect x-pos y-pos x-scale y-scale))
                (q/save "heatmap.png"))]
    (q/sketch :setup setup :size size)))
```

We're also able to output to PDF, as we'll show with the next visualization.

Visualization for communication

In the course of our work as data scientists, we may find ourselves needing to communicate with a wide variety of people. Our close colleagues and managers may be able to read and interpret our Incanter charts, but they're unlikely to impress the CEO. We may also have a role that requires us to communicate with the general public.

In either case, we should focus on making visualizations that are simple and powerful, but which don't sacrifice the integrity of the data. A lack of statistical training is no barrier to being able to understand subtle and nuanced arguments and we should respect our audience's intelligence. The challenge for us as data scientists is to find a representation that conveys the message effectively to them.

For the remainder of this chapter, we'll work on a visualization that aims to communicate a more complex set of data in a succinct and faithful way.

The visualization we're going to create is a version of one of the graphs presented in the **Wealth Inequality in America** video online at `https://www.youtube.com/watch?v=QPKKQnijnsM`. Produced by anonymous film maker Politizane, the powerful video has gathered more than 16 million hits on YouTube.

As is often the case with graphical representations like these, our data will come from several different sources.

Visualizing wealth distribution

The first dataset we'll make use of is from an article by G. William Domhoff, research professor in psychology and sociology at the University of California, Santa Cruz. The numbers we will quote next are from an article entitled **Wealth, Income, and Power** at `http://www2.ucsc.edu/whorulesamerica/power/wealth.html`.

Although the article is well worth reading in its entirety, a particularly striking graphic is a pie chart that shows the financial net worth breakdown of people in the U.S. in 2010:

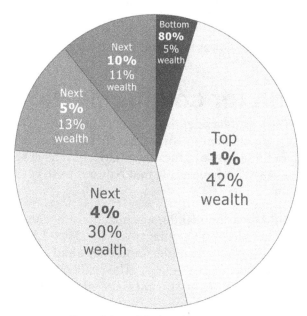

Financial wealth distribution 2010

The pie chart is striking for several reasons. Firstly, the concept that over 40 percent of the financial wealth is owned by such a small percentage is hard to comprehend. Secondly, each slice of the pie represents not just the vastly different quantities of wealth, but vastly different quantities of people, too: from 1 percent of the population to 80 percent of the population. Pie charts are notoriously difficult to read at the best of times, so this chart is doubly challenging.

 Pie charts are generally not a good way to represent data, even where the totals do conceptually represent parts of the whole. Author and programmer Steve Fenton has documented many of the reasons and provided appropriate alternatives at `https://www.stevefenton.co.uk/2009/04/pie-charts-are-bad/`.

Let's see how we could go about reinterpreting this data to make it more comprehensible. As a first step, let's extract the numbers we'll be working with that are presented in the following table:

Percentile	Total financial wealth, 2010
0-79	5%
80-89	11%
90-95	13%
96-99	30%
100	42%

A small improvement over the pie chart would be to represent the same data as a bar chart. While people generally struggle to interpret the relative sizes of the pie chart segments successfully, bar charts present no such problem. The next example simply creates a bar chart out of the earlier numbers:

```
(defn ex-10-10 []
  (let [categories ["0-79" "80-89" "90-95" "96-99" "100"]
        percentage [5      11      13      30      42   ]]
    (-> (c/bar-chart categories percentage
                     :x-label "Category"
                     :y-label "% Financial Wealth")
        (i/view))))
```

This will return the following chart:

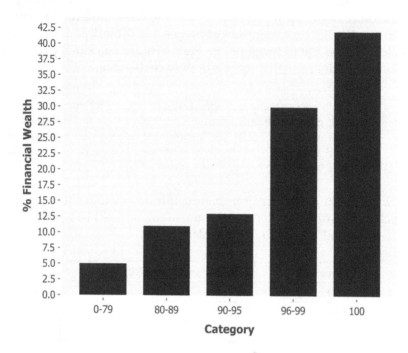

This is an improvement on the pie chart in the respect that it's easier to compare the relative sizes of the categories. A significant problem remains though: the number of people represented by each category are so vastly different. The bar to the left represents 80 percent of the population, while the bar to the right represents 1 percent of the population.

If we wanted to make this data more comprehensible, we could divide up the total into 100 equal units, each representing one percentile of the population. The width of each bar could be adjusted according to the number of percentiles it represents while preserving its area. Since each percentile unit represents an equal number of people, the resulting chart would allow us to more easily make comparisons across groups.

One way we could achieve this is by returning a sequence of 100 elements, one for each percentile of the population. The value of each element in the sequence would be the proportion of overall wealth accounted for by the percentile. We already know that the top 1 percent owns 42 percent of overall wealth, but the other groups would get a value adjusted downwards for the number of percentiles they span:

```
(def wealth-distribution
  (concat (repeat 80 (/ 5  80))
          (repeat 10 (/ 11 10))
```

```
              (repeat 5  (/ 13 5))
              (repeat 4  (/ 30 4))
              (repeat 1  (/ 42 1))))

    (defn ex-10-11 []
      (let [categories (range (count wealth-distribution))]
        (-> (c/bar-chart categories wealth-distribution
                         :x-label "Percentile"
                         :y-label "% Financial Wealth")
            (i/view))))
```

This example generates the following bar chart:

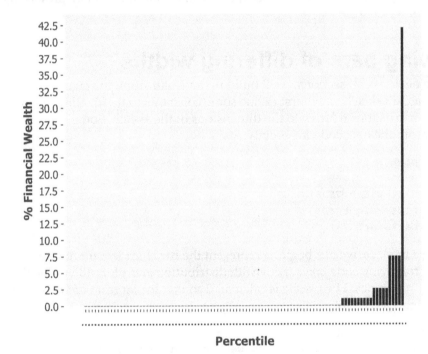

By applying a simple transformation, we're able to gain a much better understanding of the true distribution. Each bar now represents an equal proportion of the population and the area of each bar represents the proportion of wealth owned by the percentile.

Bringing data to life with Quil

The transformation in the previous section results in a chart that shows the difference between the extreme ends of the scale almost too starkly: it's hard to interpret anything but the largest bars. One solution would be to display the numbers on a log scale or a log-log scale as we did elsewhere in the book. If the audience for this chart are statistically literate, this might be the most appropriate thing to do, but let's assume that the intended audience for our visualization is the general public.

The problem with the chart presented earlier is that the rightmost bar is so large that it overwhelms all the other bars. 80 percent of the area is represented by nothing more than a few pixels. In the next section, we'll make use of Quil to produce a visualization that makes better use of space while it simultaneously preserving the integrity of the chart.

Drawing bars of differing widths

Over the next several sections, we'll build up a visualization in stages. Since we'll be drawing a Quil sketch, we'll first define some constants that will allow us to produce drawing instructions relative to the dimensions of the sketch. Some constants are omitted from the next code for brevity:

```
(def plot-x 56)
(def plot-y 60)
(def plot-width 757)
(def plot-height 400)
(def bar-width 7)
```

With these in place, we can begin to represent the bar chart in a more comprehensible way. The following code takes the wealth distribution and plots all but the final bar as a series of rectangles. The y-scale is calculated so that the largest bar we will draw will fill the height of the plot:

```
(defn draw-bars []
  (let [pc99    (vec (butlast wealth-distribution))
        pc1     (last wealth-distribution)
        y-max   (apply max pc99)
        y-scale (fn [x] (* (/ x y-max) plot-height))
        offset  (fn [i] (* (quot i 10) 7))]
    (dotimes [i 99] ;; Draw the 99%
      (let [bar-height (y-scale (nth pc99 i))]
        (q/rect (+ plot-x (* i bar-width) (offset i))
                (+ plot-y (- plot-height bar-height))
                bar-width bar-height)))
    (let [n-bars 5  ;; Draw the 1%
```

```
      bar-height (y-scale (/ pc1 n-bars))]
  (q/rect (+ plot-x (* 100 bar-width) (offset 100))
          (+ plot-y (- plot-height bar-height))
          (* bar-width n-bars) bar-height)))) 
```

The bars we've drawn so far represent the 99 percent. The final bar will represent the final 1 percent of the population. So it fits the vertical scale we've devised without disappearing off the top of the sketch, we will make the bar correspondingly wider while preserving its area. As a result, the bar is 5 times shorter — but also 5 times wider — than the others:

```
(defn ex-10-12 []
  (let [size [960 540]]
    (q/sketch :size size
              :setup draw-bars)))
```

The example outputs the following graphic:

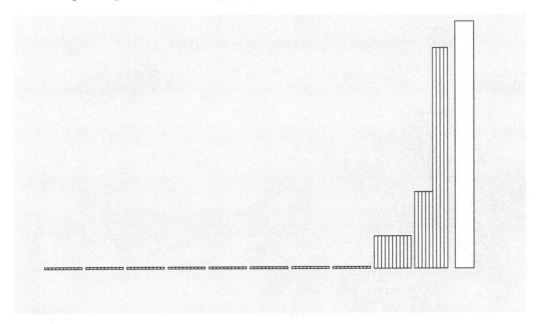

Already, we can see the relationship between largest bars more clearly, but it's not clearly apparent yet that it's a chart. In the next section, we'll add text to identify the subject of the chart and the range of the axes.

Adding a title and axis labels

One of the convenient aspects of specialized visualization tools such as Incanter is that the axes can be automatically generated for our charts. Quil provides no help for us here, but since the bar widths are known, it's not terribly hard for us to achieve. In the following code, we'll make use of the text, text-align, text-size functions to write text to our visualization:

```
(defn group-offset [i]
  (* (quot i 10) 7))

(defn draw-axis-labels []
  (q/fill 0)
  (q/text-align :left)
  (q/text-size 12)
  (doseq [pc (range 0 (inc 100) 10)
          :let [offset (group-offset pc)
                x      (* pc bar-width)]]
    (q/text (str pc "%") (+ plot-x x offset) label-y))
  (q/text "\"The 1%\"" pc1-label-x  pc1-label-y))
```

What we lose by using a nonspecialist charting library we gain in terms of flexibility. Next, we'll write a function to produce letterpress-style embossing on the text:

```
(defn emboss-text [text x y]
  (q/fill 255)
  (q/text text x y)
  (q/fill 100)
  (q/text text x (- y 2)))

(defn draw-title []
  (q/text-size 35)
  (q/text-leading 35)
  (q/text-align :center :top)
  (emboss-text "ACTUAL DISTRIBUTION\nOF WEALTH IN THE US"
               title-x title-y))
```

We use the emboss-text function to draw a large title at the center of our chart. Notice how we also specify the alignment of the text with the positions being measured optionally from the top, bottom, center, left, or right of the text:

```
(defn ex-10-13 []
  (let [size [960 540]]
    (q/sketch :size size
              :setup #((draw-bars)
                       (draw-axis-labels)
        (draw-title))))))
```

The earlier example generates the following graphic:

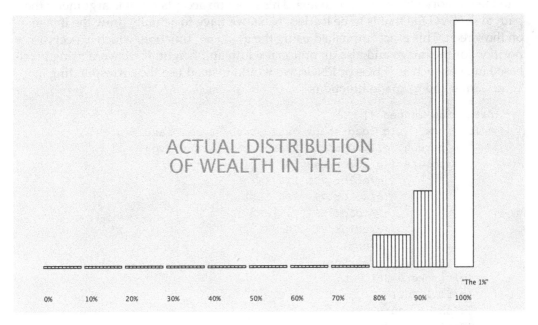

ACTUAL DISTRIBUTION
OF WEALTH IN THE US

This chart, which is a mix of bar heights and areas, and custom text visualization would be very difficult to achieve in a standard charting application. Using Quil, we have a toolbox that allows us to freely mix graphics and data with ease.

Improving the clarity with illustrations

We're getting somewhere with our chart, but it's very spare at the moment. One way to add more visual interest would be with images. In the resources directory of the example project, are two SVG image files. One is a person icon and the other is a map of the United States sourced from Wikipedia.

 Wikipedia contains a wide variety of SVG maps issued under a flexible creative commons license. For example, maps of the United States at `https://commons.wikimedia.org/wiki/Category:SVG_maps_of_the_United_States`.

The map we're using in this chapter is available at `https://commons.wikimedia.org/wiki/File:Blank_US_Map,_Mainland_with_no_States.svg` and was made available by Lokal_Profil under a CC-BY-SA-2.5 license.

Using SVG images in Quil is a two-step process. First, we have to load the image into the memory using `q/load-shape`. This function accepts a single argument: the path to the SVG file that is to be loaded. Next, we have to actually draw the image on the screen. This is accomplished using the `q/shape` function, which expects a *x*, *y* position for the image and also an optional width and height. If we were using pixel-based images such as JPEGs or PNGs, we would instead use the corresponding `q/load-image` and `q/image` functions:

```
(defn draw-shapes []
  (let [usa    (q/load-shape "resources/us-mainland.svg")
        person (q/load-shape "resources/person.svg")
        colors [(q/color 243 195 73)
                (q/color 231 119 46)
                (q/color 77  180 180)
                (q/color 231 74  69)
                (q/color 61  76  83)]]
    (.disableStyle usa)
    (.disableStyle person)
    (q/stroke 0 50)
    (q/fill 200)
    (q/shape usa 0 0)
    (dotimes [n 99]
      (let [quintile (quot n 20)
            x (-> (* n bar-width)
                  (+ plot-x)
                  (+ (group-offset n)))]
        (q/fill (nth colors quintile))
        (q/shape person x icons-y icon-width icon-height)))
    (q/shape person
             (+ plot-x (* 100 bar-width) (group-offset 100))
             icons-y icon-width icon-height)))
```

In this code, we called `.disableStyle` on both the `usa` and the `person` shapes. This is because SVG files may contain embedded style such as fill color, stroke color, or border width information that will affect the way Quil draws the shape. We'd like complete control over our representation, so we choose to disable all the styles.

Also, note that we're loading the person shape once and drawing it many times with `dotimes`. We are setting the color based on `quintile` in which the user falls:

```
(defn ex-10-14 []
  (let [size [960 540]]
    (q/sketch :size size
```

```
:setup #((draw-shapes)
         (draw-bars)
         (draw-axis-labels)
         (draw-title)))))
```

The result is shown in the next image:

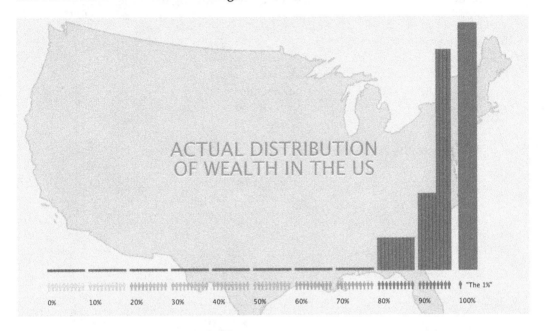

The graphic is beginning to look like one we could show people without blushing. The people icons help communicate the idea that each bar represents a percentile of the population. The bars are not very attractive yet. Since each bar represents the wealth of each person, let's represent each bar as a pile of bank notes. While this might appear to be an overly literal interpretation, it would actually make it clearer that the 1 percent bar is actually 5 times as wide as everyone else's.

Adding text to the bars

By now, it should be no surprise that we can draw the banknotes as a series of rectangles:

```
(defn banknotes [x y width height]
  (q/no-stroke)
  (q/fill 80 127 64)
  (doseq [y (range (* 3 (quot y 3)) (+ y height) 3)
          x (range x (+ x width) 7)]
    (q/rect x y 6 2)))
```

The only slight complexity in the previous code is the need to adjust the starting y position as an even multiple of 3. This will ensure that all the banknotes meet the x axis after an even number of multiples, irrespective of the height of the bar on the y axis. This is a side-effect of drawing the bars from top to bottom, rather than vice versa.

We'll add the earlier function to our sketch in the following example:

```
(defn ex-10-15 []
  (let [size [960 540]]
    (q/sketch :size size
              :setup #((draw-shapes)
                       (draw-banknotes)
                       (draw-axis-labels)
                       (draw-title)))))
```

This will generates the following chart:

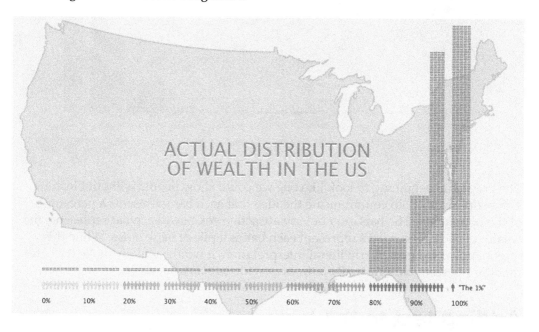

This is now a reasonably complete chart representing the actual distribution of wealth in the United States. One of the strengths of the original YouTube video link provided earlier is that it contrasts the actual distribution with several other distributions: the distribution of wealth people expected and the distribution of wealth they would prefer.

Incorporating additional data

Michael Norton, a Harvard Business Professor, and Dan Ariely, a behavioral economist performed a study on more than 5,000 Americans to assess their perception of wealth distribution. When they were shown a variety of examples on wealth distribution and asked to identify which one was sourced from the United States, most chose a distribution much more balanced than it actually was. When asked to choose their ideal distribution of wealth, 92 percent picked one that was even more equitable.

The following graphic shows the results of this study:

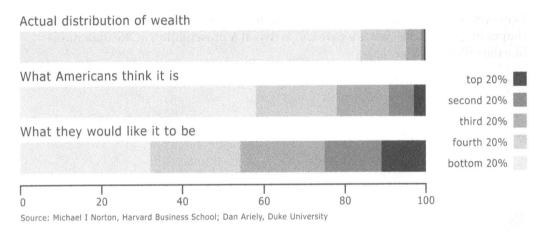

Source: Michael I Norton, Harvard Business School; Dan Ariely, Duke University

The preceding graphic was published by Mother Jones on `http://www.motherjones.com/politics/2011/02/income-inequality-in-america-chart-graph` based on the data sourced form `http://www.people.hbs.edu/mnorton/norton%20ariely%20in%20press.pdf`.

The previous chart does a good job of showing the relative differences between people's perceptions and reality for each of the 5 quintiles. We'll be converting this data into an alternative representation so, like before, we can convert the data into a table representation.

Reading off the earlier chart and with reference to the linked paper, I've arrived at the following approximate breakdown by quintile:

Quintile	Ideal %	Expected %	Actual %
100th	32.0%	58.5%	84.5%
80th	22.0%	20.0%	11.5%
60th	21.5%	12.0%	3.7%

Quintile	Ideal %	Expected %	Actual %
40th	14.0%	6.5%	0.2%
20th	10.5%	3.0%	0.1%

Let's take the *ideal* and *expected* distributions and find a way to plot them on our existing wealth distribution chart. Our bar chart already represents the relative wealth of different percentiles as an area. In order to make the two datasets comparable, we should also do the same with this data. The previous table assisted us by already representing the data as five equally sized groups, so we don't need to apply a transformation like we did with the data sourced from the pie chart.

However, let's use this as an opportunity to learn more about drawing complex shapes in Quil and see whether we can arrive at a presentation of the data more like the following diagram:

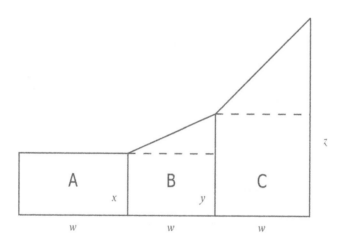

The table provides the relative areas that we want to represent by the shapes labeled **A**, **B**, and **C**. In order to draw the earlier shapes, we'll have to calculate the heights x, y, and z. These will give us the coordinates that we can plot on our chart.

The width of the areas **A**, **B**, and **C** is **w**. Therefore, the product of **x** and **w** will equal the area of **A**:

$$xw = A$$

$$x = \frac{A}{w}$$

It follows that the height of x is simply the area of A divided by w. Y is a little more complicated, but not much. The area of the triangular component of B is equal to:

$$B - xw$$

therefore:

$$y = x + \left(\frac{2(B - xw)}{w} \right)$$

We can calculate z in the same way:

$$z = y + \left(\frac{2(C - yw)}{w} \right)$$

Expanding our definitions gives the following equation for z:

$$z = \frac{A}{w} + \left(\frac{2(B - xw)}{w} \right) + \left(\frac{2(C - yw)}{w} \right)$$

If we assume that w is 1 (all our quintiles are of a constant width), then we arrive at the following equations and so on for any number of sections:

$$x = A$$

$$y = A + 2(B - A)$$

$$z = A + 2(B - A) + 2(C - (A + 2(B - A)))$$

This can be expressed as a simple recursive function. The first of our proportions will be assigned the value x. Subsequent values can be calculated from it as follows:

```
(defn area-points [proportions]
  (let [f (fn [prev area]
            (-> (- area prev)
                (* 2)
                (+ prev)))
        sum (reduce + proportions)]
    (->> (reductions f (first proportions) proportions)
         (map #(/ % sum)))))
```

The `reductions` function behaves exactly like `reduce`, but preserves the intermediate steps of our calculation. Rather than a single value, we'll get back a sequence of values that correspond to the (proportional) heights of our y-coordinates.

Drawing complex shapes

The `area-points` function defined in the previous section will provide a series of points for us to plot. However, we haven't yet covered the functions in Quil that will allow us to plot them. To draw lines, we could use the `q/line` function. The line function will accept a start and an end coordinate and draw a straight line between them. We would be able to construct an area graph this way, but it would have no fill. Lines simply describe outlines; we are not able to use them to construct colored shapes like we did with `q/rect` while making a histogram. To give our shapes a fill color, we need to build them up one vertex at a time.

To build arbitrarily complex shapes with Quil, we first call q/begin-shape. This is a stateful function that lets Quil know that we want to start building up a series of vertices. Subsequent calls to q/vertex will be associated with the shape that we're constructing. Finally, a call to q/end-shape will complete the shape. We'll draw it with the stroke and fill the styles specified in the current drawing context.

Let's see how it works by drawing some test shapes using the area-points function defined in the previous section:

```
(defn plot-area [proportions px py width height]
  (let [ys       (area-points proportions)
        points   (map vector (range) ys)
        x-scale  (/ width (dec (count ys)))
        y-scale  (/ height (apply max ys))]
    (q/stroke 0)
    (q/fill 200)
    (q/begin-shape)
    (doseq [[x y] points]
      (q/vertex (+ px (* x x-scale))
                (- py (* y y-scale))))
    (q/end-shape)))


(defn ex-10-16 []
  (let [expected [3 6.5 12 20 58.5]
        width   640
        height  480
        setup (fn []
                (q/background 255)
                (plot-area expected 0 height width height))]
    (q/sketch :setup setup :size [width height])))
```

This example plots the `[3 6.5 12 20 58.5]` series using the area-points function defined previously. This is the series of percentage values listed in the data table for the `expected` distribution of wealth in the United States. The `plot-area` function calls `begin-shape`, iterates over the sequence of *ys* returned by `area-points`, and calls `end-shape`. The result is as follows:

This isn't quite what we want. Although we're asking to fill the shape, we're not describing the full shape to be filled. Quil doesn't know how we want to close off the shape, so it's simply drawing an edge from the last point back to the first, cutting across the diagonal of our chart. Fortunately, the problem can be easily resolved by ensuring there are points at both the bottom corners of the diagram:

```
(defn plot-full-area [proportions px py width height]
  (let [ys       (area-points proportions)
        points   (map vector (range) ys)
        x-scale  (/ width (dec (count ys)))
        y-scale  (/ height (apply max ys))]
    (q/stroke 0)
    (q/fill 200)
    (q/begin-shape)
    (q/vertex 0 height)
    (doseq [[x y] points]
      (q/vertex (+ px (* x x-scale))
```

```
                (- py (* y y-scale)))))
      (q/vertex width height)
      (q/end-shape)))

(defn ex-10-17 []
  (let [expected [3 6.5 12 20 58.5]
        width  640
        height 480
        setup (fn []
                (q/background 255)
                (plot-full-area expected 0 height width height))]
    (q/sketch :setup setup :size [width height])))
```

The `plot-full-area` function adds an extra call to `vertex` before and after iterating over the sequence of *ys*. The points specified ensure that the shape is fully described before the call to `end-shape`. The result is shown in the following image:

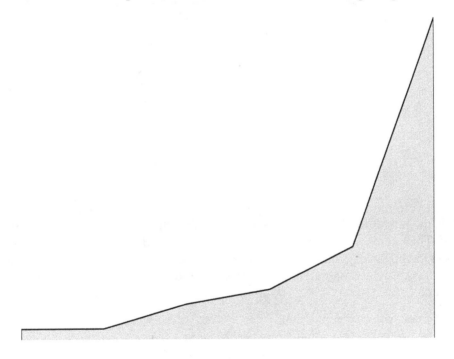

This is better, and it's starting to look like an area plot. In the next section, we'll cover how to describe more complex shapes using curves. Although curves aren't required for our area plot, it will help make the results a little more attractive.

Drawing curves

The area plot is starting to look good, but we could remove those sharp corners by making use of Quil's spline curves. Rather than building up the shape by adding vertices, we could call q/curve-vertex to smoothen out the joins between the edges.

The q/curve-vertex function implements a method of curve drawing known as Catmull-Rom splines. To draw a curve, we must specify at least four vertices: the first and last will be treated as the control points and the curve will be drawn between the middle two.

We visualize how Catmull-Rom splines work in the following diagram, which shows the path specified by points *a*, *b*, *c*, and *d*:

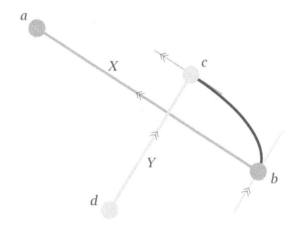

The tangent to the curve at point **c** is parallel to **X**: the line described between points **a** and **b**; the tangent to the curve at **b** is parallel to **Y**: the line described by points **c** and **d**. Thus, to draw a curve, we'll need ensure we add these additional control points at the beginning and the end of our line. Each control point is added with curve-vertex, which we call once before we iterate over our points and then again at the end:

```
(defn smooth-curve [xs ys]
  (let [points (map vector xs ys)]
    (apply q/curve-vertex (first points))
    (doseq [point points]
      (apply q/curve-vertex point))
    (apply q/curve-vertex (last points))))
```

Now that we've defined a `smooth-curve` function, we'll use it in the following two functions, `smooth-stroke` and `smooth-area`:

```
(defn smooth-stroke [xs ys]
  (q/begin-shape)
  (q/vertex (first xs) (first ys))
  (smooth-curve (rest xs) (rest ys))
  (q/end-shape))

(defn smooth-area [xs ys]
  (q/begin-shape)
  (q/vertex (first xs) (first ys))
  (smooth-curve (rest xs) (rest ys))
  (q/vertex (last xs) (first ys))
  (q/end-shape))
```

The `smooth-stroke` function will draw the shape defined by the *xs* and *ys* by creating vertices for each of them. The `smooth-area` function extends this by closing off the shape and avoiding the situation we saw previously with a fill that crosses the shape diagonally. Bringing the two functions together is `plot-curve`, a function that accepts the *xs* and *ys* to be plotted, plus a fill color, stroke color, and stroke weight to use:

```
(defn plot-curve [xs ys fill-color
                   stroke-color stroke-weight]
  (let [points (map vector xs ys)]
    (q/no-stroke)
    (q/fill fill-color)
    (smooth-area xs ys)
    (q/no-fill)
    (q/stroke stroke-color)
    (q/stroke-weight stroke-weight)
    (smooth-stroke xs ys)))
```

Let's call the `plot-curve` function on the same sequence of expected values we plotted earlier, and compare the difference:

```
(defn plot-smooth-area [proportions px py width height]
  (let [ys      (cons 0 (area-points proportions))
        points  (map vector (range) ys)
        x-scale (/ width (dec (count ys)))
        y-scale (/ height (apply max ys) -1)]
    (plot-curve (map (point->px px x-scale) (range (count ys)))
                (map (point->px py y-scale) ys)
                (q/color 200)
```

```
                    (q/color 0) 2)))

(defn ex-10-18 []
  (let [expected [3 6.5 12 20 58.5]
        width  640
        height 480
        setup (fn []
                (q/background 255)
                (plot-smooth-area expected 0 height
                                  width height))]
    (q/sketch :setup setup :size [width height])))
```

This example generates the following image:

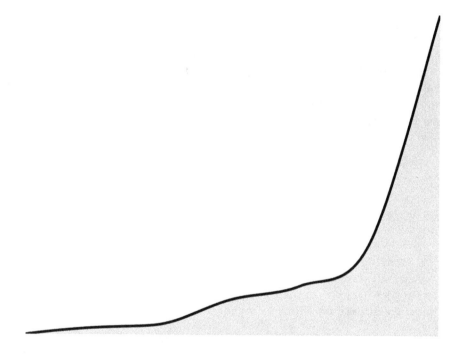

The effect of the curve is subtle, but it provides a polish to our chart that would otherwise be lacking. The previous chart shows the *expected* distribution of wealth from the study by Norton and Ariely. Before we combine this with the *actual* wealth distribution plot we created earlier, let's see how it could be combined with the *ideal* distribution of wealth from the same study.

Plotting compound charts

The earlier description shows how to create a single curved graph scaled to fit an area. As we've defined it, the `plot-smooth-area` function will fill the height we specify for every area we draw. This makes sense from a drawing perspective, but it doesn't make sense while trying to draw two comparable charts: we need to make sure they use the same scale.

In the next block of code, we'll calculate a scale based on the larger of the two graphs and then plot both using this scale. This ensures that all of the series we plot will be comparable with each other. The combined chart will fill the width and height we allot to it:

```
(defn plot-areas [series px py width height]
  (let [series-ys (map area-points series)
        n-points  (count (first series-ys))
        x-scale   (point->px px (/ width (dec n-points)))
        xs        (map x-scale (range n-points))
        y-max     (apply max (apply concat series-ys))
        y-scale   (point->px py (/ height y-max -1))]
    (doseq [ys series-ys]
      (plot-curve (cons (first xs) xs)
                  (map y-scale (cons 0 ys))
                  (q/color 255 100)
                  (q/color 255 200) 3))))

(defn ex-10-19 []
  (let [expected [3 6.5 12 20 58.5]
        ideal    [10.5 14 21.5 22 32]
        width  640
        height 480
        setup (fn []
                (q/background 100)
                (plot-areas [expected ideal] 0 height
                            width height))]
    (q/sketch :setup setup :size [width height])))
```

We plot both the `expected` and `ideal` series using the `plot-areas` function, having set a darker background to our sketch with the `background` function. In our call to `plot-curve`, we specify semitransparent white as the fill to be used. The following image shows the result:

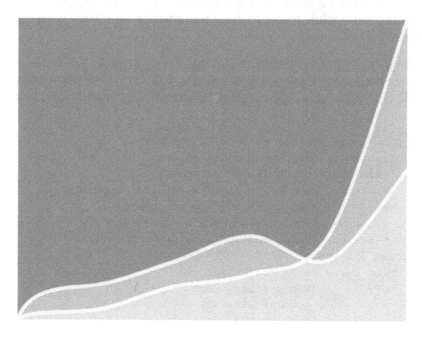

To combine this chart with the chart showing the actuals created previously, we simply need to adjust its scale to match. The highest point on this chart at the top right corresponds to a probability density of 5 percent. The 96-99th percentiles on our actual plot represents 7.5 percent of the total, each on their plot. This means that we need to draw the previous chart at 2/3 of the height of the plot we already have for the axes to be comparable. Let's do this now, and add a series of labels to the two new series while we're at it:

```
(defn draw-expected-ideal []
  (let [expected [3 6.5 12 20 58.5]
        ideal    [10.5 14 21.5 22 32]]
    (plot-areas [expected ideal]
                plot-x
                (+ plot-y plot-height)
                plot-width
                (* (/ plot-height 0.075) 0.05))
    (q/text-size 20)
    (emboss-text "EXPECTED" 400 430)
    (emboss-text "IDEAL" 250 430)))
```

Finally, we call the `draw-expected-ideal` function from our sketch along with the other functions defined previously:

```
(defn ex-10-20 []
  (let [size [960 540]]
    (q/sketch :size size
              :setup #((draw-shapes)
                       (draw-expected-ideal)
                       (draw-banknotes)
                       (draw-axis-labels)
                       (draw-title)))))
```

The finished result is shown in the next graphic:

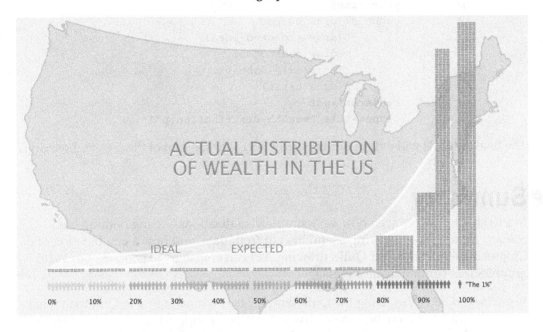

Hopefully, you'll agree that the finished chart is attractive as well as informative. Most importantly, we've generated the chart by drawing instructions from actual data. The finished result has an integrity to it that would be harder to establish if the chart were produced by hand.

Output to PDF

All the elements combined together yield a graphic of the kind that might end up in print. The drawing instructions we provided are vector-based — rather than pixel-based — so it will scale to any resolution required without loss of quality.

Rather than output to a pixel-based format using `save` as we did with the histogram, let's output to a PDF. The PDF format will preserve the scalability of our artwork and allow us to output at any resolution desired. To do this, we configure the sketch to use the PDF renderer by passing the `:pdf` keyword and also an `:output-file` path.

```
(defn ex-10-21 []
  (let [size [960 540]]
    (q/sketch :size size
              :setup #((draw-shapes)
                       (draw-expected-ideal)
                       (draw-banknotes)
                       (draw-axis-labels)
                       (draw-title))
              :renderer :pdf
              :output-file "wealth-distribution.pdf")))
```

The final example will output our finished PDF file to the root of the project directory.

Summary

In this chapter, we've seen how very simple visualizations — using nothing but colored rectangles — can bring useful insight from data, and how a combination of Clojure core functions and Quil's drawing API can enable us to generate powerful graphics that communicate a message.

We achieved all of this using the Quil library. There's much more to Quil than what we've shown here: it enables interactive animation, it supports ClojureScript output for the web, and it can produce 3D rendering as well. Visualization is a huge topic too, and we couldn't hope to provide more than a few examples to pique your interest in this chapter. By showing how even basic drawing instructions using rectangles, curves, and SVGs can combine into powerful graphics, we hope to have inspired you with the possibilities to create your own custom visualizations.

This was the final chapter of *Clojure for Data Science*. Be sure to visit the book's website at `http://clojuredatascience.com` for more information on the topics covered and links to further reading. We intend to provide an ongoing resource for data scientists in general and Clojure programmers in particular.

It was an ambitious task to convey the breadth and depth of a field as diverse and quickly evolving as data science using a language whose libraries are quickly evolving as well. Nonetheless, we hope *Clojure for Data Science* has given you an appreciation for some of the fundamental concepts of statistics, machine learning, and big data processing. This conceptual basis should serve you well, even as the technical options—and perhaps even your choice of programming language—continue evolving into the future.

Index

A

A* algorithm
  URL 423
Acbracad library
  URL 317
AcmeContent
  about 56
  inspecting 56, 57
  loading 56, 57
  sample code 56
acyclic 414
Adaptive Boosting (AdaBoost) 231
Akaike Information Criterion (AIC)
  about 512
  models, identifying 512, 513
alternating least squares (ALS)
  evaluating 405, 406
  movie recommendations 401, 402
  used, for making predictions 404
  using, with MLlib 403
  using, with Spark 403
amoeba method. *See* **simplex method**
Anscombe's Quartet 35
Apache Commons Math
  about 510, 511
  URL 510, 511
  used, for Nelder-Mead
    optimization 511, 512
ARMA model order
  determining, with ACF and PACF 500, 501
autocorrelation function (ACF)
  about 489
  ARMA model order, determining 500, 501
  plotting, of airline data 501-503
autocovariance 497

autoregressive (AR) models
  about 485-488
  autocorrelation, determining 489-491
  combining, with moving-average (MA)
    models 494-496
**autoregressive integrated moving-average
  (ARIMA) model 503**

B

B1
  about 92
  URL 92
bagging 230, 231
bag-of-words 291
balanced F-score 369
batch gradient descent 274
Bayesian view 199
Bayes theorem
  about 200-203
  with multiple predictors 203-206
bias
  about 70, 71
  high bias, addressing 229
bias term 139
big data
  code, downloading 233, 234
  example code, URL 234
  inspecting 234, 235
  records, counting 236
bigrams 309
bimodal 72
binning 16, 17
binomial distribution 175, 176
bipartite 416
bivariate linear regression 139

Thank you for buying
Clojure for Data Science

About Packt Publishing

Packt, pronounced 'packed', published its first book, *Mastering phpMyAdmin for Effective MySQL Management*, in April 2004, and subsequently continued to specialize in publishing highly focused books on specific technologies and solutions.

Our books and publications share the experiences of your fellow IT professionals in adapting and customizing today's systems, applications, and frameworks. Our solution-based books give you the knowledge and power to customize the software and technologies you're using to get the job done. Packt books are more specific and less general than the IT books you have seen in the past. Our unique business model allows us to bring you more focused information, giving you more of what you need to know, and less of what you don't.

Packt is a modern yet unique publishing company that focuses on producing quality, cutting-edge books for communities of developers, administrators, and newbies alike. For more information, please visit our website at www.packtpub.com.

About Packt Open Source

In 2010, Packt launched two new brands, Packt Open Source and Packt Enterprise, in order to continue its focus on specialization. This book is part of the Packt Open Source brand, home to books published on software built around open source licenses, and offering information to anybody from advanced developers to budding web designers. The Open Source brand also runs Packt's Open Source Royalty Scheme, by which Packt gives a royalty to each open source project about whose software a book is sold.

Writing for Packt

We welcome all inquiries from people who are interested in authoring. Book proposals should be sent to author@packtpub.com. If your book idea is still at an early stage and you would like to discuss it first before writing a formal book proposal, then please contact us; one of our commissioning editors will get in touch with you.

We're not just looking for published authors; if you have strong technical skills but no writing experience, our experienced editors can help you develop a writing career, or simply get some additional reward for your expertise.

Mastering Clojure Data Analysis

ISBN: 978-1-78328-413-9   Paperback: 340 pages

Leverage the power and flexibility of Clojure through this practical guide to data analysis

1. Explore the concept of data analysis using established scientific methods combined with the powerful Clojure language.

2. Master Naïve Bayesian Classification, Benford's Law, and much more in Clojure.

3. Learn with the help of examples drawn from exciting, real-world data.

Clojure High Performance Programming

ISBN: 978-1-78216-560-6   Paperback: 152 pages

Understand performance aspects and write high performance code with Clojure

1. See how the hardware and the JVM impact performance.

2. Learn which Java features to use with Clojure, and how.

3. Deep dive into Clojure's concurrency and state primitives.

4. Discover how to design Clojure programs for performance.

Please check **www.PacktPub.com** for information on our titles

PUBLISHING

Python Data Science Essentials

ISBN: 978-1-78528-042-9   Paperback: 258 pages

Become an efficient data science practitioner by thoroughly understanding the key concepts of Python

1. Quickly get familiar with data science using Python.

2. Save tons of time through this reference book with all the essential tools illustrated and explained.

3. Create effective data science projects and avoid common pitfalls with the help of examples and hints dictated by experience.

Practical Data Analysis

ISBN: 978-1-78328-099-5   Paperback: 360 pages

Transform, model, and visualize your data through hands-on projects, developed in open source tools

1. Explore how to analyze your data in various innovative ways and turn them into insight.

2. Learn to use the D3.js visualization tool for exploratory data analysis.

3. Understand how to work with graphs and social data analysis.

4. Discover how to perform advanced query techniques and run MapReduce on MongoDB.

Please check **www.PacktPub.com** for information on our titles